T0124896

WHO IS A
PARSI?

by

PROCHY N MEHTA

NIYOGI
BOOKS

Published by
NIYOGI BOOKS
Block D, Building No. 77,
Okhla Industrial Area, Phase-I,
New Delhi-110 020, INDIA
Tel: 91-11-26816301, 26818960
Email: niyogibooks@gmail.com
Website: www.niyogibooksindia.com

Text & Images © Prochy Mehta

Design: Shaju K. Anthony

ISBN: 978-93-91125-77-6
Publication: 2022

Printed at: Niyogi Offset Pvt. Ltd., New Delhi, India

CONTENTS

APPENDIX

FOREWORD

A proud boast of Parsis is that they belong to the world's most ancient monotheistic religion. As a matter of historical fact, they do. But presently – with the steep decline in birth-rate, the entire community is in jeopardy; it is believed, by many, that Parsi personal law[1] is largely responsible for this plight: which is precisely the theme around which this well-researched and liberally-illustrated book has been written.

When the hero of Shakespeare's tragic play: Hamlet is told that he has to avenge his father's murder (at the hands of his own uncle) he cries out in anguish:

> The time is out of joint; O cursed spite!
> That ever I was born to set it right

In Prochy Mehta's view, – for Parsis, the times are definitely out of joint, and she has valiantly strived 'to set it right": not in a spirit of acrimony or confrontation, but by invoking the more pleasurable – art of persuasion.

Modern 'Parsi-ism' is derived from the ideas and ideals expressed in that ancient, and most sacred, of Zoroastrian texts: the Gathas: in which Yasna 30 Verse 5 records: 'Truly, there are two primal Spirits,

---

1 'Personal Law' is the law that governs a person's personal and family matters; it consists of a set of settled legal principles separately applicable to a religious community. The expression 'personal law' was first mentioned in British Parliament's Government of India Act, 1935; it continues to be mentioned in the Constitution of India 1950 (in item (5) of the List III of the Seventh Schedule).

twins renowned to be eternally in conflict. In thought and word, in act, they are two: the better and the bad. And those who act well have chosen rightly between these two, not so the evil doers.' Over many millenniums, this verse has suffered attrition, and the essence of the religion is now expressed in capsule-form: 'Good thoughts', 'Good words', and 'Good deeds'. Most members of the community have not felt the need to know more about the faith; nor do the faithful look for or seek solace in gods or deities. As children, most of them have imbibed the essentials of the religion by osmosis: by observing the conduct and general behaviour of their parents and older relatives. The outward expression of the ordinary Zoroastrian's faith lies in the daily recitation of prayers, which though in a dead language (Avestan), ensures to one who recites them immense spiritual satisfaction. There is no asceticism, in Parsi philosophy – no renunciation, no monastic life, no celibacy, no mendicancy, no fasts, no mortification of the flesh. The Parsis in India – and those now scattered around in various parts (mainly) of the western world – have been reared in a tradition and culture entirely different from the adherents of the same faith in Central Asia; the latter observe the tenets of the religion far more fervently than their co-religionists in India. The late General Adi Sethna – former Chairman of the Delhi Parsi Anjuman – a great and joyful Parsi – having visited Tajikistan told me about the large community of Zoroastrians there – and that it was they who had first approached UNESCO to initiate celebrations on a global scale for the Birth Anniversary of the Prophet!

Former U.S. Presidents Jimmy Carter and George Bush were regarded as 'born-again Christians' (i.e., born of the spirit and not merely of the flesh); Parsis in India – which includes those originating from India and now living in diverse parts of the western world – are in that same sense – 'born-again-Parsis': an odd and eccentric lot, fiercely individualistic and egotistical to the core – as illustrated by the following story.

In the year 1930, my father, Sam Nariman, Branch Manager of the New India Assurance Company in Rangoon had been deputed by his Head Office in Bombay to travel to various parts of what was then British East Africa (as well as apartheid South Africa) – for opening and establishing the company's branch offices. When he landed in Zanzibar (today, a part of Tanzania) he took an evening stroll in the city; and came across a shopkeeper dressed in a Baddian with the sacred shirt (the *sudreh*) showing, and with a Parsi prayer-cap on his head; always a convivial person, my father was delighted; he greeted this gentleman, and was invited by him into his shop, and the two chatted for a while. When my father left and walked further up the same street, he was pleased to see another Parsi; also a retail merchant; my father warmly greeted him with the traditional ('Kem Chheo Sahib' - 'Greetings to you Sir') but got no response – this retail merchant turned his back on him and refused to acknowledge the greeting: 'Teme /en'/e ta pah-le/ Kem gaya?' – "how come you went to the other fellow first?', was what he wanted to know: and he happened to be the only other Parsi living in Zanzibar! This obstreperous attitude – 'hōō-panoo', as Parsis call it, persists till this day, and exhibits itself in many odd ways in different places around the world, wherever there is a sprinkling of Parsis. However, having had the advantage of travelling extensively, both in India and abroad, my wife (Bapsi) and I had always maintained that we never ever met a Parsi who was not proud to be regarded as one – even where he or she did not recite daily prayers (as 'good' Parsis should), or where he or she did not wear the *sudreh* and *kusti* (the sacred inner-shirt and thread). Pride in being a Parsi, then, has been the hallmark of members of the Community.

In a gathering of Parsis there is little solemnity, but much fun and laughter; they even make merry of their dwindling numbers! With supreme confidence they say (or at least they think, even if they do not say):

we are God's chosen few,
all others may be dammed;
there is no place in heaven for you,
we can't have heaven crammed!

As this book tells us, the Parsis in India – and those now scattered in various parts of the globe – are the followers of what was for 400 long years the established State religion in Eastern Persia. What today keeps this small and diminishing body of persons together is a faith that does not demand too much from its adherents: somewhat reminiscent of that Chief of Protocol, who had accompanied the then Queen of the Belgians on her visit to Warsaw in the 1950s; it was at a time when Poland was still dominated by the Soviets. The Belgian Queen was a deeply religious person, and the Polish Chief of Protocol was assigned to accompany her to Mass on Sunday.

'Are you a Catholic?' the Queen asked him.
'Believing, but not seriously practising. Your Majesty,' the Protocol Chief truthfully replied
'Of course,' the Queen said, 'then in that case you must be a Communist.'
'Practising, but not seriously believing, Your Majesty,' was the frank reply!

The Parsis are like that Polish functionary. Most of them are believing, not seriously practising Zoroastrians: belief in the faith then is the loose thread that binds them all together.

But what of the future? Ah, there lies the rub: it revolves around a controversial aspect of Parsi personal law as interpreted by the Courts nearly a hundred years ago. As the author of the book rightly tells us, Parsi personal law – as to conversions and as to the admission to Fire-temples, Towers of Silence and burial places –

is traditionally regarded as governed by two landmark decisions: (i) judgments of the High Court of Bombay – delivered (in 1908), by a Bench consisting of two Judges (one Parsi, the other English) in Petit vs. Jeejeebhoy (popularly known as the Soonu Petit Case), and (ii) an opinion of their Lordships of the Privy Council in the case of Saklat v. Bella (delivered in 1925)[2].

The question before the courts was not only whether the Zoroastrian religion permitted conversion of Juddins (i.e. non-Parsis) into the faith (the judges had recorded concurrent findings that it did); but also whether such conversions were permissible, according to the tenets of the religion (the judges had expressly stated that they were). But, the courts added, since their advent into India nearly 1200 years ago, Parsis had never attempted to convert anyone into their religion; and hence the practice of conversion had lapsed, by reason of a legal doctrine known, as 'desuetude': a law was said to fall into desuetude if, being of ancient date, it had, for long, been disregarded in practice. The important question raised before the two judges of the Bombay High Court, (in 1908) – as well as before three members of the Privy Council (in 1925) – the latter in an appeal from the Judgments of Judges of the then Lower Court of Burma – was whether settlers of trusts of fire-temples (Agiaries and Atash Behrams), and of the Towers of Silence in Bombay, and of the Agiary and the burial ground in Rangoon, had ever contemplated and intended that 'converts' should be admitted to these religious places; likewise, whether grantors of the lands where the Towers of Silence were located in Bombay, and where the Parsi Fire Temple and

---

2 The Privy Council was then the highest Court of appeal from judgments of Courts in British India (which then included Burma). All judgments delivered by the Privy Council were always styled as 'Opinions' – when sitting in the Privy Council (in appeals from the colonies and dominions, and from any part of the British Empire), judges in England traditionally offered advice to the reigning King (or Queen) in England, 'advice' which, by convention, was always accepted by the monarch and was final and binding in law.

Parsi burial ground was situate in Rangoon, had ever envisaged, at the dates of such grants, the admission into their sacred precincts of non-Parsis. The Bombay High Court (in 1908) – as well as the Privy Council (in 1925) – held that the Parsi community in India and Burma had grown up to be such a distinct body (almost akin to a 'caste'), and admissions from outside had been so very rare, that at the time when the trusts were created and the grants of lands were made it must have been intended (as Lord Phillimore, expressing by the opinion of the Privy Council, said): 'solely for the benefit of professing members of the Parsi community, i.e., racial Parsis or people deemed after a long lapse of ages to be racial Parsis.'

The Bombay case concerned an avowed Christian convert to Zoroastrianism. In 1902, one Mr R.D. Tata (1856–1926) – member of the illustrious and the most munificent progenitor of the Tata family, Mr Jamsetji Tata (1839–1904) – was married, in Paris, to a Christian lady whose parents were also Christians. On returning to Bombay Mrs Tata was given a Parsi name 'Soonu', and admitted into the Zoroastrian religion by the performance of a Navjote ceremony performed by duly-ordained Priests. Mr R.D.Tata claimed (and this is what was adjudicated upon) that by the conversion of the Christian lady to Zoroastrianism, and by virtue of the performance of the Navjote ceremony, his wife had become a 'Parsi professing the Zoroastrian faith', and because she had become a Parsi professing the Zoroastrian faith she was entitled to participate in the benefits of the charitable and religious institutions of the Parsis. The Special Bench of two judges of the Bombay High Court rejected this claim – after a very extensive hearing, in the course of which a host of witnesses were examined, and a very large number of books and documents (including religious books) were consulted. In his judgment, Mr Justice Davar (the Parsi Judge) said that the word 'Parsi' had a racial not a religious significance: 'Zoroastrian denotes religion, Parsi denotes community, there is no Parsi religion in existence.' His companion judge, Justice Beaman, (the English Judge) said that the word 'Parsi' had a 'caste' meaning, not a religious meaning; Soonu Tata may well have become a Zoroastrian, but she did not qualify as a 'Parsi'.

Bella's case had a different factual background. It was not decided as a case of conversion into Zoroastrianism of a person, neither of whose parents were Parsis. Bella was the daughter of a Parsi mother and a Goan father; and she was brought up since childhood by the Cowasji family (staunch Parsis) in Rangoon; at the instance of the Cowasjis, she was initiated into the Zoroastrian religion, her Navjote ceremony being duly performed by regularly ordained Parsi priests. It was claimed (by the Cowasjis on Bella's behalf) that she was therefore entitled to attend and partake of the ceremonials at the Parsi Fire Temple in Rangoon. But since this gave offence to some members of the Parsi Community there, a suit was filed by three such members (as plaintiffs in a representative capacity) against Bella and her Parsi guardians stating that the agiary was held on trust for free and unrestricted use only of the Parsi inhabitants in Rangoon who professed the Zoroastrian faith. The fact that Bella had been validly initiated into the Zoroastrian religion had been expressly denied by the plaintiffs; and since the issue was squarely raised, it was decided both by the trial court as well as by the appellate court (the then Lower Burma Chief Court) – in favour of Bella, (copies of these judgments, not otherwise easily available, have been annexed by the author). The Single Judge in the trial court at Rangoon (Justice Young) ruled that Bella, (daughter of a Goan father and Parsi mother) was validly initiated into the Zoroastrian religion (by the performance of the Navjote Ceremony); and this finding was upheld by two Judges of the Court of Appeal (of the then Lower Burma Chief Court). On a further final appeal, to the Privy Council in London, their Lordships of the Privy Council (sitting in a Bench of three members), after perusing the entire trial court record (which included a mass of evidence of over 600 pages initially taken on commission in Bombay), upheld this finding of the judges of the courts below, adding that no further rituals or ceremonials, were necessary to effectuate Bella's initiation into the religion; Bella had truly become a Zoroastrian. At the same time, however, the Privy Council also held, – following earlier dicta in the Soonu Petit Case (1908) – that it was 'settled' that as regards the racial claim (to be regarded as a Parsi) 'maternity was of no importance'. Accordingly, Bella, not being a Parsi, could not claim as of right, entry into the Parsi Agiary in Rangoon: because the founders of the Parsi Fire Temple had intended (by the trust-deed setting up the agiary) that worship in the agiary should be confined to persons who possessed the dual qualification of Zoroastrians and racial Parsis. The Privy Council said that 'the trustees of the fire temple could, if they wish, treat Bella as a trespasser', but added that 'it does not follow that they are bound so to treat her'; this was because, as a matter of law, trustees of religious trusts were not bound to exclude persons who had no legal title to share in the benefits of that trust:

My 'take' (i.e. my personal point of view) on all this is the following:

(1) As authoritatively stated by the Privy Council: the child of a Parsi mother and a non-Parsi father is entitled as of right to be recognised in law as a Zoroastrian if (and only if) such child has been initiated into the religion by a Navjote ceremony performed by an ordained priest: and he/she have the right to be so initiated, if he/she wish to profess and practice the Zoroastrian religion.

(2) Before January 1950, whether such a child could then be admitted to an agiary or Atash Behram entirely depended on the application of the ratio of judgments delivered in two sets of cases – containing diverse and contradictory conclusions viz.

First set of cases:

(i) In a decision of the High Court of Bombay in 1908 – in the Soonu Petit Case read alongwith a decision of their Lordships of the Privy Council in Bella's case (1925) – the latter originating in Rangoon: it was held that the admission of the child to an agiary or Atash Behram – entirely depended on the terms of the trust deeds by which such places of worship were established; thus, when such trust deeds provided (as they invariably did) for admission into the fire-temples of Parsis professing the Zoroastrian religion, then the child (of a Parsi mother and non-Parsi father) who had its Navjote ceremony performed was not entitled to admission as a matter of right: but the trustees could lawfully permit such child (if already initiated into the religion by the performance of the Navjote Ceremony), to enter the place of worship. In so doing, the trustees were not committing a breach of trust: since trustees of religious trusts: (so held in Bella's case) were not bound to exclude persons who may have no legal title to be in the trust premises.

Second case

(ii) in the second case there is a contrary decision of a Single Judge of the High Court of Bombay (in a decision rendered in the year 1960 – and reported in the law reports even later, in the year 1966 – Jamshed Irani vs. Banu Irani (68 Bom. L.R. 794) – a decision exhaustively dealt with by the author in Chapter 24 of the book – in which it was held (at variance with the views expressed in Petit's case (1908) as well as views expressed (by the Privy Council) in Bella's case (1925), the Bombay High Court holding that – 'Parsi' meant and only meant a person professing the Zoroastrian religion – whether in Iran or in India.

(iii) As to whether under the doctrine of precedents a single judge of the High Court of Bombay in the year 1960 could have lawfully taken a view contrary to that already expressed by two judges of the same Court in the year 1908 as well as by that taken by three members of the Privy Council in the year 1925 is debatable; but it is not at all necessary to discuss or determine this question since after January 1950 the matter is no longer governed by personal law but by constitutional law, which has conferred a separate fundamental right on 'all persons' (i.e. human beings) to freely practice their religion no matter whether they belong or do not belong to any particular race or caste – 'religion' has displaced 'race'.

(3) In the Constitution of India 1950, the 'Right to freedom of Religion' is contained in Articles 25 to 30 in the Chapter on Fundamental Rights (Part-III). And the very first Article in the 'Right to freedom of Religion' is Article 25(1) ('Freedom of conscience and free profession, practice and propagation of religion'). It specifically provides that 'subject to public order, morality and health and to the other provisions of this Part' (Part-III) all persons 'are equally entitled to freedom of conscience and the right freely to profess practise and propagate religion'. As already mentioned 'Race' or 'caste' has no place in Article 25(1): Article 25 (1) confers a distinct constitutional right on all persons (a right which is higher than a statutory right, infinitely superior to a customary right as well as a right recognised in the personal law) to freely profess and practice one's religion: i.e. like one's other co-religionists: Therefore once the child of a mixed marriage (consisting of a Parsi mother and non-Parsi father) is initiated into the religion through the performance of the Navjote ceremony by an ordained Priest, he/she is entitled as a fundamental right to

practice the religion by worshipping in the fire-temple (even if he or she is not a Parsi by race) and even if the trustees of the fire-temple object.

(4) So, after 26 January 1950, where trustees of trusts for Parsi places of worship (or places of burial) refuse to admit a child, (of a Parsi mother and non-Parsi father) then a suit for a declaration (and injunction) has to be filed in a competent civil Court: (i.e. a suit under section 9 of the Code of Civil Procedure 1908):

(i) for declaring the right of such a child to be recognised as a Zoroastrian by religion according to the undisputed law as finally laid down in Bella's case; and

(ii) for a further declaration of the right of such a child to claim admission into the Agiaries and Atashbehrams for worship on the basis of a constitutional right conferred by Article 25(1) of the Constitution of India 1950; and

(iii) for further consequential relief viz. a permanent injunction restraining the defendant trustees (and all other persons) from denying such a child entry into the fire-temple for purposes of worship.

(5) Some fundamental rights conferred in Part III of India's Constitution (The Chapter on Fundamental Rights) are enforceable only against the State (like Articles 14, 19 and 21) – which specifically, mention and make reference to the State – but rights conferred by some other Articles in the Fundamental Rights Chapter (Part III) are also enforceable against the whole world including against private persons indulging in a constitutionally prohibited practice: this has been so held by the Supreme Court of India in authoritative decisions reported in AIR 1982 S.C. 1473 (paragraph 12); and in AIR 1983 S.C. 328: (paragraph 3).

(6) The question on which there is as yet no specific decision of the Supreme Court of India is whether Article 25(1) falls within the

category of rights that are also available and can be enforced against individuals or against trustees of trusts (private or public) by which fire-temples and burial places are established. The better view is that they are; the right conferred under Article 25(1) can be enforced because:

(i) Article 25(1) in Part-III of the Constitution – unlike Articles 14, 19 and 21 – does not spell out any obligation of the State; it does not mention or even refer to the 'State': but it expressly confers a specific right of worship ('right to practice the religion') on all persons; besides, the enforcement of this right is also specifically guaranteed by the terms of Article 32 of the Constitution ('Remedies for enforcement of rights conferred by this part');

(ii) Nothing in Article 25(1) suggests that this right of worship is addressed to the State: being enforceable under Article 32, it is meant to be observed by all, including individuals and trusts. The word 'freely' in the phrase 'the right freely to profess, practice and propagate religion' in Article 25(1) lends support to this interpretation: because 'freely' means 'without anyone trying to prevent or control'. It therefore includes the right to enter and worship at a Fire Temple even though the trustees of the fire-temple trust are not agreeable or offer hindrance or resistance; the only condition necessary for the recognition and enforcement of such right is that the person so entering is a Zoroastrian by religion – even if he or she is not a 'Parsi' by race or caste.

(7) This then (as I see it) is the current state of the law, and the remedy available to enforce it.

Fali S. Nariman

Date: 9th August, 2021

(Fali S. Nariman)

New Delhi

PREFACE

The writing of my first book, *The Pioneering Parsis of Calcutta*, took me on a journey that helped me see my own city and my own people in a new light. It acquainted me with many a hitherto unknown aspect of the lives and times of the early generations of Parsis in the City of Joy. Kolkata, I discovered in awe, was once a cultural-educational hub for Zoroastrians and the city sounded the call for return to the original Zoroastrian religion. The high priests of the two agiaries in Kolkata, Dastur Kaekobad Aderbad Dastur Noshirwan and Dastur Kaikhushru Jamaspjee, and other prominent members of the community in Calcutta led what I may rightfully call a Parsi Renaissance.

My research made me realize that the tales we have heard for generations, and what has been handed down to us as history of the Parsi community in India, have often been rather fictitious. The perception, for example, that the Parsis have always been an affluent community, is a modern-day myth devoid of any true value. The story of the arrival of the Parsis in India, the most important chapter in that history, is itself shrouded in mystery.

In the present book, I attempt to set that record straight and lift the veil from the glorious history of our people. I wish to handhold the reader in this journey through the lanes and by-lanes of our history – from the time of the writing of the poem Qisaa-i-Sanjan in 1599, when Parsi recorded history actually begins, to the 20th century. Bear with me if I meander sometimes, for its no easy task. It seeks to capture 400 years' history in 300 pages.

At the heart of the issue that I want to explore in the following pages lies the titular question: Who is a Parsi? And are children born to a non-Parsi father or mother to be considered a Parsi? The Petit vs Jeejeebhoy case of 1908 as well as the Saklat vs Bella lawsuit of 1924 are two landmark events as far as settling these debates is concerned. The hearings and the judgements went a long way towards shaping the ethnic identity of Parsis in India and in southeast Asia. Both of them have been alluded to and discussed repeatedly in the following pages. Strangely, neither of these two judgements have been referred to in the Parsi Marriage and Divorce Act of 1936. It states that a Parsi is a Parsi Zoroastrian and mentions as a ground for divorce – 'the defendant has ceased to be a Parsi (by conversion to another religion)'. Finally, in Irani vs Irani in 1960 the word Parsi was identified with the Zoroastrian religion.

I have also tried to narrate stories and records of the past which show what apparently insurmountable difficulties the Parsis had to overcome at various stages of their history, particularly in the absence of a fixed set of laws to fall back on.

The census of Parsis in Bombay in 1864 pegged the Parsi population at 49,201. The professional breakup showed no Parsi beggars but there were 5,328 servants and 1,641 cooks, 180 hawkers, 176 water carriers, 7,180 writer accountants, 6,149 merchant banker and broker and 41 prostitutes amongst a total of about 70 listed occupations. They show that dignity of labour was a hallmark of Parsi community and throw up many interesting details. For example, there would be a 'leechman' whose task was to apply leeches to suck the blood of a person as a kind of medical treatment.

History books tell us that Parsis were ignorant of their religion till the middle of the 19th century having lived among the Hindus for hundreds of years. In the second half of that century, there was a general cleansing of the religion to remove the Hindu customs being followed. It was foreign scholars like A.V.W. Jackson, Martin Hauge, Friedrich von Spiegel, James Darmesteter, Lawrence Mills and others who translated and studied the Avesta and then taught the priests the true essence of their religion and its history. Dastur Dhalla, the high priest of Karachi, for example, was sent by the community on a sponsored visit to Columbia University to study under Professor Jackson. Dastur Hoshang, the high priest of the Deccan, studied under Martin Hauge at the University of Poona. Dastur Darab Peshotan Sanjana, high priest of the Wadia Atash Behram, was also a student of Professor Jackson, while K.R. Cama studied under Spiegel at the University of Erlangen in Germany.

Another key development that brought about a paradigm shift in the Parsi community in the mid-19th century was that trade links with China brought immense wealth into a section of people and the power centre shifted from the priests to the Sethias (rich people). The two court cases, Petit vs Jeejeebhoy and Saklat vs Bella highlighted this, too. In both the conflicts, it was the rich Sethias who objected to the navjotes being performed by high priests.

At the turn of the century, a new mystical movement within Zoroastrianism started gaining wide acceptance. Known as Ilm-e-Khshnoom (the Science of Ecstasy), it was spearheaded by Behramsha Shroff from Surat, who had learnt mystic and esoteric practices from the Abed Saheb-e-Dilan, living in the Caucasus Mountains. There were also the Theosophists, another small group within Zoroastrians which had caught the imagination of a few Parsis.

This created a deep chasm within the community. The priests and other members of the community who wanted to go back to Zoroastrianism in its pristine purity were labelled Reformists. And the ones who followed the new trends of Theosophy and Ilm-e-Khshnoom and wanted to follow religious practices aligned with the Hindus, came to be called the Orthodox. As would be clear to any perceptive reader by now, in actuality it was the Reformists who were the true Orthodox.

The battle between the Orthodox and the Reformist in the Parsi Community made entertaining news in all the newspapers and magazines. And there were many. The Rast Goftar started by Dadabhoy Navroji, the Journal of the Iranian Association and the Iran League Bulletin were very vocal in their support of the opening of new vistas in Zoroastrian religion, and they published many scholarly articles. Luckily for us, these publications are still available and give some real insight into the nature of the Parsi community at the beginning of the last century.

The other question that has seen the Parsi community split right down the middle is that of interfaith marriage and conversion. The letter received by the Parsi panchayat supporting the conversion of Sussaune, a French lady, and her wedding to Ratan Tata under the Parsi Marriage and Divorce Act was signed by religious scholars and some of the most eminent members of the community.

Dastur Dhalla pragmatically writes in his book *The Saga of a Soul* (1942) and I quote:'...those whose hearts have been pierced by Cupid's arrow do not pay the least attention to any objection. Lovers enamoured of their youthful sweethearts are bent upon making them their own without any consideration of the past or future. Thus mixed marriages cannot be stopped. In the years that followed the Joodin struggle (1905) we saw eight Parsis marry American wives during our various trips to America. What was strange about all these marriages was that the husband and wife did not continue with their own individual religions and get married according to the Civil Law (Special Marriage Act 1872).' (Pg 570).

He mentions two reasons for the depletion in the strength of the community.

1) 'In order to save their children from conflicts regarding their navjotes, recently young Zoroastrian men get converted into the religion of their Joodin (juddin/non-Parsi) mates prior to their civil marriage. Some have accepted Hinduism and Islam and have married according to the rites of those religions.

2) For the first time in 1200 years an ever-increasing number of girls of our community is boldly and unhesitatingly getting converted and marrying joodins.'

Hence, the Special Marriage Act of 1954 is an important landmark for the Parsis. From the date of its enactment, interfaith marriages became a reality for Parsi men and women. They no longer had to renounce their faith to marry according to the Civil Law.

Then there are other aspects of our history that need to be illuminated for modern day readers. For example, the miserable condition of our co-religionists in Iran and their rehabilitation in India is a story not known to many. Thousands of poor Iranians were accepted into the community in India, no questions asked about their ancestry. My friend Sanam Karais' grandfather was one of the first of the later wave of refugees from Iran.

Similarly, no one seems to be aware of the fact that it was the head priests of the community who had once led the call of going 'back to the original religion'. Research shows that it was a movement driven by learned priests and the educated members of society. Logic says that which was a religious duty or a tenet of the faith in 1908 has to be the same today. It was a pious duty to take care of an illegitimate child. To destroy it or give it up to the custom of its father was a great sin. Conversion was a tenet of the religion; in fact, it was an enjoined duty; prostitutes' children must be accepted into the community. The Rivayats tell us to convert slave boys and girls and servants. Zoroastrianism is a religion for all mankind said all the priests and scholars. Are we following any of these today?

These are some of the larger questions that I seek to address as we go along. Come, walk with me into the past and see us Parsis as we really were and are.

1
WHO IS A PARSI?

You must be ready to burn yourself in your own flame; how could you
rise anew if you have not first become ashes?
—Friedrich Nietzsche,
Thus Spake Zarathustra: A Book for All and None

The annals of the Parsi community are as ancient as the sun. Yet, the question – Who is a Parsi? – remains a problematic one. Over centuries, a definitive answer to this has remained elusive. And at no point in our history has it been more imperative to answer this question than it is now.

Why so? Let me share with you, dear reader, a personal experience, which in a way prompted me to take up the monumental task of writing this book.

My eldest granddaughter was born in 2006. In 2009 my daughter and son blessed us with two more grandchildren. Our fourth grandchild was born in 2013. Till 2015, all my four grandchildren accompanied us to the fire temple and participated in all the rituals to be performed. Children being few in our community, those four little ones always brought a smile on everyone's face, especially when they took a prayer book and copied us as we said our prayers.

The lighting of the 'Divo' was a special routine as my husband would hold their little hands, light a match, and make each one light an individual 'Divo'. When the priest came with the 'Alat' they would reverentially place the 'loban' (sandalwood ash from

My three Grandchildren on the first floor of the D.B. Mehta agiary in Calcutta

the holy fire) on their foreheads and take a pinch of ash home to put it on my aged mother.

In 2015, there was a change in the head priest. One day, we received a phone call from him requesting us not to bring my grandchildren to the fire temple, because my daughter had married outside the Parsi community. He, however, had no objection to intermarried men bringing their children to the agiary. I wrote a letter to the trustees asking for clarification and was informed that the trust deed was sacrosanct, and, in their opinion, they were duty bound to stop my daughter's children from visiting the only agiary in Kolkata.

Since my childhood, I had seen people outside our community hold Parsis in high esteem because of their progressive mindset, generosity and integrity. Like others in my community, I too had been taught the wisdom of our great kings – Cyrus who wrote the first Human Rights charter thousands of years ago, or Darius who paid for and rebuilt the world's largest Jewish temple. I read with fascination about Jamsetji Tata who wrote that labourers must be given a day off every week, that hospitals must be built to provide medical aid, that roads must be wide, and trees planted to give shade. All this made me proud, and I was overjoyed when I learnt of the Godrejs, the Wadias the Petits and so many others who grew wealthy and gave back generously to the society.

Hence, the patriarchy and the narrow-mindedness of some men who decided to keep innocent children of a Parsee mother out of our holiest site shocked me. I felt something was wrong. Deep down, I could not believe that a community so vibrant, so generous, so liberal, could possibly be so vindictive towards its own children. Moreover, our holy books, the Gathas were extraordinarily clear in that they not only welcomed people to our religion but enjoined upon all Zoroastrians to initiate those who chose to practise it. It was a great sin to prevent anyone from adopting Zoroastrianism. I felt I needed to enquire into this a little more.

This led to my studying the D.B. Mehta agiary trust deed and I started investigating the history of the Parsis in general and the community in Calcutta in particular and Dastur Kaekobad Aderbad Dastur Noshirwan, the High Priest of the Deccan, whom the trust deed instructs, to follow in observation of religious rites and customs. It certainly did not seem justified to me that a worshipper's right of entry to a place of worship of his own religion can be given and taken away, depending on the personal beliefs of the individual in charge of the institution. And it is not an isolated incident. Based on personal interpretations of who is a Parsi and who is not, someone from our community may be allowed into one religious institution and debarred from another one in the same city. Hence, the only solution in sight is to decide once and for all: Who is a Parsi? Are Parsi and Zoroastrian interchangeable terms?

According to folklores, Parsis trace their ancestry to a group of refugees who came by boat from Iran to escape persecution about AD 700. But this is not recorded history; it is a tale first narrated in the poem, Kisseh-a-Sanjan, written in 1599 by Mobed Bahman Kaekobad about what might have happened over a period of about 1000 years. If there was no recorded account, where did Bahman get his material from? In the introduction to the English edition, translated by Lt E.B. Eastwick, Rustomji Pestonji Karkaria writes, 'If there was no written history, there certainly was historical tradition about those early days handed down by word of mouth throughout all those centuries. And it is from this old tradition that was current in his own times, that Bahman compiled this story.'

The Iran League Quarterly (the official journal of the Iran League, Mumbai) in its Oct 1931 issue states that the Parsis are the original inhabitants of India having lived in this country from 500 BC. 'The Parsi has quite greater right to her (India's) citizenship than either the Hindu or the Muslim. These claim by right of conquest. But the Parsis claim it by right of treaty, sacrifice and service.' The book, History of the Parsis of Navsari, by Captain Hormuzdiyar Desai narrates how till 1499 Parsis lived as a tribe amongst the Hindus' following the Hindu way of life – their religious practices, customs, manner of dress, and had even adapted their language.

Dastur Dr Maneckji Nusserwanji Dhalla, the High Priest of Karachi and a renowned religious scholar, writes in his autobiography, A Saga of a Soul in 1946, 'We have been known as Iranians from prehistoric times. From the advent of Zarathustra, we have been known as Zoroastrians. From the beginning of the Akamenian dynasty two thousand five hundred years ago, we have been known as Parsis.'

Coming to the present day, the Minorities Commission of India, which identifies minorities in terms of religion, recognizes Muslims, Sikhs, Christians, Buddhists, Parsis and Jains. The word 'Parsi' is used here to refer to a religion not a race. However, who is accepted as a Parsi varies from city to city in India and from institution to institution, as noted earlier. In all cases, children – both legitimate and illegitimate – of Parsi parents are accepted. The Bandobast of 1830 by the Parsi panchayat (literally, a commission of five members) and the report the panchayat received from the priests, show that illegitimate children of Parsi men and women with Parsi partners or otherwise, were accepted as Parsis.

The Dinshaw Manockji Petit & Ors Vs Sir Jamsetji Jeejeebhoy & Ors. case heard by a division bench of Justices Dinshaw Davar and Frank Beaman of the Bombay High Court in 1908 is a watershed moment in the social history of Parsis in India. One of the plaintiffs in the lawsuit was the renowned industrialist Ratanji Dadabhoy Tata, who had married a French woman, Sussane Braire. The judgement noted that Mr Tata married a French lady in Paris. He brought her to Bombay and got one of the Shenshai High Priests, Dastur Kaikhooshroo Jamaspji, to perform the Navjot ceremony, thereby investing her with Sudreh and Kusti the sacred shirt and girdle which are the outward symbols worn by those who profess the Zoroastrian religion. He then went through with her the marriage ceremony, according to the rites and forms observed by Parsis. He then claimed that his wife had become a Parsi, professing the Zoroastrian religion, and that as such she was entitled to participate in all the charitable and religious Funds and Institutions of the Parsis.

During the hearing, Justice Beaman said that 'Parsi' and 'Zoroastrian' were used to mean one and the same thing. Ervard Sheriarji Bharucha, a member of the expert committee set up by the bench, further said, 'I would use the two terms – Parsi and Zoroastrians – as synonymous terms. This is the way in which these terms have always been used and are still used. As soon as the word Parsi is used the only idea suggested is that he is a Zoroastrian.'

Incidentally, Parsis settled outside India accept the children of both intermarried men and women. And Zoroastrian Iranis who settle down in India are also accepted as Parsis, without checking

FIGURE 6.1. "On which track??? The Parsee Punchayet Funds and Juddin case ... has been postponed ... to allow the Trustees ... to lay before [the community] the suggested compromise ... "
Source: HP (15 March 1908), 10. Courtesy of the British Library SV576.

Illustrations in the Hindi Punch *magazine referring to the Petit vs Jeejeebhoy case and the compromise solution suggested by the judges*

EXHIBIT 39.

Translation of a Gujerati translation of the article of Faith, filed before Commissioner.

EXHIBIT 39.

SUIT NO. 91 OF 1915 CHIEF COURT, LOWER BURMA.

R. S. DADACHANJI,

Commissioner.

12th February 1916.

10   O.S.
     A.S. Serial No. 805

(Translation of a Gujerati translation of the article of Faith at page 379 of the Khordah Avesta by Ervad K. E. Kanga)

ARTICLE OF FAITH

May the most righteous (and) sacred knowledge (that is to say religious instruction) (and) the good Mazdayasna religion (flourish) !

The good, true and perfect religion which * Dadar Ahuramazda sent for people of this world is the (religion) which (prophet) Zoroaster has (personally) brought. That faith is the faith of Zoroaster (and) the faith of Ahuramazda, 20   (and) which was given to holy Zoroaster (by Dadar Ahuramazda) (for spreading) (in this world).

Translation of the Khordeh Avesta; 'Every day the religious Parsi prays in his daily prayers that his religion will spread throughout the world.'

their ancestry. Writing the judgement for the bench, Justice Davar mentioned that 'the Zoroastrian religion not only permits but enjoins the conversion of a person born in another faith and of non-Zoroastrian parents... It is as much the duty of every pious Zoroastrian today to make converts as it was in the remote past... Every day the religious Parsi prays in his daily prayers that his religion will spread throughout the world.' In his notebook, Justice Beaman wrote that a compromise was suggested by the court, and that the community should regulate Conversion by framing rules to safeguard it against abuse.

Ervad Dr Ramiyar Karanjia, a religious scholar and Principal of the Dadar Athoran Institute, which trains priests and spiritual guides, mentions in his book titled *Marvels in the Life of Prophet Zarathustra* (2020), that Parsi and Zoroastrian are interchangeable terms. 'The Parsis consider Zarathustra to be their first prophet... The word Zarathustra comes from the Avestan language. In other languages the name appears as Zarthust, Zardusht, and Zoroaster. The Parsis are also, therefore, known as Zoroastrians.'

In the 18th century the affairs of the Parsi community were handled by a panchayat or committee of five. Anyone refusing to obey the decision of this tribunal was excommunicated or punished by being beaten up with a shoe. In 1777, a dispute arose between the priests and the Behdin (laity) and the British had to appoint a commission to settle the dispute. The priests claimed they had the right to marry girls of the behdin but would not allow their girls to marry the behdin men. The situation, sadly, has not changed. Girls still face discrimination.

During the controversy over Ratan D. Tata's marriage to Sussaune Briere, the trustees of the Anjuman Atash Behram had asked scholars and local priests if conversion was allowed in the Parsi religion. All of them replied that it was not only allowed but it was also a sacred duty. Now, the fact that intermarried women's children are excluded while intermarried men's children are included in the Parsi community has no basis in law or religion or ancient custom. It is also strange that admission into the Zoroastrian religion is accepted but admission into the place of worship to practice that same religion is not permitted for all Zoroastrians. The noted Parsi reformer and scholar K.R. Cama writes in a letter that a Zoroastrian cannot be punished by denying entry into religious institutions.

In 2001 at the meeting of the Federation of Parsi Zoroastrian Anjumans of India, Adi Rabadi Trustee of the D.B. Mehta Atash Adaran in Calcutta said, 'The Parsi mother's child is at least half Parsi- not necessarily the Parsi father's child.' Similarly, Hormusji Jehangir Bhabha, grandfather of Indias nuclear scientist Homi Bhabha, made a succinct observation during his cross-examination in the Saklat vs Bella lawsuit in 1916. He said, 'Parsi women, as a rule, were married to Parsis and were usually chaste. But no one can say that in every case the child of a Parsi mother was by a Parsi father.' In the same

FIGURE 7:
'MATERFAMILIAS OVER THE JUDDIN CASE JUDGMENT'
'Soonamae (Mother of seven daughters,
perusing the Juddin Case Judgment):
Good, good, very good! Serves the Madamias right! No Juddin girl, White, Brown
or Black, can now claim to be a Parsee, and no Parsee dare to marry her and
convert her to Zoroastrianism!
So now, unmarried girls have a chance!
My seven little ones!"
[Hindi Punch (6 December 1908), 12.]
[By permission of the British Library (SV 576).]

'So, now unmarried girls have a chance', 1908 Hindi Punch magazine

year, an expert committee on religion clearly stated that even an illegitimate child born of a Parsi mother should not be 'given up'. It 'would be a great sin'.

'No Juddin (non-Zoroastrian) girl, white, brown or black, can now claim to be a Parsi, and no Parsi dare to marry her and convert her to Zoroastrianism. So, now unmarried girls have a chance'– proclaimed a cartoon in the Hindi *Punch* magazine in 1908 after the Petit vs Jeejeebhoy judgement. Somehow, the judgement would be

Exhibit 72.

A Bill to define and amend the law relating to marriage and Divorce among Parsees, filed before Commissioner.

Exhibit 72.

SUIT No. 91 OF 1915 OF CHIEF COURT, LOWER BURMA.

R. S. DADACHANJI,

Commissioner.

17th June 1916.

A
BILL
TO

10

Define and amend the Law relating to Marriage and Divorce among the Parsees.

Whereas it is expedient to define and amend the Law relating to Marriage and Divorce among Parsees ; it is enacted as follows :—

1. This Act may be cited as " The Parsee Marriage and Divorce Act Short-title. 1865 ".

20

2. In this Act, unless there be something repugnant in the Subject or context—" Parsee " means or applies to a person pro-
Interpretation clause. fessing the religion of Zoroaster, and domiciled in British Parsee. India.

" Priest " " Priest" includes Dastur and Mobed.

" Marriage " shall mean a marriage between Parsees contracted after the " Marriage". commencement of this Act.

" Section." "Section " means a Section of this Act.

" High Court " means the highest Civil Court of appeal in any part of " High Court ". British India.

" Local Government " means the person authorized to administer Executive " Local Government ". Government in any part of British India or the Chief

30 Executive Officer of any part of British India under the immediate adminstration of the Governor General of India in Council when such Officer shall be author-ized to exercise the powers vested by this Act in a Local Government.

Words in the singular number includes the plural and words in the plural " Number " number include the singular.

" Gender " Words importing the masculine gender includes females.

(341)

Draft deed of the Parsi Marriage and Divorce Act describes a Parsi as a person following the religion of Zarathustra

No. 27. *Mr. Best Orthodox threatening to divide the Parsi community over the Rangoon navjote controversy.* "Open Incendiarism, " Hindi Punch, 12 April 1914, p.10. Source: University of Mumbai Library.

The orthodox threatening to divide the Parsi Community, Hindi Punch magazine, 1914

twisted later to have the opposite meaning, i.e., to allow Parsi men to marry outside the community and barring Parsi women from doing the same. As a result, more than 20 per cent of young Parsi women remained unmarried. Today, however, girls have become independent and vocal. More than 50 per cent of marriages are intercommunity, and women are demanding acceptance of their children.

The Parsi Marriage and Divorce Act of 1865, another key document in this regard, does not define the term Parsi, though the draft deed described a Parsi as a person who followed the Religion of Zarathustra in British India. It does not differentiate between the illegitimate children and legitimate children already accepted as Parsis. There are no separate castes as 'Illegitimate Children of Parsi

FIGURE 4:
"THE INTRUDER"
*"Mr. Best-Orthodox—Let me come in, ladies; it is your duty as well as your
interest to support me.
The Ladies—Not if we can help it.
(The requisition against the Rangoon Navjote Ceremony, performed by Dastoor
Kaikobad Adarbad of Poona, which created bad blood among the Parsi
community, had been sent to the Trustees of the Parsi Panchayat Funds, who,
having taken an explanation from the Dastoor now announce that there will be no
meeting of the Parsees as the Dastoor
has expressed regret for his action.)"*
[Hindi Punch (10 May 1914), 12.]
[By permission of the British Library (SV 576).]

*Two illustrations in the Hindi Punch magazine criticise the orthodox and regressive
mindset among a few Parsis—the Parsi ladies are closing the door on Mr Orthodox,
not allowing him to enter*

Women' or 'Illegitimate Children of Parsi Men' or 'Excommunicated Parsi'. In 1936, the Act was amended, and it stated that one of the grounds for divorce would be 'If he or she ceased to be a Parsi (by converting to another religion)'. It also defined 'Parsi' as 'Parsi Zoroastrian'. Here the word Parsi is used to refer to a religion.

In the 21st century, the word 'Parsi' was legally identified with religion and not race in Irani vs Irani by Mody J. in 1960 and used for both the Zoroastrians in India and Iran. Very recently, the Zoroastrians in India reached out to help their coreligionists in Iran with financial and medical assistance to fight the Coronavirus pandemic. (Appendix, p. 458)

Three independent research projects have been carried out to study and compare the DNA of the Parsis from India and Iran. A similar study was also done to match the DNA of ancient Parsis with that extracted from bones collected from an ancient Dokhma (tower of silence) excavated at Sanjan, one of the earliest Parsi settlements in India. They revealed a male orientated migration and marriage with Indian women. They also showed that the DNA of the present Zoroastrians in India and Iran are different from each other. In addition, both are different from the DNA samples found at Sanjan. In a nutshell, the Parsis have changed genetically, they are not of the 'same stock'.

It is absurd that in spite of the Parsis being such a small community, children born of a Parsi father or mother are still excommunicated, based on some law that does not exist in the first place. No matter whom a Parsi man or woman marries, his/her children will still inherit 50 per cent of their DNA equally, from their Parsi grandfather and grandmother.

Referring to the Parsi community, the fourth annual report of the minorities commission (Appendix X, Annexure IX 13) stated:

An Indian citizen is free to believe that his religion prohibits conversion of another to that religion or that it debars adoption by any person of another who does or does not profess that very religion. But, at the same time, our Constitution guarantees the fundamental rights of every other citizen who entertains the contrary belief that his religion does not contain any such prohibition. Those who profess the interpretation or views of even a majority, within a religious fold, cannot compel the minority professing to be in the same fold to either hold identical or similar beliefs or to deny the minority within the minority the same right as they are themselves entitled to enjoy. At the most the divergence of views between a majority and minority within a religious fold will justify the affixation of a description such as a 'minority' or 'dissenters', as compared with a majority or the orthodox amongst the followers of a particular faith. It cannot compel the minority to accept the majority interpretation. It would be a patent violation of the Constitution.

Justice Davar had made a similar statement in the Petit Vs Jeejeebhoy case: 'I do not see how a majority of the community can enforce their views and wishes on the minority, however small that minority might be. If that minority have certain legal rights, they would be entitled to assert and will successfully assert them in spite of any number of resolutions which the majority might pass.'

In October 2020, when Mumbai resident Bahadur Hansotia left for his heavenly abode, Ervad Yazdi Aibara, *panthaky* (priest in charge) of the Karani Agiary in Mumbai refused to perform the last rites saying Hansotia was an intermarried gentleman. The priest said his late father Nadirshah had taught him to say 'no' to performing any ceremony for intermarried people. All the practising priests of this agiary issued a statement saying they do not perform religious ceremonies for intermarried Zoroastrians (Parsianna 21st October 2020). A new controversy thus erupted which further complicated the question, 'Who is a Parsi?'

2
THE ANCIENT HISTORY
OF THE RELIGION

Then Zarathushtra said: 'Reveal unto me that name of thine, O Ahura Mazda!
that is the greatest, the best, the fairest, the most effective, the most fiend-
smiting, the best-healing, that destroyeth best the malice of Daevas and Men
—Hormazd Yasht (Hymns to Ahura Mazda), The Avesta

The faith propounded by Zarathustra is considered the most ancient of the revealed religions, but it is also one of the least known. The term Zoroastrianism was coined in 1874 by Rev. Archibald Henry Sayce. It was earlier known as Mazdayasna religion or Daena or Parsi religion. To begin with, it is not known exactly where Zarathustra lived or when the Gathas (Holy Books) were composed. The Greeks considered him a very ancient prophet and placed him around 6000 BC. Western scholars place Zarathustra between 2000 and 1000 BC.

Among what is known about Zarathustra's life is that his family name was Spitama; hence he is often called Zarathustra Spitama. His father's name was Pourushaspa literally, the owner of many horses, and his mother's name was Dugdhdova, or milkmaid. They belonged to the clan of the Hvogvas. Eleventh-century Parsi historian Al Shahrastani gives us the additional information that Pourushaspa came from Azerbaijan, and Dugdhdova from Rae or Ragha in Media (a region of north-western Iran). One feels tempted to ask, would Zarathustra, born of non-Parsi parents himself, be accepted as a Parsi in India today?

Theologians and scholars have later shown that Zoroastrian beliefs on reward and punishment, heaven and hell, the resurrection of the dead, the last judgement, the coming of the Saoshyant, a world savior who will conquer evil forever, and in the end, a renewal of existence when man, nature and all creatures are restored to their pristine glory, were beliefs which influenced Judaism, Buddhism, Islam and Christianity.

According to legends, Zarathustra left his home at the age of 21 to meditate in a cave. He had his first vision of Ahura Mazda when he was 30. The first person he converted was his cousin, Maidhyomaongha. They wandered from village to village for many years, but no one would listen to their preaching.

Finally, the Iranian King Gustasp or Vishtaspa accepted his doctrines and spread it throughout his land and beyond, as he was impressed with Zarathustra's new doctrine, but the courtiers became jealous of him. They smuggled human hair, bones and nails, and placed them under his bed. In the court, they accused Zoroaster of being a sorcerer practicing black magic. The evidence was produced. Gustasp was enraged and ordered Zarathustra to be taken to the dungeon. At this time, the King's favourite horse Aspa-siha fell very ill and could not be cured. Zarathustra heard the story and offered to cure Aspa-siha. He laid down 4 conditions before he would cure the horse.

The first was that king Gustasp should embrace the new religion. 'O good and noble king, you should be absolutely doubtless of the fact that I am the prophet of Ahura Mazda; you should resolve to be faithful to Ahura Mazda and sincerely follow the teachings of the Mazdayasni Religion,' the prophet said. The king agreed.

The second condition was that the crown prince, Aspandyar, is asked to swear on his sword that he would accept the new faith and spread it throughout the land and beyond. 'Will you be ever ready to gird up for any good cause connected to the religion and never turn back therefrom? Will you consider the enemy of the religion as your own enemy?' the prophet asked. Aspandyar knelt before Zarathustra and replied, 'I will always support the good Mazdayasni Religion with my thought, word and deed.'

The third condition was that Zarathustra is taken to the chambers of Queen Hutaosa or Ketayun, to whom he would explain the new faith, and if she was convinced of its truth, she should embrace it. The Queen replied, 'Ever since I saw you, my faith in you has been unwavering. I assure you that I will never turn back from the path of Ahura Mazda.'

His last request was for the inn keeper to be summoned and made to tell the truth as to how those articles came under his pillow. Once Zarathustra treated Aspa-siha, he sprung back on his legs and the king was overjoyed. The king recognized Zarathustra as the true messenger of Ahura Mazda and accepted him as the prophet. He exhorted all present to do the same.

Zarathustra married Havovi, the daughter of Frashoshtra who was a senior courtier in Gustasp's court. They had three sons and three daughters. The marriage of his youngest and favourite daughter Pouruchista with a man of a different clan is celebrated in the 6th Gatha. He advises the couple, 'May each of you strive with the other to attain truth.'

The religion preached by Zoroaster is unique in that it insists that each individual must choose between 'vahyo' and 'akem' or, good and evil mental faculties.

Listen to the noblest teachings.
With an attentive ear.
With your penetrating mind discriminate
Between these two mentalities,
Man, by man, each one for his own self.
Awake, to proclaim this Truth.
Before the final Judgement overtakes you.
—Yasna 30 Verse 2

Zarathustra categorized mankind into two classes: 'Ashavants' or the followers of the Truth (Asha), and 'Dregvants' or the followers of the lie (Druj). With every decision man makes, he is walking over 'Chinvato-peretu', or the bridge of the seperator, which separates the 'ashavants' from the 'dregvants'. 'Chinvat' is also the bridge of judgement which the soul must cross after the death of a person. After death the 'ashavant's go to 'Garo Demana', the house of song to commune with Zarathustra. The unbelievers, the 'dregvants' and the daeva-worshippers go to 'drujo-demana', the house of the lie.

Man's duty in this life is to play his part in the great cosmic drama of the conquest of death and evil by Life and Truth. Zarathustra wants every individual to challenge each thought and act, and having done so, to choose the right path and abide by it, for Zarathustra would have ALL MEN walk 'in the green pastures of the Divine Law and the Good Mind,' writes Piloo Nanavatty in *The Parsis*. The Zoroastrian Religion is meant for all mankind, and it is a meritorious act to bring a person into the faith. Over time, the religion of Zarathustra spread far and wide throughout the world.

It is indubitable that Zoroastrianism was the religion of the great kings of Persia. A gold tablet bears the following inscription by King Ariaramnes (c.640–590 BC) brother of Cyrus the Great: 'I Ariaramnes, great king, king of kings, king of the land of Parsa. The land of the Persians which I possess, provided with fine horses and good men, it is the great god Ahura Mazda who has given it to me, I am King of this Island.'

Darius, the king of Persia described the extent of his kingdom in the following terms: 'Darius the great king, king of kings', king of countries, son of Hystaspes an Achaemenid. This is the kingdom which I hold, from the Sacae who are beyond Sogdia to Kush, and from Sind (Indus Valley) to Lydia – this is what Ahura Mazda, the greatest of gods, bestowed upon me. May Ahura Mazda protect me and my royal house.

The image is from a rock inscription at Percepolis – ancient capital of the Persian Empire (Zoroastrian Heritage)

Trade and cultural relations existed between India and Iran under the Sassanians. The Parsasikas (Pars, Parsa; Sikas, Sakas) are referred to in the Mahabharata and the Puranas, as well as in the *Raghuvamsa* of Kalidas.

Inscriptions found at Girenar, Karli, and Nasik mention the Pallavas (Parthava, Parthian). As early as in 126 BC the Parthian king had suzerainty in Saurashtra, and the Pallavas later became the rulers of Kanchipuram. Another migratory group from Iran were the Magi priests from Sistan. They merged with the Magha or Bhojak Brahmins of southern Marwar. Historians of the Middle Ages also testify to the presence of Zoroastrians in India.

Dr J.J. Modi delivered a lecture before the Bombay Branch of the Royal Asiatic Society, on 3 March 1916, referring to the recent excavations in Pataliputra and Taxila. A mere gist of it is reproduced in *The Times of India* of 4 March 1916:'During 1915, attention was called to the great question of the influence of Ancient Iran upon India by two great archaeological excavations. The first is by Sir John Marshall at Taxila, where he excavated what he thinks to be an ancient Zoroastrian fire-temple.' Dr Modi visited this excavation in July 1915 and gave his impression in *The Times of India* of 11 August 1915.

A coin used in the Sassanian age (AD 226 –651) shows a fire altar and its sacred fire flanked by two Zoroastrian priests

The second is by Dr Spooner at Pataliputra, in modern Patna. It is financed by Mr Ratan Jamsetji Tata. This excavation has led Dr Spooner to some literary inquiries, the result of which he has embodied in a paper in the journal of the Royal Asiatic Society of England under the title 'The Zoroastrian period of Indian History'. Dr Spooner points out a wave of Persian advance in India, even up to Orissa and Assam. The paper has, as it were, 'thrown a bombshell in the peaceful camp of oriental scholars'. The object of Mr Modi's paper was to show there are many facts or evidences which point to the conclusion that, at one time, Iran had greater influence-even religious influence – upon India.'

Dr Modi says, 'The name of the city is Pataliputra means "the son of Patali",i.e.,"the Trumpt Flower". The Mouryan Kings had their capital here. The people in whose country this city is situated, are the most distinguished in all India and are called PRASSI.'

Dr Spooner points out there were Zoroastrians in India in pre-Achaemenian time (Pataliputra 490 BC). Scholars like Dr Haug and Darmesteter include India in the list of 16 counties of Iran. We find this in the works of Firdausi

Dr. D B. Spooner

Superintendent, Archæological Survey of India.

Bachelor of Arts in Classical Philology, at Stanford University, California: Student of Sanskrit in the Graduate School of the Imperial University of Tokyo, and in the Government Sanskrit College of Benares, India: Travelling Fellow of Harvard University: Ph. D. in Indic Philology, of Harvard University. Cambridge, Massachusetts, and of the University of Berlin: Member of the Phi Beta Kappa of Stanford University: Fellow of the Asiatic Society of Bengal: Honorary Member of the Calcutta Historical Society, etc. etc,.

and in the writings of several Mohammedan writers of history.

The Vendidad speaks of the Hapta Hindu, the Vedic counterpart of which is the Sapta Hindu, i.e., the seven rivers of the Punjab. There were seven branches of the Indus River in India, two of which latterly united, thus giving us the present five rivers of the

Sir Ratan J. N. Tata, Kt.

"The romance of Dr. Brainerd Spooner's discoveries at Kumrahar, near Patna, has peculiar interest for Parsis. No-one dreamt that results would follow which could issue in a paper with the title [" Zoroastrian Period in Indian History"] I have given to my lecture. It was therefore without any idea of emphasising the part the Parsi community played in the early history of India that Sir Ratan Tata offered the munificent donation of Rs. 20,000 a year for the excavations of the site where the great King Asoka had his capital......Now the spade thus unconsciously directed by a Parsi tells us that the Parsis were only returning to a land in which they had wielded vast influence a thousand years earlier"—The Rev. Dr Hope Moulton.

Sir Ratan J.N. Tata Kt.
'The romance of Dr Brainerd Spooner's discoveries at Kumrahar, near Patna, has peculiar interest for Parsis. No one dreamt that results would follow which could issue in a paper with the title "Zoroastrian Period in Indian History" I have given to my lecture. It was therefore without any idea of emphasising the part the Parsi Community played in the early history of India that Sir Ratan Tata offered the the munificent donation of Rs 20,000 a year for the excavations of the site where the Great King Asoka had his capital... Now the spade thus unconsciously directed by a Parsi tells us that the Parsis were only returning to a land in which they had wielded vast influence a thousand years earlier'—The Rev. Dr Hope Moulton.

Punjab. The Indian or Hindu name of India should therefore be 'Sindustan' and not 'Hindustan' which is derived from the Persian name 'Hindu'. Dr Modi submitted that the fact was important and suggestive. That even the people of the country should know their country by its Iranian name not Indian name.

From some Pahlavi and Persian works we learn King Gustasp of Persia had sent some relatives as missionaries to India to spread Zoroastrianism there. Traditions, recorded in some later books like the *Chandragach-nama*, the *Desatir* and *Dabistan*, support this belief. One Changragacha went to Bactria to discuss the religion. They are said to have made 80,000 Brahmins Zoroastrians.Thus, some form of Zoroastrianism may be traced to India long before the Achaemenians (*The Parsis* by Mlle Delphine Menant 1917 pp. 35–37).

The Parsis settled down as farmers and agriculturists, fruit growers, toddy planters, carpenters, and weavers. The legendary British traveler John Ogilby wrote in his famous atlas of 1670:

'They live here like the natives, free and undisturbed, and drive what trade they please...for the most part (they) maintain themselves tilling and buying and selling all sorts of fruits, tapping of wine out of the palm tree...'

Parsis today proudly talk about Dastur Meherji Rana (1536-1591) of Navsari, who expounded the Zoroastrian religion at the court of Akbar and invested the emperor with the two great symbols of the faith – Sudreh (traditional vest of nine seams worn by Zoroastrians) and Kusti (sacred girdle worn around their waists). He also installed the sacred fire, with due Zoroastrian rights. When Dastur Meherji Rana returned to Navsari he was enthusiastically welcomed by the Parsis. Akbar awarded 200 bighas of land to him as a subsistence allowance, which after his death, was increased by one half in favor of his son, Kaekobad.(Source: 'The Parsis in the Court of Akbar and Dastur Meherji Rana' by J.J. Modi)

Dasturji Meherji Rana (1510–1591)

As the Parsis had very few religious texts with them, and it was difficult for them to preserve the knowledge of Avesta and Pahlavi in their new settlements, there arose various questions regarding the finer aspects of the performance of rituals and the interpretation of religious texts. Towards the end of the 15th century, Changasha, the much-respected revenue collector 'Dahewad' of Navsari, collected all the various questions on religious matters, and, at his own expense sent Nariman Hoshang to Iran, requesting the Zoroastrians in Iran to answer the list of questions. He presented this list to the Dasturs of Yezd province, who received him cordially and answered all his questions. Nariman Hoshang returned to India around 1478. Thus started the tradition of Rivayats, questions and answers on religion between the Zoroastrians of India and the Dasturs of Iran, which lasted for nearly 300 years.

For over 600 years (1200–1837) Persian was the official language of the Delhi Sultanate and the Bengal Sultanate as well as the cultured language of poetry and literature. During the Bengal Renaissance Persian was studied by scholars, including Raja Ram Mohan Roy. From the mid 18th to the 19th century, five to six Parsi dailies were published in Calcutta. Most notable among them were The *Durbin* and the *Sultan al-Akbhar*. When Rusi B. Gimi, the noted Parsi entrepreneur started his life in Calcutta in the 1940s, he supplemented his income by translating Persian writings into English.

Persian people as well as Persian Turks settled in Bengal to work as teachers, lawyers, poets, aristocrats, soldiers, and administrators. A popular literary creole emerged mixing Persian and Bengali called 'Dobhasi'.

The October 1931 number of the Iran League Quarterly published an article on Parsis in India. It stated,

Parsis are amongst the oldest inhabitants of this beautiful and noble land: for really speaking, they had commenced settling in it since millenniums past, and not only after the fall of the Sassanian dominion as it is commonly understood. Some large bands did indeed emigrate and settle here on that occasion also; but Parsis were known to be in India during the Achaemenian, Parthian and Sassanian times (558–652 BC) as they held some

The sacred eternal fire at the Atash Behram at Yazd (Zoroastrian Heritage)
From 1960, it is open to non-Zoroastrians

portion or another of this great land as a part of their dominion
of those days. Hence it is quite long since they have become true
children of the soil; and so, they will love it and serve it with great
sincerity and devotion.

The fire at Yazd fire temple in Iran has burnt for over 1500 years. The ancient flame has been kept alive throughout various centuries and relocations and continues to burn today. The flame is one of nine Atash Behram's (Fire of Victory), the highest grade of a fire held within a Zoroastrian fire temple. The fires are created from 16 'types' of fire. This Atash Behram is the oldest and only one outside India.

In ancient times making a new fire was difficult, there was no match or other instrument to start a fire. Zoroastrian communities developed fire houses that had ever burning fires. The fire keepers were responsible to keep the fire burning, they covered the fire carefully with its ashes so that they could remove them in the morning. In this way, people did not have to make fires separately and they could take fire from the fire houses. As a result, fire houses became a necessary part of each community and fire keeping became a crucial profession. Later these fire houses were called Atash Geh in Persian.

The fire at Yazd has burned from AD 470, during the reign of the Sassanian Empire. The flame first flickered in the Pars Karyan fire temple, and then relocated to the city of Aqda, where it burned for 700 years. The fire was finally located at Yazd in 1934.

Today, the flame burns in a bronze vessel and is protected by a glass wall. The fire is kept alive by the priests who feed it dry wood several times a day.

In 1960, the Anjuman-i-Nasiri opened the doors of the Yazd Atash Behram to non-Zoroastrians who can enter the fire temple and see the fire behind the glass wall, but they are not allowed within the sanctum area that holds the fire. Entry into the sanctum area is only for the priests who tend the fire.

In the Atash Behram at Yazd even non-Zoroastrians can enter and see the fire but in India, all Zoroastrians are not allowed to enter.

3
HOW DO YOU IDENTIFY A PARSI?

He who upholds Truth with all the might of his power,
He who upholds Truth the utmost in his word and deed,
He, indeed, is Thy most valued helper, O Mazda Ahura!
—The Avesta, Ahunuvaiti Gatha

There is no universally accepted way of identifying a Parsi. In the early 19th century, Parsis were defined by their distinctive clothing, which is not applicable today. On the other hand, Zoroastrians coming from Iran and settling in India were simply identified by their Sudreh and Kusti and their knowledge of prayer lines.

Dosabhai Framji Karaka in his book – *The Parsis: Their History, Manners and Customs*, 1858, writes about the unique yet simple attire of a Parsi: The dress worn by a Parsi child consists of a single piece of garment called the jhabla, which extends from neck to ankles. The 'topee' or skull cap covers the head and completes the dress.

When a child is formally inducted into the religion with the sudreh and kusti of the Zoroastrian religion, the 'jhubla' is thrown off. The sudreh is made of linen or net, while the kusti is a thin woolen cord or cincture of 72 threads. These are generally worn at home. In Avestan language, the former is called 'Sutteher Pesunghem', which means 'the garment of the good and beneficial way'. The kusti is passed around the waist three times and tied with four knots.

At the first knot, the person says, 'There is one God, and no other is compared to him.' At the second knot, he utters, 'the religion

Till 1950 the jhubla was still in fashion

Navjote ceremony of my three grandchildren

Children wearing jhublas in the 19th century

Cartoon from Parsi Punch
(the ladies are dressed in saris with a long sudreh showing, and their heads are covered.
The men are wearing long coats and white pants and black headgear)

The long coat and white pant worn outside the house in 1800s
(Darukhanawala Parsi Lustre on Indian Soil)

given by Zarthost is true'; at the third, she says, 'Zarthost is the true prophet and he derived his mission from God', and at the fourth, 'perform good actions and abstain from evil ones'.

A waist coat, loose cotton trousers, slippers, and a skull cap are also commonly worn by Parsi men. When going out, he puts on an angrakha or loose ungirdled tunic, the sleeves of which are twice the length of the arms and are folded up in wrinkles.

Over the skull he wears a dark chocolate turban. The full dress of a Parsi man, in addition to this, consists of a 'jama' of white linen

The formal traditional dress
Darukhanawala, Parsi Lustre on Indian Soil. He is dressed in a jama and pichoree, the
traditional double-breasted ankle-length outer garment and waistband, traditional
Parsi headgear and shoes

and a 'pichoree'. The sleeves and upper portion of the former are like the angrakha, but the skirt is full and resembles an English woman's gown. The 'pichoree' is a long cloth, about a yard wide, and many yards in length and is passed around the waist in successive folds.

Parsi women are generally graceful and well formed. They are robbed of a part of their beauty by the custom of concealing their hair under a 'mathabana', a thin muslin cloth worn covering the

*A Parsi woman in traditional sari and mathabana and
long sudreh (Hindi Punch)*

head. They also wear the sudreh and kusti, and wear silk trousers with a silk vest with short sleeves called the kanchari or 'choli'. Over this is worn a sari, which is several yards in length and embroidered. The rich wear jewels, necklaces, nose rings, bangles at the wrist and ankles and sometimes even the slippers are adorned with pearls.

The dress of the modern Parsi differs from that of their ancestors in Persia and by their present coreligionists in that country. They have adapted the present costume in accordance with the agreement with the Hindu princes, who received them in India. That is why the angrakha and turban of the men, and the sari of the women resemble Hindus.

In the celebrated Saklat vs Bella lawsuit of 1914–1925, Shapurji Cowasji described Bella's mother as a Parsi – 'She was a Parsi lady: I formed this opinion from her talk and her dress when I saw her. She wore the usual Parsi dress. She had the usual Parsi features, not very dark, not very fair... When I went to see her, she put the 'kore' (i.e., the border) on her head. She wore a Mathabana. I saw the Sudreh projecting from her sari.'

The sharp nose, the unmistakable physical feature of the Parsis, was joked about in the Rangoon courtroom in the Saklat vs Bella suit. When asked to describe typical Parsi features, the lawyer, Mr Connell, pointed to Mr Hormusji and Mr Patel, two of the Parsis in the room. To everyone's delight, the magistrate replied that he would not allow them to be put as exhibits.

Jenny Rose in her book *Zoroastrianism: A Guide for the Perplexed*, writes:

> Iranian Zoroastrian immigrants who seek asylum in India under the aegis of the BPP must produce an identity card issued by a local Anjuman (Zoroastrian Council) within Iran; they must possess a sudreh and kusti, and be able to recite in Avestan the two cardinal prayers of the 'ahuna vairya' and 'ashem vahu'. It is through demonstrating such practical knowledge of daily aspects of the faith that the applicants are recognized as having been initiated into and professing the religion. They have become eligible to receive the support of the Parsi community.

From Parsi Punch (depicting the phenomenal Parsi nose)

No questions are asked regarding Ancestry. No DNA Tests are done. As Justice Beaman remarked, 'they are ready to admit any and every Irani Zoroastrian, about whose antecedent they cannot possibly know anything.'

Iranians are identified as Zoroastrians and accepted as Parsis by their possession of the sacred Sudreh and Kusti and knowledge of prayers and not by their ancestry. Why don't Parsis in India have a similar system of identification? Today, modern Parsis are not distinguishable by their dress.

4

THE BEGINNING OF THE RIVAYATS

If men come here, as co-religionists, brethren or friends ...
to seek knowledge ... let them be given that knowledge with holy words.
—Vendidād IV. 44

Parsis, as a tribe, were living in India among the Hindus till about 1499, when Behdin Changashah rehabilitated them and reminded them of their religion. This is recorded in the history of the Parsis of Navsari (a town in Gujarat where they had settled) and was recorded in court in the Saklat vs Bella lawsuit, a watershed moment in the history of the community. They had totally forgotten their religion and discarded the Sudreh and Kusti. Changashah sent missionaries to Iran to ascertain religious procedures. These were called Rivayats.

Captain Hormazdyar Jamsetji Mancherji Desai writes in the *History of the Parsis of Navsari:* 'Behdin Changashah (who lived sometime between 1400 and 1512) was the first great Parsi in the annals of Navsari. His invaluable services have been lauded at length in the narrative Kisseh-a-Sanjan.' Desai informs us that Changashah filled up a small, dried pond east of Kangavad and asked Parsis to live on that piece of land. Over the time, this area came to be known as Parsi Puri. For quite some time after that Navsari too was called Parsi Puri. Changashah also developed a colony where the Parsi 'kuvo' or well now stands and called this area Asha Puri after his father.

EXHIBIT 77

Extract from page 326 of the Journal of the Iranian Association filed before Commissioner.

EXHIBIT 77.

Suit No. 91 of 1915 of Chief Court, Lower Burma.

R. S. DADACHANJI,

Commissioner.

23rd June 1916.

DESCRIPTION OF THE CONVEYANCE OF THE FIRE OF BAHRAM TO NAVSARI BY CHANGASHAH.

A layman then appeared who had not his peer at the time. He came forward in those days to preserve the religion and many notable things (lit. signs, marks) proceeded from him. He was the Dahyovad, [49] his name was Changa, son of Asa and he solaced the hearts of the people of the Good Creed. That good-natured man would not suffer the Faith to fall into neglect in those latter days. He gave money (lit. purse) out of his own wealth to those who had no Sudra and Kusti (the sacred shirt and girdle). Many (excellent) provisions that man made for the creed. No afflicted person (ever) went to him for whom, poor man, he did not provided some relief or whose heart he did not cordially set at ease. In those times several Buhdin persons came into the Faith under his auspices (lit. by his good fortune). Indeed, my tongue cannot fully (lit. plainly) praise this layman who managed the affairs of the creed so well.

49. Phal. Dahyopat, Av. Danghu-paiti, chief ruler. Changa Asa's son Manak also is styled Dahyovad (Desai) in the Ravayat of Shapur Asa or Kama Asa of 896 A. Y., (1527 A. C.)

(121)

Extract from the journal of the Iranian Association (later changed to Iran League Quarterly) the description of the conveyance of the fire of Behram to Navsari by Changashah in the rivayat of Shapur ASA

Desai writes:

The condition of such Parsis in those times was most pitiable and heart rending. Some had no Sudreh and Kusti on their bodies and most had no footwear. Quite a few were in tatters, and some had adopted common Hindu customs and practices. Some were totally ignorant of their ancient religion. Changasha settled them in temporary camps erecting Mandwas in the area now known as Malesar... He made them give up and discard the non-Parsi customs they had ignorantly adopted.

Transcription

Exhibit 77
Extract from page 326 of the journal of the Iranian Association
Filed before Commissioner
Suit No. 91 of 1915 of Chief Court, Lower Burma. EXHIBIT 77
R.S. DADACHANJI, Commissioner.
23rd June 1916

Description of the Conveyance of the Fire of Behram to Navsari by Changashah

A layman then appeared who had not his peer at the time. He came forward in those days to preserve the religion and many notable things (lit. signs, marks) proceeded from him. He was the Dahyovad, and his name was Changa son of Asa and he solaced the hearts of the people of the Good Creed. That good-natured man would not suffer the Faith to fall into neglect in those latter days. He gave money (lit. purse) out of his own wealth to those who had no Sudreh and Kusti (the sacred shirt and girdle). Many (excellent) provisions that man made for the creed. No afflicted person (ever) went to him for whom, poor man, he did not provide some relief or whose heart he did not cordially set at ease. In those times several Buhdin persons came into the Faith under his auspices (lit. by his good fortune). Indeed, my tongue cannot fully (lit.plainly) praise this layman who managed the affairs of the creed so well.

*****

The erudite author of the *Twarikhe-e-Navsari* (History of Navsari) writes that with their prolonged stay with the Hindus, the Parsis had become almost like them. The males used to put on red Pagdhis and dhotis! Their names were mostly Hindu names such as Hasji, Fakir, Jogia, Narsang, and Dhana! The ladies had such names as Malanbai, Zilibai, Dhanabai. They used to dress and put on decorative ornaments like those of the Hindu ladies. They used wooden biers for carrying the dead and even helped in carrying the corpses. Changasashah first satisfied the economic need of the indigent Parsis and then started restoring their faith in their glorious ancient religion and put them on the right path.

It was reported in the *Parsee Prakash*, 'One Nariman Hoshang of Bharuch, was deputed by Changasha to lead a religious mission to Iran...the religious mission was organized to obtain clarifications on important religious and ritual matters from the Dasturs of Iran. This mission was very successful and led to several such delegations being sent to Iran over a period of 300 years.' The collection of all such correspondence on theological problems between the two sides then came to be popularly known as the rivayats. In the rivayats from 1516 and 1547, Changashah is addressed as first of the Parsi Behdins. Changasha is still remembered by the Parsis of Navsari among their illustrious dead at all public ceremonies; and the Behdin families there of Talati, Seth, and Patel claim descent from him.' (Patel, *Parsee Prakash* 861–62).

The well-known French traveler and scholar Anquetil du Perron also writes about Changashah:

There appeared afterwards at Newsaree a rich Parsi named Changa Shah, a faithful observer of the Zoroastrian Law. He distributed his wealth amongst the poor, provided the Parsis with Koshtis and Sudrehs, and endeavored to bring back those whom ignorance

At a village near Silvassa where the four Wadia families were located by the World Zoroastrian Association (Parsiana)

and troubled had led into many errors to the exact practice of the Zoroastrian law. To succeed in this, he applied to the Dastoors of Kerman, consulting them on different points of the Zoroastrian religion, neglected in Gujarat.

Rustum Paymaster cites from John Ogilby, a Scottish cartographer, as recorded in Atlas V (1670) pp. 218–219. 'In the course of time, these settlers forgot their origin, their religion and even their name. At length, the name 'Persian' was made to them by some men from Persia who instructed them in their religion and taught them to serve God.'

Even today Parsis have been found, unaware of their ancient religion and following Hindu customs and faith, living in abject poverty in the interiors of Gujarat, and the World Zoroastrian Assossiation is endeavouring to help them.

5
THE ORIGIN OF THE PARSIS*

Which is the one virtue that is best for mankind? Truthful speech is best, because in truthful speech there is good repute in the world and good life and salvation in Paradise.
—Pahlavi Rivāyat Accompanying the Dādestan-ī-Dēnīg

Kisseh-a-Sanjan, a poem written in 1599, is the only record of the history of the Parsis from the time they reportedly migrated to India to escape persecution. Written by Baman Kaekobad in 1599, the poem in its title refers to Sanjan in Gujarat, a place of immense historical and religious importance for the Parsis. It was here that the first Atash Behram was consecrated.

However, the fact remains that *Kisseh-a-Sanjan* is a literary work, and it makes no claims of historicity. At best, it is historical fiction. It is a pity that there is no historical record of the Parsis' arrival in India, no list of names, no count of how many men, women, or children or how many ship or ships came, and exactly when or where they landed. Travelling by sea would have been sacrilegious for the Parsis, so it is possible that they came by land.

Historian Shapurji Hodiwala in his 1920 book *Parsis of Ancient India* mentions the writer, Baman Kaekobad Hamjiar Sanjana. He writes that very little is known of him except that Baman put the finishing touch on his verses on the day of 'Khordad' in the month

---
* The author is indebted to Mr Fali S. Nariman for his inputs in this chapter.

of 'Farwandin' in the year 969 AY (about AD 1600), and that he was 'considerably advanced in age' at that time.

An English translation of *Kisseh-a-Sanjan* was made in 1844 at the suggestion of Dr John Wilson by E.B. Eastwick and published in the first volume of the journal of the Bombay branch of the Royal Asiatic Society.

Shapurji Hodiwala

Kisseh-a-Sanjan talks about five conditions set by the King before allowing the Parsis to enter his land. The conditions have often been misquoted. Hodiwala enumerates them as follows:

1) That they should give him some information about their religion
2) That they must give up the language of Iran and speak the local language of India
3) That their women should put on clothes like Hindu women
4) That they must lay aside their weapons and swords
5) That good works such as marriages should be performed in the evening.

On 25 October 1913, Hodiwala read a paper before the Society for the promotion of Zoroastrian Research, titled *The Traditional Dates of Parsi History*. This was later printed in the Journal of the Iranian Association in January 1914. In this paper, he writes, 'I have said that very few of the statements are properly authenticated and some of them are absolutely nameless. They exhibit the most bewildering diversity amongst themselves, and, if we are to believe them, the same event (the arrival of the Parsis at Sanjan) occurred in 772, 895, and 961 Vikram Samvat ie. 716, 839 and 905 AD.'

Dosabhai Framji Karaka in his book *The Parsees – Their History, Manners, Customs and Religion* (1858) makes the same point about *Kisseh-a-Sanjan.*

'Whatever information (about our history) is now in our possession, and is to any extant reliable, is gleaned from a work entitled *Kisseh-a-Sanjan*, which was compiled in the year 1599, by one Bahman a Zoroastrian resident of Nowsaree, from the traditions extant in his time.' He adds, 'various meagre and unsatisfactory traditions exist concerning the tide of emigration, the manner in which it was effected, and the total number of those who left the shores of Gulf.'

In the foreword of *Parsis of Ancient India*, Hodiwala explains:

the history of the Parsis of ancient India from the hoary past down to the 16th Century after Christ is almost a blank. Open the first volume of the Parsi Prakash, that monumental work of the Late Khan Bahadur Bomanji B. Patel, and you will find that only 3 or 4 pages have been devoted to events connected with the Parsis during the above-mentioned period.

He continues:

According to the account of the *Kisseh-a-Sanjan* about 115 years after the overthrow of the Sassanian dynasty, a number of Zoroastrians came to India and landed at Div off the coast of Kathiawar. Having stayed there for 16 years, they went to Sanjan. If we take the battle of Naharend (AD 641) to have decided the fate of the Persian Empire, it would appear that the Zoroastrians landed at Sanjan in AD 775. Some scholars, taking AD 651 (when the King Yezdagard was killed) as the starting, arrive at the starting date AD 785.

Ervad Maneckji R Unwala has got a manuscript about 150 years old, which gives a slightly different account from that of the *Kisseh-a-Sanjan.* The date is 716 AD and not 775 or 785 AD, beside

Travelling by sea would break the Parsi Purity Laws

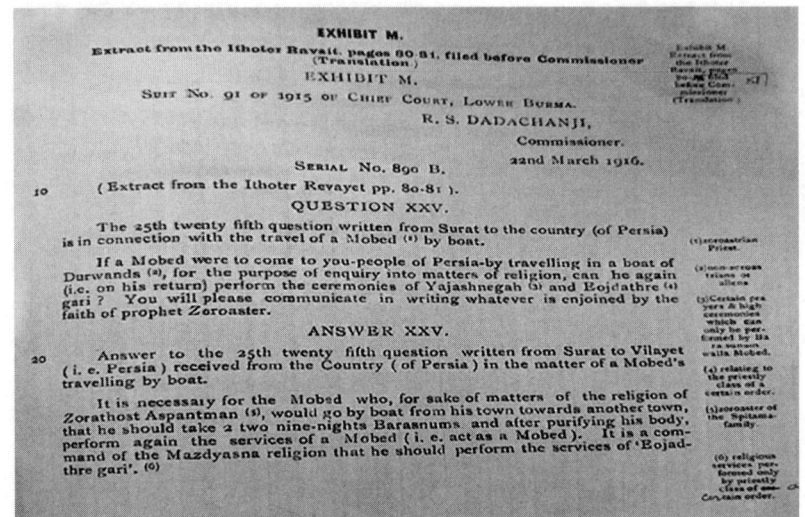

Ithoter rivayat question xxv on the purity laws

this there is no landing at Div. The reason for this difference is the accounts maybe, as suggested by Wilford, that the history of at least 2 bands of refugees has been mixed up. Such discrepancies, coupled with other circumstances, have led some scholars to challenge every detail of the *Kisseh-a-Sanjan*.

Hodiwala also says:

Nothing indeed, can be a greater error than to suppose that Bahman was a great poet, a serious historian or a man of multifarious and accurate scholarship. At the same time, he was not an ordinary man. He belonged to a family possessing remarkable literary aptitudes and it would be folly to suppose that all his statements are unworthy of credit. But it must be also recognized that he is occasionally out of his depth.

Did they come by sea? Hodiwala believes: 'It is very likely that in accordance with their tradition, they came (by land) hugging the coast – thus avoiding the dangers of the sea and the risk of breaking the rule about not defiling the sea with human impurities.'

The purification ritual to be observed after travelling by boat (over water) as recorded in the Rivayats were filed in court in the Saklat vs Bella lawsuit.

Regarding Travelling Over Water.

Transcription Of Above Rivayat

Suit No. 91 of 1915 or Chief Court, Lower Burma R.S. DADACHANJI, Commissioner

22nd March 1916. SERIAL No. 890 B. Exhibit M

(Extract from the Ithoter Rivayat pp. 80-81)

QUESTION XXV.

The 25th question written from Surat to the country (of Persia) is in connection with the travel of a Mobed by boat.

If a Mobed were to come to you-people of Persia-by travelling in a boat of Durwands (Alien in Faith) for the purpose of enquiry into matters of religion, can he again (i.e. on his return) perform the ceremonies of Yajashnega and Eojdathre gati? You will please communicate in writing whatever is enjoined by the faith of prophet Zoroaster.

Answer XXV.

Answer to the 25th question written from Surat to Vilayet (i.e. Persia) received from the Country (of Persia). In the matter of a Mobed travelling by boat.

It is necessary for the Mobed who, for sake of matters of the religion of Zorathost Aspantman, would go by boat from his town towards another town, that he should take two, nine-nights Barasnums and after purifying his body, perform again the services of a Mobed (ie. act as a Mobed). It is a command of the Mazdayasna religion that he should perform the services of 'Eojadthre gari'.

Shams-Ul-Ulama Dr Sir Jivanji Jamsetji Modi (1854–1933)

*****

Jivanji Jamsetji Modi in his book *A Few Events in the Early History of the Parsis and their Dates* (1905) writes:

> For this history (of the arrival of the Parsis), we are to a certain extent, indebted to the Qissa-i-Sanajan (ie. the story of the history of Sanjan), A Persian book written in verse in 969 Yazdajardi (1600AD). The following couplet at the end of the poem gives its date. 'It was the year nine and sixty and nine hundred (i.e., 969) Yazdajardi, when this history was written.

He thus describes his descent and his authorities for the story:

Allan Williams

A Dastur has showed me this story. O God! Keep him prosperous in both worlds. I am the poor man whose name is Bahman. My property and residence were in Naosari... My father is Kaekobad... his father was Hormazdyar Dastur. In the year nine and sixty-nine hundred (i.e., 969) Yazdajardi (1600AD), when this history was written. I have said this story as I have seen it, and as I have heard it from the words of my elders. In the month Farvandin and on the day Khordad, these verses were finished properly.

Now hear strange accounts from the words of Mobeds and from old history... I have heard it from a wise Dastur... He told me this narrative from old traditions. He told me concealed secrets of stories (ie. hitherto unpublished facts). I repeat the story from his words. I tell the secrets (ie. unpublished facts) about the work of persons of good religion.

Alan Williams in the book *Everlasting Flame*, co-sponsored by the Bombay Parsi Punchayat, corroborates the fact in the chapter *Looking Back to see the Present*, that the Qissa is a story and not historical fact.

Parsi Zoroastrians to this day believe that they came to India as migrant refugees from Iran. They believe their forefathers

Professor Alan Williams adressing the Calcutta community at a Parsi Zoroastrian Association function in 1980, Mr Rusi B. Gimi (the present author's father) was the president

travelled in one boat, arriving eventually, after many hardships, on the shores of India—This information is gleaned from the *Kisseh-a-Sanjan*, an imaginative narrative. Though it is a 'Qissa' or a story it in not 'Tarikh' or history. It is more than history. It is a multi-faceted Religious Myth.

One of the main indicators of this 'mythological' poetic nature of the text is the fluid use of temporality and his transporting of the reader into other times in a circular motion from past to present and future and back again.

It refers to one date only i.e., that of its composition in 1599. In short, events alluded to in the story stand in only vague relation to events known from historical sources.

He also mentions, 'Truly, the faithful Zoroastrians (who are always referred to as behdina⁻n, mard-e behdin, behdin-e dinda⁻r, not zartoshtiyan) are the heroes of the battles alongside their Hindu allies.' (*Parsis in India and the Diaspora* by John Hinnels and Allan Williams.) Rukshana Nanji the archaeologist, also notes, 'The word "Parsi" appears nowhere in the first half of the Qissa...the migrants were known as Behdins (people of the good faith).'

The word Zoroastrianism is of recent origin. The name 'Zoroastrianism', referring to the religion showcased in the exhibition 'The Everlasting Flame', was coined only recently. According to the Oxford English Dictionary, it first occurs in 1874 in *Principles of Comparative Philology* by the Oxford assyriologist The Reverend Archibald Henry Sayce in connection with the religion of the Persians. The term is based on the form Zarathustra, which is the Greek variety of the Iranian name of the religion's founder, Zarathustra' (*The Everlasting Flame: Exploring Religion, History and Tradition*, ed. Allan Williams, Sarah Stewart and Almut Hintze).

Allan Williams in his essay on the Kisseh-a-Sanjan writes that the author Bahman Kay Kobad is by no mean an invisible or shrinking figure in the text and he fashions his story, to bring to the fore certain interests which he, as a Sanjan priest in Navsari, represented in his day. (Referring to the once violent dispute between the Sajana priests and the Bhagarsath Priests of Navsari.) The Qissa is written by a Sanjan Priest bent on proving his own sect's case against the rival Bhagarias Priests of Navsari.

Gyaneshwer Choubey in his genetic research and the DNA of the Parsi community, came to the conclusion that it was a male oriented migration. This would be highly unlikely, that our ancestors would have run away to avoid persecution and have left their women and children behind. Maybe they had come as traders and settled down along the coast.

Archaeologists Rukshana Nanji and Homi Dhalla conclude that the Persians came as traders and communities of these traders had settled on foreign shores as far as China and often their numbers were not negligible. That the Zoroastrian migrants to Sanjan were basically a mercantile group is borne out by records as well as by excavated material. Andre Wink goes further and adds that the migration was not so much due to religious persecution as much as 'a readjustment of commercial patterns which had arisen long before Islam, and, to an extent at least, a response to new opportunities in the transit trade between the Islamic world and al-Hind' (Wink 2002: 105) ('Landing at Sanjan' by Rukshana Nanji and Homi Dhalla in *Parsis in India and the Diaspora*).

Nanji and Dhalla further mention:

> The Parthian and Sasanian contact with India and Gujarat in particular is also historically known and well documented. Hence a trading outpost with a community of foreign settlers, both Arab and Persian, at Sanjan is not unexpected. Such a trading outpost may well have existed prior to the migration, as is indicated by the presence of early ceramic types in the lowest levels of the excavations. The migrants may well have been aware of this settlement and may have made a conscious decision to migrate to Sanjan. It is logical to suppose that they had contact with the mainland and would therefore have taken an informed decision to relocate themselves at the most hospitable and suitable point on the west coast. The idea that a shipload of migrants buffeted by the winds was tossed ashore at Sanjan by sheer chance needs to be recognized as a myth. From the tenth century onwards Bharuch, Khambat and Chaul were known to have similar communities of Arab and Persian Zoroastrians.

What we know is not based on historical fact. Most of our history is simply a surmise or assumption based on the little knowledge available. When did we come? Did we come by land or sea? How

A family staying at a village near Silvassa in Gujarat, located and assisted by the World Zoroastrian Association (Parsiana)

many people came? How many men, women, and children? Where did we land or enter India? Did we really come to escape persecution? Or were we just travelling traders? What were the names of these people? These are questions only about the coming to India. What happened from then to 1599? Innumerable such questions had no definite answer for almost 1000 years in this land. Yet, Parsis claim they trace their ancestry to the original emigrants who came to India.

Shernaz Cama, in a chapter on Languages and Texts in the book *Threads of Continuity* (2016) says, 'In India the new spoken language or Parsi Gujrati dialect emerged. A unique blend of Imperial Persian and Dubra or outcast Gujarati, and it was acquired through mingling with agriculturists and other workers, who must have been the first point of contact for the refugees.' The World Zoroastrian Organization (WZO) is still discovering 'Parsis' staying in the remote villages of Gujarat living in abject poverty and trying to rehabilitate them. Testing the DNA (which has not been done to date) of these recently discovered Parsis might reveal a lot about the unknown past.

Origin of the Parsis.

As narrated by Mr Fali Nariman

The Kisseh-a-Sanjan (literally the story of Sanjan), is the oldest extant account we have of the Parsis in India. It was written by Bahman Kaekobad of Navsari in 969 AY (AD 1600) in Persian verse; it has been translated several times into Gujarati and English and was much better known to the Parsis 70–80 years ago, when it played its part in some of the controversies that then agitated the community. A study of the Kisseh-a-Sanjan was first published as an Article in 1971 by Dr H.E. Eduljee who later at the instance of Dr (Mrs) Piloo Jungalwala, a well known Zoroastrian scholar, decided to embark on a full scale study which is now published by the K.R. Cama Oriental Institute – as *Kisseh-a-Sanjan* by Dr H.E. Eduljee (1991).

According to this account when the rule of Yazdargir the IIIrd ended with the battle of Nihavand the followers of Zarathushtra fled to the mountains of Kohistan,and lived there for a hundred years. From there they went to Hormuz (on the Persian Gulf) where they spent another fifteen years but there was no peace. A Dastur (Priest) who was also an astrologer advised them to leave for India. Setting sail, they came to the island of Diu and stayed there for nearly twenty years. They learnt some Sanskrit in Diu, and when they ultimately set sail for Gujarat in their small boats they were met by a violent storm. They prayed and vowed that if they landed safely they would erect a Fire Temple (an Atash Behram) as an offering of thanks. The storm abated, and they ultimately landed in Sanjan!

The ruler of Sanjan was Jadi Rana. The leader of the Parsis, a Dastur, went to him and asked for asylum. The Rana replied that he would grant asylum if the Dastur explained to him the Zoroastrian beliefs and practices and accepted certain conditions. The Dastur (who thought on his feet, as modern-day lawyers are trained to do!) explained the religion in pleasing Sanskrit (in the form of 16 shlokas) making it appear to be not too distant from the Hinduism practised at that time: after all, survival was at stake and the religion had to be portrayed in some acceptable form to those from whom sanctuary was sought! The ruler was impressed. The Parsis were allowed to land and build their settlement which they called Sanjan – and later (AD 790) with the Rana's permission and help they also built the Atash-Behram[1]. The ruler appears to have imposed five conditions for their continued stay in India:

(1) that they should speak the Gujarati language;

(2) that their women should dress in saris;

(3) that their marriages should be performed after sunset (a local custom at the time);

(4) that they should till the soil diligently; and

(5) that they should never bear arms. Each one of these conditions was faithfully carried out[2].

---

1 There is however a contrary oral tradition - perhaps better known; certainly more pleasing to the ears The Zoroastrian Chief Priest not knowing the language of the Yadav ruler is supposed to have asked for asylum in India in sign language. The ruler is supposed to have sent back a cup filled to the brim with milk thereby signifying that there was no place in this country for refugees.escape the astute Whereupon the Chief Priest, a man of considerable worldly wisdom, is supposed to have added sugar to the milk without disturbing the contents. The significance ofthis gesture did not escape the astute Yadav Rana. Here were people telling him that they were intelligent enough to co-exist with his own people, the sprinkling of sugar meant that not only would they not disturb them, but that they would actually sweeten their lives. See Tanya Luhrmann 'The Good Parsi' (Oxford University Press), 1996 pages 78–79: she characterises this story as an 'old chestnut'!

2 In John Stuart Mill's classic essay on 'Liberty' (written in 1859), it is shown how a self denying habit of centuries can get transmitted in a Man's genes! The example given in a footnote in that essay, is of the Parsis in India who (it is said) having promised the Hindu Ruler who gave them refuge that they would not eat beef continued to honour the promise generation after generation, and when a Mohammedan ruler a few centuries there after said that he would permit them to remain if they abjured eating the meat of pig (i.e. pork) the Parsis agreed and again this was a promise which successive generations of Parsis observed. I recall (says Nariman) that my own grandparents never touched beef or pork – without even knowing the true reason why!

6

PARSIS IN MUGHAL COURT

I attribute (the creation of) all things to Ahura Mazda, the Good,
the Righteous, the Holy, the Resplendent, the Glorious, to whom belong all
good things – the World, Order or Righteousness (prevailing in the world), and
the luminous, with whose light all brilliant objects shine.
—Yasna XII.1

A footnote on page 197 of vol. IX, part II (section titled 'Gujarat-Population') of the *Gazetteer of the Bombay Presidency* mentions names of eight Parsis who visited the Mughal Court.

The first was Meherji Rana who invested Akbar with the sacred shirt and girdle in AD 1580, and in reward became the high priest of Navsari.

The second was Meherji's son Kekobad, who went to Delhi to seek redress, as the Nawab of Surat had tried to take away the Emperor's grant of 200 acres. Kekobad was successful, and in a paper dated the 10th of Aspandád, in the 40th year of Akbar's reign, he received an additional grant of a 100 acres.

The third was Mulla Jamasp, a priest of Navsari. In AD 1619, in return for his present of jasmine oil, Emperor Jahangir gifted him a piece of land named Ratnagiri near Navsari.

The fourth was Rustam Manek who went with the head of the Surat factory to Delhi in 1660.

The fifth person, Sorabji Kavasji, was of great service to the English in 1760 when they obtained command of the Surat castle and the post of Mughal Admiral. He returned to Surat bringing dresses of honour and a horse to the heads of the English Company at Surat (Despatch from the Surat Chief in Council to the Bombay President and Council, 3rd May 1760, in Briggs' 'Cities of Gujarastra'). It is said that Sorabji Kavasji, who had been taught watch-making by a European, first went to Delhi in 1744 to mend a favourite clock of the Emperor. The Emperor, probably Muhammad Shah (AD 1719–1748) was so pleased with Sorabji's skill that he honoured him with the title of Nek Sat Khan, (ie., Lord of the Lucky Hour), gave him a lien on the customs revenue in Surat and the rank of a chief of 500 horse and 300 foot soldiers. Nek Sat Khan was an ancestor of the well-known Ardesher Bahadur, Kotwal of Surat.

The sixth was Kavasji Rustomji, third son of the high priest of Udvada, who is said to have gone to Delhi as Nek Sat Khan's assistant. He was given the title of Mirzan Khosru Beg and also a piece of land near Surat, which his family, now known as the Mirza family, enjoyed for several years. Mirzan Khosru Beg's skill as a watch maker descended to his third son Kaioji who was a watch-repairer to Bajirav Peshwa. After Bajirav's fall (AD 1818) Kaioji went to Bhavnagar (a native state in Kathiawar) with a clock of Bajirav which the Bhavnagar Chief had bought. In Bhavnagar, he made a clock for which a tower was built, which is still in order.

The seventh was Kalabhai Sorabji, son-in-law of Nek Sat Khan. He is said to have gone to Delhi to meet his father-in-law and received an estate in Rander (in Surat).

The eighth was Mancherji Kharshedji Seth, a wealthy merchant and well-known Dutch broker who, some time before AD 1784, visited Delhi, supposedly at the emperor's request, who had heard of Seth's generosity.

It was from Bombay that the Parsis began their commercial relations with China, approximately around 1756. From there the Parsis extended their connections with Pegu, Moulmein, Rangoon,

Mecca, Jeddah, Muscat, Mauritius, and the coast of Malay, trading in timber, rice, sugar, asafoetida, cotton, and spices. Along the Malabar Coast, they traded with Calicut, Cannanore, Alapi, Travancoro, Tellicherry, and other places. One of the kings of Mysore had deputed one of the Parsi merchants to improve the trade, commerce, and the revenue of that Province half a century back. Even the Imam of Muscat entrusted several commissions to a well-known Bombay firm.

7
THE BOMBAY PARSI RIOTS IN 1832

Truth is good.
Indeed, it is best.
It is happiness.
Happiness comes to him, who, for the sake of truth, follows the path of truth.
—Ashem Vohu Prayer

Today it might sound unbelievable that a full-scale riot broke out in Bombay in 1832 over dogs. And it might sound even more incredible that the ever-so-gentle, decorous, well-bred Parsis led it from the front.

Noted industrialist and author J.R.B. Jeejeebhoy described Bombay in the middle of the 19th century as a 'rowdy and corrupt place' where 'clashes between governors and chief justices were common' and 'bribery was rampant' (*Bribery and Corruption in Bombay*; 1952). Many of the poor Parsis lived in typical Bombay 'chawls' where residents shared a common toilet and bath. The community in the late 18th and early 19th century was clearly divided between the educated and affluent class (the Sethias) and the masses who lived in chawls.

On 7 June 1832, the Parsis called a strike in Mumbai in protest against government action against street dogs. Faced with the menace of stray dogs, the government had decided to kill them. However, it relented when, in 1830, a deputation of eminent citizens led by Sir Jamshedji Jeejeebhoy proposed that the dogs be captured and released elsewhere. But this reprieve did not last long.

The Parsis called a strike because on 6 June, the dog squad had entered the houses of many Parsis and had taken away their dogs. The Parsis entreated them not to do so and asked them to release the captured dogs. There were some skirmishes between the Parsis and the members of the dog squads. It was then decided in a meeting of a hundred-odd Parsis that all the food and grain shops would be closed on the 7th of June, food supply to the English stopped, and a general strike be called. They indicated their program to the shops inside the Fort and the bazaar outside the Fort. The rich Parsis were not with them and were unaware of their plans.

Most of the rioters were of the lower class like cooks, and water-carriers; some middle-class gentlemen also joined them. On that day, they closed the shops, and stopped the supply of roti and bread being sent for the soldiers at Colaba. Many of the Khatki (butcher) people, who transported the meat did not support the strike; when they were carrying the meat, they were beaten up and the meat thrown into the moat surrounding the Fort. The Portuguese Christians, who also supplied bread to the soldiers, were threatened and the bread spoilt. This rioting continued till 10am.

Their action spread terror in the English. The Magistrate wrote to the Town Major asking him to send troops as the Parsis were Rioting. He did not respond for a long time. The British regiment in Colaba did not receive its bread. The British who were going to offices were waylaid. They obstructed the car of Sir John Awdry, the Chief Justice of the Supreme Court, and threw some garbage and a dead Goose into his car. The Magistrate arrested many of them and appealed to Sir Jamshedji Jeejeebhoy and other prominent Parsis to control the situation. Their efforts failed. The rioters were too excited and would not listen. At about 3 o'clock in the afternoon, the British troops from Colaba were stationed in the Fort with instructions to shoot if required.

The Parsi gangs, seeing the armed troops, dispersed and ran away. Many were captured and jailed and some were sentenced to jail for 2 or 3 years. These riots led to the Englishman distrusting the Parsis. This situation was corrected when the British were convinced that the upper-class Parsis did not support the rioters and were in fact against them. (*Frontline* 16 October 2013 Story of 2 Riots.)

Stray dogs were being removed from the city for the fear of rabies

Here is an incident between Parsis and Europeans reported in *The Times of India*, Bombay, on 14 August 1878:

A Parsi named Maneckjee Aspandiarjee was yesterday charged before the hon'ble Mr Dosssabhoy Framjee, at the Girgaon Police Court, with assaulting a European woman named Dina Trickee Trackee, residing in the Cursetjee Sooklajee Street. It appears that on the night of the day previous, the defendant, while passing along the street, 'made faces' at the complainant and otherwise annoyed her. She came down from the verandah of her house and held the defendant, whereupon he bit her hand. Upon the evidence the defendant was convicted, and fined Rs 25 or in default, to rigorous imprisonment for 14 days.

Yes, it was quite a different community then.

On 9 July 1888, *The Times of India* reported another incident involving Parsis and Europeans at Parel. A young man named were made by

We here subjoin a table showing the pro-
fessions and number of Parsees as given in
the last census of Bombay, which cannot fail
to be interesting. The number here given,
denotes the females and minors, as included in
the profession of the head of the family:

Annuitants, independents	2,657
Auctioneers	128
Bakers, confectioners	1,417
Bullock drivers	97
Cane workers	474
Clothiers, drapers, mercers	328
Cotton workers or retailers	124
Domestic servants	5,468
Fishmongers	13
Grain dealers	5
Hawkers	347
Horse dealers, drivers	2,025
Iron dealers	8
Jewellers and watchmakers	1,125
Labourers	41
Liquor sellers, distillers, palm wine drawers	5,227
Marine store dealers	37
Medical men	577

Census showing Parsi population by profession in about 1850 (The Parsees: Their
History, Manners, Customs, and Religion by Dosabhai Framji Karaka)

MCarthy accidentally struck a Parsi on the leg and was verbally
abused in public. 'MCarthy called him a *cagra* (crow) and with that
about 12 Parsis got onto him with their umbrellas'; Both sides
acquired supporters; 500 on the Parsi side. A constable who was
present 'quietly went into the other street'.

Again in 1851, the Muslims of Bombay rioted over a picture of
Prophet Mohammed shoddily drawn by a Parsi and published in a
newspaper called *Chitradyanadarpan*. A drop of ink had fallen on the
prophet's eye, seeming to have blinded him in one eye. The Muslims

152   **THE PARSEES.**

Merchants, bankers, or brokers	61,298
Money changers, assayers	1,535
Oil dealers	163
Pensioners	1,274
Policeman	1
Priests	5,656
Printers, stationers, bookbinders	616
Schoolmasters	2,056 •
Tailors, embroiderers, tent makers	172
Tavernkeepers	826
Vagrants	127
Water carriers	1,584
Wood workers and dealers	4,101
Writers and accountants	11,028
Total	**110,544**

*Census showing Parsi population by profession in about 1850 (*The Parsees: Their History, Manners, Customs, and Religion *by Dosabhai Framji Karaka)*

were incensed by this and believing that the Parsis wanted to insult their prophet, rushed with clubs in their hands to attack the Parsis. They could not be controlled. Looting broke out in the bazaars. The army was called in to control the situation which continued for over a month. Parsi children and women feared to go out of their houses. Finally, a reconciliatory meeting was organized, the publisher of the picture apologized, and many Muslim and Parsi gentlemen drove in carriages through the streets as a mark of truce.

In 1874, communal violence broke out again over a biography of the Prophet written by a Parsi. This was reported in the Gazette on 14 February 1874. 'Seven Muslims and four Parsis were admitted in the Jamsetjee Hospital. Several injured were treated. A Muslim cemetery lay between Parsi houses and the Queens Road at Sonapur. As a funeral procession marched towards it on Sunday, Feb 15, Parsis threw stones at the processionalists. The police blamed the Muslims for initiating the riot and the Parsis for retaliating.'

This was the social condition in Bombay in the 19th century. A census (mentioned in Karaka's *The Parsees: Their History, Manners, Customs, and Religion*) in about 1850 shows that Parsis were engaged in all kinds of works – from vagrants and servants to bankers and doctors.

In the Saklat vs Bella lawsuit, during the cross examination of J.D. Nadirshaw, one of the first pupils of K.R. Cama's religious madrasa and member of the 'Expert Committee on Religion', he described the community members who were leading the litigation against Bella as 'agitators of ignorant masses'. The community was clearly divided in their behavior based on their social upbringing and education. Dadabhai Naoroji describes this difference in great detail in his speech about the manners and customs of the Parsis.

8
SELF-GOVERNMENT THROUGH PARSI PANCHAYAT

May I think of you as the first and last – the be all and end all of everything – always. As the father of the highest mind. May I behold You in my mind's eye as the true creator of truth – the lord over the actions of the living?
—AHUNAVAITI-YAS. 31.8

There is no record of the history of the laws governing Parsis before the 18th century. The community was quite different from the Parsis of today. Having no Personal Law of their own, Parsis were governed by British Law, except in matters of marriage and divorce which were controlled by the Parsi Panchayat. The two common methods of punishment were beating up a person with the shoe or declaring him 'out of caste'. Even then, the priests and the behdin (laity) had major disputes on the issue of inter-caste marriages.

Dosabhai Framji Karaka, the first Indian chairman of the Bombay Municipal Corporation, in his book *The Parsees: Their History, Manners, Customs, and Religion* (1858), wrote extensively on the laws and the internal government of the Parsis in the 18th century.

He writes:

The affairs of the Parsis seem generally to have been managed by a Panchayat, or committee of five selected from their most influential and wisest men. We have no record of the early history of this body, and are in ignorance as to what laws it was guided by,

Dossabhoy Framjee Karaka, C.S.I.

(1829—1902)

The First Indian Chief Presidency Magistrate in Bombay and the First Indian Chairman of the Bombay Municipal Corporation

Mr. Karaka began life as a journalist, and going to England in 1858-59, wrote there "The Parsis, Their History, Manners, Customs and Religion." He was the first Indian Chief Presidency Magistrate (Acting) in 1874, the first Indian Chairman of the Bombay Municipality, 1875, and a Member of the Bombay Legislative Council. He took a very active part in the public life of Bombay, and his "History of the Parsis" is even to-day considered as a monumental work and is widely read both in India and in England.

in its early existence, in the decision of the religious, social, and other disputes,'

The panchayat was the court of justice, and its decisions were never disputed by the contending parties. Anyone refusing to obey the decision of that tribunal was excommunicated from the caste, and his co-religionists held no further intercourse with him. He was not invited to their feasts, religious ceremonies, funeral processions, or marriage festivals. He could not attend the Fire Temple; nor if he died while in this state of disgrace, could he receive the rites of Parsi burial. Priests were prohibited from performing any religious ceremonies in his family. In fact,

PARSEES OF WESTERN INDIA

This Record

OF

THEIR HISTORY, MANNERS, CUSTOMS, AND RELIGION,

IS AFFECTIONATELY DEDICATED·

BY

DOSABHOY FRAMJEE.

all communication between the party excommunicated and his countrymen was entirely stopped.

All Parsi religious and social rights were suspended.

There had been violent clashes between the priests and the Behdin in 1777. The dispute rose out of a regulation made by the panchayat of Bombay which prohibited the behdins from giving their daughters in marriage to the *andiaroos* (the priestly class). 'The panchayat took this step, in order to counteract an ordinance which, the priests had passed among themselves, to the effect, that the andiaroos should continue to receive in marriage, the daughters of the behdin, but that they should not bestow their own females upon them. The panchayat, therefore, prohibited the giving of daughters in marriage to the priests, and thus sought to deprive them of the unfair advantage they had gained for themselves.'

The cause of the quarrel owed its origin to an andiaroo contracting his son in marriage to the daughter of a behdin, in defiance of the regulation passed by the panchayat. So great was the excitement, that the Government was compelled to take notice of the event and a committee composed of European gentlemen, was appointed to investigate into the cause of the disputes and give a report upon the best mode of bringing about a satisfactory settlement. 'They gave their opinion, that the bandobast made by the andiaroos was unfair, and fully warranted the behdin in withholding their daughters from them. That the resolution passed by the andiaroos was calculated to enrich and aggrandize their own caste, and as the behdins, were excluded from marrying the daughters of the priests, their own women and property were carried into the other caste without any reciprocal advantages being gained by the laity... The commissioners observed that the behdins had every right to put a stop to this unequal intercourse by the Regulations of 1777.'

Dosabhai Framji further writes: 'This state of affairs continued till the middle of the 18th century, when the panchayat found that they could no longer rule their countrymen. Under the old system offenders were punished by being beaten with the shoe: but this mode of punishment it was found almost impossible to enforce when the Parsis were under British rule. In 1778 the panchayat petitioned the then Governor, William Hornby, requesting legal power to inflect this punishment. The prayer was granted:'

Hornby's order dated 5 July 1778 read: 'To the Parsis not of the Priest Class – You are hereby empowered to meet and enquire into all the matters that are committed by your caste contrary to what has been agreed to by the majority of the Caste, and to punish the offender agreeable to the rules of your caste, so far as not permitting them to come to your feasts, or beat them with shoes, but no other corporal punishment.'

The dispute, however, was not resolved even at the turn of the century. Here is an extract from the minutes of a consultation, dated the 21 April 1786:

'The President acquaints the board that some religious disputes at present subsist in the caste of Parsis, Which he is apprehensive, from the nature and temper of these people, may be attended with disagreeable consequences unless properly settled and recommends that a committee be appointed to enquire into the rise of the disputes and to report upon the mode of finally settling the same... The names of Messrs. John Forbes, Edward Revenscroft, and James Stevens senior, are appointed to form the same.'

William Hornby

'The Commission further reported that the Regulation of 1777, which was the immediate cause of the dispute, was equitable in principle. That the fault lay with the priesthood whose selfishness had caused the agitation.'

To prevent such problems in the future the Commissioners recommended a panchayat should be formed and its authority defined and derived from the Government. 24 names were suggested and 12 were selected in 1787 to form the panchayat, to do strict justice to all parties without, fear, favor, or affection to anyone.

But as Dosabhai Framji writes, 'By the end of the 18th century this punchayat was again powerless.'

A similar situation exists today where men claim a right to marry women outside their community but do not give men from other communities the right to marry the women belonging to their community, thereby leading to an 'unequal intercourse'. Many Parsi girls remained unmarried because of this. Today the question of acceptance into the community/religion is even more problematic with more than 50 per cent of the marriages being interfaith.

9
THE MAZGAON DOCK NAVJOTES

O Ahura Mazda! Ever since I first conceived Thee in my mind,
I have taken Thee as worthy of worship with good mind, as the Father
of good mind, as the rightful Creator of Righteousness,
as the Lord (ruling) over all the deeds of this world.
—Yasna XXXI

The navjote of 11 persons born to intermarried couples, performed at the Mazgaon docks in Maharashtra by several priests in June 1882, was an important event in the annals of the Parsi community vis-á-vis the question of their identity. Among the priests who performed the navjotes, was present someone who most Parsis revere as a saint, Dastur Jamshedji Sohrabji Kukadaru.

The *Parsi Prakash* records that a group of poor dock workers living and working in the Mazgaon docks appealed to various priests and High Priests and also petitioned the Bombay Parsi Panchayat for being admitted to the Parsi fold, as being born to intermarried parentage. About 200 prominent Parsis collected funds and eminent Dasturjis performed the navjote ceremony, in the presence of a large gathering on 26 June 1882. Eleven navjotes were performed (four males and five females, age ranging from 35 years to 77 years, and two children) on persons born of intermarried parentage. The event was also reported in the *Mumbai Samachar* and *Jam-e-Jamshed*.

After the ceremony, there arose a dispute among the priests on the correct procedure to initiate a Juddin (non-Zoroastrian) into the religion. In one of his books, late 19th century religious scholar Dastur Darab Peshotan Sanjana had laid out the correct rituals to be performed on such occasions. According to him the initiates were over 35 years old and their navjote had not been performed earlier, technically they had forfeited the right of entry into the religion and were looked on as converts.

Mumbai Samachar wrote on 27 June 1882: 'Some Zoroastrians here under the leadership of Seths Navroji Nassarvanji Minocherji Wadia and Nanabhai Dhanjibhai Banaji, having each raised a subscription, had the rites of putting on the sudreh kusti performed for the children of non-Zoroastrian mothers' wombs living in Mazgaon in the Fort in the deceased Maneckji Seth's Garden by Dastur Jamaspi Minocherji Jamaspasana, his son, Ervad Firozji Dastur Jamaspji, Dastur Jamshedji Sohrabji Kukadaru, and Ervads Khurshedji Minocheherji Kateli, Kavasji Maneckji Katrak, Khursedji Rustamji Madan, Rustumji Barzorji Ranji, Dadabhai Framji Pavri, and Hormusji Tehmulji Jamaspasana. On this occasion, Dastur Pesotenji Behramji Sanjana put out a handbill that these rites should have been performed in a more suitable manner, and until they were performed according to his belief, he entreated the sudreh-wearers to stay away from the Marhum Seth Hormasji Wadia Atashbehram. As a result of this incident, just as there is much partisanship within the Parsi community, so too is there hatred.'

The phrase that deserves attention in this report is 'performed for the children of non-Zoroastrian mothers' wombs.' It makes clear the fact that the objection was to the performance of the navjote on children of non-Zoroastrian mothers, implying that all children born of Zoroastrian mothers were accepted.

Justice Davar wrote in his judgement in the Petit vs Jeejeebhoy case that after the navjote, 'the other High Priest, Dastur Peshotan – between whom and Dastur Jamaspji there always existed great rivalry and unfriendliness – issued handbills and distributed them

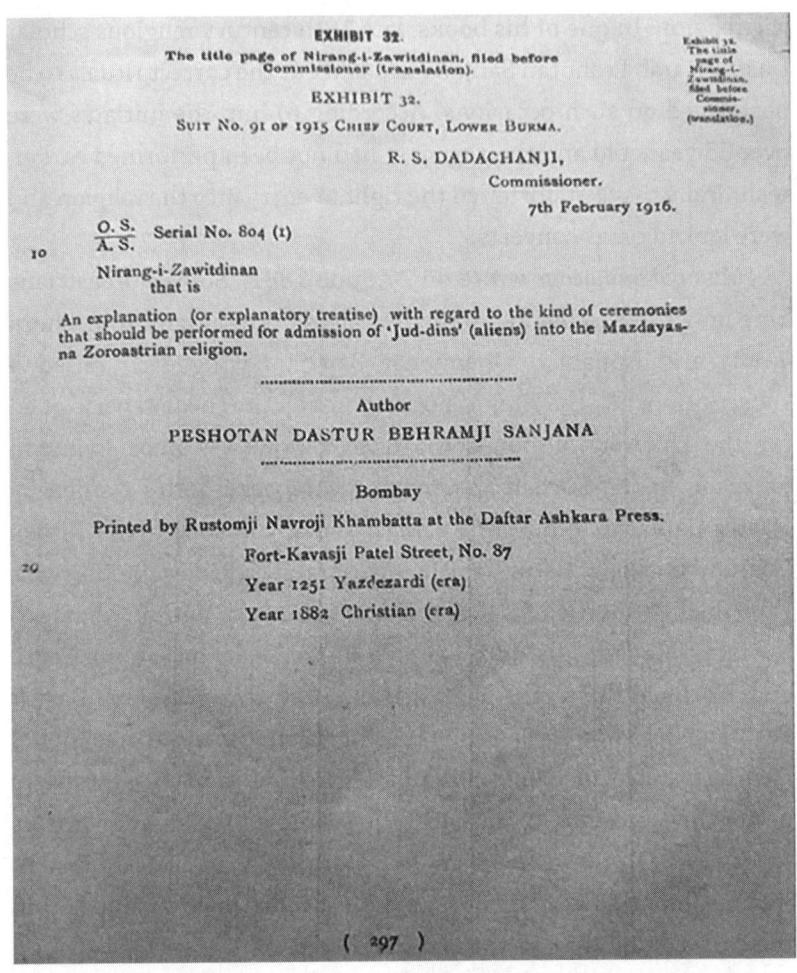

Book written by Peshotan Dastur Behramji Sanjana after the Mazgaon Dock navjotes, explaining the ceremonies to be performed for the navjote of a juddin (of another faith)

amongst the people assembled as soon as the Navjote ceremony was over, stating that as he was not aware what ceremonies had been performed by Dastur Jamaspji in admitting Juddins in the Zoroastrian religion, he would not allow the newly admitted men and women in his Atash Behram. He subsequently published a pamphlet stating therein what, according to him, were the ceremonies to be performed before admitting Juddins into the Zoroastrian Religion.'

Justice Beaman of the Bombay High Court (1908) comments that notwithstanding the conflicting opinions, the Mazgaon Dock Navjotes show beyond doubt that conversion was accepted:

> The case of the Mazgaon Converts is useful for the same purposes. It is, in my opinion, quite immaterial to enquire whether they were converted, or, for that matter, whether they were capable, in the broad general sense of becoming Converts. It may be that they were all the illegitimate children of Parsi fathers. What is important and material is, that in their case, in quite recent times, two eminent Parsi Divines engaged in a heated controversy as to what ceremonies were, and what were not, essential to conversion. This shows, again, with convincing clearness, that conversion—in the abstract at any rate, and as a theoretical religious tenet—was perfectly familiar to the Parsi Community, not only in the remote past but in our own time. Scattered about the voluminous papers which have been laid before us, there is plenty of evidence to support this view.

With no birth control in existence, Parsi women most probably had children with 'alien' men, but as they were of a Parsi woman's womb born they were accepted. Men, however, had a problem, of having their children born of 'alien' women accepted into the fold. The illegitimate children of Parsi men, mostly with 'dubra' (an out-caste Gujarati) women, and how they were being 'smuggled into the community', was discussed in great detail in the Petit vs Jeejeebhoy lawsuit.

10

THE MAKING OF
PARSI PERSONAL LAW I*

If ye will only know and learn these Laws,
Which Mazda hath ordained for ye, O men, -
The Laws of Happiness, the Laws of Pain, -
That Falsehood brings on age-long punishment,
That Truth leads on to fuller, higher, Life, -
Upon all such the Light Divine shall dawn.
—YASNA 30.11

Parsis had lived for a thousand years in total ignorance of their religion. They had no laws of their own. The panchayat, the earliest existing administrative body, was unable to control the community. Bigamy, adultery, and prostitution had become so rampant that they threatened the very rubric of the society. A series of events spread across decades finally went into the making of the Parsi Personal law. This chapter takes a chronological look at those events, which have been discussed in detail in the subsequent chapters.

A detailed study of these events will make it evident that historically, the children of Parsi women, whoever the father was, were always accepted by the community, socially and by religious diktats. There never existed any legal or religious custom of discrimination against intermarried women and their children.

---

* The author is indebted to Mr Fali S. Nariman for his inputs in this chapter.

However, legitimate children of Parsi intermarried women or men became a reality only after the Special Marriage Act of 1954.

A) In August 1830, 8th Bid of Swaran 1886 St and the 14th day of the 11th month of 1299 (Yezd), a *bandobast* was made by the Parsi Panchayat. It objected to the fact that both men and women of the community had 'issues' with 'aliens' and these children were being initiated into the religion and community. (See Annexure for details)

B) The minute of Framji Cowasjee Banaji to the Bombay Panchayat exposing the extent of the level of social corruption of the Parsi community. (See Annexure for details)

C) In 1865 the first Parsi Marriage and Divorce Act was promulgated. It stated that a Parsi marriage is between a Parsi man and Parsi woman and laid down restraints on the extramarital affairs of both men and women. This Act was repealed only in 1936 (see Annexure for details)

D) In 1872, The Special Marriage Act was promulgated allowing interfaith marriages, but the spouses had to give up their respective religions. (See Annexure for details)

The words 'Parsi' and 'Zoroastrian' were being used interchangeably. Justice Davar in an obiter dictum in the 1908 judgment made an attempt to differentiate between the two. This differentiation was not accepted by all Parsis and was disputed judicially much later in 1960 by Justice N.A. Mody of the Bombay High Court, in his judgment in Irani vs Irani, however, the Parsi Marriage and Divorce Act, 1936 for the first time statutorily defined a 'Parsi' as meaning a 'Parsi Zoroastrian'.

E) In 1908, the Petit vs Jeejeebhoy judgment by Justices Davar and Beaman established that conversion was a basic tenet of the Zoroastrain religion. The Saklat vs Bella case, which commenced in Rangoon in 1914, ended in London in the ultimate judgment of the Privy Council in October 1925. The Judges of the Chief

Court of Rangoon (single and appellate) had held that the Fire Temple Trust was a trust for a religion and not for a race, and since Bella was 'converted or initiated' into the Zoroastrian religion, the suit by the Trustees of the Rangoon Fire Temple for declaration and for injunction should be dismissed. However, in the final appeal to Their Lordships of the Privy Council – the ultimate court in London (Bench of three judges) held that although Bella was in fact converted or initiated into the Zoroastrian religion, she was not entitled as of right to worship in the Fire Temple in Rangoon since the benefits of the temple trust were confined to persons who possessed a double qualification – that of being Zoroastrians as well as being racial Parsis; and Bella, though born of a Parsi mother and though initiated into Zoroastrian religion, was not a 'racial Parsi', since her father was a Goan, Lord Phillimore (delivering the opinion of the Privy Council) said that in the view of the Privy Council 'it was settled that as regards the racial claim, maternity is of no importance.' The Privy Council, whilst refusing to grant the reliefs in the Trustee's suit for declaration and injunction as prayed, did however issue the following declaration: 'that Bella was not entitled as of right to use the Fire Temple, or to attend or to participate in any of the religious ceremonies performed therein' – only because Bella was not a 'racial Parsi'.

F) The Special Marriage Act of 1954 permitted a couple in an interfaith marriage to retain their respective religions.

Annexure:

Re A) the *bandobast* of 1830 by the Parsi Panchayat.

The *bandobast* of 1830 was made to stop both Parsi men and women from having extramarital affairs and bringing the children born under these circumstances into the community. It also recommended stringent action against the priests who did not follow their orders. This *bandobast* mentioned that children of Parsi women with non-Parsi men, though illegitimate, were being accepted into the community. The Panchayat wanted to stop this existing custom. Child marriage was allowed, and couples would be married at a very young age. Divorce was an expensive procedure. Couples who were incompatible often just drifted apart. This may have been one of the reasons for the extramarital affairs of men and women. The *bandobast* is transcribed below:

Exhibit D

Copy from the Record No.6, filed before Commissioner (translation) In the Chief Court of Lower Burma.
SUIT NO.91 OF 1915 Serial No. 975
P. 51 (Copy from Record No.6). NEW BANDOBAST is made.
R.S. DADACHANJI Commissioner.

In the name of the Holy Providence Who arranges the affairs of both the worlds through the hand of nature and Who guides His favourite Mazda Yasnas of the pure Mazda Yasna Sect for 'Bandobast in respect of His Sacred Faith, through Zoroaster AspantmanAnosheh-rawan (i.e., of blessed soul), and by the help of the blessed soul of Prophet Zoroaster deputed by Him, a new 'Bandobast' is made for enabling the excellence of righteousness to reach to the Mazda - Yasna followers of the good faith and for keeping them aloof from vice.
On 11 August 1830, (corresponding with Wednesday the Bid of Shrawan 1886 St. and the 14 day of 11 month of 1299 Yezd), the entire large and small Anjuman of the Zoroastrian religion met in the Aderan* of Sheth Dadibhai Nasherwanji and made the

Bandobast mentioned below (viz.) that our people invest their issues by alien mistresses with Sudreh and take them into our religion that as regards those, who were admitted into the faith up to this day, it is done and finished, but that none should be taken hereafter, and that pukka resolutions are made this day about those (above) matters and about the forbidding of adultery committed with women of our own and alien community by some foolish persons out of us who go astray.

Those resolutions are stated below, and all Zoroastrians should act according to them.

First: As our people commenced to take the issues born of alien mistresses only recently, into our faith, and as they commenced to admit the issues born of alien women as lawful (issues) wickedness increased very much in the followers of our religion. These *bandobasts* are therefore made. They are recorded in this record of our Panchayat, and it is decided to print copies thereof and distribute them amongst all of the Zoroastrian race.

And it is resolved that letters in the name of our *anjuman* congregation be written and posted to other out station leaders and a few words as would seem fit, be written to them also on this matter, so that the admission of issues of those mistresses into the faith would cease in all respects, and fail in that behalf, nor allow them to be invested with sudreh and kusti not give permission for their marriage and exposures in dokhmas. Those letters should be written in this manner with several particulars and posted to all the out stations.

Second: That hereafter no one should invest the issue born of a mistress and brought down from out station by anybody or who may be in Bombay, with sudreh and take him/her into the faith, that we should not accept the fact of the investiture of sudreh got performed by any one at any place or village after going there, and moreover, if any mobed would go to any place whatever either in Bombay or Chhasti outside Bombay or in the out stations and surreptitiously invest such issues with sudreh, that Mobed should be forbidden from performing all Mobedi Services, and no one should give (Ashodad) contribution to him on every good or bad occasion, and if any Behdin or Mobed acting against the *bandobast* of our *anjuman* would bring down the issue born of an alien mistress and invest him/her with Sudrehh, he should be out of our *anjuman* and awarded any other punishment appropriate in the view of our *anjuman*.

Third: That of anyone would hereafter bring down from any out station or Bombay, the issue born of a mistress and keep him in his house with his family, his house will be put out of the fold of our *anjuman*; and no one should invite the master of that house and feed him on his table and that no one should visit his place on occasions of joy or sorrow. If anyone would not act according to this writing, he will be guilty before our Panchayat. Approved. The punishment thereof will be one appropriate in the view of the *anjuman* in addition to what is written above.

Fourth: That in case the issues of such a mistress would come from some out station and they had been invested with sudreh but if no one would give 'pukka' proof of their putting on the sudreh prior to this *bandobast* of ours, their sudreh should not be accepted, and they should not be exposed in dokhmas also and the party bringing them (issues) should also be punished.

Fifth: That at present, in Bombay as well as in outstation places good, respectable and manly persons commit such 'wicked' actions: Our Panchayat Members should privately send word to them or write open letters that they should abstain from such actions. And if they would not listen to them at all, they should be disgraced by the large and small *anjuman* in a manner deemed proper, with a view to their desisting from wickedness; and that if such persons would not desist from such wicked actions they will be awarded such punishment as will be fitting in the view of the members or the *anjuman*.

Sixth: That no man having a wife of the first or second marriage should commit adultery with a woman of our own or alien community. If he will commit that act and if the leaders of the *anjuman* will know of it, through a witness, they will disgrace him after awarding such strict punishment as would be suitable.
If the adultery of any one either male or female will be definitely known to another person and if he will conceal the guilt of those two persons, he shall be guilty before the *anjuman*.

Seventh: If any woman of our community having a husband will commit adultery with another man of our or alien community she as well as the procuress – if there be one and if she be known or caught who has caused such actions to be committed, shall get punishment in accordance with our ancient usage, from the large and small *anjuman* and they (the latter) shall not allow such male in any assembly and shall keep him aloof in all matters and disallow him from entering every Dare-Meher. Besides the *anjuman* shall award such other punishment as they would think fit.

Eighth: That at present our people remain in foreign countries for many years (for sake of business) and some go there keep mistress and spend their days in licentiousness and they do not return home or take any notice of their wives. It is therefore advisable that letters in the name of our *anjuman* be written to them and their family sent to their 'mooluks' (own country) abroad if they can be sent there, and if that party be willing to return he should be sent for within a short period and made to live with his family. And in case that person would not agree to either of the two alternatives, the woman concerned shall wait for her husband for 8 to 10 years. Then after the expiry of) that period if the woman of her own will and pleasure ask for permission to take another husband, she will be permitted to do so. But if the said man would return (from abroad) and ask for permission to take another wife it should be refused and the *anjuman* should do what appear good to them, after considering his condition. On this arrangement being made, it will be advantageous in many other respects.

Ninth: That letters in the name of our Bombay Anjuman should be addressed to the leaders of places abroad where Zoroastrians reside and where some of them may have kept Jud-din women and got issues of Zoroastrian descent born of them, stating that their whole Anjuman having met together, had made "Bandobast" in respect of issues born of Mistresses and that they (leaders) should, by their God Who is one, write and send to the Bombay Anjuman, definitely within one month, the names and surnames including age, of those Zoroastrians who have kept mistresses and got issue born of them; and the leaders of the (Bombay) Anjuman will arrange for the passage money of those who will bring such issues together with letters signed by leaders of outstation Anjuman if there be any and if they think it proper, they will give order for taking them(issues) into our Zoroastrian religion. But the decision in the matter is, that permission will be given for investing Sudreh to this issue who will arrive in Bombay within 3 months of the date of receipt of the Bombay Anjuman's letters. Approved.

(Sd.) JIVANJI JAMSHEDJ MODI, Secretary Parsi Panchayat.

The Panchayat used its power to try to control the Priests who accepted the children of Parsi men and women, with alien men and women, by preventing them from performing prayers and rituals and thus depriving them of their livelihood. The bandobast states: If any woman of our community having a husband will commit adultery with another man of our or alien community, she as well as the procuress – shall get punishment. The bandobast clearly shows that women too committed adultery with alien men and the children thus conceived were being accepted as Parsis.

Re B) the minute of Framji Cowasji Banaji (first Justice of Peace in Bombay)

Dosabhai Framji Karaka in his book on the manners amd customs of the Parsis writes, 'Common sense suggests that a body professing to do justice with one law for the rich and another for the poor cannot command any moral respect whatever.' Parsi men and women at this time had scant regard for the ties of matrimony and the Parsi Panchayat was not taking sufficient steps to stop this evil. This is confirmed in the Minute of Framji Cowasji Banaji:

Extract from *The Parsees: Their History, Manners, Customs and Religion* by Dosabhai Framji Karaka, objecting to the totally immoral behavior of the Parsis:

The following is a short extract abstract of Framjees minute, from a literal translation of it published in an English newspaper some years ago. The minute was addressed to the members of the panchayat, and it fully exposes the extent to which corruptions had reached the Parsee community, and the utter apathy and carelessness with which the Panchayat overlooked the unhappy state of things.

Framji Cowasji Banaji 1767–1851 (History of Rast Goftar)

'I have resolved' said Framji, 'that' I shall not join with you in transacting any of the panchayat's business. Individuals calling themselves Zoroastrians have now become so reckless, that they look upon bigamy and other monstrous sins as anything but sinful. I can site numberless instances of persons in this place, who have not only deserted their lawful wives and joined in matrimony with others, in defiance of the rules of our community, as also of many who are recklessly living and spending their existence in the houses of unprincipled women. You, who call yourself members of the panchayat, will not only take no notice of these affairs, but will allow such sinful persons to participate in all the rights of Zoroastrians, You will not bring such offenders to punishment, but on the contrary, sometimes think very lightly of their offences. It cannot be said that you are not cognizant of this growing evil, and if you do not discharge your trust faithfully, what answer will you give to your Maker on the Day of Judgement.'

See Kholasa-i- Punchayat, edited by Sir Jamsetji.

With the passing of the Parsi Marriage and Divorce Act, 'The Panchayat was virtually extinguished and performed no other functions than those of trustees to certain charitable funds.'

Re C) the Parsi Marriage and Divorce Act 1865

In 1865, the Parsi Marriage and Divorce Act was passed. Rules and regulations were made to maintain the sanctity of the marriage vows. These laws were made to resolve problems which existed at that time mainly bigamy, adultery, forced prostitution and child marriage. However, adultery was defined as 'having sex with a woman other than a prostitute.'

The Parsi Panchayat had ceased to have any control over the Parsis, and there was no law generally applicable to them. A Law Commission was appointed to look into the custom and usages of the Parsis. The legal difficulties faced in the case of Cursetjee vs Perozebai, daughter of Framji Cowasji Banaji, culminated in the Parsi Marriage and Divorce Act of 1865: Perozebai (13), the daughter of Framji Cowasji Banaji, and Ardaseer Cursetjee (15), were married in 1830. In 1836, the husband rejected his wife and remarried without a divorce. In 1843, Perozebai instituted a lawsuit against her husband for the restitution of conjugal rights and a nullification of the second marriage under the English Ecclesiastical system. The Courts (the

Privy Council) denied her jurisdiction under ecclesiastical law and having no Parsi Personal Law regarding marriage and divorce, the situation had a detrimental effect on the morality of the Parsis.

Framjee Nusserwanji, Chairman of the Managing Committee Parsi Law Association reported to Sir George R. Clerk, Gov. and Pres. In Council, 9 March 1861 para 9 J.D. 1862 21/468:429–59, 'The temporal rights and incidents derived from marriage nay, the very nature of the marriage contract itself are left wholly unascertained, remarriages are without authority: the ties of family are relaxed; morality is infringed, successions are become uncertain; and the female sex amongst us is denied the certain protection and recognition which it enjoys amongst other communities.' Between 1860 and 1861 the incidence of bigamy among the Bombay Parsis reached over 26 cases as noted in the *Rast Goftar* of 2 October 1864, where it was reputed that the Privy Council judgment had 'no mean influence on the social morality of the Parsis'.

The *Bombay Times* 28 August 1856 commented: 'By the highest legal authority, the Supreme Court is debarred from entertaining suits relating to marriage and divorce, and other kindred matters arising in the Parsi Community; the necessity of action therefore is the more apparent on the part of Government to stay the current which at the moment is drifting Parsi Society into anarchy.'

The *Bombay Times* 23 August 1859, reported, 'The Parsi Panchayat has fallen so much into universal contempt, that the Parsis are no longer able to restrain their feelings.' In addition, the Moffusil Parsis followed a different law and custom from the Parsis in the Presidency towns. Letter of Framjee Nusserwanji Cowasji Chairman of the Managing Committee, Parsi Law Commission to Sir George C. Clerk, Gov. and Pres. in Council, Bombay, 9 March 1863, in J.D. 1862 21/468-429-59. 'The mistake of their authors lies in their assuming, without proof or argument that the usages to which they wish to adhere in preferences to the provisions for adoption, are the old usages of Persia. The truth is that they are no such thing. They are Hindoo usages, adopted by the Parsis long after their landing in Gujrat.'

And Navsari, which was the centre of the Parsi population, from the 18th century, was ruled by the Gaekwad of Baroda. 'Since the Parsi Desais of Navsari helped the Gaekwad clan in establishing its seat of power at Baroda, the Navsari province had the unique distinction of being exclusively governed by the Gaekwads from Baroda, even though the neighboring provinces were not under their governance.' (From the *History of the Parsis of Navsari* by Capt. Hormazdyar Jamshedji Mancherji Desai) This situation continued till independence in 1947.

Parsis in India were following three different systems of law.

1) British Common Law for the Parsis in the Presidency towns.
2) Mofussil Parsis followed their own personal laws and customs which were different from those of the Parsis in the Presidency towns.
3) The Parsis of Navsari and of the territories of the Gaekwads were ruled by the Gaekwad of Baroda till 1947.

'To remedy the situation the Parsi Marriage and Divorce Bill was introduced in 1865. In the draft bill, the meaning of Parsi was given as 'a person professing the religion of Zoroaster and domiciled in British India'. However, this definition was not included in the Bill as introduced and enacted into law.

Under the Act of 1865, marriage was only between a Parsi husband and Parsi wife, so marriage of a Parsi with a non- Parsi could not be had or registered under this law.

A 'priest' meant a Parsi priest and the marriage had to be solemnized 'according to the Parsi form of ceremony called

TABLE.

A man shall not marry his—

1 Paternal grand-father's mother.
2 Paternal grand mother's mother.
3 Maternal grand-father's mother.
4 Maternal grand-mother's mother.
5 Paternal grand-mother.
6 Paternal grand-father's wife.
7 Maternal grand-mother.
8 Maternal grand-father's wife.
9 Mother or step-mother.
10 Father's sister or step-sister.
11 Mother's sister or step-sister.
12 Sister or step-sister.
13 Brother's daughter or step-brother's daughter, or any direct lineal descendant of a brother or step-brother.
14 Sister's daughter or step-sister's daughter, or any direct lineal descendant of a sister or step-sister.
15 Daughter or step-daughter, or any direct lineal descendant of either.
16 Son's daughter or step-son's daughter, or any direct lineal descendant of a son or step-son.
17 Wife of son or of step-son, or of any direct lineal descendant of a son or step-son.
18 Wife of daughter's son or of step-daughter's son, or of any direct lineal descendant of a daughter or step-daughter.
19 Mother of daughter's husband
20 Mother of son's wife.
21 Mother of wife's paternal grand-father.
22 Mother of wife's paternal grand-mother.
23 Mother of wife's maternal grand-father.
24 Mother of wife's maternal grand-mother.
25 Wife's paternal grand-mother.
26 Wife's maternal grand-mother.
27 Wife's mother or step-mother.
28 Wife's father's sister.
29 Wife's mother's sister.
30 Father's brother's wife.
31 Mother's brother's wife.
32 Brother's son's wife.
33 Sister's son's wife.

A woman shall not marry her—

1 Paternal grand-father's father.
2 Paternal grand-mother's father.
3 Maternal grand-father's father.
4 Maternal grand-mother's father.
5 Paternal grand-father.
6 Paternal grand-mother's husband.
7 Maternal grand-father.
8 Maternal grand-mother's husband.
9 Father or step-father.
10 Father's brother or step-brother.
11 Mother's brother or step-brother.
12 Brother or step-brother.
13 Brother's son or step-brother's son, or any direct lineal descendant of a brother or step-brother.
14 Sister's son or step-sister's son, or any direct lineal descendant of a sister or step-sister.
15 Son or step-son, or any direct lineal descendant of either.
16 Daughter's son or step-daughter's son or any direct lineal descendant of a daughter or step-daughter.
17 Husband of daughter or of step-daughter, or of any direct lineal descendant of a daughter or step-daughter.
18 Husband of son's daughter or of step-son's daughter, or of any direct lineal descendant of a son or step-son.
19 Father of daughter's husband.
20 Father of son's wife.
21 Father of husband's paternal grand-father.
22 Father of husband's paternal grand-mother.
23 Father of husband's maternal grand-father.
24 Father of husband's maternal grand-mother.
25 Husband's paternal grand-father.
26 Husband's maternal grand-father.
27 Husband's father or step-father.
28 Brother of husband's father.
29 Brother of husband's mother.
30 Husband's brother's son, or his direct lineal descendant.
31 Husband's sister's son, or his direct lineal descendant.
32 Brother's daughter's husband.
33 Sister's daughter's husband.

Note.—In the above table the words "Brother" and "Sister" denote brother and sister of the whole as well as half-blood. Relationship by step means relationship by marriage.

(**Gazette of India, 9th September, 1865, pp. 9-81, 982.**)

Table of cosanguinity in the Parsi Marriage and Divorce Act

"Ashirvad" by a Parsi Priest in the presence of two Parsi witnesses.' (The word Parsi in this Act seems to denote religion) The law states, No marriage contracted after the commencement of this Act shall be valid, if the contracting parties are related to each other in any of the degrees of consanguinity or affinity prohibited among Parsis . And set forth in a table from No. 1) a man shall not marry, his paternal grandfather's mother to No. 33) his sisters son's wife. This table of consanguinity gives equal weightage to relationship from the man's side and the woman's side.

Regarding gender a note was added in the draft saying,'words importing the masculine gender includes females.' This signifies men and women were to be treated as equals.

Bigamy was not allowed and any priest 'knowingly and wilfully' solemnizing such marriage could be convicted. Continued absence of husband or wife for seven years was made a ground for dissolution of marriage.

Divorce could be granted to any wife on the ground that her husband was guilty of adultery with a married woman, or fornication with an unmarried woman not being a prostitute, or of bigamy coupled with adultery, or of adultery coupled with cruelty, wilful desertion over two years, or of rape, or of an unnatural offence, or if a prostitute is openly brought into the house to stay in the place of abode of a wife by her own husband.

Divorce could be granted to a husband on the grounds that his wife was guilty of adultery.

Clause 4 of the Act states no Parsi shall after the commencement of this Act contract any marriage in the lifetime of his or her wife or husband, except after his or her lawful divorce.

Fali Nariman in his book *Before Memory Fades* explains, 'Before the year 1865, Parsi Zoroastrians living in India, like all other religious communities, were not enjoined to be monogamous. Men folk could lawfully marry and marry again. But when my mother's ancestors in Calicut decided to marry again, during the lifetime of his first wife, it was his sons (the Burjorjees of the second generation) who rebelled, and in protest they left home, setting out in a sailing boat, and landed finally in the port of Rangoon.'

The Law Commissions explanation given for introducing this clause was that 'Before the year 1865, when the Act came into force there was no restriction as regards marrying by a person in his or her partners lifetime.'

Infant marriage which had become common was now not allowed. The husband had to be a minimum of 16 years and the wife 14.

D) The Special Marriage Act of 1872

In the Special Marriage Act of 1872, the word Parsi is used with reference to religion. Today people attempt to make a differentiation between Parsi and Zoroastrian, maintaining that Parsi only means a Race. Historically the word Parsi was identified with religion. The word Zoroastrianism was first coined only in 1874.

Under the Special Marriage Act, couples professing different religions could marry by declaring that they had renounced their religion. Any person irrespective of religion, Hindu, Muslims, Buddhists, Jains, Sikhs, Christians, Parsis or Jews can perform a marriage under this Act.

Before this Act came into existence, interfaith couples could only marry under personal law by either of the spouses converting to the other's religion. Rattanbai Petit became a Muslim and married Mohammed Ali Jinnah. Suzan Briere converted to Parsi religion and married Ratan Tata (father of J.R.D. Tata) under the Parsi Marriage and Divorce Act.

To marry under the Special Marriage Act of 1872 the parties had to give up their respective religions. So, a Parsi man could not be married to a non-Parsi woman. He would no longer be a Parsi if married under the Special Marriage Act. This provision was deleted when a new law was enacted-the Special Marriage Act of 1954.

E) The Parsi Marriage and Divorce Act of 1936

This Act replaced the Parsi Marriage and Divorce Act of 1865. The bill was introduced in the Council of State in 1935 by Sir Phiroze Cursetji Sethna. This Law was welcomed since it promoted the rights of women. The grounds for divorce were equalized between the sexes, and the prostitution exemption was removed, for the first time a husband's relations with prostitutes was to be counted as adultery and formed, a basis for divorce. Polygamy was banned. The law states that a spouse could claim a divorce if the partner 'ceased to be a Parsi (by conversion to another religion),' clearly equating the word Parsi with religion. Further it identifies a Parsi as a Parsi Zoroastrian. Compelling a wife to submit herself to prostitution was now forbidden. (Prior to this Act, the children born of prostitutes or of adultery with 'alien' men were accepted into the community as Parsis. There was no mention of a separate caste of 'Parsi Illegitimate Children.')

This Act also required that the contracting parties in a marriage should not be related to each other in any of the degrees of consanguinity as set forth in schedule 1. (See Table of Cosanguinity, p. 107) This list gave equal weightage to ancestry from the male and female side.

'In 1865 the Parsis of the towns and the Mofussil area were consulted (in the making of the law). In the 1930s the consultation process extended to Parsi groups in China and Persia also.' (Extract from the Council of State Debates. Vol. 1 No. 9)

Some of the major changes were as follows.

1. Grievous hurt caused by the man or the woman on their husband or wife was explained in detail. Grievous hurt included.
   a) emasculation,
   b) permanent privation of the sight of either eye.
   c) permanent privation of the hearing of either ear
   d) privation of any member or joint
   e) destruction or permanent impairing of the parts of any member or joint

f) permanent disfiguration of the head or face; or

g) any hurt which endangers life.

2. 'Parsi' means a 'Parsi Zoroastrian'

3. In grounds for divorce these following clauses were included:

Clause 32e) where the defendant has infected the plaintiff with venereal disease or, where the defendant is the husband, has compelled his wife to submit herself to prostitution.

Clause 32i) that the defendant has ceased to be a Parsi (by conversion to another religion).

In Clause 32e) We see once again (bandobast of 1830) that Parsi husbands would and could force their wives into prostitution.

In Clause 32i) The amended law of 1936 implemented the draft deed of the 1865 Parsi Law Commission where they had given an explanation for the word Parsi that it 'means or applies to a person professing the religion of Zarathustra'.

This clause seems to negate the obiter dictum made by Justice Davar in 1908 differentiating between a Parsi and a Zoroastrian. In this Act of 1936, the word Parsi is clearly connected with the followers of the Zoroastrian religion. It is strange, but there is no mention of the court cases which tried to determine who is a Parsi and differentiate between Parsi and Zoroastrian. The word Zoroastrian is only mentioned once in the entire act.

In addition, The Parsi Marriage and Divorce Act of 1936 clearly states that a Parsi ceases to be a Parsi by conversion to another religion. Yet, Parsis claim that one who is born a Parsi is always a Parsi no matter what religion is being followed.

F) The Special Marriage Act of 1954.

This Act made it possible for an interfaith couple to marry and retain their religion. It is only after this date that Parsi men or women could have legitimate children with 'alien' men or women.

This was an Act of Parliament of India to provide a special form of marriage for the people of India and all Indian nationals in foreign countries, irrespective of their religion or faith followed by either party. Marriages solemnized under this act are not governed by Personal Laws.

The 3 main objectives were.

1) To provide a special form of marriage in special cases
2) To provide for registration of certain marriages and
3) To provide for divorce.

This Law is applicable to

1) Any person irrespective of religion.
2) Hindus, Muslims, Buddhists, Jain, Sikhs, Christians, Parsis or Jews can perform marriage under this Act.
3) Inter-religious marriages can be performed under this Act.
4) The Act is applicable to the entire territory of India and extends to intending spouses who are both Indian nationals living abroad.

Requirements:

The Marriage performed under the Special Marriage Act of 1954 is a Civil contract and accordingly there need be no rites or ceremonies.

A Parsi man or woman marrying under this act could now continue being a Parsi. The acceptance of the legitimate children of intermarried Parsi men or women became a reality only after this Act of 1954.

('Parsi' is used in this Act to mean a religion.)

11
THE LOVE STORY
OF RATAN AND SUSAUNE

O Spitama (Zarathushtra)! Never break your promise, whether it is given to an
evil person or a righteous co-religionist, because a promise is the same for both
(whether given to) an evil or a righteous person.
—Meher Yasht, 2~

Businessman Ratanji Dadabhoy Tata's marriage to a French woman,
Susaune Briere, in 1903, made news all over the world. The marriage
was solemnized by observance of Parsi rites under the Parsi Marriage
and Divorce Act of 1865. It was only possible because Susaune
converted to a Parsi. Under this act a marriage was between a Parsi
man and a Parsi woman. This is why conversion, which was a tenet
of the religion, gained so much importance at that time. It gave the
Parsis an opportunity to follow their hearts and still remain staunch
in their faith. If they had married under the Special marriage act of
1872, they would have had to renounce their religion. Today, couples
following different religions can marry under the Special Marriage
Act of 1954 and still keep their individual faith.

This is a love story of two people born almost a generation apart,
in two different continents and how the wheels of fortune brought
them together.

Ratan D. Tata (nephew of Jamshedji Tata) was in Paris hoping
to trade in pearls and silk. He wanted to learn French, so his uncle
Jamshedji appointed a teacher named Madame Briere. It was here

Sussaune Briere   *Ratan D. Tata*

that he met and fell in love with the teacher's beautiful daughter Susaune, slim, tall, with beautiful golden hair. She was 20. Ratan informed his uncle Jamshedji about his feelings for the beautiful lady, and his desire to marry her. He was prepared for an angry refusal but, instead, was delighted when Jamshedji readily gave his consent. The wedding was held in 1902 and Jamshedji attended the ceremony in Paris and even delivered a heart-warming speech in the presence of Dadabhoy Navroji.

After the wedding, Jamshedji took Ratan D. Tata and Susaune (now called Sooni after her golden hair) to Britain and hosted a party at Kingston-on-Thames. It was said to be the largest gathering of Parsis hitherto held west of the Suez Canal.

Jamshedji left no stones unturned to make it a grand success. He took his guests on a pleasure ride on the Thames from Westminster to Kingston. A guest present on the cruise writes:

'He played the host to perfection, though he depreciated in courtly manner, the numerous expressions of thanks. His friends Jamshedji and Lady Jeejeebhoy had cut short a tour of Scotland in order to be present. Sir Mancherji Bhownagree represented the House of Commons; Mr Dadabhoy Navroji, doyen of the Parsi residents in England, brought his family.'

Raising a toast to the newly weds, Sir Mancherji Bhownagree said:

'I may recall as an example of enlightened sentiments of our host, that recently an event has happened in his family, which I am told, would have been impossible without his sanction and consent. I have the great good fortune to have on my right hand a lady of French nationality who is associated in life and fortune for the rest of her days with Mr Tata. If am rightly informed, Mr Ratanji Tata, the lucky possessor of that bride, had some misgivings as to how the projected union would be regarded by the head of the family. The fact that in spite of his many years of orthodoxy, Mr Jamshedji Tata gave his ready consent to the alliance, is one more proof of his progressive tendencies and his interest in the social advancement of the community.'

Susaune wrote letters to her mother and these letters give an insight into the intense love she shared with Ratan D. Tata. She writes – 'I only have to look at Ratan (*mon petit*) and I am truly happy! My husband makes me feel safe, content, protected.'

She reveals to her mother that the religious-minded Ratan was planning to do her navjote and then marry her again by Parsi rites – 'the official sanction has been given only this morning by the High Priest and Ratan wants the ceremony on Sunday... It will be attended by a whole lot of important Parsis.' The navjote and wedding were attended by 60 dasturs, when only one was necessary according to scriptural requirements.

'I will wear an "ijar" and will be wrapped in a white cashmere shawl. But what is most significant is that at the same time the priest will marry us and then no one will give me another thought. I will be allowed to enter the temple or stay in a house where a Parsi lies dead.'

After the navjote and wedding performed by Dastur Kaikhushru Jamaspji, head priest of the Anjuman Atash Behram and Dastur Minocher Jamaspji, she writes to her mother describing the event in detail. (Available with the Tata Central Archives) Here is an excerpt:

Darling mother .... Here I am, at last a Parsi. Everybody is happy for me and so am I. I spent five sleepless nights filling my head with the prayers I had to learn – now I feel exhausted. Let me however try and recount the ceremonies of my conversion and our marriage that took place at Mr Sethna's big house. At 4 pm I was made to sit in a small room next to the huge salon in Mr Sethna's house where the ceremony was going to be performed. A dastur with his face hidden sat opposite me. I recited some prayers with him, ate a piece of pomegranate and then raised my lips in a gesture of sipping a cup of pewter which contained the urine of the cow. It is supposed to purify but of course nobody really drinks it – not even touch it with their lips – but it is a custom that has existed since the beginning. Ratan asked me not to tell you about this (he finds it distasteful). Don't therefore talk of it. Normally, a dastur is present but this time, he remained on the other side of the partition. The wife of a dastur and the beautiful Meherbai Tata were with me. They dressed me in an 'ijar' and confined my hair in a *matte bonu* and draped a white cashmere shawl around my shoulders. Then feeling very pale and nervous, and with my feet in sapats I entered the drawing room where there were waiting at least 60 dasturs when only one is really necessary. I was made to sit with my back to everyone facing the high priests and I started to recite the prayers with him. After 15 minutes or so, he placed my hands in the sleeves of the sudreh and left, then all the Parsi ladies, the wife of Mr Kanga, the daughters of Meherbai and the wife of the dastur held up before me a white sheet to shield me from view. I put on the sudreh, my blouse and a white sari with a silver border. When I was ready, the High Priest returned but this time we stood – he standing just behind me. Then, while I held his little fingers, he tied the kusti around me. Then seated again there were more prayers with the priest showering my head with pieces of pomegranate, rice and coconut. There it ended and I was led into the midst of all our friends who were waiting to congratulate me. Soon only our close friends remained, and the drawing room was prepared for our wedding which had to take place before sunset. I read out aloud, the pledge to the *Zoro faitehr*, in French, and then the ceremony began. Ratan and I sitting side by side and the dasturs started to pray and showering us with rice. It took about 25 minutes. When everybody except the family and Mr Kanga had left, we all drank champagne and then quietly we returned home."

They were married for 21 years, and had five children – Sylla, Jamshed (J.R.D.), Rodabeh, Darab and Jimmy. As they were married by Parsi religious rites, all the children were accepted as Parsis. During the war, Susaune served as a volunteer and contracted TB in Paris. In 1923, her health was deteriorating. Ratan D. Tata was engaged in the struggle to establish Tata Steel in India. Every day, she would wonder whether he would arrive in Paris in time to see her.

Finally, on the day he got on to the ship to leave for Paris, he received a cable that Sooni was no more. With a heavy heart, he proceeded to France and brought his children back to India where they stayed in the house Ratan was building for his wife. He called the house 'Sunita' in her memory.

12
TWO LEADING CASES INVOLVING PARSIS*

As you realize not the eternal truths, and recognize not the better life, I come to you all to guide you in the right selection between the two sides That we may thence live in accordance with Truth and Right.
—The Avesta, Ahunuvaiti Gatha; Yasna 31, 2

In the early years of the ninentieth century one of the questions that engaged the Parsis in Bombay (as it was then known) was whether the Zoroastrian religion permitted the conversion into Zoroastrianism of a person not born of Zoroastrian parents. A subsidiary – but live – question that haunts (and taunts) the Parsi community in the current twenty-first century viz. is whether the child of a Parsi Zoroastrian mother and a non-Parsi-father should be admitted to the Zoroastrian religion if they so desired

In the year 1903, Mr R.D. Tata married a French lady in Paris and brought her to Bombay; he got one of the High Priests of the Deccan to perform her Navjote ceremony investing her with a sudreh and kusti; He then went through a marriage ceremony according to the rites and forms observed by the Parsis. He then claimed that his wife had become a Parsi, who professed the Zoroastrian religion and as such she was entitled to participate in all the charitable and religious events. He also claimed that she was entitled to enter

---

* The author is indebted to Mr Fali Nariman for his inputs in this chapter.

the Fire Temples, and on her death to have her body taken to the Towers of Silence. The claim was vehemently denied. Public meetings were held and Mr Tata and his French wife (by then re-named Sooni) were denounced. A suit came to be filed in the year 1906 against the trustees of the Parsi Panchayat in Bombay and the principal question raised in the suit was whether a person born into another religion, and converted into Zoroastrianism was entitled to the benefits of the religious institutions and Funds managed by the Parsi Panchayat at Bombay. The answer given was a firm 'no'.

The suit was heard – not before a Single Judge of the High Court as was customary but by a Special Bench of two Justices of the High Court of Bombay – Justice Davar (a Parsi judge) and Mr Justice Beaman (an English judge). The case took a long while to be ultimately decided. Much evidence was led of religious-experts and others. During the hearing one of the judges – (Justice Davar), reportedly an egoist – also had a weakness for publicity; during the hearings in Court he returned home each evening in his two-horse – carriage (there were no motor cars at that time) by taking a detour through the densely populated Parsi locality of Allbess Baug: Where hordes of Parsis came out saying to him, 'Saheb Apra Dharam Noo Nam Rakhjo'. (Sir, keep the flag of our religion flying!).

In his separate judgment in the case handed down in November 1908, Justice Davar held[1]:

---

[1] Sir Dinshaw M. Petit vs. Sir Jamsetji Jijibhai (1909) 11 Bom. Law Reporter 85. In the course of evidence recorded in the suit the plaintiffs attempted to convince the Court that many converts had from time to time, in comparatively recent times, been admitted to the Fire Temples and the Tower of Silence – but Justice Davar said that 'far from proving anything of the kind, all that the evidence revealed was that many mofussil Parsis kept alien mistresses had illegitimate children by them and brought up those children as orthodox Parsis'. The defendant trustees in the suit admitted all along that the bastard children of a Parsi father were eligible and could be admitted to the Zoroastrian communion; what they denied was the right of any foreign convert, 'in whose vein no Parsi blood runs, to become a member of the Parsi community and as such to share in the benefits of their public religious and charitable endowments'. (a sentiment also concurred by the second judge Justice Beaman).

(1) that the Zoroastrian religion not only permitted but enjoined the conversion of a person born in another religion and of non-Zoroastrian parents.

(2) that, although such conversion was permissible, the Zoroastrians, ever since their advent into India 1200 years ago, had never attempted to convert anyone into their religion; that there was not a single instance proved before the Court of a person born of both non-Zoroastrian parents ever having been admitted into the Zoroastrian religion.

(3) That this well-established and ancient usage prevailing in the community viz. that of non-conversion, must override such of the tenets of its religion 'as are shown to have fallen into desuetude and conflict with ancient usage prevailing in the community (sic).'

Justice Davar said that anyone who professed the religion of Zoroaster – be he an Englishman, Frenchman or American – did become a Zoroastrian, the moment he was converted to the faith – not a Parsi: 'But how can he become a Parsi?'; the judge queried, refuting the argument that Mr R.D. Tata's wife (on conversion) was now a Parsi, and the Judge went on to give an example:

'Supposing a Parsi lady becomes a Christian and marries a Frenchman, can it be said that she had become a Frenchwoman? And if she adopts Christianity and marries an Englishman, does she become an Englishwoman?'

One had only to see how the word 'Parsi' had come into existence (the judge said) and what it was meant to designate, to realize that the word 'Parsi' had a racial significance, whereas the word 'Zoroastrian' referred to the person's religion.

Justice Beaman – who wrote a separate judgment but one that concurred in the conclusion given by Justice Davar (though not in his reasoning) – described the religion as practised in India for a hundred years as one having a distinctive caste-badge: being a member of the Good religion was (he said) being a member of 'the Parsi caste'.[2]

Each of the judges (in the Bombay case) held that the properties vested in trustees of the Parsi Panchayat and the Towers of Silence and the fire-temples, (subject matter of private trusts) were only for members of the Zoroastrian religion who were also Parsis – 'i.e., descendants of those who came to India centuries ago from Persia', since Sooni Tata was not a Parsi, though she was undoubtedly a Zoroastrian by conversion, she could not partake in the benefits of all that Parsi Zoroastrians of Bombay could.

---

2 The English judge (Justice Beaman) in his judgment rationalised his own decision as follows: 'When, 150 years ago, leading members of Indian Zoroastrians talked about dedicating Temples and Towers to the Zoroastrian community, or for the benefit of all of the Holy Mazdiasni faith, we must reflect how those ideas presented themselves to the speakers. For Many hundreds of years the Zoroastrian community in India had meant one thing - and one thing only to them - their own select people. And the Holy Mazdiasni faith, as far as they knew, was professed by that select body and by them alone. The religion - originally the principal, if not the only social and tribal bond - had long since been converted also into a distinctive caste badge. Being a member of the good religion was doubtless at that time synonymous with being a member of what we may now, I think, fairly call the Parsi caste. The subject of conversion was unquestionably, as a theoretical dogma, recurrently in the air, but it was growing constantly to be more and more imperatively conditioned by purely caste considerations. As I have said, I think it likely that had these founders of the trusts been asked whether they were prepared to accept converts, they would have replied that they would not object to duly-accredited and approved converts. And what they would have had in mind was a regular convocation of Elders on each case as it arose, to decide whether the person proposed was eligible and desirable, much as members are admitted into and exclusive club. Had they been further told that this would be impossible that they must choose between accepting any covert or none - that accepting any meant accepting all converts indiscriminately; and had it been further pointed out to them that the probabilities were immensely in favour of hundreds of the most undesirable people, for every single desirable person, offering themselves for conversion; looking to the constitution of the society, I cannot doubt for a moment that they would have unhesitatingly said that, whatever might be the abstract religious dogma, they meant their benefactions for their own people, the members of the Indian Zoroastrian community, that is to say; those who, as in the case of every other caste, were born into it'.

A few years later a case similar to that of Sooni Tata – but far more pathetic in consequence – originated in Rangoon Burma – (then part of British India) – It went up all the way from the then Chief Court of Rangoon (Single Judge and Division Bench) to the Privy Council in London in what is popularly known as Bella's Case[3]: The facts were as follows: a child Bella – presumed to be (though not proven to be) born of a Parsi mother and a father who was a Goan Christian – was taken into the home of the Cowasjis (a well-known Parsi family in Rangoon) and brought up by them as their own child. When Bella was fourteen years of age, her Navjote ceremony was also performed: and she was taken to the Parsi Fire-Temple in Rangoon where facing the sacred Fire she went through all the ceremonies like other worshippers – but this gave offence to a number of orthodox members of the Parsi community in Rangoon.

A suit was filed by the trustees of the Parsi Fire Temple for relief by way of declaration and injunction preventing Bella from entering the Parsi Fire Temple in Rangoon, but the suit (on the evidence led in court and in Commission in Bombay) was ultimately dismissed by a Single Judge of the Chief Court of Rangoon. The first appeal from the judgement was also dismissed-the case was decided in favour of Bella. The Trustees of the fire Temple in Rangoon then appealed to the ultimate final Court of appeal in London – His Majesty's Privy Council – where (in October 1925) Lord Phillimore (sitting in a Bench of three Judges) and applying the same reasoning, as in the Sooni Tata case, (decided by the Bombay High Court in 1908) reversed the Judgments of the Judges of the Chief Court of Rangoon and held that the Parsi Fire Temple (established in private trust) was intended for the benefit of professing members of the Parsi Community, i.e., racial Parsis, and that in the lordships view since it was 'settled as regards the racial claim that maternity is of

---

3 Saklat v. Bella AIR 1925 Privy Council 298: Judgements that of the Privy Council also reported in 28 Bombay Law Reports 161.(PC)

no importance' Bella (child of a Goan father) had no right to enter the Fire Temple! The consequence of this decision – was that even though ultimately Bella was later married to a Parsi by race and a Zoroastrian by religion (one Dhanjisha Kolapore) she was no longer accepted as a Parsi by the small Parsi community in Rangoon. This was the unfortunate culmination – in the 20th century – of the darker and inequitable side of the vexed question: who is a Parsi? It is hoped and expected that during the current 21st century it will get established in courts of law in India that biologically maternity is as important as paternity to establish even a racial claim to be a Parsi.

13
THE MAKING OF PARSI LAW II

If a pious man or woman with firm belief is accepted into
the Zoroastrian religion and taken into the community,
then the Zoroastrian religion has no closed-door policy.
—Darab Dastur Peshotanji Sanjana in a letter to Ratan D. Tata

I. Petit Vs Jeejeebhoy (1908)

The Petit vs Jeejeebhoy case of 1905-1908 established the rights of
Parsi men to have their illegitimate children initiated into the faith
and it confirmed that conversion was a tenet of Zoroastrianism. The
social (not religious) reasons given for not converting Juddins to
Zoroastrianism were very explicitly depicted in the cartoon from the
Hindu Punch (p. 30). The letter of Dastur Kaikhusru Jamaspji stated
that the religion of Zarathustra is meant for the whole world. The
judges had offered a compromise solution 'to allow conversion with
safeguards,' but it was not accepted by the defendants. There was a
very special need for conversion to be allowed. It was the only way a
couple could marry under the personal law of the Parsis which was the
Parsi Marriage and Divorce Act. Susaune was converted and she then
married Ratan Tata as a Parsi under the Parsi Marriage and Divorce
Act. There was no discussion in court on intermarried men and women
and their offspring as this situation did not exist at that point in time.

Ratan D. Tata (father of J.R.D. Tata) had obtained an 'approval to
his wife's admission, from Mr Jivanji Modi (Secretary of the Bombay

Panchayat) and from Dastur Darab' and letters were written to him by them explaining the ceremonies to be performed.

Letters by Jivanji Modi and Dorab Dastur Peshotanji Sanjana to Ratan D. Tata Giving Permission to Perform his Wife Susaune's Navjote

Bombay 8 February 1903

Gracious Seth Ratanji Dadabhoy Tata

Respected Sir, we have received your letter dated 7 February. I would like to thank you for your gracious invitation to participate in this Navjote ceremony that is going to take place today. For this invitation I consider that you have kind feelings for me. Because of certain items, I am sorry that I will not be able to attend the gathering.

You have said in your letter that you had read the public sermon which we have published, and that you are planning to act accordingly. I am very happy to know this.

If a pious man or woman with firm belief is accepted into the Zoroastrian religion and taken into the community, then the Zoroastrian religion has no closed-door policy. This is our humble opinion that we have expressed in our sermon.

Signed
Darab Dastur Peshotanji Sanjana

*****

Colaba, 8 February 1903

'If any lady or gentleman of another faith with a true belief wishes to enter the Zoroastrian Religion, are there any restrictions?' is the question being asked of me. I am taking permission to inform you that according to my understanding there is absolutely no restrictions.

Signed,
Jivanji Jamshedji Modi.

*****

'He (Ratan Tata) obtained the approval of his wife's admission, though in guarded terms, from Mr Jivanji Modi and from Dastur Darab, the two principal witnesses for the Defendants, on this part of the case, as will appear from their letters' (Justice Davar, Petit vs Jeejeebhoy)

Dastur Darab Dastur Peshotan Sanjana

Ratan Tata then converted Susaune Briere a French lady, to a Parsi and married her under the Parsi Marriage and Divorce Act. The navjote and wedding were performed by Dastur Kaekhusru Jamaspji High priest of the Anjuman Atash Behram in Bombay, Banaji Atash Behram, Head Priest of Banaji Agiari Calcutta, The Cama Bay Agiary, Soda Waterwalas Agiary and the Godiwalas Agiary in Bombay. He was also in charge of the *panthaks* of Aden, Colombo, Lahore and Lunouli, and Dastur Minochere Jamaspjee, High Priest of the Anjuman Atash Behram.

Justice Beaman wrote in his judgement in the Petit vs Jijibhoy case, 'she was publicly admitted by a person corresponding in our religion, let us say, to the Archbishop of York; everyone knew of it; leading citizens English as well as Parsi, were invited to be present at the ceremony. The priest who aught to know says that she was fully and regularly admitted'. Sixty priests including high priests were present at the navjote and wedding, where only two priests were necessary. This must have been an attempt by the priests to show their solidarity with Ratan Tata.

When asked in court, if he would 'allow Mrs Tata into the fire temple of which you are the Head Priest?' Dastur Kaekhusru Jamaspji said, 'I would. As she has become a Zoroastrian, I would have no objection.' (Judges' notebook Petit vs Jeejeebhoy)

The Anjuman Atash Behram (the Highest Grade of Fire Temple) had a consensus that Zoroastrian religion does not prohibit the admission of persons of other communities into the religion and they wrote to the learned foreign scholars for confirmation if Mrs Tata could now enter the firetemple. The scholars replied as the lady has become a Zoroastrian, any question of her admission to the Fire Temple has been removed.

R.D. Sethna and N.N. Katrak, the trustees of the Anjuman Atash Behram, were plaintiffs supporting Ratan Tata in the Petit vs Jeejeebhoy case.

Letter of the Anjuman Atash Behram to Foreign Scholars in Religion

Dear Sir

Anjuman Atash Behram
10, Sirdar's Building Bombay
23rd June 1903

We have the honour to submit for favour of your opinion a question of Parsi religion which has been exercising the minds of the Parsi community of Bombay for some time past. The question has arisen under the following circumstances.

A young educated lady of French birth and parentage, having expressed a strong desire to embrace the religion of Parsees or Zoroastrianism, a High Priest of the Parsees of Bombay performed her Navjote, i.e, the ceremony of investing her with the sacred shirt and thread which are recognised by Parsis as the essential symbols of the faith of Zoroaster: All the rites and formalities observed in admitting children of Parsee parents in the Zoroastrian fold were performed and observed in the case of this lady and in addition to these she underwent a purificatory ceremony imposed by orthodox Parsee sentiments upon those who are supposed to have contracted gross impurity or contamination. The ceremony was performed by an orthodox High Priest assisted by other High and subordinate Priests, the latter subject to the spiritual jurisdiction and control of the High Priest of Navsari, which is recognised to be the stronghold of Parsee religious orthodoxy, and several leading and enlightened members of the Parsee lay community took part in the function. The young lady made a voluntary and full declaration of her new faith and her acceptance of its fundamental doctrines and teachings.

Sometime after this event a question was raised as to whether she could be admitted into the Parsee Atash Behram or Fire Temple for prayers, and the question was taken up by the Fire Temple, on whose behalf your valued opinion regarding the question now solicited, and which is known as the 'Zartoshti Anjuman Atash Behram,' i.e. Fire Temple of the Zoroastrian community. At a meeting of the Governing Body of the Fire Temple held on 22 February 1903, six of the members present voted in favour of her admission, and eight desired to have the opinion of European savants versed in Parsee scriptures before coming to a decision, and hence this reference to you. We may mention here that there is a consensus of opinion among our Avesta and Pahlavi scholars who, on being consulted, have given their opinion on the preliminary general question that Zoroastrian religion does not forbid the admission of persons of other communities or castes into the Zoroastrian religion.

We may also inform you that about a year ago, a Parsee, older than the French lady, born of Parsee parents and brought up as a Parsee, but who had since renounced Zoroastrianism and became a convert to Christianity, was some years after such conversion re-admitted into the Parsee religion by another High Priest of the Parsees of Bombay, and that shortly before the conversion of the French lady yet another Parsee High Priest, renowned for his learning and piety, publicly admitted into the Parsee religion the children of a Parsee father by a non-Parsee mother not united in wedlock, and that several years ago another High Priest performed a similar ceremony on children of Parsee fathers by non Parsee mothers of low castes living in concubinage, many of them so admitted being considerably older than the French lady in question. In none of these cases was a question of their eligibility to admission into Parsee Fire Temple raised, and they have been freely recognized as Parsees, and admitted to all social and religious rites of members of that community. The case of the French lady being unique and quite novel, has naturally provoked keen controversy, the opposition resting their case mainly if not entirely on the social and material side of the larger question of conversion of members of other faiths to the religion of Zoroaster a side which we may state is quite beyond and outside the scope of subject of the reference made to you, which is restricted solely to the religious object We, therefore, request that you will be so good as to consider all the above facts, and favour us with your opinion on the question of admitting the lady into our Fire Temple. The question being one of great importance to the Parsee community. We trust your opinion will be as clear and full as possible.

Apologizing for the trouble, and thanking you in anticipation,
We are,
yours very faithfully
SD. Sorabji Rustomji, Sharpurji Byramji Katrak, Honorary Secretaries

Replies to the Above

(1) The letter of inquiry which you did me the honor of sending was received after I returned from Persia, where I had been making an interesting journey in connection with my Zoroastrian studies. In reply I beg leave to say that if all the requirements had been complied with, as your letter indicates, I should think that the lady had become accepted as a Zoroastrian, and that any question of admission to the Fire Temple had thereby been removed. Such at least would be my understanding of the spirit of Zoroastrianism so far as my knowledge goes.

Respectfully yours,
SD. AV Williams Jackson (New York)

*****

(2) The point is raised that these religions, the Christian and the Zoroastrian, are inherently mutually too antagonistic to admit of a transfer from the one to the other that I deny in cases where the two religions are philosophically considered, though the popular aspects of them must be worlds apart.

If it is asserted that the race of Europeans is especially alien to the Iranians, that is an error; all are Indo-germanic.

Finally, it is practically contrary to universal usage for the member of a religious community, who value their religion as helpful or necessary to salvation, to forbid any sincere person from sharing in such parts of its privileges as are thus deemed to be necessary to their eternal spiritual welfare.

I gather that you do not request my opinion as to the expediency of creating a distinction with reference to the inheritance or transfer of property in the case of converts, you simply ask for my results as above cited which I willingly afford you.

The main question which should come before us is whether the original Zoroastrian Religion discouraged the admission of proselytes. Upon this the community can then proceed to statutory action. To that point I would answer that this is to the last degree improbable as a fact, while it is positively contradictory to the letter and spirit of the original documents.

SD.
Yours obediently
Lawrence H. Mills, Professor of Zend Philosophy at Oxford University July 18th, 1903.

*****

Prominent members of society
and some of the trustees of the
Anjuman Atash Behram who were
petitioners in the Petit vs Jeejeebhoy
case included:

1) Ratan D. Tata (Father of
   J.R.D. Tata and a priest of the
   Bhuggasarth sect of Navsari)

A V Williams Jackson, Professor,
University Of Columbia

2) Ratan Jamsetji Tata (son of
   Jamshetji Tata and a priest of
   the Bhuggasarth sect of Navsari)

3) R.D. Sethna (Trustee Anjuman Behram)

4) N.N. Katrak, (Trustee Anjuman Atash Behram)

5) Dinshaw Maneckji Petit (founder of the Persian Zoroastrian
   Amelioration fund)

6) Rustumji Byramji Jeejeebhoy.

Their plea in court was 'whether a person born in another faith
and subsequently converted to Zoroastrianism and admitted into that
religion is entitled to benefits of the religious trusts and funds in the
management of the defendants, i.e., becomes a member of the Parsi
community professing the Zoroastrian religion.' They were supported
in this view by other intelligent members of society who individually
signed and sent a letter to the Bombay Parsi Punchayat. Their letter,
printed below, expressed the view that conversion, which was a tenet
of the religion, was not being looked on favourably for socio-religious
reasons. They also noted the fact that the Parsi Panchayat did not
have any authority to pass laws for the community or to stop any
Parsi from practicing what he thought was a tenet of his religion.

Their letter of support of Ratan Tata was recorded as an Exhibit
in Saklat vs Bella:

EXHIBIT A 18.

Protest forwarded to the Trustees of the Parsi Punchayet Funds, filed before Commissioner.

R.S. DADACHANJI,

Commissioner,

20 June 1916.

Bombay, 28 October 1904.

To

SIR JAMSETJI JIJIBHOY, Bart.

HORMASJI EDULJI ALBLESS, Esq.,

JAMSEDJI CURSETJI JAMSEDJI, Esq.,

MERWANJI MANCHERJI CAMA, Esq.,

AND

BOMANJI DINSHAW PETIT, Esq.,

Trustees of the Parsi Punchayet Funds and Estates.

1. The proposal to place before a meeting of the Parsi Anjuman certain resolutions which are said to have been adopted by the Committee appointed to consider the several questions embodied in the requisition to the Trustees of 13 July 1903, makes it necessary for us to address you with regard to your past and future action in the matter.

2. You are aware that, besides being subject to the general law of British India, the Parsis have special Acts of the Indian Legislature to regulate their law of marriage and succession. There is no other constituted authority to which the Parsis are subject with regard to religious, social, domestic and personal matters.

3. There have been from time to time what have been called meetings of the Parsi Anjuman, but they can claim no higher

authority than general gatherings like, for example, public meetings of the citizens of Bombay convened by the Sheriff or people who have established by practice a claim to call them. The functions of such meetings are largely, in their very nature, of a formal, ceremonial and limited character.

4. Among the Parsis a practice has sprung up by which such meetings among them are convened by the Trustees of what are called the Parsi Punchayet Funds. It scarcely needs to be said that there is no such body among the Parsis as the Punchayet. The Trustees themselves are creations of diverse trust-deeds executed by individual Parsis. The Parsi Anjuman has, as a body, no voice in the election of these trustees. Vacancies among whom, as is well known, are filled up by the surviving Trustees. It is not known whether such appointments are in legal accordance with the provisions of the various trust-deeds, which have never been generally made known or published. Such as they are, these Trustees have taken upon themselves to call public meetings of the Parsis. It should be added that the present and last Sir Jamsetji Jijibhoy, Bart were elected at such public meetings to occupy the position of what may be most nearly described as Life Chairman.

5. Holding the place of trustees of the Parsi Punchayet Funds and Estates as above mentioned, a requisition signed by a certain portion of the Parsis was sent to you, wherein you were requested to appoint a Committee comprised of a few Parsis of education, wealth and position to enquire (1) whether it was desirable, looking at the present religious and social condition of the Parsis, to receive non-Zoroastrians into the Zoroastrian religion, and (2) if desirable, under what conditions and ceremonies they should be so received. The contention that the Parsi religion did not enjoin or permit conversion was tacitly and indirectly abandoned by the requisitionists, and they asked only for an enquiry on the

basis that, according to the tenets of the Zoroastrian religion, conversion was enjoined and permitted.

6. On receipt of the said requisition the Trustees, instead of proceeding to appoint a Committee in accordance with the terms of the requisition, preferred to convene a meeting of the Anjuman by a notice dated 29 July 1903.

7. We think that the course persued by the Trustees was a course open to serious objection. Though the immediate business, to be placed before the meeting, was only the appointment of a Committee, the course adopted was capable of the construction that a general meeting of Parsis, without rules or constitution or legal validity, was a suitable machinery for discovering and determining grave religious and social questions effecting Parsis. More serious still was the further assumption involved in the action of the Trustees, that any number of Parsis could require or restrain a single individual of the Community from practicing a tenet of his religion on the score of social or other considerations.

8. The meeting of Parsis, so called as aforesaid, was held on 2 August 1903, and passed the following resolution:

*****

The Committee thus appointed was comprised of 195 members.

9. The proceedings of this committee have been so fully reported in the Parsi papers that there is no need to refer to them in detail here. A very small number of members, scarcely a fifth of them, appear to have taken part in its deliberations. Over a hundred and fifty of them have held themselves completely aloof, and at no time have members exceeding 40 taken part in the voting.

10. We learn that a report containing the resolutions passed by the Committee will be soon submitted to you to be placed before a public meeting of the Parsis which you will be required to convene.

11. We have pointed out above that the resolution of the public meeting convened by you on the 2 August 1903 confined itself to the appointment of a committee, and we venture to think that it is not incumbent on you to convene any meeting to receive the report of the Committee.

12. We desire to point out that it will not be in the best interests of the Parsi Community to convene any public meetings for the consideration and determination of the questions involved in the report of the Committee. A public gathering of a Community indefinite in its dimensions like that of the Parsis, possessing no constitution or law, will be readily admitted to be too incohesive, unorganized and miscellaneous a body to consider and pronounce upon religious and social questions. It cannot be held to possess either fitness or power, or authority for such a task, when, as in the present case, the action proposed by the Committee goes the length of requiring Parsis to abandon what they might hold and believe as tenets of their religion confessedly for social and extra religious reasons, such action cannot for a moment be admitted as within the cognizance or competence even of an Anjuman meeting properly and validly constituted.

13. For the reasons and under the circumstances above stated we think that it would be wise and in the best interests of the peace, harmony and welfare of our community that no further action in the shape of calling a public meeting of the Parsis should be taken by you. It is hardly necessary to say that those members of our Community who have definite views on the various questions that have been discussed by the Committee are perfectly welcome not only to hold them but to endeavor to propogate them in every right and legitimate manner, but we would venture to point out that the propagation of such views should be left to the operation of moral forces alone. Every one

is free to try and educate public opinion of the community, and it is to that that we should all look for all such changes and reforms as may be considered desirable in the interests of the Community. We sincerely trust that the adoption of such a course would in every way promote the well being, harmony and progress of the Community which we have no doubt all Parsis, however they may differ in their views, have fully at heart.

The above Protest was signed by

Sir Dinshaw Manockjee Petit, Bart.

D.N. Bahadurjee, B.A., Bar-at-Law.

The Hon. Sir Pherozsha M. Mehta, K.C.I.E.

F. Sorabji Talyarkhan, Bar-at-Law.

Sir J. Cowasjee Jehangir Kt.

F. Pestonji Talyarkhan, Bar-at-Law.

The Honourable Khan Bahadur Darasha R. Chichgar

Rustom D.N. Wadia, M.A., Bar-at-Law.

Khan Bahadur Muncherjee C. Murzban, C.I.E.

M.D. Dadiset, Bar-at-Law.

Rustomjee Byramjee Jeejeebhoy.

H.H. Wadia, B.A., Bar-at-Law.

Dinsha Eduljee Wacha.

N.N. Saher, Bar-at-Law.

Meherwanjee F. Murzban.

J.C. Bilimoria, Bar-at-Law.

H.J. Dadiset.

Ardeshir Framjee, B.A., LL.B., Solicitor.

D.J. Tata.

Hormasjee N. Vakil, Solicitor.

R.J. Tata.

F.R. Wadia, M.A., LL.B., Solicitor.

Jamsedjee Ardeshir Wadia.

J.D. Gandy, B.A., LL.B., Solicitor.

Bapujee Sorabji Patel.

Rustom K.R. Cama, B.A., LL.B., Solicitor.

Cursetji Sorabji Patel.

D.F. Mulla, M.A., LL.B., Solicitor.

Cowasjee D. Dubash.

D.F. Wadia, B.A., LL.B., Solicitor.

Dadiba Merwanjee Dalal.

Framjee Dorabjee, B.A., LL.B., Solicitor.

Rustamjee Dossabhoy Settna.

Fardunjee M. Kanga, B.A., LL.B., Solicitor.

L.N. Banajee, Bar-at-Law, Prothonotary, High Court.

Darasha Bezonji Mehta, M.A., Solicitor.

Jahangir Dossabhoy Framjee, Bar-at-Law, Special

F.E. Dinsha, B.A., LL.B., Solicitor.

Collector, City Improvement Trust.

Rustamji Merwanjee Patel, M.A., LL.B., Advocate,

Jahangir D. Neemuchwala, B.A., LL.B.,

Judge of the Court of Small Causes. Solicitor.

R.D. Sethna, B.A., LL.B., Bar-at-Law, Registrar,

Jahangir, B. Baman-Behram, B.A., High Court. LL.B., Solicitor.

Pheroz H. Dastoor, M.A., Presidency Magistrate.

Sorabjee D. Bastawala, B.A., LL.B., Solicitor.

C.M. Cursjtee, B.A., (Oxon.), Bar-at-Law, Judge,

Kekhashroo F. Seervai, B.A., Solicitor. Small Causes Court.

H.C. Coorlewala, Income Tax Collector.

Jahangir K. Dadachanji, B.A., LL.B., Solicitor.

Framjee Eduljee Daver.

Ratansha E. Koyar, B.A., LL.B., Pleader.

Dinshaw Muncherjee Panthaki.

Cawasjee B. Sethna, B.A., LL.B., Pleader.

Eduljee Mervanjee Dubash.

Rustam Barjorji Paymaster, B.A., LL.B., Pleader.

Rustam S. Paovalla.

Ardeshir D. Daver, B.A., LL.B., Pleader.

Cawasha S. Paovalla.

B.D. Mulla, B.A., LL.B., Pleader.

Cowasjee Jehangir.

Sorabjee J. Dalal, B.A., LL.B., Pleader.

Munchersha S. Mehta.

Hormazdiar Pheroz Dastoor, B.A., LL.B., Pleader.

R.D. Tata.

K.N. Kharas, B.A., LL.B., Pleader.

M.N. Wadia, B.A., Secy., Municipal Corporation.

F.S. Doctor, B.A., LL.B., Pleader.

J.M. Framji Patel.

Phirozsha Burjorjee Surveyor, B.A., LL.B., Pleader.

N.R. Chichgar, Editor, Akhbar-e-Sodagar.

Nadersha N. Commissariatevala B.A., LL.B., Pleader.

Dinshaw D. Davar, Bar-at-Law.

Jahangir Jivanji Gazdar, B.A., LL.B., Pleader.

H.A. Wadia, Bar-at-Law.

Nusserwanji Jivanji Gazdar, B.A., LL.B., Pleader.

P.J. Padasha, M.A., Bar-at-Law.

Surgeon Lieut. Col. J.K. Kanga I.M.S.

Dr. Ardesher D. Mody, L.M. and S.

Dr. N.N. Katrak, L.M. & S.

Dr. Dara M. Dastoor, L.M. and S.

Dr. Hirjibhoy J. Appoo, L.M. & S.

Dr. H.N. Seervai, L.M. and S.

Dr. Merwanji Cooverji L.M. & S.

Dr. M.D. Cama, L.M. and S.

Hirjee Pestonjee Dinsha Adenwalla.

Dr. K.M. Gimi, L.M. and S.

P.D. Seth.

Dr. D.R. Burdi, L.M. and S.

Bhikhaji Limjibhoy Panday.

N.A.F. Moose, L.C.E., F.R. CH.S. Director,

Limjee N. Parakh. Government Observatory.

K.B. Dadi-Barjor, B.A., L.C.E.

Sheriarjee Dadabhoy Bharucha.

Pestonjee Dorabjee Khandalewalla L.C.E.

Dadabhoy Bapujee Lam.

Jamsedji Dadabhoy Nadersha, L.C.E.

Shoshiosh K.R. Cama.

K.R. Wacha, L.C.E.

Pheroz C. Sethna, B.A.

Manekji Sheriarjee Bharucha, L.C.E.

N.H. Patak.

Maneksher K. Nadersha, L.C.E.

Phirozsha Dadabhoy Bhedwar, B.A.

Dinshaw D. Daruwalla, L.C.E.

F.L. Panday.

Ardesher Cawasjee Dadachanji, L.C.E.

P.M. Chichgar.

Peshotan Hormasjee Dastoor, L.C.E.

A.J. Billimoria, B.A.

Meherjibhoy N. Kuka, M.A.

Rustam B. Behaman Behram.

Jeejeebhoy P. Mistri, M.A.

H.S. Seervai.

Pestonjee Ardesher Wadia, M.A.

M.C. Tarachand.

Behramgor T. Anklesaria, M.A.

Pestonjee Framji Bhaonaggri.

R.P. Masani, M.A.

Munchersha B. Godres, B.A.

Pirosha Bezonjee Wacha, M.A.

Pirosha Pestonjee Mistry, B.A.

Sorab Jamshedjee Bulsara, M.A.

Shapurji Sheriarji Bharucha, B.A.

K.D. Kanga, M.A.

Sorab Naoroji Kanga, B.A.

Darab Dinsha Kanga, M.A.

Jahangir Pestonjee Pavree, B.A.

Ratanjee Furdoonji Gorewalla, M.A.

C.D.M. Limjee, B.A.

Jamshedjee Palanjee.

Bahaman H. Dastoor Jamasp-Asa, B.A.

F.F. Karaka

H.E. Bamjee, B.A.

Dadi B. Lam.

Hirjeebhoy Dadabhoy Mulla, B.A.

Phirozsha Dadabhoy Lam.

Pirosha Hormasjee Vakil, B.A.

D.M. Tabak.

Hormasjee Hirjibhoy Chinoy.

A.D. Gandhy, B.A.

Shavaksha N. Soongerwalla, B.A.

B.K. Dadachanjee, B.A.

Hormasjee N. Peston-Jamas, B.A.

    And many others

This list reads like a who is who of the community and learned priests. They were in favour of conversion which, they considered, was a tenet of the Religion.

*****

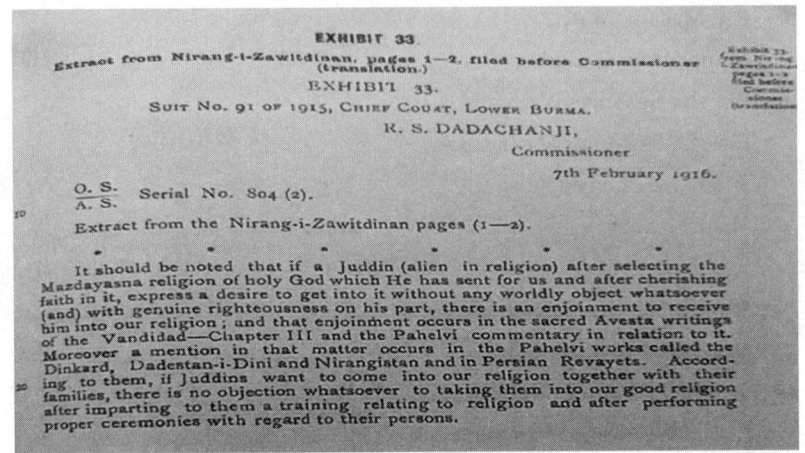

Nirang-i-Zawitdinian a book written by Dastur Darab explaining the ceremonies to be performed for the conversion of Juddins (non-Parsis)

The Nirang-I-Zawitdinian was quoted to show conversion was a tenet of the religion and that, Juddins, if they want to be admitted, they, together with their families, should be admitted into the religion. It is an enjoinment of Mazdayasna religion.

Exhibit 33

Transcribed

Extract from Nirang-i-Zwaitdinian, pages 1-2, Filed before R.S. DADACHANJI, Commissioner 7th February 1916. Serial No. 804

Extract from the Nirang-i-Zawitdinan pages (1-2).

It should be noted that if a Juddin (alien in religion) after selecting the Mazdayasna religion of holy God which He has sent for us and after cherishing faith in it, express a desire to get into it without any worldly object whatsoever (and) with genuine righteousness on his part, there is an enjoinment to receive him into our religion, and that enjoinment occurs in the sacred Avesta writings of the

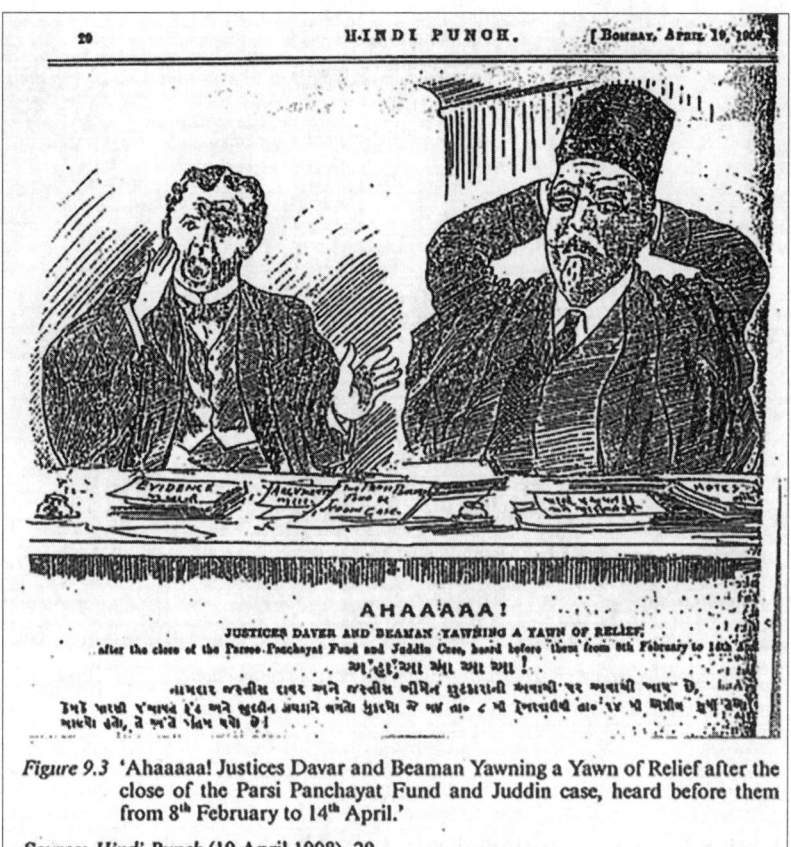

Figure 9.3 'Ahaaaaa! Justices Davar and Beaman Yawning a Yawn of Relief after the close of the Parsi Panchayat Fund and Juddin case, heard before them from 8th February to 14th April.'

Source: Hindi Punch (19 April 1908), 20.

The Petit vs Jeejeebhoy case was closely covered in the press

Vandidad-Chapter III and the Pahelvi commentary in relation to it. Moreover, a mention in that matter occurs in the Pahelvi works called the Dinkard, Dadestan-i-Dini and Nirangistan and in Persian Revayets. According to them, if Juddins want to come into our religion together with their families, there is no objection whatsoever to taking them into our good religion after imparting to them a training relating to religion and after performing proper ceremonies with regard to their persons.

EXHIBIT 59.

Extract from the Report of Sub-Committee of experts in religion, filed before Commissioner (translation.)

EXHIBIT 59.

SUIT No. 91 OF 1915 CHIEF COURT, LOWER BURMA.

R. S. DADACHANJI,

Commissioner.

O. S. Serial No. 803 (I)   29th March 1916.
A. S.

(Extract from the Report of the Sub-Committee of experts in religion, in the matter of the question of admitting aliens into Zoroastrian religion.——Page 6).

•   •   •   •   •   •   •

From this, we see that there is no restriction of any sort in our Scriptures against admitting aliens (lit: persons belongings to other religions) into the Zoroastrian religion, nay there is an enjoinment. Not only that, but even after the immigration here, such a restriction was not believed in. Then, no necessity for allowing such a special restriction, appears even at present. Although under the present circumstances, it does not appear proper that the Zoroastrians should, as Missionaries, spread the religion amongst others as there are no means and opportunities for that purpose, it seems right to take those who want to get into the religion voluntarily as shown above, after due investigation.

•   •   •   •   •   •   •

Extract from the report of experts in religion supporting conversion.

*****

Justice Beaman mentioned some social reasons why conversion was being avoided, 'We are told among other things........that unscrupulous European women would pretend to be converts, in order to marry eligible Parsi young men, and so there would not be enough husbands to go around. The Parsi maidens, we were told would be deserted; and one high priest even assured us that, owing to this lamentable tendency, he knew of a Parsi virgin of forty still looking out in vain for a husband. This is the merest absurdity ".

Extract from the Report of Sub-Committee of experts in religion, filed before Commissioner translation EXHIBIT 59. Suit No. 91 OF 1915 CHEIF Court, Lower BURMA. (Transcribed)

R. S. DADACHANJI Commissioner

29th March 1916. O. S. Serial No. 803 (1) A. S

(Extract from the Report of the Sub-Committee of experts in religion, in the matter of the question of admitting aliens into Zoroastrian religion, p. 6).'

> From this, we see that there is no restriction of any sort in our Scriptures against admitting aliens (lit: persons belongings to other religions) into the Zoroastrian religion, nay there is an enjoinment. Not only that, but even after the immigration here, such a restriction was not believed in. Then, no necessity for allowing such a special restriction, appears even at present Although under the present circumstances, it does not appear proper that the Zoroastrians should, as Missionaries, spread the religion amongst others as there are no means and opportunities for that purpose, it seems right to take those who want to get into the religion voluntarily as shown above, after due investigation.

*****

Justice Davar surmised, 'In the olden times, the Parsis were a poor community. A great many of those settled in Bombay and the larger cities of Gujarat had to go out into the interior to earn their livelihood.'

> While in these remote villages–far from their homes and their families, some of these Parsis took to having unlawful intercourse with women whom they took into their quarters as their mistresses. The women whom they could persuade to live with them were necessarily from the poorer and the lower classes. In the Districts of Gujarat, a low caste of Hindus, known as Dubras, abound, and most of the Parsis settled in remote villages took to themselves mistresses from this caste. It was not unusual in those

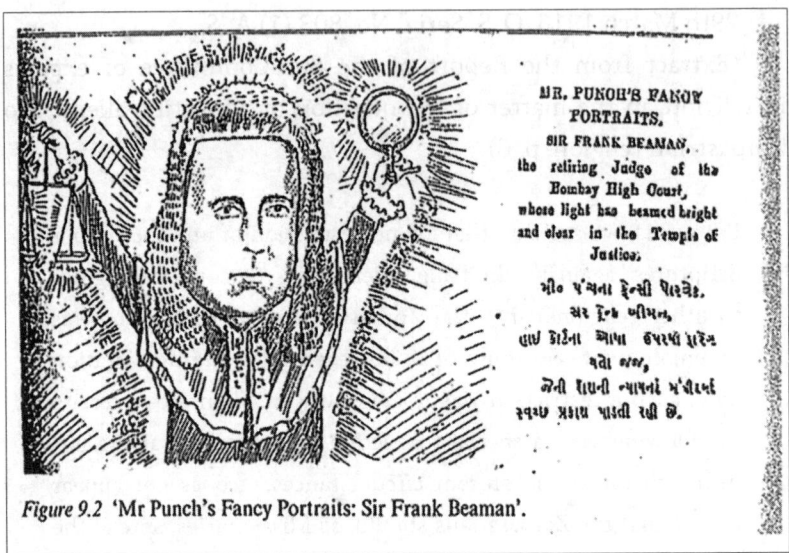

Figure 9.2 'Mr Punch's Fancy Portraits: Sir Frank Beaman'.

(*Source:* Hindi Punch, *27 October 1908*)

days for Parsis, in some of the cities of Gujarat, to introduce Dubra women in their houses ostensibly as servants and subsequently treated them as mistresses. Alliances such as these sometimes resulted in the birth of children.

Justice Beaman explains that Parsi men had lax morals and were having illegitimate children with Dubri (low Caste) women:

All that the evidence has revealed is that many mofussil Parsis kept alien mistresses, had illegitimate children by them, and brought up those children as orthodox Parsis. The Defendants have admitted all along that the bastard children of a Parsi father are eligible and may be admitted into the Zoroastrian communion. 'These alleged instances may be dismissed as cases of illegitimate children or adopted children or, at the highest, cases of persons smuggled in as converts.' They will admit all the illegitimate children of Parsi parents, begotten of prostitutes or kept mistresses, but they will not admit the noblest, most exemplary foreigner. What the defendants deny is the right of any foreign convert, in whose veins no Parsi blood runs, to become a member of the Parsi Community. This is not religion; it has nothing to do with Religion: it is essentially distinctly irreligious; but it is pure unadulterated Oriental Caste.

We have abundant evidence to show with what disapproval the better class – the class from where these Founders came from – regarded the lax morals of the Moffusil Parsis. It was not only because that conduct was irreligious – though, that too, doubtless weighed with them – but because it was lowering to the status of the Community. Keeping Dubri mistresses and having Dubri children, was not only shocking to the correct Zoroastrian, as a marital offence – an offence, too, against his religion – but because the Dubri woman belonged to a very low caste. It may be doubted whether at that time the same disapproval would have been extended to intermarriages – real marriages – with men of equal or superior rank. (This was the compromise solution given. Allow selective conversion).

He continues:

'All the priests and Dastur's have consistently replied: By all means let Converts use our endowments, if they are converts who will do credit to us. The early history of the Parsis, or rather the Zoroastrians, shows conclusively that such marriages often did occur, and that no one dreamed of stigmatizing them as religious sins.'

It has been suggested that Justice Beaman yielded to Davar because he was the weaker judge in several ways. *The Times of India's* obituary of Beaman noted his submissiveness: 'after having taken throughout a strong line in favour of recognising the rights of converts to Zoroastrianism, at the end he somewhat weakly gave in to his more practical and masterful colleague and became party to a monumental judgment which has been freely criticised.' ('Ex-Bombay Judge' 1928: 11)

Writing the judgement for the bench, Justice Davar mentioned that 'the Zoroastrian religion not only permits but enjoins the conversion of a person born in another faith and of non- Zoroastrian parents... It is as much the duty of every pious Zoroastrian today to make converts as it was in the remote past.' Justice Beamon states, that it would be a 'practical absurdity, that you have a great religion ordering conversion, and yet refususing to allow all Converts any lot or part in its public communion.'

Justice Davar mentioned there was a well-established usage or custom of non-conversion. Justice Beamon observed that you 'cannot rely on a custom of NOT MAKING CONVERTS, to abrogate the positive command of the religion. There cannot be a custom of not doing a thing. As long as the cardinal dogmas of the religion itself have remain unchanged, their efficacy, where, as here it is freely admitted, cannot be impaired, much less destroyed, by the inability or unwillingness to obey them. It is as much the duty of every pious Zoroastrian today to make converts as it was in the remote past.'

While it was declared in court that conversion was a tenet of the religion, there followed a lengthy and detailed discussion on the illegitimate children of Parsi men and women and their right of entry into the religion. The illegitimate children of Parsi women, being born of a Parsi 'woman's womb' were being accepted as Parsis. The illegitimate children of Parsi men and their rights, were discussed in great detail. They were taken as cases of conversion, as there was no way of proving they had been fathered by Parsi men.

No decision was given in court as the ladies who were seeking clarification regarding their rights as converts, were not party to the suit. The case did not go into appeal and to date, no decision has been given by the courts on the rights of converts born in

SIFTING!

[Justices Davar and Beaman [delivered their judgment on
Friday last (27th Nov.) in the famous Parsi Juddin Case. They
have found that the defendants—the Trustees of the Parsi Punchayat Funds—were not validly appointed trustees ; that the Trust
Deed of 1884 was invalid so far as the power of appointing successors which the Deed purported to confer on the Trustees was
concerned ; the Court however would appoint them, together with
the present Sir Jamsetjee, Trustees for life ; the Court dismissed
the suit so far as it sought relief on all points relating to the conversion of Juddins and their right to participate in the charitable funds and institutions in the possession and under the management of the defendants.]

મેદા ને ખુલ્લા ચાલવા બેડેલી ભાઈઆા.
[બહુ માઠે જમા બીઠ વારૂ.]

Justice Davar and Beaman delivered their judgement on Friday last (27 November) – the famous Parsi Juddin Case. They have found that the defendants – the Trustees of the Parsi Panchayat Funds – were not validly appointed trustees, that the Trust Deed of 1884 was invalid as far as the power of appointing successors which the deed purported to confer on the trustees was concerned; the courts however would appoint them, together with the present Sir Jeejeebhoy, trustees for life; the court dismissed the suit so far as it sought relief on all points relating to the conversion of the juddins, and their right to participate in the charitable funds and institutions in the possession and under the management of the defendants. (Hindi Punch 1908) another religion. However, the conversion of Sussaune to a Parsi was accepted and the couple were married under the Parsi Marriage and Divorce Act the personal law of the Parsis, under which only a Parsi man could marry a Parsi woman. Their children, the renowned J.R.D. Tata, along with Rodabeh, Sylla, Darab and Jimmy were all accepted as Parsis.

*****

II) Replies to letter sent by Anjuman Atash Behram to Priests and Scholars:

Seth Rustomji Dosabhai Sethna, (R.D. Sethna) trustee as well as the chairman of the Anjuman Atash Bahram, at the time of Ratan Tata's wedding to Sussaune Briere, wrote to priests and scholars to clarify if conversion was a tenet of the Zoroastrian religion and if Sussaune, after conversion, should be allowed into the Fire Temple. He received the following replies:

Sir.
I have received your letter of this current month dated the 16th, and I am taking the liberty to answer the questions being asked in it.

Any person of another faith, man or woman, who with a firm belief, free will, and a desire, wishes to enter our religion to perform his Navjote and accept him into the Zoroastrian religion.

If once an individual either born to people of another faith or born to a Zoroastrian has a Navjote performed and has made the necessary solemn declaration in the presence of the priest thereby being accepted into the Zoroastrian Religion, from that point that person should be considered for all the rights as a Zoroastrian. This is my humble opinion.

Signed
Ervad Sheriarji Dadabhai Bharucha

*****

I am taking permission to answer the question asked in your letter dated 16th of this month. Any person of another faith, man or woman, with a firm belief, free will, and a desire to enter into our religion, then to perform his Navjote and to accept him into the Zoroastrian religion, according to my thinking there is no restriction in our religion. If his Navjote is done according to the customs, and he makes a declaration of faith, then according to my opinion he should be considered a Zoroastrian.

Signed
Ervad Edalji Kersaspji Antia

*****

Respected Sir,

I am taking the opportunity to answer in the shortest possible way the question asked in your letter of the 16th of this month. Any non-Zoroastrian, with his own understanding or with an explanation provided by a Zoroastrian, that could understand the faults of his own religion, and at the same time understands the purity, truth, and Ashoi of the Zoroastrian religion, and of his own free will openly declares and desires to become a Zoroastrian, and is deeply wanting his Navjote to be performed to enable him to be recognized as a person of the Zoroastrian religion, and this person keeps the sign of a Sudreh and Kusti on his body, then to such a person there is no restriction to accept him into the Zoroastrian religion as it is declared * Not only that, but to accept these people into the Zoroastrian religion is the duty of every Zoroastrian. In this manner those who have become a new Zoroastrian should be given the same benefits and rights of the existing Zoroastrians.

If we create difficulties and delay in the process of initiation of these people who request to become Zoroastrian, then this is comparable to stopping someone from correcting his path of wrong deeds to changing to good deeds.

*INSTRUCTED

Signed,
K.R. Cama

*****

In 1903, after Ratan Tata's marriage to Sussaune under the Parsi Marriage and Divorce Act, the view of priests and religious scholars was sought on whether conversion was permitted. These are some of their replies:

Respected Sir,

Received your letter on 16. February I am taking the liberty to answer the questions you have asked According to the customs and rituals of our religion there is no objection to initiating into the Zoroastrian religion a person of another religion man or woman who because of the beauty of the Zoroastrian religion, and who with the goodness of his heart, is attracted toward this noble religion, and wants to join our own religion.

You Respected Sirs, must be aware of the fact that about 21 years ago the late Dasturji Jamaspji Minocher Jamasp Asa had accepted into the Zoroastrian religion several Zoroastrian children with Non-Zoroastrian mothers boys and girls - and had performed the necessary ceremonies. At that time also there were many questions and discussions. On that occasion because of the suggestions from several friends, I had published a booklet named 'Judeeno ne Mazdayasni Din Ma Dakhal Karva Rava Che Te Vishawnee Shahadato' (The Argument in Support of Accepting non-Zoroastrians into the Mazdayasna Religion). I am enclosing a copy of the booklet for you, Sir. On reading this booklet you will note that there is no objection to accepting into the Zoroastrian religion with great care and religious ceremony any person of other faith

Signed
Ervad Tahmurasp Dinshah Anklesaria

*****

Sir,
In reply to your letter of this week, I am taking the liberty to write to you. There is absolutely no objection in the religion to accepting, after the necessary rituals, people of other faiths with a true belief and noble intentions and wishing to enter the Zoroastrian religion. However, it is my opinion that based upon today's time, place, and conditions, this particular question should not be looked at from the religious point of view – that is whether the religion says it accepts or does not accept. We should look at it through the cultural point of view. I would like to inform you that for this we have to keep some reservation and create some law and order.

Signed
Ervad Jivanji Jamshedji.

*****

III. The Obiter Dictum of justice Davar

In the Petit vs Jeejeebhoy case, during the course of his judgement, Justice Davar made an observation (an 'obiter dictum' an opinion which is not legally binding) as to who is a Parsi. Justice Beaman confirms this is obiter in his independent judgement, 'As it is, the

FIGURE 6.2. "Mr. Punch's Fancy Portrait" of Justice D. D. Davar in everyday dress.
Source: HP (7 June 1908), 12. Courtesy of the British Library SV576.

Justice Dinshah Davar

whole of my brother Davar's otherwise valuable and instructive judgement on this part of the case is merely obiter.' The later Parsi Marriage and Divorce Act of 1936 simply mentions that a person ceases to be a Parsi by converting to another faith: Parsi is defined (for the first time) in the 1936 Act as meaning 'Parsi Zoroastrian'.

That the Parsi community consists of Parsis who descended from the original Persian emigrants into India in consequence of Mohameddan persecution and who profess the Zoroastrian faith.

The descendants of the Zoroastrians in Persia who were not amongst the original emigrants, but who are of the same stock and have since that date, from time to time, come to India and settled here, either permanently or temporarily, and who profess the Zoroastrian religion.

The children of a Parsi father by an alien mother, if such children are admitted into the religion of their fathers and profess the Zoroastrian religion.

Parsis in India often quote this description of a Parsi made by Justice Davar to claim that Parsis are patrilineal, and hence the children of intermarried men can be accepted but the children of intermarried women, are not accepted by the community. In fact, the obiter dictum highlights the opposite. Parsi women and their children, legitimate or illegitimate, were always accepted as they were born out of a Parsi woman's womb. The men had trouble in proving their parentage of their illegitimate children and having them accepted into the community and the religion. Justice Daver's obiter dictum champions the cause for the acceptance of the illegitimate children of Parsi men.

The most important fact is that there was no evidence that in 1905/1908 there were any intermarried Parsi men and women.

If they married under the Parsi Marriage and Divorce Act 1875 both had to be Parsis as the Act only recognized a marriage between a Parsi man and a Parsi woman. Sussaune Briere was converted to a Parsi and married Ratan Tata under the same Parsi Marriage and Divorce Act. If they were married under the Special Marriage Act 1872 both would have to, have given up their religion and as such they would not be Parsis. Both partners had to be Parsis for a legal Parsi marriage.

The 3rd clause in Davar's obiter dictum refers to illegitimate children of Parsi men whom the community was having difficulty accepting into the community.

'It becomes all too plain that illegitimate children of Parsi fathers were in the same way smuggled into the Community, especially in the mofussil, where the Parsis were scattered and under no communal control......There was too much dirty linen of this kind, in too many reputable Parsi families, for anyone to be over eager to wash it all in public for the sake of a doubtful principle'.

This obiter dictum has not been accepted by Justice Young of the Chief Court of Rangoon in his judgement in Saklat vs Bella in 1920 nor by Justice Modi, Judge High Court of Bombay, in Irani vs Irani in 1960.

The 1st clause accepts as Parsis those who are the descendants of the original immigrants. Nowhere is it mentioned that only men are descendants. In the draft of the Parsi Marriage and Divorce Act of 1865 it is specifically mentioned that men and women are equal and regarding gender the General Clause Act of 1897 specifically provided that in all Central Acts words implying the masculine gender included females. The Table of Cosanguinity in the Parsi Marriage and Divorce Act gives equal weightage to descendants and ancestry from the man and woman's side.

On Page 35 of his notebook, Justice Beaman had recorded that the judges had suggested a compromise in the case.

'Compromise on the lines suggested by the court.' (Illustration from Hindu Punch, p.27)

'After having heard the plaintiff's case, and some indications at least of the line which the defendants propose to take, we think it right to intimate to the parties (without in any way prejudicing the final result should our suggestions not be accepted) what appears to us to be a reasonable solution. Our desire is to put to an end as soon as possible to this litigation.'

'We suggest that we might declare that the Zoroastrian religion permits conversion but that the Community (in a matter to be settled after further discussion) should regulate conversion by framing rules to safeguard it against abuse.'

'We cannot help thinking that if all parties are reasonable, a settlement could be come to along these lines, and we invite council to consider what we have said, and if they are in substantial agreement with us, to advise their clients accordingly. We have felt for some time, that the course of litigation has been, and is taking is out of all proportion to the interests at stake. We think the course has given offence and caused much indignation throughout the Community whose social and private affairs have been drawn within the scope of the enquiry; and we think it can be stopped, upon perfectly fair and satisfactory terms, it is in the interests of the parties and the public that it should be stopped as soon as soon as possible.'

On 5 March 1908, Beaman Justice writes: 'Lowndes for the plaintiffs says that his clients are ready to accept the compromise on the lines suggested with a few minor alterations of details. Strangman (for defendents) says that his clients are advised that they cannot accept the compromise.'

At the beginning of his independent judgement, Justice Beaman makes a very succinct observation about the term Parsi Community professing the Zoroastrian faith which is much used in trust deeds.

'Firstly, they were used by an English draftsman. The draftsmen thought, as probably everyone else thought at that time, that the Parsi Community was a phrase of sufficiently precise and definite connotation; and that there could never be any question of the class denoted. Secondly, the qualifying words "professing the Zoroastrian Faith" were inserted not to exclude converts to, but converts from, the Holy Zoroastrian faith. About that there can be no serious doubt; and if not expressly admitted, it was impliedly admitted during the progress of the case, over and over again. The Parsis of Bombay were beginning to be exercised in mind over the cases of converts to Christianity; and they naturally wished to make it clear that no such Converts, though originally of the Parsi community, would be allowed to share the benefits of the funds and properties.'

IV. The Orthodox Justice Dinshah Davar

In Jewish courts ne'er sat an Abbethdin
With more discerning eyes, or hands more clean:
Unbrib'd, unsought, the wretched to redress;
Swift of dispatch, and easy of access.
—Absalom and Achitophel, John Dryden

Dinshah Davar was the first Parsi judge of the Bombay High Court. Fierce and intimidating, he was best known for his unusually harsh sentencing of Bal Gangadhar Tilak on 22 July 1908, for an article in *Kesari* where he referred to the killing of two European women at Muzaffarpur by terrorists: A six-year prison term and a fine of Rs 1000. None other than M.A. Jinnah appeared for Tilak and moved a bail plea, but Davar would have none of it. It is said that even Davar's son, the barrister and future judge J.D. Davar, refused to speak to him for a period after the Tilak sentence. Ironically, it was council Davar who got Tilak out on bail about 10 years prior to that when Tilak was arrested and tried for sedition before the Bombay High Court in July 1897.

As the presiding Judge in Petit vs Jeejeebhoy case, he left his indelible mark in the judgement. He tried to offer his orthodox views in the Saklat vs Bella case too but fell sick and passed away during the long trial. (The cartoon below from the *Hindu Punch* depicts Davar as an intervenor in Saklat vs Bella.)

He did not even accept the views expressed by the expert committee on religion appointed by the court. The expert committee signed a report giving the view that conversion was a tenet of the Zoroastrian religion. The members of the committee were stalwarts such as K.R. Cama, Sheriarji Dadabhai Bharucha, Behramgore Tehmuras Anklesaria, Dastur Peshotan Sanjana, Cowasji Edalji

FIGURE 8:
"THE GREAT DADGAR DAVAR"
from "The Rangoon Romance (Bella and the Anjuman)"
[*Hindi Punch* (7 June 1914), 14.]
[By permission of the British Library (SV 576).]

Justice Davar, representing the orthodox, made an attempt to intervene in the Saklat Vs Bella Case in 1914

Kanga, Pestonji Cooverji Motivalla, Bomanji Nasharwanji Dhabar, Jeevanji Jamshedji Modi and Dastur Kaekhusru Jamaspjee.

Its report said, 'The Expert Committee is most emphatic in its opinion... Such candidates alone who are admitted to the din (religion) after the performance of ceremonies in this way shall be entitled to all the rights as a Zoroastrian.' But Justice Davar was not convinced.

He was outspoken on his views on the Zoroastrian religion. As a witness in a 1915 defamation case between Parsi organization's he described his position on a range of controversies over religious reform. His views were orthodox on every issue. He became more orthodox over the course of his adult life. In 1897 he supported the invalidation of trusts funding Zoroastrian death ceremonies and in 1915 testified that it 'was a portion of Zoroastrian ritual which must be observed' ('Jame' Defamation Case 29 April 1915).

Similarly, at the beginning of Petit vs Jeejeebhai, Davar was open to the idea of allowing ethnic outsiders to convert to Zoroastrianism and to benefit from the Parsi trusts. He even encouraged the defendant's lawyers to accept compromise terms that he and Justice Beaman had drafted in March 1908. (Cartoon, 'on which track') It was only in the later stages of the case that Justice Davar changed his mind, turning towards orthodoxy and opposing the idea of conversion.

As a matter of fact, Davar was a leader of the orthodox camp. By popular accounts, he would take the long way home after presiding over Petit vs Jeejeebhoy to greet crowds of supporters in orthodox neighborhoods. After his death, the *Hindi Punch* commented that the 'Best Orthodox section' had lost its 'Din-shah', punning on his name to imply that he was king (Pers. Shah) of the faith (Pers. Din)

On the bench he drew on his knowledge of Parsi life, doubting representations placed before him if they contradicted his own personal knowledge. His later judgments favored religious orthodox outcomes. The rule of law ideally requires that decision makers have no connection to the parties or their social world. But Davar was embedded in the social life of the community, and he gave his orthodox vision of community identity the force of law.

The Zoroastrian Conference headed by Dastur Dhalla, the head priest of Karachi in its journal wondered aloud if 'Justice Davar's personal involvement in the case (Saklat vs Bella), as a sitting High Court Judge was not a breach of professional duty' (Journal of the Iranian Assossiation Vol. 1, 5 August 1915).

The Petit vs Jeejeebhoy judgement was not an impartial judgement. One further connection reinforced Davar's ultimate identification with the orthodox in Petit vs Jeejeebhoy. His son, Jehangir D. Davar, was married to the former Miss Virbaiji J. Jeejeebhoy, a member of the family of one trustee defendant, Sir Jamsetjee Jeejeebhoy (Mitra Sharafi, *Judging Conversion to Zoroastrianism Behind the Scenes of the Parsi Panchayat Case 1908*).

Jehangir Vimadalal was the lawyer leading the case against Bella in Saklat vs Bella. He was a key witness in Petit vs Jeejeebhoy and his views on Parsi eugenics had a noticeable effect on the outcome of the case. He was an orator and doyen of Parsi orthodoxy as well as a prominent theosophist and follower of the Zoroastrian mystical Ilm-e-Khshnoom. He was an ardent eugenicist and had published two books opposing the admission of outsiders into the Zoroastrian religion based on eugenics. The Bombay solicitor drew on the writings of European race theorists like Gustave Le Bon and Houston Stewart Chamberlain, and tailored the global eugenics movement in the Parsi context.

Vimadalal's view was that intermarriage between dissimilar races produced unhealthy children. In his book *Racial Intermarriage, Their Scientific Aspect*, he writes that mixed offspring tended to be a 'low type of progeny, that suffered from atavism, or reversions, reviving pathological defects from the deep past'. Careful cross breeding in animals and plants could produce exceptional results according to Vimadalal. But human beings could not be matched in the same way. Intermarriage would have to be allowed completely or not at all. He concluded that free

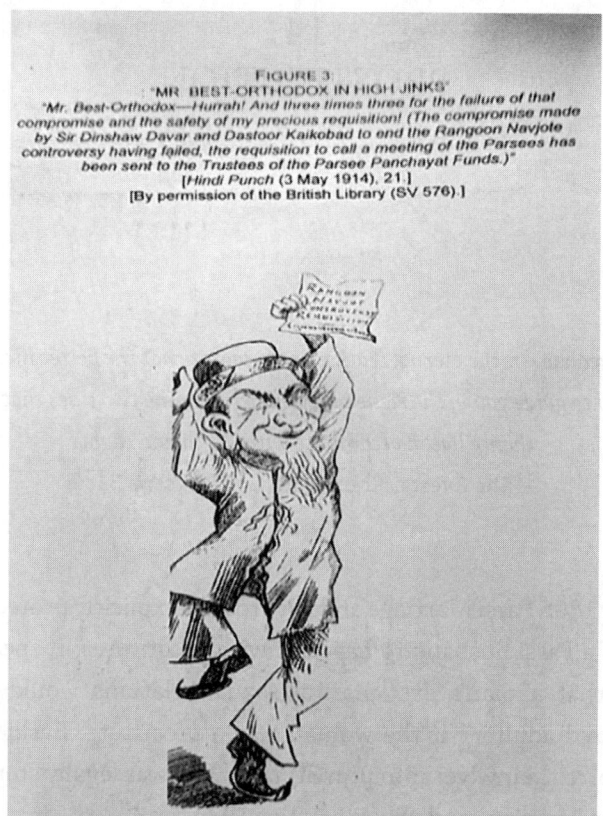

FIGURE 3
"MR. BEST-ORTHODOX IN HIGH JINKS"
"Mr. Best-Orthodox—Hurrah! And three times three for the failure of that
compromise and the safety of my precious requisition! (The compromise made
by Sir Dinshaw Davar and Dastoor Kaikobad to end the Rangoon Navjote
controversy having failed, the requisition to call a meeting of the Parsees has
been sent to the Trustees of the Parsee Panchayat Funds.)"
[Hindi Punch (3 May 1914), 21.]
[By permission of the British Library (SV 576).]

The cartoon depicts Dinshah Davar's role in Saklat Vs Bella

and continuous crossing would destroy the Parsi character. He writes, 'It is difficult to imagine what a shocking conglomeration of hybrids, mongrels, pariahs, half castes, and no castes of all kinds we should have amidst us in a short time. If all restrictions against alien marriages were done away with a stroke.'

Justice Dinshah Davar was also very involved in the Bella case trying to put pressure to stop Dastur Kaekobad Aderbad Dastur Noshirwan from performing Bella's Navjote, but he passed away during the course of the proceedings.

14
PROSTITUTION
AND MALE LEGAL PRIVILIGES

As you realize not the eternal truths, and recognize not the better life, I come
to you all to guide you in the right selection between the two sides that we may
thence live in accordance with Truth and Right.
—The Avesta, Ahunuvaiti Gatha; Yasna 31, 2

The 1865 Parsi Marriage and Divorce Act explicitly protected the right of a Parsi husband to have sex with prostitutes. It specifically stated that a man's extramarital sexual relations would not be considered adultery if the woman was a prostitute. Besides, men could force their wives into prostitution. This was legally stopped by the Parsi Marriage and Divorce Act of 1936.

The Parsi Law Commission had explained it reasons. It had said 'Illicit intercourse with courtesans carried on casually and beyond the precincts of the conjugal residence' was not enough to dissolve a marriage. The prostitution exemption ended at the threshold of the matrimonial home: 'the gross and flagrant violations of the feelings of a wife involved in the establishment of a kept mistress under the marital roof ought not to be regarded as falling within the just limit of exception.' It was not the extramarital nature of the sexual intercourse that was the problem but the lack of discretion. All children born of prostitutes were accepted as Parsis.

The occupation-wise Census of Bombay in 1864 mentioned 41 Parsi Prostitutes, 4 per cent of the total Parsi female population.

95

LXI. — (*continued*).

were returned as present in BOMBAY on the night of the 1st February 1864.

CASTE OR RACE.	Printer, Stationer, Book binder—dealer	Prostitute	Purveyor, or Bumboat-man and Market boat-man	Saltmaker—dealer	Scavenger, Sweeper	Schoolmaster, Teacher	Silk-worker—dealer
Boodhist or Jain	..	..	..	..	..	19	26
Brahmun	173	58	2	17	..	720	89
Lingaet	90	1	..	..	..	..	113
Bhatia..............................	0	..	3	..	*..	90	110
Hindoo of other Caste	2,323	6,026	1,783	695	47	1,033	3,785
Hindoo Out-caste	..	77	171	..	1,031	..	..
Mooculman	1,083	3,215	1,826	208	315	556	1,275
Negro-African	..	..	161	..	..	..	..
Parsee.............................	575	41	58	4	..	376	71
Jew	7	..	..	12	..	51	21
Native Christian	252	36	86	336	27	99	98
Indo-European.....................	27	5	..	..	2	16	0
European	0	41	37	..	..	81	22
Chinese	..	..	0	..	..	..	..
	4,482	9,536	4,136	1,302	2,355	2,981	5,580

Cencus Of 1864 by Occupation Listed 41 Parsi Prostitutes.

The exemption did not exist in the British laws. There, adultery was defined as sexual intercourse with any woman other than the wife. That Parsi Law did not replicate English Law on prostitution reflected a deliberate choice made in the mid-nineteenth century. It was an example of the ways in which Parsi lawmakers did not replicate English law, but pulled away from it, on points that mattered to them.

The fact of the acceptance of Parsi prostitutes and their children was discussed at length in court in both Petit vs Jeejeebhoy and Saklat vs Bella lawsuits as these children were possibly born to Parsi women and non-Parsi men.

Until 1936, when the Parsi Marriage and Divorce Act was amended, husbands would invariably try to argue in divorce cases filed by their wives, that the other woman was a prostitute. (See Parsi Chief Matrimonial Court 4 September 1880; Suit No 5 of 1895; 1893 to 1903 PCMC Notebook, I:215)

The Parsi polemicist Muncherjee Cowasjee Lungra, who wrote under the pseudonym 'Mansukh', lambasted the Act for protecting husbands' rights to have sex with prostitutes.

Travel allowed Parsi men to frequent brothels in China and European 'Madams' in England. The transgression took place in a spirit of fun and merriment. When questioned by their wives they responded it was perfectly legal. Mansukh complained, 'Parsi Law invited men to live like the Hindu king, Raja Gopichand, who was legendary for his immense harem (albeit of wives not concubines)' (Mansukh 73-74 'Raja Gopichand').

Mansukh lamented the indifference of Parsi priests and leaders towards the purchase of sexual services by Parsi men (Mansukh 79). Early Zoroastrian leaders complained that Parsi men depleted their fortune this way. 'They gamble and whore and indulge in other vices', grumbled Dinshaw Wacha to Dadabhoy Naoroji in a letter on 6 August 1904.

The Act of 1936 eliminated this patriarchal privilege in theory more than in action. Both before and after 1936, Parsi wives accused their husbands in courts of visiting prostitutes and keeping mistresses. (K.J. Khambata, 'New Law of Marriage and Divorce among Parsis, A Progressive Measure', 17 July 1936.) The lawyer

FIGURE 4.2. Title page from Mansukh's book (1888) criticizing Parsi matrimonial law. *Source*: Mansukh. ©The British Library Board 14146.e.25.

Mansukh criticized Parsi matrimonial law

P.P. Ginwala, in his essay 'Prostitution' argued for the legislation by appealing to marital etiquette: 'it was better for a man to take a mistress or visit prostitutes than to pester his wife when she was not interested.'

Exhibit 71.

Extract from Jame-Jamshed, newspaper in native character, dated 5th July 1870, filed before Commissioner (translation).

Exhibit 71.

SUIT NO. 91 OF 1915 CHIEF COURT, LOWER BURMA.

R. S. DADACHANJI,

Commissioner.

17th May 1916.

10   O. S.
      A. S.   Serial No. 801 (19)

JAME JAMSHED, DATED 5TH JULY 1870.

Thereafter, on 21st July 1870, 25 respected Zoroastrian gentlemen of this place had sent a written protest to Sir Jamsetji Jijibhai Bart. the President of that meeting, to the effect that " We understand the name of ' Entire big and small Anjuman ' given by you to the meeting held on 3rd July 1870, as objectionable.   The meeting that was convened by you and other fifteen gentlemen of your side cannot be called an ' entire big and small Anjuman meeting '.   In our Bombay Zoroastrian population there is not an acknowledged person or
20 body who can, by virtue of authority, convene and assemble the entire big and small Anjuman and who can oblige a Zoroastrian who would not attend that meeting or who would give his vote against the majority of that meeting, to follow according to the resolution passed by it (meeting).   If some 100 or 200 persons of the Zoroastrian population would like to obtain a decision on a supposed difficulty by sending an application to other fifteen or twenty gentlemen and getting a public meeting convened in that behalf and if those fifteen or twenty gentlemen on adhering to the president of the meeting of 3rd July, would, thereupon, call a public meeting and pass resolutions therein, will that meeting also be called " the entire big and small Anjuman " and will its resolutions obtain that weight and authority ?   And in the same way, if how many soever
30 public meetings would assemble, will their resolutions bind all the Zoroastrians ?   If such a thing would take place, there would be a large number of authorised bodies in our population and dangerous irregularity cannot but follow out of it.   The business transacted in the above meeting of 3rd July appears to us to be devoid of mature consideration and to be defective.   We believe that the power of removing from Society, prostitutes and also persons, committing other offences against morality, lies in the hands of all of us. But the resolutions passed by you with the object of not considering as a Zoroastrian, the prostitute who would be professing Zoroastrianism and forcibly obliging her not to observe Zoroastrianism not only that—but of preventing the
40 issues born of her from entering into or following Zoroastrianism, shows extreme ignorance about the elements of Zoroastrian religion, in accordance with our understanding, instead of its being in agreement with the dictates of that religion.

(339)

39

The Parsi panchayat, it may be mentioned here, wanted to proclaim prostitutes and their children, out of caste. The religious scholar, K.R. Cama and other prominent citizens protested against this in writing and rejected the proposal.

A letter written by prominent citizens objecting to resolution of the Parsi panchayat to outcast prostitutes and their children was published in the weekly, *Jam-e-Jamshed*.

Transcription

JAM-E-JAMSHED, Dated 5 July 1870.

Thereafter, on 21 July 1870, five respected Zoroastrian gentlemen of this place had sent a written protest to Sir Jamsehdji Jijibhai Bart. the President of that meeting, to the effect that 'We understand the name of entire big and small Anjuman given by you to the meeting held on 3 July 1870, as objectionable. The meeting that was convened by you and other fifteen gentlemen of your side cannot be called an entire big and small Anjuman meeting of Bombay Zoroastrian population there is not an acknowledged person or body who can, by virtue of authority, convene and assemble the entire big and small Anjuman and who can oblige a Zoroastrian who would not attend that meeting or who would give his vote against the majority of that meeting, to follow according to the resolution passed by it (meeting). If some 100 or 200 persons of the Zoroastrian population would like to obtain a decision on a supposed difficulty by sending an application to other fifteen or twenty gentlemen and getting a public meeting convened in that behalf and if those fifteen or twenty gentlemen on adhering to the president of the meeting of 3 July, would, thereupon, call a public meeting and pass resolutions therein, will that meeting also be called the entire big and small Anjuman and will its resolutions obtain that weight and authority? And in the same way, if how many, so ever public meetings would assemble, will their resolutions bind all the Zoroastrians? If such a thing would take place, there would be a large number of authorized bodies in our population and dangerous irregularity cannot but follow out of it. The business transacted in the above meeting of 3 July appears to us to be devoid of mature consideration and to be defective. We believe that the power of removing from Society, prostitutes and also persons, committing other offences against morality, lies in the hands of all of us.

But the resolutions passed by you with the object of not considering as a Zoroastrian, the prostitute who would be professing Zoroastrianism and forcibly obliging her not to observe Zoroastrianism not only that-but of preventing the issues born of her from entering into or following Zoroastrianism, shows extreme ignorance about the elements of Zoroastrian Religion, in accordance with our understanding, instead of its being in agreement with the dictates of that religion.'

The following gentlemen had (put) their signature on this protest—

Messrs Khurshedji Nasserwanji Camaji, Sorabji Shapurji Bengalee, Dossabhai Framji Karaka, Rustomji Kawasji, Bahadurji, Kharshedji Rostomji Camaji, Hormasji Bapuji Vicaji, Jamshedji Jivanji Soonawala, Ratanji Bomanji Dubash, Kharshedji Framji Khory, Rustomji Nasseerwanji Khory, Manekji Dhanjishaw Doctor. Kharshedji Manekji, Kharshedji Shroff. Dosabhai Ratanji Kohla, Framji Edulji Davar, Dosabhai Beramji Pesikaka, Jijibhai Jangirji Lam, Jehangirji Burjorji Vachha, Pestonji Jehangirji Taleyarkhan, Jamshedji Palonji, Pallonji Kapadia. Bomanshaw Kavasji Vakil, Framji Shapurji Doctor, Pestonji Hirjibhai Unwalla.

*****

The Bandobast of 1830 and the Parsi Marriage and Divorce Act of 1936 also put legal restraints on Parsi men from forcing their wives into prostitution. 'Prostitution was problematic not just ethically, but also because staunch defenders of communal

EXHIBIT 4.

Circular No. 88 of St. year 1926, filed before Commissioner (translation).

EXHIBIT 4.

SUIT No. 91 OF 1915 CHIEF COURT, LOWER BURMA.

R. S. DADACHANJI,

Commissioner.

25th January 1916.

CIRCULAR No. 88 OF ST. YEAR 1926.

In the matter of the Bombay Parsi Panchayet Funds.

Bombay, Dated 1st August 1870.

14th day of 11th Month of the Shenshahi year 1239.

To

Sheth Rustomji Jamshedji Jijibhai.
" Hirjibhai Hormasji Shethna.
" Kharshedji Fardunji Parakh.
" Merwanji Framji Panday.
" Dinshaji Manakji Petit.
Trustees of the Panchayet Funds.

SIRS,

20 As resolved in your meeting held on 28th October 1239 Yez. (corresponding with) 16th July 1870, your letters dated 3rd November Yez. (21st July) asking for answers to four questions and bearing your signatures were sent together with the four questions to Dasturjis Pesotanji Beranji Sanjana, Jamaspji Minocherji Jamaspasana and Dasturji Sorabji Rustomji Mullafiroze. In order to consider over the matter of giving answers to these questions in accordance with the enjoinment of religion, these three Dasturs had twice met in the school hall of the Sir Jamshedji Jijibhai Bart. Charitable Institute, Fort Bombay. The Dasturs had called Sheth Mancherji Hormasji Cama and the Secretary Mr. Nasserwanji Beramji on those occasions. After fully investigating with the 30 help of religious books and in other proper ways, in connection with those questions, they have sent the answers unanimously prepared by them, stating them opposite to their respective questions, together with a letter over their signatures dated 9th November (Shen) or 27th July A C. I have put up that letter and questions and answers together with this Circular, which please note.

Sirs,

I am your humble servant,

MERWANJI NAVROJJI,

(Clerk) Mehtaji.

(139)

15

Letter to priests by Parsi Panchayat. Acceptance of Prostitutes' Children

boundaries found that it brought people of different communities into intimate contact with each other.' (The Parsi prostitute crisis of 1870 highlighted anxieties over intercommunal sex. See 'Morality among the Parsis' 29 June 1870, *The Times of India*)

QUESTION III.	ANSWER TO QUESTION III.
If such a prostitute had, after repentance & performance of proper ceremonies of the faith, social intercourse	Such issues after attaining the age of 15 years, want to be admitted into Zoroastrian religion after exercising

(141)

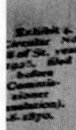

with Zoroastrians again, but if she had during her condition as a prostitute, given brith to one or more issues and if she had taken them with her (into Zoroastrian society) can we take such issues into Zoroastrian religion or not ?

their sense of understanding and regard for the faith, they should be admitted after having been imparted with instructions and knowledge of the Zoroastrian faith and invested with Sudra and Kusti. But such children who are less than 15 years age or more than 15 years but who have not entered into Zoroastrianism should be regarded as Juddins and should not be given any right whatsoever as a Zoroastrian.

The reply of the priests

The 1936 Parsi Marriage and Divorce Act introduced a clause that a woman could claim a divorce if her husband forced her into prostitution. Children born of these forced acts of prostitution were, however, accepted as Parsis.

Transcribed

Circular No. 88 of St. year 1926, filed before Commissioner (translation).

EXHIBIT 4

SUIT No. 91 Of 1915 CHIEF COURT, LOWER BURMA,

R. S. DADACHANJI,

Commissioner.

25th January 1916.

CIRCULAR No. 88 OF ST. YEAR 1926.

In the matter of the Bombay Parsi Panchayet Funds.

Bombay, Dated 1st August 1870.

14th day of 11th Month of the Shenshahi year 1239.

Letter to priests by the Parsi Panchayat and their answer regarding acceptance of children of prostitutes, as recorded in court in Saklat Vs Bella:

To

Merwanji Framji Panday.

Hirjibhai Hormasji Shethna

Kharshedji Fardunji Parakh

Meherwanji Framji Panday

Dinshahji Maneckji Petit

Trustees of the Panchayet Funds.

SIRS,

As resolved in your meeting, held on 28th October 1239 Yez. (corresponding with) 16th July 1870, your letters dated 3rd November Yez. (21st July) asking for answers to four questions and bearing your signatures were sent together with the four questions to Dasturjis Pesotanji Beranji Sanjana, Jamaspji Minocherji Jamaspasana and Dasturji Sorabji Rustomji Mullafiroze. In order to consider over the matter of giving answers to these questions in accordance with the enjoinment of religion, these three Dasturs had twice met in the school hall of the Sir Jamshedji Jijibhai Bart. Charitable Institute, Fort Bombay. The Dasturs had called Sheth Mancherji Hormasji Cama and the Secretary Mr. Nasserwanji Beramji on those occasions. After fully investigating with the help of religious books and in other proper ways, in connection with those questions, they have sent the answers unanimously prepared by them, stating them opposite to their respective questions, together with a letter over their signatures dated 9th November (Shen) or 27th July A C. I have put up that letter and questions and answers together with this Circular, which please note.

Sirs,

I am your humble servant,

MERWANJI NAVROJJI,

(Clerk) Mehtaji.

*****

Question III.

If such a prostitute had, after repentance & performance of proper ceremonies of the faith, social intercourse with Zoroastrians again, but if she had during her condition as a prostitute, given birth to one or more issues and if she had taken them with her (into Zoroastrian society) can we take such issues into Zoroastrian religion or not?

*****

Answer to Question III.

Such issues after attaining the age of 15 years, want to be admitted into Zoroastrian religion after exercising Their sense of understanding and out of regard for the faith, they should be admitted after having been imparted with instructions and knowledge of the Zoroastrian faith and invested with Sudreh and Kusti. But children who are less than 15 years in age or more than 15 years but who have not entered into Zoroastrianism should be regarded as Juddins and should not be given any right whatsoever as a Zoroastrian.

This letter was sent by the Parsi Panchayat to learned priests in 1870 asking if children of Parsi prostitutes should be accepted into the community. The priests answered if their Navjote was done, they should be accepted.

15
THE MAKING OF
PARSI PERSONAL LAW III

Common sense often makes good law.
—William O. Douglas

I) The Saklat Vs Bella case revisited

(See Transcription of Judgements of 1918 and 1920 in Appendix)

Bella was the child of a Parsi mother and a non-Parsi father. Both her parents died when she was just a few months old, and she was brought up by Sapoorji Cowasji and his wife as their own child. The head priest of the Deccan, Dastur Kaekobad Aderbad Dastur Noshirwan, who was also a high priest of the Parsis of the Deccan, Malwa and Madras, and Late Ervad D.B. Mehta, Zoroastrian Anjuman Atash Adaran, Calcutta and had 23 *panthaks* (diocese) under his charge, a very learned and knowledgeable priest, went with his wife from Calcutta to Rangoon to perform Bella's navjote. He also performed the navjote of Sapoorjis wife and then married the couple under the Parsi Marriage and Divorce Act. In his telegram to Meherwanji, brother of Sapoorji, he writes, 'I must stick to my promise, have performed similar navjotes after resolution of Punchayat. I am an independent Dastur... I must follow my conscience.'

The Saklat vs Bella lawsuit was filed in court for an injunction prohibiting Bella from entering the Fire temple. This was not granted, and Bella was given the right of entry in the Chief Court of Rangoon Judgements. When the case went to the Privy Council in the final appeal, Bella was no longer described as the daughter of a Parsi mother but 'as there was no legal evidence in finding that her mother is a Parsi.' Bella was now viewed as a convert to the religion The Privy Council determined that the respondent Bella has no right of entry into the temple. However, no injunction was given prohibiting her entry, but it was left to the trustees to decide to allow her to enter. The Privy Council held 'This of itself would warrant no ground of complaint.'

It was confirmed in the judgements, that conversion was a tenet of the religion,

That children of non Parsi fathers can be initiated into the Zoroastrian Religion,

The children of Parsi prostitutes were accepted as Parsis and

The words Parsi and Zoroastrian were being used interchangeably.

Most importantly, it was recorded in court that the navjote of a child of a Parsi Mother is 'not Conversion but Initiation into the Faith.'

The questions asked in court were:

Can the child of a non-Parsi father be initiated into the religion?

Whether the ceremonies performed were correct.

Is Bella entitled to the benefit of the fire temple trust?

Bella's lawyer was the Pahlavi scholar Dhanjisha Meherjibhai Madan, the author of 'The Complete Text of the Pahlavi Dinkard', an ancient religious book of the Parsis 'which gives us an idea of the opinions of some of the Sasanian Dasturs on various social, economic, philosophical and religious questions.' A school was established in this learned scholar's name in Jamshedpur, called the D.M. Madan School for Girls. While reading the full court transcripts of the Saklat vs Bella judgement I had wondered aloud, how the lawyer Mr Madan was so well informed about the religion and the Pahlavi language. In his cross examinations of some of the witnesses, he discussed parsing and phrasing of the Pahlavi script and details about the Zoroastrian religion only a scholar would know. It is only recently that I found out that he was himself an expert on religion, a student of Martin Hauge and a friend and contemporary of the learned Dasturs who were selected as experts on religion. Opposing him in court was Jehangir Vimadalal a preponent of the eugenics theory, an orator and doyen of Parsi Orthodoxy as well as a prominent theophysicist and devotee of the Zoroastrian mystical Ilm-e-Khshnoom.

Justice C. Young of the Chief Court of Rangoon in his judgement 23 April 1918 states, (Transcription in Appendix)

'This raises 2 main questions, the first being, could Bella seeing she was the daughter of a non- Zoroastrian father become a Zoroastrian and be duly initiated – in other words is Zoroastrianism a missionary religion and secondly, was she in fact initiated or in other word were the ceremonies performed sufficient for this purpose.'

'As regards the first question........ I am in complete agreement to the conclusion arrived at on the same point by Sir Dinshaw Davar and Sir F Beaman J J, namely that the Zoroastrian religion not only permits conversion but enjoins the conversion of a person born in another religion and of non- Zoroastrian parents.'

'Every day the pious Zoroastrian prays that the knowledge and propagation and belief in the good religion of Mazda be spread all over the seven regions of the earth.' 'Kerfeh Mazda' (see translation, p. 28).

"In the 18th Century we find the priests referring to Persia on questions of conversion, in the books called the RIvayats. "Behdin (Parsi laity) is he only who propagates the Good Religion" was the gist of their reply. To convert servants working in the household to the Zoroastrian religion is a pious duty, not to do so is a sin. The person who puts obstacles in the way is a great sinner.

Picture of Bella

Transcription

Translation from The Rivayats of 18 April 1773 as recorded in court in Saklat Vs Bella (see photocopy in Appendix).

Prayer Book Page 221

Translation of extracts from a small Gujarati printed book on pages 52, 53 and 54, containing proof (in support) of the matter that it is lawful to admit Juddins into the Mazdayasni religion, second edition, compiled by Tehmuras Dinshaji Anklesaria.

Rivayat

About 132 years ago, on the occasion when the late Mulla Kaoos went to Persia from India, taking with himself his son Peshotan who is well known by the name of Mulla Pheroze, certain Zoroastrian gentlemen of Surat and Broach, namely, Dasturs Darah *valade* (i.e. son of) Dastur Sohorab, Kavoos Munajjam valade Dastur Faredum, Kavus valade Dastur Rustam Sanjana, Noroj valade Dastur Framaraj, Rustam alias Padshah valade Dastur Framaraj, Behedins (i.e. laymen) Sohorab alias Nekasayetkhan valade Kavus shah and 14 other gentlemen sent 78 questions in writing, through the late Mulla Kavus Rustam Jalal, to the Zoroastrians of that time of the whole of Persia and requested them to send their answers.

The Zoroastrians of Persia, on the sixth day of the eighth Kadmi month of the Yezdezardi year 1142 (18 April 1773) having written and completed the answers to those questions (and) the undermentioned Dasturs and Behedins having put their signatures and seals thereon, sent them to India. The names of the persons who have signed them are (as follows) Dastur

Dasturan Marjban Valade (i.e., the son of the) late Dastur Hosang and 17 other gentlemen. These questions (and) answers are now in existence (and they are) with certain gentlemen. Out of those (questions), the 13th question and answer hereof given by the aforementioned Zoroastrians of Persia are translated from Persian and given below:

Question–13

Here in India Parsis buy Hindus' sons and daughters as *gulams* (slaves) and *kani jaks* (female slaves) and utilize them, to (do) their household work, and teaching them Avesta (they) invest them, according to the tenets of the Zoroastrian religion, with Sudreh Kusti (sacred shirt and thread) and having got prepared by their hands *Darun* (i.e., small wheat bread) for Ghambars and other (ceremonies or festivals), get the same consecrated, and in the same manner all the mobeds and Behedins of India eat and drink food and water (touched) by their hands, but when they (gulams and koni jaks) die, the said mobeds and Behdin do not allow their corpse, to be placed in the dokhmas saying 'They are children of durvands' (literally infidels, unbelievers, meaning non-Zoroastrians). therefore it is not proper that their bones should lie in the same place along with the bones of the Behedin. Now when those (gulams and kani jaks) were living, (the mobeds and behdins) got all the works relating to religion (relating to religious ceremonies done by their hands and when they die they prevent their corpses) being placed in Dokhmas, such being the case, it is requested that you will be good enough to explain whether it is or it is not lawful to place their corpses in Dokhmas.

Answer-13

As regards the matter of buying (1) Juddins' sons and daughters
(we say) that the mobeds and behdin should first take into
consideration the religion and the tenets of the religion and the
safety of their own persons and property in order that (by so
doing they) may not suffer any sort of harm. Alter having been
satisfied with regard to the aforesaid matter, if they buy Juddins
children and having taught them Avesta if they take them into the
good Mazdayasni religion, then that is a great meritorious act. But
this (1. e. the following) is a matter much to be condemned and ill
becoming the followers of the good Mazdayasni religion that the
Behdin of India, when the aforesaid children were alive, partook
of the food (touched or prepared by their hands) and yet when
they die, they should utter improper words with regard to the
dead bodies of those poor paupers. Their argument to the effect
that they are Juddins' children and therefore it is not proper that
their corpses may be put in the dokhmas along with the corpses
of behdins. To utter such words is improper, unproductive of
any good and adverse to meritorious acts. And the person who
puts obstacles in this matter and does not put their corpses (And
does not let their corpse be put) in dokhmas is an extremely
great sinner in the religion, and he is Ruhsiah (black faced) in the
presence of Meher and Sarosh. Therefore, it behoves the mobeds
(and behedins of India that they should give due respect to the said
children and that they should send their dead bodies to dokhma
according to the tenets of the Mazdayasni religion, this will be a
cause of satisfaction to Ahura Mazda (God) and Ameshaspand
(angels). We (Zoroastrians of Persia) have heard from the lips
of Dastur Kavus to the effect that some of the dasturs, mobeds
and behedin of India have put restrictions at all places (asking
people) not to teach Avesta to such children and not to take them

into the Mazdayasni religion. This is a thing very much opposed to (common sense). My dear co-religionists in the third chapter of the Vandidad, Dadar Hormazd (God) has directed the holy Zoroaster that he should publicly propound the Mazdayasni religion to all people (that is to say, he should preach religion) and that having shown (them) the good way, should himself acquire, by the benefit thereof, greatness and fame. Further, in the times of Hoshedarmah, Hoshedarbami and Soshiyos all the Juddins will be brought into this better Mazdayasni religion.

So, it appears also from the said authorities that it is lawful according to the Mazdayasni religion to admit into the religion the children of the above description. By doing such an act, great religious merit is acquired. And those who prevent (people) from doing so are the persons encouraging Juddins. And to call such persons as behdin is opposed to common sense. Behdin is he only who propagate the good religion.

Justice C. Young, continues in his judgement:

'And today we find questions referred by the Parsis of Bombay to the most learned in their religion and the answers given in the affirmative, and two of plaintiffs own witnesses one being the High Priest of the Shenshai sect, (Dastur Kaekhusru Jamaspji) the larger of the 2 Parsi sects and differing from the other merely on chronological questions and himself a leading member of this Expert Committee and the other being the Deputy High Priest, (Dastur Darab Sanjana) admitting that conversion was not only permitted but enjoined by the religion. In the face of these proofs and admissions might easily be multiplied, it seems idle to discuss further the doctrine that Zoroastrianism is a missionary religion, which I take to be admitted. It would be equally idle to deny that for one cause or another the Parsis for many years have not as a rule attempted to convert, that there are few if any authenticated instances in recent times and that many Parsis while admitting the theory set their faces sternly against the practice of conversion.'

The court appointed an Expert Committee on Religion to decide on religious matters. They gave the opinion that conversion was not only permitted but enjoined by the religion. There was a difference of opinion on the ceremonies to be performed. Dastur Kaekhusru Jamaspji decided that a navjote ceremony was required and Dastur Darab Sanjana wanted the longer Barashnum ceremony.

The Judge states that the priests decide who should enter the religion and what conditions the initiate must fulfill:

'So far as I can see in the Zoroastrian religion the power of admitting persons into the fold lies with the priest.' 'The priest has to satisfy himself.

(a) that the initiate really and sincerely desires to enter the faith

(b) that he believes in its doctrines, and

(c) That he is sufficiently acquainted with them for the purpose, and when he is so satisfied himself, the Nahn, Navjote and investing with Sudreh and Kusti, the outward and visible signs of Zoroastrianism, are all that is requisite.

(d) And that no harm of any kind would be done to the Mazdayasnams themselves.'

He concludes his judgement 'All that the defendant asks is permission to pray in the temple of her faith...... The suit stands dismissed.'

The case went in appeal and on 28 July 1920, (transcription and photocopy in Appendix) Justice A. McGregor gave a judgement saying

'The first defendant is a member of the Parsi Community of Rangoon and that she has been duly initiated into the Zoroastrian Religion; and therefore, she is entitled to the benefits of the Fire Temple Trust.'

Justice McGregor expressed his view that the navjote ceremony is not conversion but initiation into the religion: 'The expression 'conversion' has been used throughout but that implies that the person concerned had before professed another faith. In the present case Bella never had any other religion.' This was never dissented in the judgement of the Privy Council.

Justice Mcgregor confirmed that Zoroastrian religion enjoins conversion: 'That the Zoroastrian religion not merely recognizes but enjoins conversions cannot be disputed'. 'On the available evidence it must be held that the conversion of children of non-Parsi fathers is not contrary to the religion.'

He explains the social grounds which were affecting the matter:

'The Parsis had acquired wealth and they had charitable institutions and the right to share in these would affect their views. All sorts of undesirable persons attracted by these benefits might seek to become Zoroastrians in order to share in them. But these are not considerations that can affect the fact of the matter. Conversion was enjoined as a pious duty and mere neglect of that duty cannot remove tenet from the religion, no custom can be established by non-performance. That would be a contradiction in terms for a custom is created by regular consistent and continuous performance. I would therefore hold that the child of a non-Parsi father can be initiated into the religion.'

The meaning of Parsi and Zoroastrian was still being debated in 1920 and Justice Mcgregor concludes that, 'Parsi' and 'Zoroastrian' are being used interchangeably:

'There is abundant indication throughout the case that the words Parsi and Zoroastrian are interchangeable and synonymous.'

'There is therefore no reason to saying that the expression Parsi means and was intended to mean Parsis 'as a race.' He explains,

'In the Parsi Marriage and Divorce Act of 1865, the word Priest is defined as a Parsi priest and includes Dastur and

EXHIBIT 6.

Deed of Settlement (paras 1 to 4 only) of Sir Jejeebhoy's Parsee Benevolent Institution filed before Commissioner.

EXHIBIT 6.

SUIT No. 91, OF 1915 CHIEF COURT, LOWER BURMA.

R. S. DADACHANJI,

Commissioner.

25th January 1916.

Deed of settlement of Sir Jamsetjee Jejeebhoy's Parsee Benevolent Institution.

THIS INDENTURE, made the Ninth day of January, in the Year of Christ One Thousand Eight Hundred, and Forty nine, between Sir Jamsetjee Jejeebhoy, of Bombay, Knight, Parsee, of the first part; Nowrojee Jamsetjee, Bomanjee Hormusjee, Dadabhoy Pestonjee, Hormusjee Bomanjee Sett, Jejeebhoy Dadabhoy, Cursetjee Rustomjee, Cursetjee Jamsetjee, Cursetjee Furdoonjee Manockjee Limjee, Dossabhoy Sorabjee, Moonshee and Manockjee Nusser-wanjee, respectively of Bombay Esquires, Parsees, of the second part; and the several other Parsees who may hereafter become members of the Society by these presents constituted, of the third part; and The Honourable East India Company, of the fourth, part. Whereas the said Sir Jamsetji Jejeebhoy and the parties hereto of the second, part and other members of the Parsee Community, for the purpose of mitigating, as far as in their power lies, the evils of poverty and the ills consequent on infirmity and old age, amongst the Parsee Community and for providing for the Education of poor and other Parsee children are desirous of forming themselves into a society, to be called " Sir Jamsetjee Jejeebhoy's Parsee Benevolent Institution," in the manner hereinafter mentioned and set forth. And whereas, in order to carry such intention into effect, the said Sir Jamsetjee Jejeebhoy has agreed to contribute the sum of Three hundred Thousand Rupees and Fifteen shares in the Bank of Bengal, and on the part of Lady Avaboye the wife of the said Sir Jamsetjee Jejeebhoy, has also agreed to contribute five shares in the Bank of Bengal and the said parties hereto of the second part have also agreed to contribute Thirty-five Shares in the Bank of Bengal, for the use of such Society to be appropriated by such society for the purposes, and in the manner hereinafter mentioned; and whereas in order to promote the benevolent objects of the said Society, and to preserve the funds agreed to be contributed as aforesaid from loss, and to obviate inconvenience which might otherwise arise in the investment thereof, the said Honourable East India Company have agreed to become the perpetual Trustees of the said Society, and also to allow and pay, for the use of the said Society, interest at the rate of six per cent. per annum on the said sum of three hundred thousand rupees; and whereas in order to obviate all doubts respecting the meaning of the word Parsee in this Indenture, it is hereby declared that the word Parsee means in this Indenture throughout a person or persons professing the religion of Zoroaster. Now this Indenture witnesseth that the said Sir Jamsetjee Jejeebhoy and the abovenamed parties to these presents of the second part do for themselves severally, and for their respective heirs, executors and adminis-

(113)

The Deed of Trust of The Sir Jamsetjee Jeejeebhoy Trust Fund identifies a Parsi as a person professing the Religion of Zoroaster (Fouth line from the bottom)

Mobed. The word Parsi is used throughout, sometimes as referring to a Parsi man or woman where it has a racial significance possibly, and at other times in a sense that clearly refers to the religion e.g.- marriages are to be solemnized according to the Parsi form of ceremony.'

'In Act X of 1865 section 331 the exempted persons are defined by their religions and in Act XX1 of 1865, a similar Act for Parsis it is urged that they are also referred to by their religion. In Act III also the legislature speaks of the persons professing the Parsi Religion.'

'In the deed of settlement of Sir Jamshedji Jeejeebhoy Parsi Benevolent Institution (Exhibit 6, p. 181) a definition of Parsi is given to remove all doubt. – 'It is hereby declared that the word Parsi means in the indenture throughout, a person professing the religion of Zoroaster.'

'In Exhibit 1(A) the general Trust Deed of the Parsi Punchayat Property we find the expression 'the Parsi Religion.'

'It seems clear from these that the word 'Parsi' and 'Zoroastrian' were interchangeable, and this is not denied.'

Justice McGregor pointed out the differences between the 'initiation' of Bella, daughter of a Parsi mother and the 'conversion' of Suzanne Braire:

'There are differences between the Bombay case and the present one. There the plaintiffs were the champions of a French lady, Mrs Tata, who had been converted to the Zoroastrian religion, and their object was to enter into the use of certain properties. Here the first defendant is Parsi on the mother's side.' 'She is not a convert to the religion in the sense Mrs Tata was a convert. The object of the plaintiff is to exclude her from the Rangoon Agiari which she has been attending.'

He explains Justice Davar's reasoning on social grounds of non-acceptance of Suzanne Braire in his next statement:

'Lastly - It seems to me in the present condition indiscriminate conversion is very unlikely to occur.' 'This is with reference to Justice Davar's judgement - if the plaintiffs contentions prevailed, the community would soon cease to exist as a community by reason of rapid invasion of all paupers, sweepers Dubras of Gujrat who would no doubt be attracted to the Holy Mazdayasni Religion by reason of the 53 lacs of rupees in the possession of the defendants and the other advantage of belonging to the Holy Zoroastrians of Bombay.'

He pronounces his verdict:

'I may say, here, that 1st Defendant is a member of the Parsi Community of Rangoon.'

Then he explains the meaning of the word Parsi.

'The Government of India in the various acts relating to Parsis has not concerned itself to define the term (Parsi). It is a reasonable influence that it does not want to commit itself to any precise definition. I doubt myself whether this term is definable. It is impossible to say, of any individual Parsi now living, that he is descended from the male line from the Parsi immigrants 1,300 years ago. A Parsi, it seems to me, is to be described, rather than defined, as a member of the well-known community having, as a community, a certain origin and history, distinctive customs and above all a distinctive religion.'

He concludes 'The first defendant is a member of the Parsi community of Rangoon and that she has been duly initiated into the religion; and therefore, she is entitled to the benefit of the Fire Temple Trust.'

Finally, in 1924 the case went in appeal to the Privy Council. By this time, Bella's adoptive father Sapoorji Cowasji, had passed away and there was no one to fight her case.

The Judgement was as follows:

'They claim an Injunction to restrain the defendant Bella from entering and the other defendant, now dead, from bringing her into the temple to perform religious ceremonies.'

He explains his thought process:

'They can treat her as a trespasser. But it does not follow that they are bound so to treat her.' 'But the mere claim of A that B shall not share in such a benefit because B is not within the terms of the foundation is not one that courts would encourage'. 'The intrusion of an unbeliever into a place of worship might well be a case of substantial interference with the devotion of worshippers. But the plaintiffs have failed to make out that Bella was not a Zoroastrian' 'If it were a question of caste and worshippers of a higher caste would be defiled by the presence of a lower caste.... This would be a serious disturbance......But this claim is again not established.' 'That a beneficiary or two or three beneficiaries of a trust for public purposes may bring a suit for trespass against an intruder is a novel principle of jurisprudence; and the case is not made stronger by the suggestion that several other beneficiaries agree with them.' 'It must be established that the juxtaposition of the two sets of persons is so repugnant to their habits of mind that the entrance of one set into the temple entails the departure of the other, so that it is as it were trespass to the person'.

And he refuses the injunction:

'As already stated, no such case has been established and No Injunction can be Granted'

'The Judges in the Chief Court took the view that the fourth issue (is Bella entitled to the benefits of the fire temple) might also have been decided in favour of Bella, i.e., that her mother was a Parsi, but that this fact was unimportant. Their lordships agree with this. In their view it is settled that as regards the racial claim, maternity is of no importance.'

This would be totally unacceptable today when women and men enjoy equal rights.

'But upon the whole, their lordships feel that the plaintiffs have failed in the greater part of their suit, and that giving to them of a declaration is an indulgence....that a declaration be made, namely, that Bella was not entitled as of right, to use the temple..... But if the trustees permit her that of itself furnishes no ground of complaint.'

In the final plea made against Bella the plaintiffs had made a change from the original plea. Bella was no longer depicted as the child of a Parsi mother. Instead, they pleaded.

(j) 'For that this Court erred in holding that the respondent Bella's mother was a Parsi, it should have held that there was no legal evidence to justify the Court in finding as a fact that her mother was a Parsi.'

Dastur Kaekobad Aderbad Dastur Noshirwan High Priest of the Deccan and of the Calcutta Late Ervad D.B. Mehta Zoroastrian Anjuman Atash Adaran performed Bella's navjote In his cross examination in Saklat Vs Bella. He states that Bella was a Parsi 'because her mother was a Parsi'. When asked if the fire temple would be desecrated if Bella entered, he replied, 'No'. And on being further questioned why not? he replied,

'Because she is born of a Parsi parent, a Parsi mother.'

In 1918, N.N. Burjorjee, A.B. Mehta, N.S. Pavri, D.N. Cooper, Rustum H. Hirjee, K. Nowrojee and others petitioned the court to be added on as defendants in the case Saklat vs Bella. (Transcript of judgement in Appendix). They petitioned that the case involves questions of great importance to the Parsi community, and they disagreed with the orthodox views of the plaintiffs and in their opinion, Bella was entitled to worship at the fire temple.

'They ask to be added in order to represent their own views and those of the members of the Parsee Community in Burma who agree with them.'

FIGURE 6:
"A TORRENT OF FIRE"
[*Hindi Punch* (6 September 1914), 16.]
[By permission of the British Library (SV 576).]

Picture of Dastur Kaekobad in the Hindi Punch *in 1914*

They claimed, 'The issues are far reaching and important. One raises the question as to who are entitled to the benefit of the Fire Temple Trust and another the still wider question as to whether it is possible for the daughter of a non-Parsi father to be initiated (a) into the Zoroastrian religion (b) into the Parsi Community. The Plaintiffs are the more orthodox or as the opponents would probably say the more narrow-minded section of the Parsees who would prohibit conversion and deny that anyone not being the child of a Parsi father can be a Parsi.'

The judge however ruled 'the plaintiffs have brought this suit against persons they allege to be wrong doers. They have no wish to sue all members of the community who disagree with them on questions of doctrine in order to have it declared, which view is correct.'

The suit was for action against two individuals only and not a declaration of doctrine for the community.

'Let us assume that a Parsi gentleman marries a non-Parsi lady converts her and seeks to introduce her into the Fire-Temple, are they to have no chance of being heard if the decision in this case is that no person not born of a Parsee father is entitled to worship there? I do not think so. They are not interested and will not be bound.'

'The practical result of which would be to convert the suit from one for an injunction against alleged wrongdoer into a suit for a declaration as to doctrine - the competence of which I doubt. (Transcript of judgement attached in Appendix)

Neither Justice Davar's obiter nor the Saklat vs Bella judgement is binding on the community. More important is the fact that even in 1918 and to date conversion of a person born in a different faith was accepted and the rights of converts not decided.

Today as the situation exists, Bella, being the adopted child of a Parsi father, would be accepted as a Parsi, no questions asked as to where her ancestors came from or who her real father is, no DNA

(839)

Certificate under Section 6 of the Parsi Marriage and Divorce Act being Act XV of 1865	
Date and place of marriage.	Jubilee Hall, Rangoon. 20th December 1920. Parsi Roaj 12th, Maha 4th, Yezdezerdi 1920.
Name of the husband and wife.	Dhanjishaw Jamasjee Kolapore and Goolbai (Bella) Shapurjee Cowasjee.
Condition at the time of marriage.	Bachelor and Spinster.
Rank or Profession.	Nil. and Assistant to the Singer Sewing Co., Rangoon.
Age.	Thirty one. & Twenty.
Residence.	18, Pagoda Road, Rangoon.
Name of the father or Guardians.	Dr. Jamasjee Framjee Kolaporewalla and Mr. Sapoorjee Cowasjee.
Rank or Profession.	Doctor and Merchant.
Signature of officiating priest.	M. D. Dastoor, A. Sorabji Chothana.
Signatures of the witnesses.	Sorab Burjorjee, B. N. Burjorjee.
Signature of father or guardian when husband or wife is an infant.	D. J. Kolapore; Bella S. Cowasjee; S. Cowasjee, Guardian.

S. Cowasjee.

Bella married Dhanjisha Kolapore under the Parsi Marriage and Divorce Act by Parsi rites and by Parsi priests. Mr Sorab Burjorji (grandfather of Mr Fali Nariman) signed as a witness for Bella

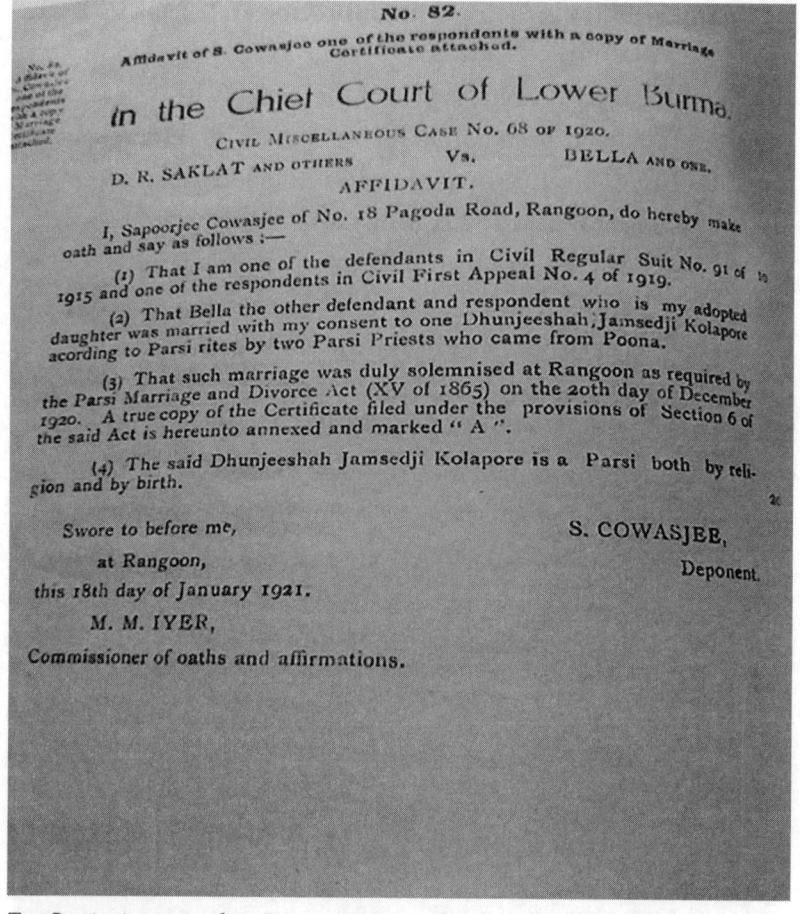

No. 82.

Affidavit of S. Cowasjee one of the respondents with a copy of Marriage Certificate attached.

In the Chief Court of Lower Burma.

CIVIL MISCELLANEOUS CASE No. 68 OF 1920.

D. R. SAKLAT AND OTHERS   Vs.   BELLA AND ONE.

AFFIDAVIT.

I, Sapoorjee Cowasjee of No. 18 Pagoda Road, Rangoon, do hereby make oath and say as follows :—

(1) That I am one of the defendants in Civil Regular Suit No. 91 of 1915 and one of the respondents in Civil First Appeal No. 4 of 1919.

(2) That Bella the other defendant and respondent who is my adopted daughter was married with my consent to one Dhunjeeshah, Jamsedji Kolapore according to Parsi rites by two Parsi Priests who came from Poona.

(3) That such marriage was duly solemnised at Rangoon as required by the Parsi Marriage and Divorce Act (XV of 1865) on the 20th day of December 1920. A true copy of the Certificate filed under the provisions of Section 6 of the said Act is hereunto annexed and marked " A ".

(4) The said Dhunjeeshah Jamsedji Kolapore is a Parsi both by religion and by birth.

Swore to before me,   **S. COWASJEE,**

     at Rangoon,   Deponent.

this 18th day of January 1921.

M. M. IYER,

Commissioner of oaths and affirmations.

Two Parsi priests went from Poona to Rangoon to perform Bella's wedding by Parsi rites to Dhanjeeshah Kolapore

test required. Rules of adoption do not allow the adoption agency to reveal the identity of the parents who give the child for adoption.

To end the story, Bella was accepted as a Parsi and she married Mr Dhanjishaw Jamsetji Kolapore by Parsi rights, in a ceremony called Ashirvad, and the wedding was registered under The Parsi Marriage and Divorce Act under which only a Parsi man can marry a Parsi woman.

II) Hormusji Bhabha's Cross Examination In Saklat Vs Bella

Hormusji Jehangir Bhabha, father of Meherbai (wife of late Dorab Jamsetji Tata) and grandfather of the father of India's nuclear program Homi Bhabha gave the most modern and acceptable interpretation of 'Who is a Parsi' in his cross examination as a witness in Saklat vs Bella. He was the President of the Iranian Association which was very vocal in its support of Conversion as a tenet of the Zoroastrian religion, and of Dastur Kaekobad Aderbad Dastur Noshirwan who initiated Bella into the Zoroastrian religion. The association covered both events extensively in articles written in its journal. In the cross examination he made a very succinct statement which highlighted the sad state of marital affairs in the community in 1916: 'Parsi women as a rule were married to Parsis and were usually chaste. But no one can say that in every case the child of a Parsi mother was by a Parsi father.' Similarly, Adi Rabadi, trustee of the Mehta Atash Adaran in Calcutta opined 'The Parsi mother's child is at least half Parsi- not necessarily the Parsi father's child!' ('Arnavaz Mama', report on the Inauguration of the Federation of Parsi Anjumans of India Meet at Jamshedpur, 2001.)

Hormusji was a polymath. An MA from Bombay University, he was director of public instruction in Mysore state; fellow and member of the syndicate of Bombay University, member of the council of the late Mr Tata's Institute of Science; member of the panchayat of the Sir J.J. Benevolent Institution, member of the executive committee of the Dand Sassoon Reformatory; member of the Committees of the J.N. Petit Parsi Orphanage, the Alexandra Native Girls' English Institution, the J.N. Petit Institute, President of the Iranian Association and Chairman of the standing committee of the Zoroastrian Conference.

Some extracts from Hormusji's cross examination in court in Saklat vs Bella, where he gave evidence to support Bella (daughter of

Hormusji J. Bhabha (Gene.com)

a Parsi mother and non-Parsi father) and was questioned by lawyer Vimadalal (who wrote the book *Racial Intermarriages: Their Scientific Aspect*, 1922, based on Eugenics) are given below.

Q) Is it generally known to educated Parsi society whether conversion of non-Zoroastrians into the Zoroastrian faith is or is not permitted according to the tenets of the religion.

A) It is generally known that such conversion is permitted by the tenets of our religion.

Q) Is the preponderant majority of educated and enlightened Parsis and those capable of independent thinking for or against the inclusion of juddin converts into their own community as members of the Parsi Community

A) Such converts are accepted as members of the Parsi Community.

Q) The Parsi Community has insisted on the father being a Parsi if a child is to be considered a member of the Parsi community on the ground that the child must have a Parsi boon which proceeds from the father. (Question by Lawyer J.J. Vimadalal).

A) I do not know what you call the Parsi community that has so decided. I believe that there must be and there are many of my opinion in the community, so that it is not a case of the unanimous opinion of the whole community.

Moreover, I do not think that such questions can be settled by a majority of votes in a community, the minority having a right to hold their own opinions independently of the rest of the community.

Secondly, it seems absurd to make a distinction between the part contributed by the father and that contributed by the mother in the birth of the child. The two parts can be compared only to factors each of which would be useless without the other.'

Lawyer Vimadalal tries to pressurize Mr Homi Bhabha into saying it's a custom to accept children of Parsi fathers only.

Q) From your knowledge of Parsi custom please tell us who have been regarded in India amongst Parsis as members of the Parsi community

A) If you want me to classify the members of the Parsi community I would give the following classification.

(1) the descendants of Parsi fathers and Parsi mothers

(2) the descendants of Parsi fathers and non-Parsi mother

(3) in rare cases the children of Parsi mothers by non-Parsi fathers

(4) those who are not born either from Parsi fathers or Parsi mothers but who have for various reasons by adoption, conversion or otherwise been admitted into the Parsi religion and thus enjoy the rights of being members of the Parsi community.

Q) When you speak of the regular customs in our community to admit all children one of whose parent is a Parsi, you refer to the custom of admitting children of Parsi fathers by alien mothers.

A) I meant children either of whose parents whether father or mother was a Parsi.

Q) There can be no regular custom as to children whose mother alone was a Parsi since no such case is known to have occurred.

A) Of course not, because Parsi women as a rule were married to Parsis and were usually chaste. But no one can say that in every case the child of a Parsi mother was by a Parsi father.

Q) The knowledge that conversion was a tenet of the Zoroastrian religion became general knowledge after the discussion of the Committee Experts on the juddin question.

A) Yes, after the report that was so.

Q) Do you know of your own personal knowledge if Parsi families were living in the vicinity of the family in which the Mohammedan servant was converted to Zoroastrianism.

A) Yes

Q) Will you give the relationship of that family with you.

A) It was in the family in which my wife's sister was married.

III) The hue and cry over Parsi 'boon'

'They were children of Parsi 'olad' or *boon* (i.e., seed)'. This phrase was repeatedly used in both the Petit vs Jeejeebhoy judgement in 1908, and the Saklat vs Bella judgement. It was believed that the male sperm contained a fully formed baby, and the womb was only a receptacle for growing the seed. Science of reproduction has progressed. We know today that a child carries equal DNA (seed) from both parents. In other words, we are now aware that the Parsi *Boon* comes from both the mother and the father.

In Petit vs Jeejeebhoy Justice Daver mentions why illegitimate children of Pasi men should be accepted. He says, 'The reason for regarding such children with favor and allowing them to be invested with Sudreh and Kusti, was that they were taken to be children born in the faith of their fathers... They were the children of Parsi 'boon' (i.e., seed); they were children of Parsi 'olad' (i.e., origin).'

Justice Beaman in his independent judgement in the same case says, 'What the defendants deny is the right of any foreign convert, in whose vein no Parsi blood runs, to become a member of the Parsi Community.'

In Saklat vs Bella, J.C. Daji, one of the witnesses, said in evidence, 'The main principle has been that boon or seed and the olad or descent of a child, it owes to its father. Upon that principle, children of Parsi fathers are supposed to have the Parsi seed in them' D.B. Master in his cross-examination, said, 'having as their father a Parsi and I think that is accepted as it is considered that the seed comes from the Parsi father.'

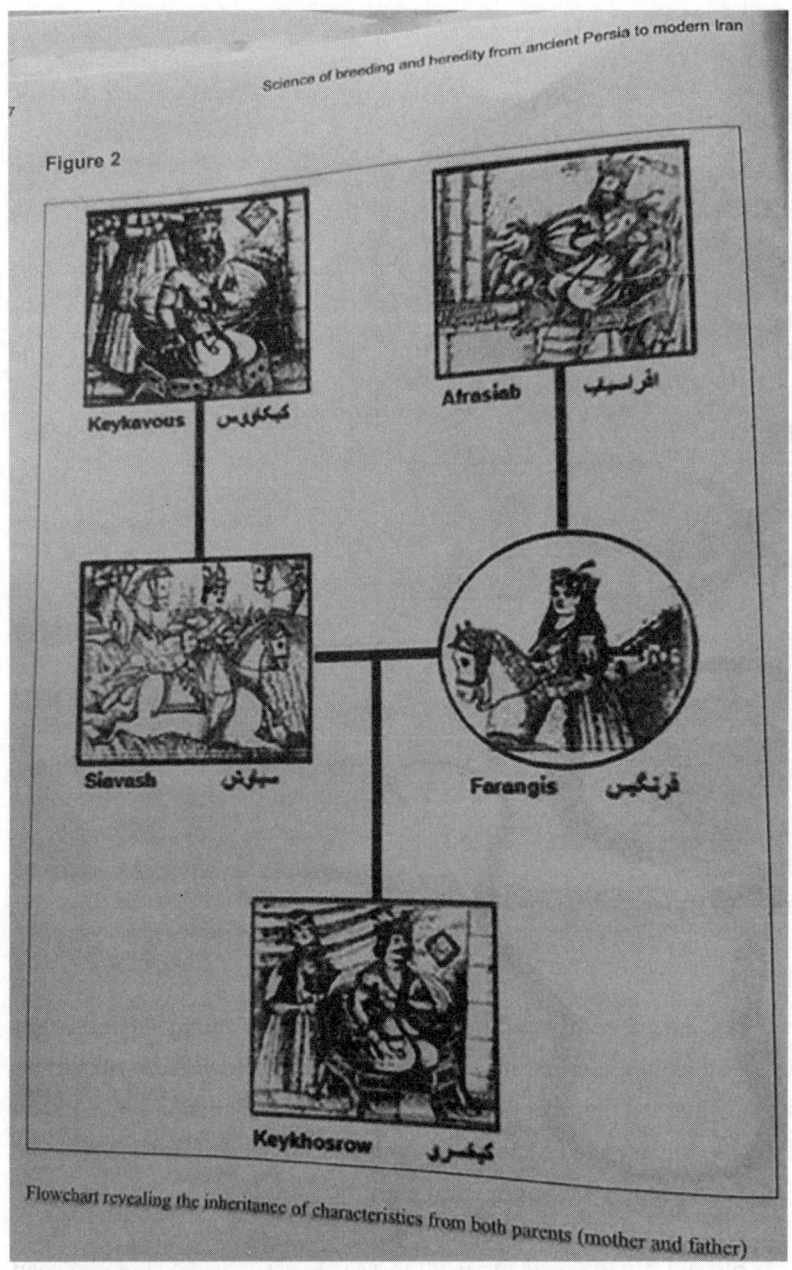

Legend: Flowchart from Ancient Iran, revealing the inheritace of characteristics from both mother and father.

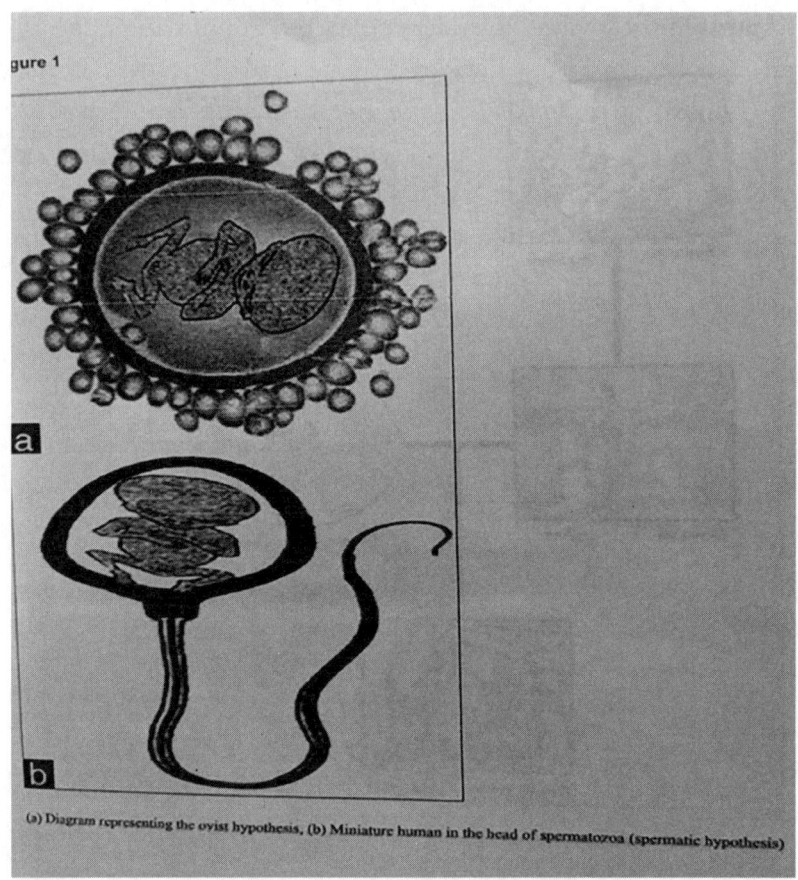

(a) Diagram representing the ovist hypothesis. (b) Miniature human in the head of spermatozoa (spermatic hypothesis)

Preformation Theory: This theory envisioned a miniature human in the head of the sperm (Spermatic Hypothesis) which would be deposited in the uterus to grow and mature

D.R. Saklat, another witness, made the point, 'Among Parsis descent is traced from males because if an issue has got blood from his father, we consider it a member of the community.' N.J. Gamadia said, 'A Parsi father's child is called a Parsi because it has the seed of the father.'

Parsi seed, Parsi boon, Parsi olad,

What are they referring to?

Greek philosophers believed that man's semen contains all human characteristics, and the female uterus is only the vessel to nurture the sperm. This idea, called the Preformation Theory, presupposed a miniature human was in the head of the spermatozoa.

However, in the *Indian Journal of Human Genetics* Jan-April 2012, Ardeshir Khorshidian in an article entitled 'Science of breeding and heredity from ancient Persia to modern Iran' writes:

'About 1700 years BC, the prophet Zoroaster declared equal rights for men and women to choose their "own ways," or choose their path. There is much evidence that ancient Persians believed in the equal contribution of women and men towards producing a child, and all its hereditary characteristics.'

'Even more surprising are the phrases in Vendidad book, which were gathered by Mobedans in the Mad dynasty about egg extraction (gamatese) from animal reproductive organs(*gonads*) and their storage for future conception.'

'Centuries later, Western philosopher beliefs were contrary to Persian knowledge. The Greek philosophers believed that man's water (semen) contains all human characteristics, and the female uterus is only responsible for nurturing the development of the fetus.' After detection of the spermatozoid by Nicholas Hartsaoker it was suggested that there was a miniature human being in the sperm that transformed into a fetus.

'This was called the Preformation Theory.'

'The general concept was that the male component is the contributor of complete human features. The female component is the uterus that will nurture the seed from the father's semen to fruition, granting the seed all the hereditary features and the woman none.'

16
IRANIAN ASSOCIATION'S LETTER TO THE PARSI PANCHAYAT ON THE RANGOON NAVJOTE

There is only one path and that is (the path) of Truth.
All other paths are not proper.

—Mino-ī-Kherad

The Iranian Association was established in Bombay in 1912. Its president was Homi J. Bhabha (grandfather of nuclear scientist Homi Bhabha). The vice-presidents were J.A. Dalal, and L.N. Banaji; and committee members included D.F. Gimi, Padumji Desai, M.F. Anklesaia, P.A. Engineer, Jamshedji Nadirshaw, N.N. Katrak, D.M. Madan (Bella's lawyer) N.N. Kanga and Ardesher Servai.

The objectives of the association were:

1) to maintain the purity of the Zoroastrian religion and remove the excrescences they have gathered around it
2) to expose and counteract the effects of such teachings of theosophists as tend
   a) to corrupt the religion of Zarathustra by adding elements foreign to it, and
   b) to bring about the degeneration of a progressive and virile community like the Parsis, and make them a body of supertitious and unpracticed visionaries.

3) to promote the measures for the welfare and advancement of the community.

A letter sent by the Association to the Bombay Parsi Panchayat in 1914 gives us a glimpse of what transpired behind the scenes during and after Bella's navjote in Rangoon by Dastur Kaekobad Aderbad Dastur Noshirwan. The account is so vivid that one can relive the event through these pages. In point 14 of the letter, it is mentioned that a resolution (which was not accepted) of the Parsi Panchayat in 1905 wanted to deny the acceptance of the children of intermarried men and the children of alien parents on both sides. Children of Parsi mothers and alien fathers were not mentioned in the resolution. The letter also records that 'acceptance of children by alien fathers and Parsi mothers is tacitly recorded in the Panchayat Trust Deed' (Point 15).

It protested against the Parsi Panchayat passing resolutions which it had no authority to make. And it made the point that a minority and the majority in a religious institution also had a right to follow their beliefs. The members of the Association expressed their support and solidarity with Dastur Kaekobad Aderbad Dastur Noshirwan, (who performed Bellas navjote), and recognized and acknowledged his religious knowledge in glowing terms.

It was opposed to the idea of a lay body like the Anjuman making any authoritative pronouncements on religious matters against the declared unanimous opinion of a chosen body of religious experts, and also going the length of requiring other Parsis to abandon, confessedly for social and extra-religious reasons, what they hold and believe to be tenets of their religion, and what a committee of experts had declared to be special enjoinments of their religion and their prophet.

This letter was signed by Homi J. Bhabha President, of the Iranian Association. (Grandfather of Homi Bhabha the founder of India's Nuclear Physics Program).

This letter clearly shows that conversion was accepted as a tenet of the Zoroastrian religion, and that the Parsi panchayats attempt to stop conversion for social reasons was being objected to by many prominent community members.

The learned Dastur Kaekobad Aderbad Dastur Noshirwan was later honored by the community who selected him to represent them at the Parliament of Living Religion where he spoke about the Zoroastrian religion as a monotheistic religion meant for all mankind.

Transcribed: (Photocopy in the Appendix)

THE IRANIAN ASSOCIATION, To
The Hon. Sir Jamshedji Jeejeebhoy Bart
Jamshedji Cursetji Jamshedji Esq.
Bomanji Dinshaw Petit Esq.
Sir Cowasji Jehangir Bart.
Mancherji Pestonji Kharegat Esq. I. C. S.
Hormasji Ardeshir Wadia Esq., Bar-at-Law
Naoroji Jehangir Gamadia Esq.
Trustees of the Charitable Funds and Immoveable properties of the Parsi panchayat of Bombay.

Gentlemen,
We understand that a requisition said to be signed by a very large number of Zoroastrian ladies and gentlemen has been forwarded to you as Trustees of the Charitable Funds and Immoveable properties of the Parsi Panchayat of Bombay, and that you are therein asked to convene a general meeting of "Parsi Zoroastrians" in order to pass resolutions expressing strong disapproval of Shams-ul-Ulama Sardar Dastur Kaekobad Aderbad Dastur Noshirwan of Poona for having performed a

certain Navjot ceremony at Rangoon. You have also asked to help the requisitionists and others to meet together and adopt other proper measures for safeguarding the interests of our community. On behalf of the Iranian Association, we are directed to address this representation to you in the matter, and we trust it will be given fair consideration before you arrive at a final decision in regard to the aforesaid requisition.

1. In the first place, we believe it is essential for us to bring to your recollection a few prominent facts which are gleaned from the history of our community in this city. In remote times, when the Parsi population in Bombay was small, and when it was conveniently possible for the whole community to meet together for the discussion and determination of matters affecting the general body of the community, it appears that meetings of the general Anjuman or "Panchayat, " as it was then called, were held. Later on some of the powers of the " Panchayat " were delegated by common consent to a few individuals elected in general meetings of the whole "Anjuman, " and in course of time this smaller body to whom such powers were assigned, came itself to be designated as "The Panchayat." With the growth of the community and the natural unsuitability of the larger or the smaller Punchayet" to take any action in the name and on behalf of the community, the powers of the "Punchayat" altogether vanished, and the only function of the smaller "Punchayat" was to control and manage the funds and properties of the community which were committed to its care. The smaller Panchayat " in its turn came in course of time to delegate its functions to a few of its members, who styled them- selves Trustees of the Funds and Properties of the Parsi Punchayet, and who further arrogated to themselves the power of appointing their successors, as

also other functions which were at one time exercised by the "Panchayat," including the power of convening, when occasion arose general meetings of the community, known as Meetings of the Anjuman.

2. The meetings that were thus called were necessarily and at all times, of a formal, or ceremonial and limited character. In any event at no time did the Panchayat, large or small, profess or attempt to legislate for the community. It never ventured to be set up as a propounder or interpreter of the tenets of Zoroastrian religion and never did it dream of questioning or repudiating them for social or other reasons or of pronouncing verdicts on the actions of individuals in religious matters, or in regard to the performance or non-performance of religious duties.

3. About a decade ago, attempts are made by a certain section of the community to induce the then Trustees of the Parsi Panchayat to convene a meeting of the Anjuman, with the object of passing certain resolutions on very delicate questions of religious and socio-religious character. On that occasion, an initially signed representation of a number of leading Parsees, bearing date the 28th October 1914 was forwarded and submitted to those Trusteees, in which various reasons were given to demonstrate the inadvisability and impropriety of calling such a meeting. After pointing out there in the facts that the Parsi community was bound to render obedience only to the general law of India and the special laws affecting it, that there was no such body as the Parsi Punchayet or any other authority possessing any powers to control the action of its members, that the meetings from time to time convened by the so-called Trustees of the Parsi Panchayat under a modern practice, adopted for the sake of convenience, were of a formal, ceremonial or limited character, whose conclusion

had no binding force or validity, they requested the Trustees not to convene a general meeting of the Anjuman in the best interests of the community, for the preservation of peace and harmony among its members, on the ground that a general meeting of the kind was by its character and composition unfitted to deal with delicate questions of a religious and socio religious character. We are grieved to find that this advice was disregarded by the then Trustees, mainly and ostensibly on the ground that they were bound by a promise given at a previous meeting of the Anjuman to submit before it the report of a committee which was appointed at the said previous meeting.

4. The aforesaid representation had made clear that the course sought to be adopted of placing delicate questions relating to religion and society before a mass meeting of the Anjuman, "was capable of the construction that a general meeting of Parsis, without rules or constitution or legal validity, was a suitable machinery for discussing and determining grave, religious and social questions affecting Parsis. More serious still was the further assumption involved in the action of the Trustees that any number of Parsis could require or restrain a single individual of the community from practicing the tenets of his religion, on the score of social or other considerations." In spite of this warning, a meeting was held on the 16th day of April 1905 when certain resolutions of a dictatorial character were adopted, and other resolutions were carried at the meeting the purport of which was to subject to a social ban or ostracism any member of the community who offended against the prior resolutions.

5. You are also aware that after these resolutions were adopted, they were submitted to learned counsel for opinion and advise as to their legal validity and efficacy. You are also

aware that the joint opinion of 2 councils was obtained, even before the said meeting was held, as to the validity and legal effect of such resolution, if adopted, at a general meeting of the Anjuman by a large majority. The unanimous opinion of council in this matter was, to cite the words of Mr. Inverarity, "Such resolutions would have no legal effect. D. D. Davar (now the Hon. Justice Sir Dinshaw D. Davar) expressed himself thus, "I do not see how a majority of the community can enforce their views and wishes on the minority, however small that minority might be. If that minority have certain legal rights, they would be entitled to assert and will successfully assert them in spite of any number of resolutions which the majority might pass". The Hon the Chief Justice Sir Basil Scott, who was the Advocate General, was asked if the Parsi Community assembled at a public meeting, either unanimously or by a large majority, could give expression to its views, so that they may hereafter at all times be binding upon and unchallengeable by the Parsi community. He said: "In my opinion they cannot effectually achieve this result. "The contention of the signatories to the representation of the 28th October 1914 were thus in substance borne out by the opinion of eminent lawyers.

6. The then Trustees accepted this opinion, and, to a certain extent even acted upon it despite the resolutions of the aforesaid Anjuman meeting of the 16th April 1905. Two years after the said meeting, in April 1907, they filed their written statement in the famous Suite 689 of 1906, which has become known as the Panchayat Case. They disregarded therein one of the resolutions of the aforesaid meeting, and deliberate chose to treat the same as if it was never binding on them or on the whole community, in whose interests and on whose behalf they professedly defended the action brought against

them. In paragraph 14 of that written statement dealing with, the rights of children of Parsi fathers by alien mothers, which purported to be taken away and denied for all time to come by one of resolutions of the Anjuman meeting of the 16th April 1905, the Trustees observed "The right of this latter class of persons to the benefit of the trusts of which these defendants are Trustees has been questioned from time to time, and the majority of the community are against their inclusion in the Parsi Community. Having regard to the usage and practice for a good many years of admitting this class of persons into the said community and to the benefit of the said trusts, the defendants have recognized such rights, and have not disputed the same."

7. It was expected after the wide publicity that was given to the legal opinions above cited, and after the determined manner in which the then Trustees decided to act upon those opinions that it would not occur to any thinking Zoroastrians to indulge any longer in the futile endeavor to enforce one or more of the resolution of the 16th April 1905, more particularly because it was well known that those resolutions were entirely antagonistic to the wishes of a certain section of the community, who challenged the right of the Anjuman either to pass them, or to give them any binding aspect or legal validity, and more particularly also because an enlightened section of the community that could never be neglected, was opposed to the idea of a lay body like the Anjuman making any authoritative pronouncements on religious matters against the declared unanimous opinion of a chosen body of experts, and also going the length of requiring other Parsis to abandon, confessedly for social and extra- religious reasons, what they hold and believe to be tenets of their religion, and what a committee of experts

had declared to be special enjoinments of their religion and their prophet.

8. As large number of requisitionists have taken organized steps in view of certain events that have recently happened to induce you to convene a meeting to enforce the resolutions of the meeting of the 16ᵗʰ April 1905, and to pass other proper resolutions for the protection of the community. "we are asked by our Association to remind you of the aforesaid facts, and for the reason hereinafter stated, to request you, in the best interests of the peace, harmony and welfare of our community not to take any steps or action in the shape of calling a public meeting of the Paris or the purpose intended by the requisitions.

9. In the first place, a public gathering of the community, indefinite in its composition, and possessing no constitution or law, will be readily admitted to be too heterogeneous and unorganized a body to consider and pronounce upon religious and social questions. It cannot be held to possess either capacity and authority for such a task and fortified as you are by the legal opinion of eminent counsel, who have unanimously declared that resolutions adopted by such a meeting, by however large a majority, can have no binding effect on anybody, and no legal validity whatever, you can very safely and wisely decide to say that you would not call a meeting for a purely futile end.

10. Secondly as we have said before the right to convene such meetings of the Anjuman so called was arrogated to themselves by the gentlemen who from time to time held the office of and styed themselves as, Trustees of the Charitable funds and Immovable properties of the Parsi Punchayat of Bombay. It is now decided by the judicial authorities that the powers thus arrogated to themselves by the Trustees, and

their very appointment, were illegal and invalid. You are not successors of the Trustees under the old agreement, nor have you been appointed to hold any of these powers which the trustees under the old arrangement exercised, except those specially conferred on you for a limited purpose. Four of your number have been nominated by the High Court and the other 3 elected by the 'Anjuman Committee', in pursuance of the scheme framed and sanctioned by the Court, and your functions are now restricted to the custody and management of the funds and properties vested in you as Trustees and you are not authorized to convene any such meeting of the Anjuman, as it was customary for those holding office as trustee in the past to do. Our Association therefore submits, that you will see your way not to convene the meeting which you are now asked to do, and because you as Trustees have no special power or authority to do so and because it is not your express duty to convene meetings of the nature set out by the requisitionists.

11. Thirdly, your help is specially requisitioned in the present instance to convene a general meeting for the expression of an opinion amounting to a vote of censure on Shams-ul-Ulma Sardar Dastur Kaekobad of Poona for a certain religious ceremony performed by him at Rangoon. Neither the Anjuman at Bombay, nor you have any concern with the affairs of the Rangoon Anjuman or the acts of the Poona Dastur. And again, neither you nor the Anjuman have any jurisdiction or authority over them.

12. Fourthly, it must be deemed the height of presumption, if not impertinence on the part of the requisitionists when they ask you to help them in their desire to vent their wrath upon a gentleman in the position of Sardar Dastur Kaekobad whose religious learning and knowledge of the Zoroastrian

Scriptures are well known and have received well merited recognition at the hands of His Majesty's Government the coveted title of Shamsul-Ulama on the occasion of the historic Darbar at Delhi; whose zeal and fervor for his religion have never been questioned during all his life; who by his sincerity and honesty of purpose and genuine concern for the welfare of his co-religionists has been an ideal Dastur and an exemplary Pastor of his flock; who has won the esteem and veneration of all who come into close contact with him. The report of the expert committee submitted to the Anjuman in 1905, and now in your possession, points out the unerring nature of Dastur Kaekobad's action, and the learned high priest can very well cite in support of what he has done the following weighty pronouncement of the Hon. Mr. Justice Beaman in the Panchayat case.

"It is as much the duty of every pious Zoroastrian to-day to make converts as it was in the remote past "Our Association submit further that no Anjuman however constituted, however large its numbers may be, and however "representative" its character, can ever have the right to pronounce an opinion which could be respected, on the acts of a duly constituted minister of religion like Dastur Kaekobad, and our Association, as far as they are concerned, feel that it will be setting a most lamentable precedent to give opportunities to any one section of the community to grow indignant with, and express its denunciation of a Dastur's action, only because he did not yield to the pressure that was brought to bear on him on extra-religious grounds from performing what he, as a Dastur, considered, was a religious duty what indisputably is in conformity with the precepts of our holy faith.

13. Fifthly, we say that it is puerile to allege and argue that

whatever the tenets of the religion might be and whatever the conscientious opinion of Dastur Kaekobad may be in the matter, he had no authority or right to go against the weight of the "collective conscience" of the one-sided Anjuman which adopted various resolutions on the 16th April 1905, forbidding the performance of the navjote ceremony in certain cases, although, as a matter of fact, the disputed Navjot forms a class by itself, and is not included in those resolutions. We beg to point out that the Trustees of the Punchayet who convened the meeting of the 16th April 1905. and who attended and participated in it, did not themselves, as we have above indicated, choose to follow the dictates of this so-called "collective conscience" of the Anjuman, even when they were not only ostensibly, but to all intents and purposes, lighting a case on behalf and in the interests of the Anjuman. And apart even from the general contention that such an ill-organized and ill-constituted body like the Anjuman has no power, authority or fitness to make weighty, valid or binding pronouncements on such questions as it did in 1905, we say that the resolutions arrived at by the Bombay Anjuman could under no circumstances be held to be morally binding or capable of exercising an influence on the conduct of a recognized Dastur like Shams ul-Ulama Sirdar Dastur Kaekobad of Poona, or capable of being made applicable to the affairs of a faraway city like Rangoon. We submit that your assistance has been very wrongly been involved on the present occasion in the present circumstances.

14. We have said in the last paragraph that the Navjote ceremony performed by Dastur Kaekobad at Rangoon, in the matter of which the requisitionists ask you to convene a meeting can in no way be said to be in contravention of any of the resolutions passed at the 16th April 1905. We may be

permitted to set out and explain this point in greater detail. You will remember that the de facto Trustees of the Parsi Panchayat got a notification published in the newspapers of Mumbai over the signature of their Secretary Shams-ul- Ulama Ervad Jivanji Jamshedji Modi, dated the 9th day of February 1905, to the effect that only the persons who could prove their descent from Zoroastrian parents on both sides would be entitled to the benefit of the Trusts, Vested in them. You will remember that by another notification dated the 3rd March 1905, your Secretary published an Explanation in the newspapers to the effect that Zoroastrian residents of Persia, coming to India, and also the children of Parsi fathers by alien mothers would be entitled to rank as beneficiaries of these Trusts, according to ancient usage and custom. Soon after the publication of these notifications, on the 16th April 1905, the Anjuman meeting on which your requisitionists rely, was held.

Your records will show that on that occasion, Dr. N. H. Sukhia of Bombay, in accordance with a notice of motion which he had sent some time prior to the meeting to your Secretary, proposed and got carried a resolution to the effect that children of Parsi fathers by alien mothers, born after the date of the meeting, should no longer be considered as members of the Parsi community, or admitted into the Zoroastrian religion. The Trustees under whose auspices the meeting which passed the resolution was convened, deliberately contravened the said resolution, as we have shown already in paragraph 6 herein. We wish to emphasize the fact that the only other substantive resolution which was adopted at the meeting was aimed against the admission of children born of alien parents on both sides, as proselytes into our community.

You will thus see that nowhere, either in the two circulars of the Trustees of 1905, or in the resolution adopted by the Anjuman meeting of the 16th April 1905, was any reference made to the possible case of children of alien fathers born of Parsi mothers. This case seems for one reason or another to have been entirely lost.

15. We shall state further that your Secretary was subjected to a fairly long cross-examination in the course of the Panchayat case. Your records, no doubt, contain the full shorthand notes of the proceedings of that memorable case. If you will turn over the notes of evidence recorded on the 31st March 1908, you will find various questions put to Dr. Modi by Mr. Lowndes, counsel for the plaintiffs in the case, which were all directed to point out that paragraph 14 of the written statement did not contain an exhaustive classification of the Parsi community.

We are here concerned only with that portion of the cross-examination in which reference is pointedly made to page 7 of your Trust Deed of 1884, in which there is a clear recital showing that children of Parsi prostitutes (who may be presumed to be in some cases children of alien fathers by Parsi mothers) have been considered to be entitled to claim the benefit of Zoroastrian Trust properties to a certain extent. Dr. Modi was asked to say plainly if the Trust Deed was wrong. His answers as recorded were as follows: - "It is more a question for lawyers than laymen. I am not prepared to say it is wrong. If a case arises, I will consult my solicitors."

16. We do not propose to comment on any of these facts or on the evidence of your Secretary, recorded in Court as above. We only wish to point ostensibly through oversight, the two circulars issued by the Trustees omitted to refer to the case of the children of alien fathers born of Parsi mothers and the result

of it was that the mover of the proposition was kept off the scent and prevented from moving, as we believe it would have been done, an ominous resolution prohibiting the admission of every sort of admixture of blood into our community.

Your Secretary, so cautious and so keen sighted, by the admission he made in Court and the answers he gave to the question put to him, showed that he was all along unaware of the rights which have been enjoyed by custom by the children of alien fathers by Parsi mothers. May we ask if under these circumstances you are prepared to allow a penal resolution to be adopted against an outsider for this oversight of your Secretary and your Anjuman? You have not, your Anjuman of "Parsi Zoroastrians" has not passed any resolution prohibiting the admission into the religion of such children.

And yet your requisitionists without hesitation want you to assume, and have the temerity to declare that Dastur Kaekobad has "openly violated the unanimously adopted resolutions of the Anjuman," and they have not scrupled to say in language to which our Association must take strong exception, "that he has herby done an act pernicious to the community and the religion." and argued that the resolution of your Anjuman never had at any time, neither have they now, any binding character whatever. But even assuming that they did have such a character, and the violation thereof would necessitate the uproar that has been now raised in our community, or justify the demands of the requisitionists, we ask you, to judge dispassionately and to say if requisitionists are right in saying, as they unhesitatingly do, that Dastoor Kaekobad has been disrespectful to those resolutions.

17. We would add that even if, for the sake of argument, the resolutions of 16th April 1905 be taken as binding on Dastur Kaekobad, and secondly, if by parity of reasoning,

the Anjuman's resolution applied equally to the case of the children of alien fathers by Parsi mothers, as to the case of the children of Parsi fathers by alien mother.

It is impossible to bring the Navjote Ceremony performed by Dastur Kaekobad at Rangoon within the scope of the penal resolution adopted by the meeting of 1905, in as much as according to the admitted facts that have come to light, the child was born prior to the date of the said meeting, and was therefore, according to the wording of the resolution, exempted from it.

18. We trust we have made clear our contention that the whole requisition is misconceived, and based entirely on a misapprehension of facts, and is therefore valueless. We refrain from referring to the doubtful method is misrepresentations by which the agitation against the Rangoon Navjot has been created and maintained, the artifices by which signatures to the requisition have been obtained, and the personal animus against the learned Dastoor which seems to pervade all the actions and representations of the promoter of the requisition. To these and such like matters brought to light by the press we trust you will give due consideration when you judge the importance, urgency and genuineness of the requisition. We fully hope that you will not lend your support to a movement made expressly for the purpose of discrediting the character and actions of a learned High Priest in the discharge of his duties, demeaning him in the eyes of the general public. Such measures as are contemplated by the requisitionists cannot reflect credit on the good sense of the community or promote its interests. They can only cause dissensions in the community, such as would but interfere with its future progress and happiness. For these reasons, we earnestly appeal to you, in the name of our Association

not to associate yourselves in any way with this objectionable movement of the requisitionists, and to desist from calling a mass meeting of Parsi Zoroastrians," as they propose.

Alice Buildings, Fort.
Bombay, 7th May 1915

We have the honor to be, Gentlemen, Your most obedient servants.

H.J.BHABA
President.
BYRAMJEE HORMUSJEE
P A WADIA
Joint Honorary Secretaries
True copy.
JIVANJI JAMSHEDJI MODI
Secretary, Parsi Punchayet, 12th February 1916

Dastur Kaekobad Aderbad Dastur Noshirwan was honoured by the Zoroastrian community to represent them at the Parliament of Living Religions, 1924.

At the Parliament of Living Religions held at the Imperial Institute, London, 22 September to 3 October 1924 in a report by William Loftus Blake, he writes,

'A short description of the Parsi religion is given by Dastur Kaekobad who addressed the audience.'

'They are Persians by race and religion, and preserve the faith taught in the sixth century BC by Zoroaster. Here again the conference was well served by a lucid paper by Shams-ul-Ulema Dastur Kaekobad Aderbad Dastur Noshirwan, Ph. D. first class Sardar and High Priest of the Deccan. Poona. India, whose simple exposition of the basic principle of Zoroastrianism, a universal religion, was much appreciated.'

'The Dastur's paper though short, was simple and clear, and removed, I thought, the whole subject from the realm of controversy in which it is so often wrapped. The whole paper was interesting as evidence of the way in which the followers of so many religions nowadays, have given up the exclusive demands of their faith. For it is upon the principles that harmonize with the idea of a universal religion that emphasis is laid. Within all the faiths, as with all the nations, the desire for union is being increasingly felt. After a brief account of Zoroaster as a religious reformer of ancient Persia—or rather of Iran of which Fars was one province only—he affirmed that the Zoroastrian theology was a monotheism.......The ethical conceptions of Zoroaster were described, followed by a view of the hereafter.'

17
THE PARSI BHIKARI FUND AND THE DNA OF THE PARSIS OF INDIA AND IRAN

By Thy perfect Intelligence, O Mazda Thou didst first create us
having bodies and spiritual consciences, And by
Thy Thought gave ourselves the power of thought, word, and deed.
Thus leaving us free to choose our faith at our own will.
—The Avesta, Ahunuvaiti Gatha; Yasna 31, 11

The arrival of the refugees from Persia from 1872, followed by the loss of income and unemployment triggered by the depression in 1920 created an economic and financial crisis in the Zoroastrian community. The 'Parsi Bhikari Fund' was set up to look after the poor Parsis. This may be the reason why a lot of emphasis was put on keeping control over the community's funds which was one of the reasons for not allowing conversion. Today, a hundred years later, these factors should not act as a deterrent to the initiation and acceptance into the religion of the intermarried girls' and boys' children.

In India and Iran, the great depression had a devastating effect on the Parsis. Dr M.E. Pavri, the honorary joint secretary of the Parsi Bhikari Fund wrote in his report: 'At the moment, the most acute and vital question that affects the whole of the Parsi community is unemployment. It is up to the leaders --- Parsi Panchayat Akabars, Trustees of different Trust Funds, and the wealthy Sethias of the Parsi community to search for its causes and find out ways and means to temporarily alleviate-if it is not possible

There Was Extreme Poverty In The Parsi Community. Advertisment For Donations To The Parsi Bhikari Fund (Parsi Lustre On Indian Soil).

to remove the distress immediately and entirely. Our community could not naturally escape from the disastrous repercussions of the world-wide trade depression which has sapped the world dry of its happiness for the last ten years or so. The acuteness of the major problems of our community was vividly illustrated in the Report issued by Mr. Dinshaw J Irani with the help and guidance of Lady Ratan Tata, Mr and Mrs J K Mehta and Sir Phiroze Cursetji Sethna, but unfortunately it still remains unsolved. Schemes have been mooted and discussed only to be shelved.'

He lists some of the causes of this distress:

Genuine poverty due to natural deficiencies and defects of body, mind and soul (character), or to unforeseen circumstances.

Sir Cusrow N. Wadia has been a great industrialist, businessman and philanthropist. Sir Cusrow and Sir Ness Wadia, jointly with their late revered mother Baiji Jarbai, have spent more than the colossal sum of thirty million rupees solely for the benefit of the Parsi Community, apart from the huge sums they have given away in cosmopolitan charities. The splendid residential colony of "Cusrow Baug" in Bombay is the latest monument of their great benefaction. Hence it is with regret that the Parsi Community hears of Sir Cusrow's retirement from Bombay and going to Europe for settling there. He, however, carries with him their grateful remembrance and prayers for his health and happiness. He belongs to the family of the great Master Builders who supplied fleets of men-of-war and merchantmen to the British Government.

سر خسرو این وادیا یکنفر کارخانه چی و کاسب و نوع پرست بزرگ بوده
است سر خسرو و سر نسروان باتفاق مادر محترمهٔ مرحومهٔ ایشان بایجی زر بائو پیش
از مبلغ هنگفت سی ملیون روپیه فقط از برای اعانه به ملت فارسی صرف کردند علاوه
بر این مبلغ زیادی بعنوان دستگیری بفقراء هر ملتی بدون تعصب ملی هزینه نمودند
مستعمرهٔ مسکونی با شکوه خسرو باغ در بمبئی آخرین ساختمان یادگاری احسان و کرم
بزرگ ایشانست از این جهت ملت فارسی از شنیدن کناره گیری سر خسرو از بمبئی
و عزم بانگلستان از برای اقامت در آنجا نهایت متأسفند ایشان از خانوادهٔ کشتی
ساز بزرگی هستند که از برای دولت انگلیس جهازات جنگی و تجارتی بسیار ساختند

Sir Cusrow N. Wadia in the Iran League Quarterly, April 1934
Cusrow Baug in Bombay was built by him

Another class of able-bodied people, due either to inefficiency or weak character or to laziness and indifference to make any effort to stand on their own legs and earn their livelihood by honest means, depend on doles which do them more harm than good. The dole system in such cases leads undoubtedly to indolence and is a sort of an incentive to begging.

Emulating the 'Smart' set and living beyond their means, lack of correct education, adoption of a higher standard of living, and the advancement of other communities which closed the doors on avenues which were the main preserve of the Parsis were cited as reasons for the economic problems of the community.

The Great Famine of 1871-72 in Persia occasioned an extensive pan-Parsi effort to provide relief to the Persian Zoroastrians afflicted by the calamity. Parsi communities based in Amoy, Cannanore, Poona, Surat, Ahmedabad, sent sizeable donations to Messrs. Godrez Mehrban & Co., a mercantile firm in Bombay that was the chief organizer of the relief efforts. Through networks involving British Political Agents and military personnel in Muscat and Bushire and prominent Zoroastrians in India and Persia, the funds and food provisions were distributed among the famine struck coreligionists (*Bombay Gazette*, 7 Sept 1871)

Efforts were also directed towards organizing the passage of groups of Persian Zoroastrian famine refugees from Bandar Abbas via Kurrachee to Bombay. The first group of 29 refugees that arrived in Bombay on 6 June 1871 had the cost of their passage defrayed by Messrs. Nicol & Co., the managers of the steamers. In Bombay, the refugees were accommodated at an asylum for Persian Zoroastrian migrants. (Ibid. 22 September 1871)

'In a letter of Dr E.W. West published in the 'Sir Jamshedji Jeejeebhoy Madressa Jubillee' Volume (1914), he says: 'In 1511 four Iranian traders brought a Maktab to Gujrat, in which the Iranian Parsis estimate their own population in Sharafabad and Turkabad at 400, in Yazd at 500, in Kirman at 700, in Sistan at 2,700, and in Khorasan at 1,700. 'nafar'. Supposing 'nafar' means head of the family, this would imply a total Parsi population of between 25,000 to 30,000 Parsis in Persia probably no more than then in India.' (Delphine Menant, 1917, P 108)

The Parsi Zoroastrians who fled Persia for Bombay in the 19th century were often supported by local Parsi families. The most famous story of the Persian (Parsi) refugees is that of Kai Khusran-i-Yazdyar, who fled from Kerman to Bombay to save his daughter the beautiful Gulistan Banu from being abducted by a wealthy Muslim. At the age of 12 years, Gulistan Banu popularly called Gulbai Vellati (Gulbai the foreigner) was married to Framji Bhikaji Pandey. A famous Bombay Parsi. Her husband, Framji, would help several Persian Zoroastrian migrants to settle in Bombay. He was called the 'father of the Irani Parsis'. This movement to help and relocate the Parsis of Persia to India was called the Zoroastrian Ameliorating Society. In Persia the Society was referred to as the 'Anjuman-e-akbar-e-Parsian' or the Society of Parsi Nobles.

As the number of refugees coming to India increased, they were housed at the asylum for Persian Zoroastrian Migrants. Over time, the constraints of space in the asylum caused by the increasing number of refugees, prompted Cowasjee Jehangir to construct a chawl to house about 200 migrants. The chawls were typically four to five stories tall, with eight or 16 tenements on each floor. The tenements are referred to as 'kholis'. A central staircase serviced the building and gave access to a long passage which ran the length of each floor. A typical feature of chawl architecture is that long passage which is open on one side and has a row of doors on the other side, each door being the entrance of a tenement. Each floor had a common block of toilets. There was little privacy.

Questions about the avenues of employment for the famine refugees in Bombay were raised in the English and Gujarati

A Zoroastrian family in Yezd

press. A limited set of job opportunities were proposed for the refugees- as domestic servants, as soldiers and as agriculturists. It was suggested that as domestic servants, the refugees would help ease the 'servant problem' in Bombay. The shortage and unreliability of servants was a common and uniting discourse among the native and European populations in the city. A letter written under the pseudonym A Parsee to *The Bombay Gazette* (3 June 1871) noted:

'The want of male servants and female servants is increasing day after day, and to what amount of imposition and baseness we are subjected

Mr. M. C. Murzban.

Khan Bahadur Muncherjee Cowasjee Murzban (1839–1917). (The Parsis. Vol. 1. No. 1., January 1905, p. 5.)

by these classes, which have become so odious, every Parsee employer knows to his cost. Let some large number of needy Persians be sent for and permitted to place themselves in active competition with these classes as soon as they become fit for it, and our annoyance and anxieties as regards them will commence ceasing.'

Khan Bahadur Muncherji Cowasji Murzban (1839–1917) was an architect and he was inspired to build these chawls in Bombay after the style of the Peabody Estates of London, an ambitious housing project for London's poor. He set up the 'Garib Zoroastrian Rehethan Fund,' through which he raised funds for the housing project. In his speech he said:

'Even now with the keen competition of the several sections of the native community, the Parsees, it need hardly be observed, held their own in the several walks of life; but the fact was that if they remained apathetic and inattentive to the growing requirements and wants of their community, there was every danger of their lagging behind, in the race of life...As was observed in all parts of the world, with the increase of population there has been an increase of poverty among the Parsees...

It would be needless to describe the condition of the houses generally occupied by the poor, which were, as a rule, situated in low-lying, crowded, ill-ventilated, and filthy localities, where all sorts of diseases raged rampant, gradually destroying like the cankerworm the physique of the working class, who might be called the backbone of their community. (Hear, hear.) (*Times of India* 1 April 1889)

Upto the early 20th century there was extreme poverty in the community. The influx of Parsi refugees from Persia must have exasperated the problem. Parsi philanthropy was at its height but the need was endless. This may have triggered the social reason of not wanting to accept intermarriage for both men and women.

Manekji Limji Hataria (1813–1890)

Manekji Limji Hataria's forefathers were among the Zoroastrian immigrants who came to India from Safavid, Persia (1501–1772) and settles in Surat. His family moved to Bombay when he was five. He was an avid traveler and trader and in 1854 he was appointed by Sir Dinshaw Petit and Framji Pandey as the first emissary of the Society for the Amelioration of the condition of Zoroastrians in Persia known

BAI MOTLIBAI WADIA HOME FOR PARSI WOMEN

We have constantly been hearing the cry against misdirection of Parsi Charity in the baneful system of dole-giving which has done so much in sapping the morale of the community. People therefore have heard with some relief, that N. M. Wadia Trustees have taken a step in the right direction in opening a home for destitute Parsi women. Lady Cowasji Jehangir (Jr.), Sir Shapoorji Billimoria, and Mr. and Mrs. R. P. Masani have been taking a leading part in the scheme, and the Institute is placed in charge of two experienced supervisors. It is hoped to provide suitable work for every inmate, for fifty of whom provision is made in the home at present.

Causes Sapping the Morale of the Community: The Remedy

As the inmates will be selected from women living on doles, the Trustees will have the opportunity to know how many of these would be willing workers. They will thus be able to mark out the real unemployed from the habitual beggars among the women living on doles. This will enable them to regulate charity and discourage all idleness.

Regulation of Charity

If the experiment is successful the Trustees contemplate extending the institution and also providing a similar one for males.

SIR CUSROW WADIA

We hear with regret the retirement of Sir Cusrow Wadia from Bombay's business life, and his intended settlement in England and France. The Parsi settlement in Colaba which is being raised to commemorate his name, will keep his memory always fresh here.

A Munificent Family

The Parsis and the general community in Bombay remember the benefits conferred on Bombay by Sir Ness and Sir Cusrow Wadia, and their late revered mother through their various munificent charities.

A report on the charitable work being done by Parsis for their community in the Iran League Quarterly, April 1934

in Persia as Anjuman-e-
Akbar-Parsian. He was
given explicit instructions
to enquire into and report
upon the social, political,
and intellectual condition of
the Zoroastrians in Persia.
His mission to Iran was
not without risk to himself,
and he took to travelling
well-armed.

In Bombay, a meeting
of Parsi leaders on 11
January 1855 reviewed his
report and initiated plans
for fundraising for schools,
fire temples and a dokhma
and an effort to procure a
partial or total remission

Manekji Limji Hataria (1813-1890)
(The Parsis, 1917)

from the Jazya tax imposed on Zoroastrians by the Qazar Rulers.
The tax was of an amount of 667 Tomars (a tomar was equal to
10-shilling Sterling), (*Parsi Prakash*, p. 654).

To aid the Zoroastrians of Iran the Zoroastrians of India
funneled money to Iran for Hataria to distribute. Hataria encouraged
the Zoroastrians to immigrate to India. He noticed that most of
the Zoroastrians were illiterate. With the funds collected by the
Amelioration Society he set up schools for boys and girls in Iran.
He used this money to also rebuild dokhmas and Fire temples. The
Great Atash Behram at Yezd and the Atash Behram at Kerman were
extended and repaired by him.

He built prayer halls, lodging houses *Badgirs* or wind towers,
and *ganats* or subterranean water channels to irrigate fields. He

Twin Towers of Silence, south of Yezd City (Zoroastrian heritage) (use of dokhmas is banned in Iran)

delivered food, clothing, and medicine to elderly Zoroastrians and built orphanages for parentless children and arranged marriages for the poor.

In his report to the society, Manecji described the wretched conditions of the Zoroastrians in Iran:

'Dear Sir; This noble group (the Zoroastrians of Iran) has suffered in the hands of cruel and evil people so much that they are totally alien to knowledge and science. For them even black and white, and good and evil are equal. Their men have been forcefully doing menial works in the construction and as slaves receive no payment. As some evil and immoral men have been looking after their women and daughters, this sector of Zoroastrian community even during daytime stays indoor. Despite all the poverty, heavy taxes under the pretexts of land, space, pastureland; inheritance and religious tax (*jizya*) are imposed on them. The local rulers have been cruel to them and have plundered their possessions. They have forced the men to do the menial construction work for them. Vagrants have kidnapped their women and daughters. Worse than all, community is disunited. Their only hope is the advent of future saviour (Shah Bahram Varjavand). Because of extreme misery, belief in the saviour is so strong that 35 years earlier when an astrologer forecasted the birth of the savior, many men in his search left the town and were lost in the desert and never returned. I found the Zoroastrians to be exhausted and trampled, so much that even no one in the world can be more miserable than them.'

The *Iran League Quarterly* on the death anniversary of Maneckji Hatari quoted from Mr Sorab Wadia's speech on that occasion, 'Instead of spreading the holy gospel of Zarathustra he had to prevent it's extinction from the hearts of the small band of his adherents in Iran. He had striven hard for full forty years and gained his object by perseverance, wisdom, sympathy, and sacrifice. At the time when oppression had reduced their numbers to a paltry seven thousand, Seth Maneckji went to their help and not only saved them from extinction but provided for their growth and expansion by a life prosperity and peace.' (April 1934 *Iran League Quarterly*)

A Report in the *Iran League Quarterly*

The Pestonji Dossabhoy Marker Boys' Orphanage And Day School, Yezd

P. P. Baruah

Ceremony Of Laying The Foundation-Stone Of The New Premises

The Iran League Quarterly June 1933

Mr. Pestonji Marker, the well-known Iranophil citizen of Bombay, conferred an additional boon on the Zoroastrians of Yezd by purchasing a large plot of land near the Bunder Abbas-Teheran Main Road, in the vicinity of Elyas in Yezd, for creating new premises of the Orphanage and School.

It was a sore need; and the economical, and none the less progressive and efficient, administration of the Orphanage by the Iranian Zoroastrian Anjuman of Bombay, combined with the munificence of Mr. Marker, has enabled the Anjuman to embark on a scheme of having their own building for their institutions.

A pleasant function took place when the Foundation VA Stone was laid at Yezd in the afternoon of the 12th of April last. It was the anniversary of the founder's mother's demise and the foundation day of the Orphanage exactly ten years back. Dr. Minocher Rustom Vesuna, the Medical Officer of Sir Ratan Tata Medical Hall and Bai Dinamae Desai Dispensary, opened the proceedings by delivering in fluent Persian a speech welcoming His Excellency the Governor of Yezd who was kind enough to postpone for the purpose his departure to Isfahan, and all the other guests. About a hundred well-known citizens including Persian Government officials and the medical officer of the English Missionary Hospital had gathered. In requesting His Excellency Mirza Ovessi to lay the stone Dr. Vesuna gave a brief history of the institution. It was followed by a suitable speech by one of the orphans. Then the Governor laid the foundation stone and amidst cheering applause he paid a very eloquent tribute to the high aims and ideals of Mr Peshotan Marker. He said that Mr. Marker's name would be perpetually remembered by the Iranians as one of the foremost benefactors. His services to the regeneration of the ancient community was as unique as they were spontaneous and timely. His Excellency expressed his personal interest and sympathy for the poor Zoroastrians of Yezd and invoked heavenly blessings for Mr. Marker and his family who, he said, were contributing such a large share in their educational, ethics and economics uplift.

Mary Boyce On The Conditions Of The Zoroastrians

'In 1963 when Mary Boyce arrived in the region to study them, she discovered gloomy, fortress-like buildings virtually devoid of any furniture or greenery. They were low and airless. No badgirs adorned their roofs. The primary consideration of the builders had been defense. The ideal solution would have been to build upwards, erecting high, tower-like houses as are found (for example) all over Scotland. But in Iran, Zoroastrians were not allowed to build their homes any higher than a man could reach (or any taller than the houses of Moslems). They could only build downwards, creating dark honeycombs of subterranean rooms with adobe walls several feet thick to withstand attack. The Zoroastrians were physically greater in stature than their Moslem neighbors and they could have put up a fight if they had to. But it seldom happened. The penalty for killing a Moslem was certain death: to kill a Zoroastrian meant incurring only a modest fine, usually waived by the authorities. Better, therefore, to prevent attacks in the first place.'

'Entry to the houses was via a single door from a narrow lane just wide enough to allow a fully-laden donkey to pass. The Law stated that the door of a Zoroastrian dwelling could be secured by only a single hinge, so a series of doors had to be built (one after the other) to prevent forced entry. Finally, at the end of a gloomy corridor, a narrow door - the smallest of them all - led into a bare, central courtyard or rikda.

'There were no windows. Sometimes glass bottles could be seen protruding from the walls of the entrance lane. But these served as spyholes rather than windows, defense being uppermost in the minds of these persecuted inhabitants. The only light to enter the house was through the tiny courtyard or via irregular gaps in the doors or ceilings. In some of the buildings the courtyard had been covered over completely to prevent intruders gaining access from the roof. The result was total darkness and oppressive claustrophobia. It is ironic that Zoroastrians, with their sophisticated theologies of light, should have been forced to live in such shadowy, enclosed buildings.'

An article in tenets.zoroastrianism.com titled 'Zarathustri Pilgrimage Sites in Iran' quotes Prof. Edward G. Browne from his 'A Year Amongst the Persians' (the year being 1887–88): 'Up to 1895, no Parsi was allowed to carry an umbrella. Up to 1895, there was a strong prohibition upon eyeglasses and spectacles; up to 1885 they were prevented from wearing rings; their girdles had to be made of rough canvas, but after 1885, any white material was permitted. Up to 1896, the Parsis were obliged to twist their turbans instead of folding them. Up to 1898, only brown, grey, and yellow were allowed for body garments but after that, all colors were permitted, except blue, black, bright red or green. There was also a prohibition against white stockings and up to about 1880, the Parsis had to wear a special kind of peculiarly hideous shoe with a broad, turned-up toe. Up to 1885, they had to wear a torn cap, up to about 1880, they had to wear tight knickers, self-coloured, instead of trousers. Up to 1891, all Zoroastrians had to walk in town and even in the desert, they had to dismount if they met a Mussalman of any rank whatever.'

The Zoroastrians of India made every effort to improve the living conditions of thousands of their Iranian co-religionists, financially, socially and politically in Iran and also accepted and rehabilitated them into the community in India no questions asked about who they had descended from.

DNA of Parsis in India and Iran

Three independent studies have been done on the DNA of the Parsis of India and Iran and their affinity to the DNA of the people of the Indian subcontinent. All three come to the conclusion that it was a male oriented migration from Persia with assimilation (marriage) with Indian women.

They also conclude that the DNA of the early migrants, (DNA analysis of bones found in ancient Sanjan Dokhma) was different from the DNA of the extant Zoroastrians in India today. And that the the DNA of the extant Zoroastrians in Iran is quite different from the DNA of the extant Zoroastrians in India today. In a nutshell, that original stock of immigrants who migrated from Iran no longer, genetically exists.

1) 'Population Affinities of Parsis in the Indian Subcontinent' by Manjari Jonnalagadda, Shantanu Ozarka and Veena Mushrif Tripathy in 2009.

   They used DNA recovered from skeletal material from a Dokhma recently excavated at Sanjan by the World Zarthusti Cultural Foundation (WZCF) and the Indian Archaeological Society and compared it with extant Parsis. The conclusion they came to was that 'Sanjan Parsis share close affinities with Sarai Khola (10000–4500 BC) whereas extant Parsis share closest affinities with groups from Harappa (3300–1600 BC).'

   That 'Sanjan and extant Parsis are observed to be similar to contemporary Maharashtrian Groups than the Central Asian and South Asian Groups. However, as against Sanjan, extant Parsis show closer affinity to low caste Mahars and High Caste Marathas and tribal Madia Gonds.'

   They expected the relationship between the Sanjan Parsis and extant Parsis to be very close. 'However, contrary to the expectation it is seen that extant Parsis and Sanjan samples are distinctly separated from each other.' And 'in the given population set, these results presented may be considered considerably reliable.'

2) 'The Genetic Legacy of Zoroastriansism in Iran and India: Insights into Population Structure, gene flow and selection'. 2017, Researchers are Saioa Lopez, Mark J. Thomas, Lucy Van Drop, Naser Ansari-Pour, Sarah Stewart, Abigail L. Jones, Erik Jelinek, and others.

They took samples from Iranian Zoroastrians, Indian Zoroastrians and Zoroastrian Priests from India. They found evidence of admixture from 2 different sources. 'In all Indian cases one source of admixture is best represented by a modern-day Indian population. The second source is generally represented by an an ancient Neolithic sample from Europe or Anatolla, or a modern group close to Iran such as Armenia, Lebanon, or Iraqi Jews. In the case of Iranian Zoroastrians, no such admixture was inferred'.

'We detected admixture in the Parsis dated from 27 to 32 generations ago between one predominantly Indian-like source and one predominantly Iranian-like source.'

They conclude 'the Parsis (of India) descend from an admixture event between ancestral groups consisting predominantly of males with Iranian-related ancestry and females with Indian related ancestry.'

3) Like Sugar in Milk: reconstructing the Genetic History of the Parsi Population a Research paper by Gyaneshwar Chaubey, Qasim Ayub, Veena Mushrif-Tripathy, Rakesh Tamang, Kurush Dalal and others funded by World Zarathusti Cultural Foundation, Parsi Foundation and others. The contribution of the Parsi Community of India and Pakistan by donating samples, and by Dr Shernaz Cama, Director Parzor Foundation for her help and critical comments have been gratefully acknowledged in the research paper.

'The present-day Iranian population exhibited a striking difference from the Parsis, (in India) mainly in carrying an additional European component and substantially lower south Asian ancestry.'

They also concluded that the 'mtDNA (maternal DNA) in the Parsi cluster was closer to the Indian and Pakistani cluster.' 'The contrasting patterns of maternal and paternal

BACK TO THE LAND

Two Iranian Gentlemen Farmers

Bayram Zack

WHEN the Irani refugees came to Bombay, penniless and jobless, their first instinct was to take whatever menial jobs came their way. These were mostly as servants in Parsi households or as lowly assistants in the fire temples. Some of them however felt that this was not the life for them and they decided to go and live on farms and orchards as they had done back in Iran.

At Golwad, some three hours away by train from Bombay, there is a small concentration of Irani farmers—and their unquestioned leader and dean is 80-year-old Bayram Zack.

Bayram is a bit vague about dates but otherwise still remembers vividly the time

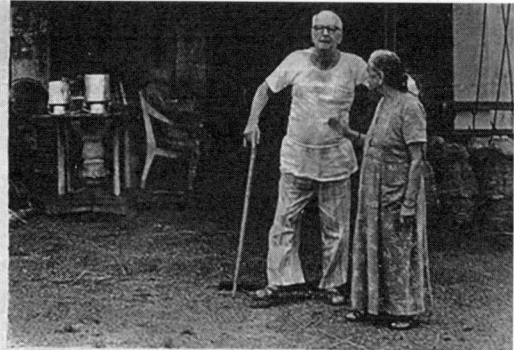

ALTHOUGH BAYRAM ZACK OWNS ALMOST 80 ACRES OF LAND, he lives in a bc which serves as his living room, bedroom and godown. He continually teases his wife a her expensive tastes.

THE ZACKS GROW RICE and vegetables as well as chickoos and mangoes. They own the largest number (over 2,000) of toddy trees in Thana district. Bayram's son, Dinshaw, does his rounds of the fields.

"I CAN STILL DO A MAN'S WORK," boasts 80-year-old Zack, the Elder. But he gets tired soon and spends most of the time sitting in his frontyard, supervising his workers.

he came here from Iran. "I was about this high," he says, pointing to his waist. His family was fairly prosperous so he came from Yezd to Bandar Abbas by palkhi. "At Bandar Abbas some Muslims tried to kidnap me, but my palkhi-bearers were loyal and saved me from them." He tells the story with much gusto and many dramatic flourishes.

Luck seems to have followed Bayram all the way to Bombay, for, whilst still a young boy, he was adopted by a rich Parsi

lady, Dhunbaiji Hakim. He came to Go to recuperate after an illness and liked place so much that he decided to stay

Though basically a farmer, he has tried his hand at many other jobs. He been in turn, a building contractor, a t tapper, a salesman and many other th "I can still do a man's job," he likes to l but actually gets tired after a little and spends most of his time sitting i front yard supervising his workers playing with his three huge dogs and small great-grandchild.

Despite the fact that he owns almo acres of land and has given away huge of money to charity—"I donated the sum of Rs 2 lakhs left to me by my ac

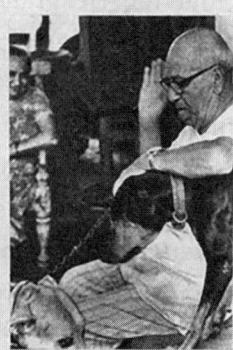

GEORGE AND MARY are Zack's far dogs and barely ever leave his side. too live with the family in the same "l

Story of Irani refugees settled in India in the illustrated Weekly.

ancestry support a largely female based admixture from the South Asian population to the Parsis'

The DNA analysis of all the studies suggest a male based migration. But history tells us that the migration was to protect the women and children from the ravages of war crimes. The story of the escape of Gulistan confirms this. Why would the Zoroastrian men only migrate leaving their women and children behind? It is beyond logical thinking to accept a male dominated migration. We really do not know much of our history and our limited knowledge is from the poem Kisseh-a-Sanjan written in 1599. We can only speculate. The knowledge of our past does not match with the conclusions arrived at by our DNA analysis. Who exactly were the Parsis?

My childhood friend Sanam Kermani Karais family was originally from Iran. Her grandfather Byram Zack's story was narrated in the Illustrated weekly of 1970. He tells of his escape from Iran, how he was adopted by a rich Parsi lady Dhunbaiji Hakim, in India and his present lifestyle as a feudal Lord. (Appendix: *Illustrated Weekly,* 1970, 'Irani Zoroastrians'). Her DNA as a recent refuge from Iran, and my DNA as a supposed earlier refuge from Iran, are totally different. Mine is more than 50 per cent South Asian whereas hers has no such admixture.

18
THE MEHTA VANSHAVALI (FAMILY TREE)

I am who I am because who they were.
—Anonymous

The DNA analysis of my family members reveals that we have an admixture of mostly South Asian (between 50 to 70 per cent) and mostly Middle Eastern (from 25 to 45 per cent) DNA. This analysis has been done by California-based genomics firm 23andMe. However, my family tree from AD 1300 does not mention any admixture. All members have been included into the community as Parsis.

The Mehta family has a Family Tree which starts from approximately AD 1300. It is written by Edulji Navroji Mehta in 1921 with a foreword by Dastur Dr Maneckji Dhalla. The families' original title was Talati which was changed at the time of Ramji to Mehta. The tree is depicted as having a solid trunk and there are two main branches — Ramji and Bhaiji. We are the descendants of the Bhaiji branch. From approximately AD 1300 to AD 1640 the solid trunk of the tree has only a few names depicted on it — Kamdin Talati, Kela Talati, Thumba Talati, Vejai Talati, Hapa Talati, Kadva Talati, Kama Talati, Hacha Talati, Behram Talati, Chanda Talati, Behram Talati. And then RAMJI and BHAIJI — the two main branches start with about 6000 family members including Zubin Mehta, the renowned music conductor.

Edulji Navroji Mehta writes, 'I have found the history of this family from the *Disa Pothi* (death register) and Twarikhe Navasari of

Ramji Sagar, Behram Chanda Behram, Kama Kadwa Hapa, Vijal Kela Kamdins etc. Except this I have not found details from other sources.' I have not been able to obtain the details of those who changed their Mehta surname. Moreover, the details of birth, marriage and death counting should be considered imperfect."

'The priests in order to keep their profession intact, have preserved the family history. The behdins (Lay people) do not have to follow their family history. In some houses there were many notes written by the elders, but instead of preserving them they were sold and destroyed in the hands of the stationer. Although, reminding them often, many members have not given details about the relatives. This family was very vast and old; thus, many members have settled in Navsari, Surat, Ahmedabad, Bombay, Nagpur, Jabalpur etc. Those who have settled in Navsari, their details have been collected with the help of 'disa kothi'. But the members settled in other cities, especially those descended from Bhaiji Sagar, and their family history is not obtained by me. I admit there are many defects in this book. Morover in order to examine proof I have not paid careful attention.'

The author thus clarifies that even this detailed record is not a perfectly correct record.

Till 1640 the names are Hindu sounding names which fits in with the theory that Parsis lived as a tribe amongst the Hindus till Changasha found them and retaught them their religion. Most of the 'admixture' which is of 'Mostly South Asian' DNA must have occurred at this time. But there is no record of this admixture. More than 50 per cent of our DNA is 'Mostly South Asian' but there are no 'Mostly South Asian' ancestors. All must have been included into the community and accepted as Parsis.

Even this detailed family tree has no record before AD 1300 and just a sketchy outline till 1640. Is it possible for ordinary Parsis, with no family tree, to trace their ancestry to approximately AD 600?

PREFACE.

In every country and every age it is the desire of men to know their lineage and pedigree, but the attainment of this knowledge is not possible for all. In our Zoroastrian community, while the BEHDINS or laymen have been unable to trace their lineage, the ATHORNANS, or the priestly class, have succeeded in preserving records of ttheir pedigree to a certain extent, because they have to share the profits of their sacerdotal work and functions. The priests of Naosari have preserved their pedigree with exactness since they came to Naosari. A Mobéd (priest) of Naosari is not considered fit to share the above-mentioned profits till he has attained the ranks of Navur and Murtub, and when he has reached these ranks the fact is noted in a book called the Feheresht. When the son of a Mobéd attains the dignity of Navur, his name and those of his father, grand-father, great-grandfather, and great-great-grandfather, with the family name or surname, are noted down in the Feheresht. In this manner at Naosari, since the arrival of the first Athornan named Zurdoosht Mobéd, who went there on Roz Din in the month of Furvurdin 551 Yezdezardi, till to-day, that is for a period of 717 years, such notes have been kept in the Feheresht. All such notes have been kept with great care since our arrival in Naosari, but we have no record of any kind from the time we came from Persia down to our arrival at Naosari. History records that Zoroastrians came to India from Persia in 85 Yezdezardi. From that time till they came to Naosari a period of 466 years elapsed; but we have not our own records about the Zoroastrians throughout this long period. There are only four names before that of the Mobéd Zurdoosht of whom mention has been made, and these are the names of Homjiar, Ramiar, Shapoor, and Shehriar. I cannot place implicit trust in these names, because all the Mobéds in India carry their lineage back to Shapoor Shehriar. They say that Ramiar and Dhaval were the sons of Shapoor. Also according to them Homjiar was the son of Ramiar and Mobéd the son of Homjiar. Zurdoosht and Behram were the sons of Mobéd. The progeny of Zurdoosht live at Naosari and Surat, while those of Behram live at Broach. The famous and well-known Nureeosung was the son of Dhaval. It is said about Nureeosung that he founded the well-known Atushbehram at Udvada 1,178 years ago. If that is so, he must have lived in that distant period. Mobéd Hom Behmuniar, who belonged to Nureeosung's family came to Naosari in A.D. 1271. Between him and Nureeosung we find six names:—Khoorsheed, Behmuniar, Khooshmusta, Khoojusta, Mobéd, and Nureeosung. If we assign a period of two centuries to these six generations, then Nureeosung must have lived in A.D. 1071, i.e., the time of Nureeosung comes 300 years after the foundation of the Atushbehram. From this it is clearly proved that if we consider the Atushbehram of Udvada to have been founded by Nureeosung, then we certainly err in our calculation of generations and pedigree; moreover, the supposition that the Mobéds of India carry their lineage to Shapoor Shehriar is certainly open to question. The Atushbehram was founded immediately after our arrival in India, and if it was inaugurated according to our present custom, many Mobéds must have been engaged to perform the ceremony, and of course they must have belonged

Preface to the geneaology of the Parsi priests of Navsari.
(Year of Yezdezardi starts at 631, accordingly AD 551Y is 551+631=AD 1182)

More interestingly, in the Preface of the book on the genealogy of the Navsari Parsi Bhuggasarth priests written in 1899, by Rustumji Jamaspji Dastur Meherjirana, he mentions that the Behdin or laymen have been unable to trace their ancestry and even the Naosari priests can trace their ancestry to only AD 1182.

The Family Tree of the Mehta Family from 1300 to 2020; the two main branches are from Ramji and Bhaiji

Ancestor Report

Generation I	
1 (0)	Samara Mehta Vyas
Generation II (Parents)	
2 (1)	Sandeep Vyas relationship with Sanaya Mehta
	Married/ Related to:
3 (1)	Sanaya Mehta relationship with Sandeep Vyas
Generation III (Grandparents)	
6 (3)	Numazar Mehta married to Prochy Gimi
7 (3)	Prochy Gimi married to Numazar Mehta
Generation IV (Great-Grandparents)	
12 (6)	Dorabji Mehta relationship with Khorshed
	Married/ Related to:
13 (6)	Khorshed relationship with Dorabji Mehta
Generation V (Great Great-Grandparents)	
24 (12)	Dhunjisha Mehta relationship with Dinbai Mehta Born 1877, died 13 Dec 1929, 51 or 52 years Dhunjisha Dorabji Mehta studied till the age of 11 in Gujarati before his paternal uncle, Meherwanji, called him away to Calcutta where he received an English education till the 7th standard. He began working with his uncle in 1897 and in 1901, he took charge of the Canton branch.After his father died, he became a partner in M.N. Mehta and Co. and took charge of the Head Office. Finally in1926, he began his own firm, Dorabji Mehta and Sons, in Calcutta.
25 (12)	Married/ Related to:
	Dinbai Mehta relationship with Dhunjisha Mehta

Generation VI (3rd Great-Grandparents)	
48 (24)	Dorabji Mehta relationship with Bhikaiji Mehta Died 6 Jun 1911 Dorabji Nanabhai Mehta studied at the Branch School in Bombay until his father's business collapsed and the family returned to Navsari. When Nanabhai managed to get a job there, the boy returned to study in Bombay. Later, he was called to Taipei by his maternal uncle - E. N. Mehta to handle that branch of the business. In 1897, he took charge of his brother, Meherwanji Mehta's business in Canton. He was an honest and upright man and well respected by the local Chinese inhabitants. He expanded the business and became a partner in the firm. He spent the better half of his life in that region and was much loved by the people there. After his death, his brother Meherwanji built a hospital in Navsari in his memory.
	Married/ Related to:
49 (24)	Bhikaiji Mehta relationship with Dorabji Mehta Died 6 Mar 1923
50 (25)	Shapurji Mehta 1st relationship with Manekbai Mehta, 2nd relationship with Dhunbai P. Ragi Died 9 Aug 1900 Shapurji Faramji Mehta ran the Canton branch of E. N. Mehta and Co. Well in Damka Mohalla 10 July 1888 Pucca Road in Damka Mohalla 21 August 1896 Renovated Well at Navsari's Mota Bazaar 15 September 1897
	Married/ Related to:
51 (25)	Dhunbai P. Ragi relationship with Shapurji Mehta

Generation VII (4th Great-Grandparents)	
96 (48)	Nanabhai Mehta relationship with Navazbai Mehta Died 21 Sep 1891
	Married/ Related to:
97 (48)	Navazbai Mehta relationship with Nanabhai Mehta Died 27 Apr 1889
98 (49)	Pestonji Mehta married to Baiai Mehta Died 6 Oct 1916
	Married/ Related to:
99 (49)	Baiai Mehta married to Pestonji Mehta Died 3 Apr 1912
100 (50)	Faramji Mehta 1st relationship with Motibai D. Baria, 2nd relationship with Baiai D. Mehta
	Married/ Related to:
101 (50)	Baiai D. Mehta relationship with Faramji Mehta Died 6 Apr 1831
Generation VIII (5th Great-Grandparents)	
192 (96)	Manaji Mehta relationship with Hansibai Jeevanji Mehta Died 26 Jun 1861 Manaji Pestonji Mehta was the munim of Gopalrao Meheral of Gandevi.
	Married/ Related to:
193 (96)	Hansibai Jeevanji Mehta relationship with Manaji Mehta Died 1864
	Married to:
195 (97)	Manekbai married to Navroji Mehta Died 13 Oct 1872
196 (98)	Burjorji Mehta relationship with N.N. Died 12 May 1869

	Married/ related to:
197 (98)	N.N.
198 (99)	Kavasji Mehta relationship with Jeevanbai Mehta Died 18 Jun 1883
	Married/ related to:
199 (99)	Jeevanbai Mehta relationship with Kavasji Mehta Died 30 Oct 1883
200 (100)	Navroji Mehta married to Manekbai (Allready listed above as number 194)
	Married to:
201 (100)	Manekbai married to Navroji Mehta (Already listed above as number 195)
Generation IX (6th Great-Grandparents)	
384 (192)	Pestonji Mehta relationship with Dhanabai Died 19 Dec 1792
385 (192)	Married/ Related to:
	Dhanabai relationship with Pestonji Mehta Died 29 Jan 1818
388 (194)	Chandjibhai Mehta married to Jeevanbai Died 29 Jan 1860
	Married to:
389 (194)	Jeevanbai married to Chandjibhai Mehta Died 20 Aug 1844
392 (196)	Faramji Mehta relationship with N.N. Died 17 May 1791
	Married/ Related to:
393 (196)	N.N.
396 (198)	Manaji Mehta relationship with Hansibai Jeevanji Mehta (Allready listed above as number 192)
	Married/ Related to:
397 (198)	Hansibai Jeevanji Mehta relationship with Manaji Mehta (Allready listed above as number 193)

398 (199)	Navroji Mehta married to Manekbai (Allready listed above as number 194)
	Married to:
399 (199)	Manekbai married to Navroji Mehta (Allready listed above as number 195)
Generation X (7th Great-Grandparents)	
768 (384)	Hirji Mehta relationship with Hansai Died 17 May 1770
	Married/ Related to:
769 (384)	Hansai relationship with Hirji Mehta Died 17 Apr 1798
776 (388)	Jamshedji Mehta married to N.N. Died 18 Nov 1801
	Married/ Related to:
777 (388)	N.N.
784 (392)	Pestonji Mehta relationship with Dhanabai (Allready listed above as number 384)
	Married/ Related to:
785 (392)	Dhanabai relationship with Pestonji Mehta (Allready listed above as number 385)
Generation XI (8th Great-Grandparents)	
1536 (768)	Darabji Mehta relationship with N.N. Died 20 Sep 1748
	Married/ Related to:
1537 (768)	N.N.
1552 (776)	Jeejeebhai Mehta married to Chanibai Died 28 Nov 1784
	Married to:
1553 (776)	Chanibai married to Jeejeebhai Mehta Died 3 Aug 1787

Generation XII (9th Great-Grandparents)	
3072 (1536)	Ramji Mehta married to N.N. Died 5 Feb 1736 Ramji Sagar was an important person in Navsari and was given a lot of respect by the Nawabs of Surat. He was probably the first person to adopt the surname Mehta; before that, the family had been known as Talati. Parsi Prakash (Vol-1 Pg-23) writes that Ramji Sagar was a contemporory of Meherwanji Darabji Dordi who died in 1742. The latter was a 7th generation ancestor to Dr. Jehangir Beramji Dordi (FRCS) Ramji Sagar and his brother Bhaiji Sagar were involved in brokering a peace between the Bhagarias and the Sanjanias, after riots broke out in Navsari in the 17th Century. Ramji was adopted by his paternal uncle, Kavas.
	Married/ Related to:
3073 (1536)	N.N.
3104 (1552)	Sohrabji Mehta married to N.N. Died 6 Jan 1744
	Married/ Related to:
3105 (1552)	N.N.
Generation XIII (10th Great-Grandparents)	
6144 (3072)	Sagar Talati married to Rajabai Died 20 Jan 1673 Sagar was a prominent citizen of Navasri and interacted with the Mughal court. His name is recorded in the (?) offices of Surat.
	Married to:
6145 (3072)	Rajabai married to Sagar Talati
6208 (3104)	Ramji Mehta married to N.N. (Already listed above as number 3072)

	Married/ Related to:
6209 (3104)	N.N.
Generation XIV (11th Great-Grandparents)	
12288 (6144)	Behram Talati married to Malahi Died 20 Jan 1640
	Married to:
12289 (6144)	Malahi married to Behram Talati
Generation XV (12th Great-Grandparents)	
24576 (12288)	Chanda Talati married to N.N.
	Married/ Related to:
24577 (12288)	N.N.
Generation XVI (13th Great-Grandparents)	
49152 (24576)	Behram Talati married to N.N.
	Married/ Related to:
49153 (24576)	N.N.
Generation XVII (14th Great-Grandparents)	
98304 (49152)	Hacha Talati married to N.N.
	Married/ Related to:
98305 (49152)	N.N.
Generation XVIII (15th Great-Grandparents)	
196608 (98304)	Kama Talati married to N.N.
	Married/ Related to:
196609 (98304)	N.N.
Generation XIX (16th Great-Grandparents)	
393216 (196608)	Kadva Talati married to N.N.
	Married/ Related to:
393217 (196608)	N.N.
Generation XX (17th Great-Grandparents)	
786432 (393216)	Poma Talati married to N N
	Married/ Related to:

786433 (393216)	N N married to Poma Talati
Generation XXI (18th Great-Grandparents)	
1572864 (786432)	Hapa Talati married to N.N.
	Married/ Related to:
1572865 (786432)	N.N.
Generation XXII (19th Great-Grandparents)	
3145728 (1572864)	Vejal Talati married to N.N.
	Married/ Related to:
3145729 (1572864)	N.N.
Generation XXIII (20th Great-Grandparents)	
6291456 (3145728)	Thumba Talati married to N.N.
	Married/ Related to:
6291457 (3145728)	N.N.
Generation XXIV (21th Great-Grandparents)	
12582912 (6291456)	Kela Talati married to N.N.
	Married/ Related to:
12582913 (6291456)	N.N.
Generation XXV (22th Great-Grandparents)	
25165824 (12582912)	Kamdin Talati married to N.N. He is the first known ancestor in this family. Calculating backwards, he must have died circa 1300 AD.

19
SEE YOU IN COURT!
ARE PARSIS LITIGIOUS BY NATURE?

If ye will only know and learn these Laws,
Which Mazda hath ordained for ye, O men,-
The Laws of Happiness, the Laws of Pain,-
That Falsehood brings on age-long punishment,
That Truth leads on to fuller, higher, Life,-
Upon all such the Light Divine shall dawn.
—Yasna 30.11

If one studies the history of the Parsi community in India in minute detail, one will come across a plethora of lawsuits and pitched battles in courtrooms which have played a key part in shaping the community's life and times. This is rather surprising because as individuals, Parsis on an average are not acrimonious at all.

Mitra Sharafi, the US-based socio-legal historian, gives a detailed analysis of the Parsis' affinity to go to court in her book *Law and Identity in Colonial South Asia*. We have already discussed in detail two lawsuits which have left their marks on how Parsis attempt to identify themselves. For years, Parsis lacked a personal law and did not have any well-defined rules to govern their lives. Who could be a member of the community was very much debated in the 1900s and is still being shrouded in uncertainty?

Parsi Trust lawsuits occasionally involved large numbers of community leaders opposing each other on points of religious doctrine and practice. Fighting for a principle meant fighting to the end. It meant not compromising. The opposing views were openly discussed in journals and newspapers and cartoons published in the press reveal the sentiments of the people. For example, we have the cartoon of the young ladies pushing out Mr Orthodox who wants them to sign a petition against Bella (p. 33) and another of the Petit vs Jeejeebhoy case as a train at the crossroads waiting to be informed which path to follow, when a compromise solution, of accepting conversion under guidelines, was offered by the Judges. (p. 27)

Mitra Sharafi details many marital cases which went to the Parsi Chief Matrimonial Court (PCMC). These appeals in court give an insight into the moral behavior of Parsis. Bigamy, adultery, prostitution, impotency, illegitimate children etc were very much a part of Parsi life. In fact, in 1936 in the amended Parsi Marriage and Divorce Act, forced prostitution on a wife by a husband was additionally introduced as a ground for divorce.

Most marital discord cases, however, did not go to court as it was an expensive procedure. Child marriage being the norm and divorce expensive, many couples, on not finding themselves compatible, just drifted apart without divorce. It is only when the situation went out of hand or maybe, the families' honor was at stake, did divorce cases go to court.

Sharafi writes, for those cases that did go to court evidence had to be collected first. 'Making Enquires' was the term used for extracting information from social networks within the community. Through it, wives, discovered that husbands had entered bigamous marriages or had admitted to being impotent. Making enquires occasionally meant getting help from professionals. Suspicious wives sometimes hired detectives like the Irish Private Eye, Charles Edward Ring. Ring followed many husbands to clandestine meetings with other women in private apartments. ('Marital

Patchwork Colonial South Asia: Forum shopping from Britain to Baroda', 2010 by Sharafi)

Husbands also went all out to collect evidence against their wives, particularly when alleging extramarital pregnancy. In court they produced birth certificates of the children in question and cross examined the keepers of death registers from the Dokhmas, where the bodies of still born babies were exposed to vultures. (Suit No.5 of 1893 PCMC Notebook)

The challenge was in proving that conception had occurred after the husband's last date of access to his wife. There were no DNA tests, so cases often hinged on timing. In an 1883 case, a husband claimed he had not access to his wife in Bombay because he was in Hyderabad, and she had given birth to three children in his absence. In another case in 1914, a man estranged from his wife accused her of tricking him into a brief reconciliation during which they had sex three times. He claimed she was already pregnant and was trying to make her extramarital pregnancy look marital. (Suit No.3 of1914 PCMA Notebook)

By asking around, husbands claimed to learn that their wives were having affairs or working as prostitutes. (Suit No.4 of 1895 PCMC Notebook). In another case in 1903, a husband reported that a tip led him to a maternity hospital where he found his estranged wife with a newborn baby, that could not be his. (Suit No.4 of 1903 PCMC Notebook)

In some cases, Parsis sued to save their reputation. Others felt their reputations were already so tarnished by rumor that exposure was a price worth paying for divorce. The classic example was the cuckold estranged husband. Two scenarios were most common. In the first, a husband learnt that his wife had become pregnant from their last meeting. He might then confront her with the new baby at the lying-in-hospital, send a photographer, take her picture with the child, produce a birth registry entry or even read an obituary of the child (when deceased), in a Parsi newspaper. (Suit No.3 of 1914 PCMC Notebook)

In a second scenario, a husband would discover that his wife had been living as a prostitute. The evidence was usually locational. For example, the husband would claim that his wife had been frequenting places like Suklaji Street or Kamathipura both known for their brothels. Most of the times the evidence was gesture or clothing based. A husband claimed he had seen his wife at Kamathipura, sitting in front of a house with three Mussalman women on each side, just as a prostitute would sit. "I say like a prostitute because she had a black sari on and nothing on her hair." (Suit No.4 of 1895 PCMC Notebook)

In one 1932 case, a woman's mother took her to see a lawyer on learning that the woman's husband had brought his mistress to live in the marital house. (Suit No.9 of 1932 PCMC Notebook)

There were times when intervening neighbors determined the presentation of facts. Having observed the Muslim driver of a married woman's father sneak into the bedroom while she was alone in the house, a group of Parsi neighbors became convinced that the two were having an affair. Their suspicions were confirmed when they entered the house and pulled the man out from under the marital bed. Rather than expose the pair, the neighbors decided to give the woman (and her marriage) a second chance. When the matter finally went to court the neighbors explained "We decided to keep the marital relations intact between husband and wife and hammered the co-defendant as if he were a thief." The neighbors chased the man out of the house and down the road on that pretext. (Suit No.1 of 1927 PCMC Judges Notebook.)

Whether husbands were violent, or wives were cheating, their spouses were often advised not to spread the news for the sake of preserving the family reputation. In one 1920 case, the mother of one plaintiff husband advised him to keep quiet when he heard his wife was being unfaithful. She said, "I should only expose myself by exposing my wife." (Suit No.7 of 1920 PCMC Notebook). In another case the parents of a woman whose husband was impotent opposed the idea of getting an annulment. They wanted "to avoid scandal" (Suit No.6 of 1933 PCMC Notebook)

Formal arbitration bodies also existed around 1930, run by groups like the Parsi League of Honor, The Grant Road Parsi Association, and the Irani Association. They specialized in advising couples in their marital disputes before they went to Court. With the help of arbitrators, the parties in these cases often agreed in writing to stay married but live separately and for the husband to make maintenance payment to the wife. (Erachshaw Dosabhai Toddiwala v. Dinbai wife of Erachshaw Dosabhai Toddiwala ILR 45 Bom 318, 1921, at 322).

These cases show that there was no sanctity of the marital bonds for both men and women. Extramarital affairs and illegitimate children were the norm. Children born out of these relationships were accepted into the society as Parsis. There was no separate caste of Parsis called 'Illegitimate Children of Men' or 'Illegitimate Children of Women'. All were Parsis.

20
ADOPTION IN THE PARSI COMMUNITY*

Adoption – because family isn't made from blood, it's made from love
—Anonymous

The status of Parsi customary law on adoption is not clear – the better view being that the personal law of Parsis did not, or at any rate no longer, recognises adoption amongst Parsis.

In one of the earliest of decisions of courts – in the year 1802 – a case arising in Bombay – the consequences of a Parsi adoption were accepted, the English judge characterising Parsi ceremonies to be the same as that of Hindus and holding that 'in little else but their faith they will be found to differ materially from Hindoos and they may safely be pronounced to have no law' (Pastonjee v. Veeiji: a decision of the Sadr. Diwani Adalat).

But nine years later – in Vol.-I Bombay Sadar Adalat Reports p.23 (1811) – the Sadr. Adalat Court upheld an arbitration award of a High Priest holding that an adopted son was entitled to two shares of property, one from his biological father and another from the person who adopted him!

And later, in the year 1835, in the case of Homabee v. Punjeabhare Dorsabhare 1835 (1) Sutherland's Judgments 68 at p.70 it appears that the Privy Council – after the promulgation

---

* The author is indebted to Mr Falis. Nariman for his inputs in this chapter.

of Regulation IV of 1927 – held that the adoption of a son by a Parsi was 'clearly a valid and legal adoption to all intents and purposes (sic)'.

It also appears, from an Opinion (of 15 February 1982) given by High Priest Dasturji Dr Firoze Kotwal that it was 'a long cherished tradition amongst Parsis in India that they can adopt as son a male-member of their own community even when they are alive'; and for this opinion an ancient document dated 4 June 1676 of the entire Anjuman of Navsari ('strong hold of parsi-ism') has been relied upon by Dasturji Firoze Kotwal which laid down that 'a Parsi could adopt another Parsi of his own choice during his lifetime'.

However, all the above 'law', or 'custom and usage', appears to have been set at naught in the decision of the High Court of Bombay (where the vast majority of Parsis have been and still are located): in the case of Kershaji Dhanjibhai v. Kaikhushru Kolhabhai (AIR 1929 Bombay 478 = reported in 31 Bom. L.R. 1081) where a Division Bench of two judges of the High Court of Bombay stated that it appreciated counsel's statement that although the lower court had found in his client's favour that in the then Indian Princely State of Baroda where the parties were domiciled, the custom of adoption did prevail among the Paris, yet it had also held that this custom would not prevail in British India as regards immovable property situate there!

The court then added:

'It is elementary international law that the law which governs the land of a particular nation is the law of that nation. Consequently, land in British India is governed by the law of British India as the lex loci and not by the law of the domicile of the temporary owner.

It follows, therefore, that, having regard to the law of British India, and the statutory provisions which govern succession amongst Parsis[1]; it is abundantly clear that there is no room in the law of British India for such a custom amongst the Parsis as is now put forward, accordingly, the bulk of the points taken in appeal by the appellant must fail.'

There is no later case taking a different view. Besides, one must have regard to the provisions now contained in the Hindu Adoption and Maintenance Act, 1956 – an Act that expressly states – in Section (2): dealing with the 'Application of the Act' – that the Act also applies to any other person who is not a Muslim, Christian, Parsi or Jew by religion...'.

Parsis have not had a general law of adoption in India despite repeated representations: made to government only for one reason – that Muslims by religion abhor adoption since it is prohibited by the Koran; it has been settled law for more than one hundred years that the Mohammedan law – i.e. the Mohammedan Personal Law does not recognise adoption as a mode of filiation. The Adoption of Children's Bill of 1972 was introduced by the Government of India in Parliament – which enabled, but did not compel, members of different faiths to adopt; but it was strongly opposed by Muslim Members of Parliament – leading to the Bill being withdrawn. It has never again been revived.

An afterthought.

Adoption is a legal process that creates a parent-child relationship between persons not related by blood. This is the general meaning

---

1 The reference to the 'Statutory provisions which govern succession amongst Parsis' is to Chapter-III (Special Rules for Parsi Intestate) in the Indian Succession Act, 1925 – Sections 50 to 56 which do not recognise 'adopted' sons or 'adopted' daughters of Parsis dying intestate as their lawful heirs.

of adoption, but for Parsis, it is not so straightforward. A Parsi can adopt a son to perform funeral ceremonies, but such adopted person will not inherit any portion of the deceased's estate, except under his will.

Such an adopted person is called 'Palak' or 'Dharm-putra'. A Palak is appointed by the adoptive parent in their lifetime, while a 'Dharm-Putra' is appointed after the death of the person for performing of funeral ceremonies.

Parsis can adopt a child only under the Guardians and Ward Act,1890. This Act allows guardianship but does not allow complete adoption and thus, makes the child a 'ward' and the interested couple their 'guardian'. The child does not become their own child, and thus does not inherit the parent's property or name.

The Act allows guardianship only till the child is a minor. The relationship lasts till the child attains the age of 21. After completing the age of 21, he/she will not remain as 'ward' and will be considered as an individual.

Today, children 'adopted' under the Guardians and Wards Act by Parsi men, are being accepted as Parsis. They are initiated into the religion and allowed entry into the fire temples. This privilege is not extended to inter-married Parsi women who similarly adopt.

As these 'adopted' children are not biological children of Parsis they cannot trace their ancestry 'to the original emigrants into India from Persia who profess the Zoroastrian Religion' (Justice Davar's obiter dictum), nor can they be 'the descendants of these original emigrants'. No DNA tests are done to check the ancestry of these children.

21
SIR HENRY MAINE AND THE SPECIAL MARRIAGE ACT OF 1872

Ahura Mazda shall grant perfection and immortality (to the man)... who
through his thoughts and actions becomes his friend.
—Yasna XXXI

In British India, each religion had its own personal law for marriage and divorce. The Parsis had their Parsi Marriage and Divorce Act of 1856. It states that a Parsi marriage is between a Parsi man and a Parsi woman. Under this law a Parsi could marry only a Parsi.

The origin of civil marriage legislation in India dates back to Henry James Summer Maine and James Fitzjames Stephen, who succeeded him. Sir Henry Maine (1822–1888) was a British jurist and legal historian who pioneered the study of comparative law, notably primitive law and anthropological jurisprudence. As a member of the council of the governor-general of India (1863–69), Maine was largely responsible for the codification of Indian law. In 1869 he became the first professor of comparative jurisprudence at the University of Oxford and, in 1887, a professor of international law at Cambridge. He was knighted in 1871 (*britannica.com*).

Sir James Fitzjames Stephen, first Baronet (1829–1894), was a British legal historian, Anglo-Indian administrator, judge, and author noted for his criminal-law reform proposals. The older brother of the literary critic Sir Leslie Stephen, Sir James practiced law from

Sir Henry Maine

1854 and contributed articles on a wide range of topics to various periodicals, especially the *Pall Mall Gazette*. As the member of the British viceroy's council in India (1869–72) responsible for legal matters, Stephen devoted himself to the codification and reform of Indian law (*britannica.com*).

Maine's views on Indian society and laws in the 1860s were noticeably challenged by Indians who contested his energetic observations of young natives throwing off centuries worth of religious practice and marrying out of love rather than duty. Love marriage was a new concept, made possible by the gradual cessation of child marriages.

In 1872, they enacted a law for civil marriage in India. It was called The Special Marriage Act of 1872 that allowed Indians to marry outside their castes or communities and made the state witness to such unions.

However, this law contained a peculiar anomaly for a civil marriage law. It contained a compulsory statement of excommunication from one's religious community. The Special Marriage Act was applicable only if people were willing to take themselves out of their religious communities and outside the boundary of their ethno-religious groups.

Another way of getting married was to convert to either of the spouse's religion. For example, Ratti Dinshaw Petit converted to the Muslim religion and married Muhammad Ali Jinnah or Suzanne Braire converted to the Zoroastrian religion and married Ratan Tata (father of J.R.D. Tata)

In 1954, the Special Marriage Act was amended whereby any two citizens of India, weather professing the same or different or no religion could marry. After independence, the law of civil marriage was amended. In a secular state the right to marry whomever one pleased should not be conditional on a rejection of religion. C.C. Biswas, Minister of Law and Minority affairs in Nehru's cabinet, introduced the Bill in Parliament in 1954 with this explanatory note:

> The first is...marriage under this law will not require the parties to forswear their religion or to declare that they do not belong to any religion. The Bill if passed, will permit of inter-religious marriages. Religious differences are put out of the way altogether. Government feels that the time has come now when religious differences should not stand in the way of a couple getting together, if they feel that their lives are cast together, and the

fact of their marriage should not in any way affect their religious beliefs. That is the change' ('Parliamentary Debates: House of the People', Vol. V, Part11, 5-21 May 1954 Sixth session, Lok Sabha Secretariat, New Delhi, Columns 7807-8.

The Special Marriage Act was intended to have uniform civil application, marriage would be a civil contract. But it also aimed to protect religious freedoms in that now it did not require persons to surrender their faith. Nehru's government did not believe that marrying out should require social excommunication or a self-renunciation of faith.

A legal marriage between a Parsi and an 'alien' did not exist till 1954.

Under the Special Marriage Act of 1954, Parsi men and women could continue to follow their religion and marry a person from another faith. The question of acceptance of the legal children of religiously intermarried Parsi men and women could arise only after 1954. So, there cannot be any 'centuries-old' established custom regarding the acceptance of children of intermarried men and women.

Intermarriage in the Parsi community is not unusual. According to statistics gathered by the *Parsiana* magazine in 2021, more than 50 per cent of marriages are interfaith marriages. With so many Parsi men and women marrying out, parents accept the marriage and the grandchildren within the home and community in which practices and beliefs cannot be policed by trustees of wealthy trust funds.

22
DADABHOY NOWROJI ON THE PARSI RELIGION

Standing at the Bridge of Judgment, The evil soul beholds the path of the righteous, But the evil of his actions, the words of his evil tongue, prove to be his fetters, In fear, he finds that he fails.
—Vohu-Khshathra Gatha; Yasna 51, 13

Dadabhoy Naoroji, one of India's greatest social and religious reformers, wrote a magnificent book called 'The Parsi Religion 1861'. He has highlighted the difference between the 'Old Class' and the 'Young Class' in matters of custom and religion. He says, 'The Parsi Religion is for all and not for any particular nation or people.' He is very critical of the priests and their lack of knowledge of the religion and the absence of religious education for the community. He wished to remove from the Parsi religion, the Hindu customs not enjoined by their religious books nor authorized by the practice of their Persian ancestors, which were being followed. He wanted the Zoroastrian religion to return to its pristine purity. He describes the 'Zarthosti Community' and the 'Parsi Religion'. He uses Zarthosti to describe the community and Parsi to describe the relgion.

Naoroji read a paper on the Parsi Religion at the Liverpool Literary and Philosophical Society, on 18 March 1861. He started by giving a short account of the present state of the knowledge of the Parsis about their religion. 'As a body, the priests are not only

*Dadabhai Naoroji, father of religious and
social reform of the Parsis.*

ignorant of the duties and objects of their own profession, but are
entirely uneducated, except that they are able to read and write, and
that, also, often very imperfectly.' He continued, 'Their work consists
of reciting certain prescribed prayers on various religious occasions;
to go to the fire temple or seashore, and say a prayer for anybody
that chooses to give a halfpenny; and to depend upon charities
distributed on various joyous or mournful occasions. They do not

understand a single word of those prayers or recitations, which are all in the old Zend language.'

He further said, 'Far from being the teachers of the doctrines and duties of the religion, the priests are generally the most bigoted and superstitious, and exercise much injurious influence over the women.' But he says the situation is improving now. There are, perhaps, a dozen, among the whole body of professional priests, who lay claim to a knowledge of the Zend Avesta, the religious books of the Parsis. But they have only learnt the meanings of some words of the book, without knowing the language, either philologically or grammatically.

Dadabhoy was a religious reformer, and started a society called the Rahnumae Mazdayasne Sabha (guides on the Mazdayasne Path). He rued the fact that Parsis were ignorant about their religion.

'Such being the state of knowledge of the religious book by the guides and teachers among the Parsis, it may be easily conceived what could be expected from a layman. The whole religious education of a Parsi child consists in preparing by rote, a number of prayers in Zend, without understanding a word. 'Under these circumstances, a Parsi has not much opportunity of knowing what his creed really is; the translation, besides, of the Zend books, in the present vernacular of the Parsis, being of very recent date.'

At the end of the prayer book there are a few questions and answers on religion which he relates:

There is a dialogue, appended to the Khordeh Avesta (small Avesta)... The subject of the dialogue is thus described:

"A few questions and answers to acquaint the children of the holy Zarthosti community with the subject of the Mazdiashna religion (i.e. of the worship of God).

Dialogue between a Zarthosti master and pupil:

Q: Whom do we, of the Zarthosti community believe in?

A: We believe in only one God, and do not believe in any
        besides Him.'

What is the form of God, what is our religion, what are our holy
books, what commands did God give us, what is God's name, are
there any miracles recorded, what commands has God sent us, and
other questions are asked and replies given.

He gives extracts from the holy book the Yazashne, which is
divided into 72 chapters called 'Ha'.

He quotes from the '46 Ha'.

'May all men and women of the world become my followers and
become acquainted with thy exalted religion, that I may rise in thy
praise and in thy religion with prayer'; He says 'The Parsi religion is
for all, and not for any particular nation or people.'

He concludes 'At the present I gave some account of the present
imperfect knowledge of the Parsees about their religion, I do not
however mean to blame them for it. A handful of persecuted exiles
living in a foreign land, surrounded for 1200 years by idolatry, and
persecuted at times by religious fanaticism, it is rather a matter of
surprise, as with the Jews, that the Parsees have preserved their
national type and character, and their original worship. Though they
have not altogether escaped contamination and have adopted many
superstitious ceremonies and notions of the Hindoos.'

Mr Dadabhoy said, after his speech that 'no member need feel
any delicacy in putting any questions to him on the subject of the
paper.' Dr Ihne said he had brought with him a French work, by M.
Menant, containing an excellent digest of the Parsi creed, which,
according to it, was briefly as follows- 'There is one God, He is
Eternal, there was nothing before Him, and all things are by Him.
The universe was truly created by Him and is not an emanation
from Him'. Hormuzd established religion for all mankind, and not
for some only.' 'This is a quote from *Les Parsis* by D. Menant which

was later translated into English by Miss Ratanbai Ardeshir Vakil in 1902.

Dadabhoy was trying to remove the Hindu customs which had entered into the religion and establish the Parsi religion as a monotheistic religion meant for all mankind.

The Manners and Customs of the Parsees by Dadabhoy Naoroji

In a Paper read before the Liverpool (Philosophical) Society 13 March 1861, Dadabhoy Naoroji said:

> Under ordinary circumstances it may not be difficult to give a general account of the existing manners and customs of a people; but in the case of the Parsis, in the present transition state of their social and intellectual condition, it is difficult to say what the whole community generally observe and believe.
>
> There is at present nearly as great a difference between one portion of them and another as there was between Englishmen and Parsis twenty years ago. The English education of the last twenty years has worked a great change. That change, however, is not general; nor is it looked upon with satisfaction and approval by one portion. The educated, not having arrived at their present knowledge by the gradual process of self-made progress, with struggles and amidst difficulties, and by the efforts watched and sympathized by the whole community; not having earned but inherited the treasure; a large and sudden chasm separates them from the uneducated in their sentiments, ideas, habits of thought, opinion, and customs. This difference is so wide and marked, that in describing the present condition and customs of the Parsis, statements about one portion will sometimes be altogether inapplicable to another.

Just as the influence of English education has operated on their mental condition, the example of English modes of life and domestic habits and arrangements has worked a revolution in their social condition. These changes, both mental and social, are confined to certain portions, though exercising more or less influence upon the general body of people.

He describes the domestic life of the older way of life, which is similar to life in the villages today.

No tables and chairs, sitting on mats, eating from thalis with their hands, women not eating with the men. Saying of the Kusti prayers in the morning and rubbing their face with *nirang*, followed by saying of the Kusti prayers, if he' gets his head shaved, or have had a nightly issue, or takes a bath or after his morning ablutions.' The nirang he explains is 'the urine of cow, ox or she goat, and the rubbing of it over the face and hands, is the second thing a Parsi does after getting out of bed; Now he should not touch anything with his hands' and in order to wash out the nirang he either asks somebody else to pour water on his hands, or resorts to the devise of taking hold of the pot through the intervention of a piece of cloth, such as a handkerchief or his Sudreh. He first pours water on one hand, then takes the pot in that hand and washes his other hand and face and feet'. 'They sometimes eat together from the same plate, but they have to take care not to put their fingers in their mouth but fling the morsel into the mouth from a little distance...while thus taking the meal together, the water must also be drunk from a copper pot without touching the lips'. Every meal is preceded by doing the Kusti prayers and then again prayer before going to bed.

He describes the Parsi customs of birth, marriage and death and bemoans how Hindu customs were being observed. These 'staunch, orthodox, unchanged Parsis belong to the Old Class in contradiction to the Young Class, by which name the educated and the reformers are known.'

'Many of the customs and ceremonies in connection with marriage, death and birth, says the Young Class, are not at all Parsi; they are almost all Hindoo. To abolish them.... an association has been formed to discuss and show the reasons why Parsis should have nothing to do with them, as being neither enjoined by their religious books, nor authorized by the practice of their Persian ancestors. This association is named Rahanumaee Mazdiashnans, Rahanumae means The Guide and Mazdiashnans means Worshippers of God.'

An anti Rahanumae society was formed called Raherastnumae Mazdiashna. The promoters of these two bodies met often, and published pamphlets to refute each other's views. 'And the result has been that the reformers found themselves the more strengthened by the intolerant bigotry and weakness of arguments of their opponents.'

He ends the paper:

'The school master is abroad, and reform and progress, is the order of the day. God speed them, is the hearty prayer of one who is proud of his race and hopeful of its destiny.'

These two lectures clearly bring out the existing sharp differences in opinion among the Parsis in religion and customs.

23
THE IRAN LEAGUE QUARTERLY

Zarathustra was the greatest of all the pioneer prophets who showed the path of freedom to man, the freedom of moral choice, the freedom from the multiplicity of shrines which draw our worship away from the single-minded chastity of devotion.
—the Religion of Man, Rabindranath Tagore

The Iran League, Bombay was an organization established by prominent Parsis with the aim of reviving and strengthening cultural and other ties between Iran and India. Sir Hormusji C. Adenwala was its first President. Its journal *The Iran League Quarterly* was like a community magazine. It highlighted the achievements of the community, commented on world events (the World Wars, for example) and the effects they had on particularly, India, Iran, and the world. It also tried to educate the community on Zoroastrianism through the newly interpreted Gathas. It also aimed to show the connection between Iran and India which the Parsis of both the countries had forgotten. Reading the Quarterly issues of the Iran League takes us back to the 1930s and shows us the life and times of the Parsi community of the past.

In November 1924, Ahmad Shah Qajar landed in Bombay and was presented with a silver casket by The Iran League. On another occasion, the League and the Iranian Zoroastrian Association jointly sent to Reza Shah presentation copies, in a silver casket, of Poure-Davoud's Persian translation of the Avestan Gathas and the Yashts.

Sir Hormusji C. D. Adenvala, the venerable Chairman of the Iran League, has returned to India after a grave illness in England. This esteemed member of the Community was greeted with genuine pleasure by friends and admirers when he stepped on the shore of Bombay on 15th February 1931.

سر هرمزجی سی. دی. عدن والا رئیس انجمن ایران لیگ پس از ناخوشی سختی در انگلستان هندوستان برگشت این عضو محترم ملت فارسی را دوستان و دوستدارانش در هنگام قدم گذاشتن بساحل بمبئی از صمیم قلب پذیرائی نمودند

Hormusji C.D. Adenvala, Chairman of the Iran League being welcomed back after his illness (Iran League Quarterly, *April 1934*)

As the first president of the League, Hormusji Adenwala's aims, and objectives are stated clearly:

In the October 1931 issue, the editor, Sohrab J. Bulsara, in his editor's note wrote that the Parsis are the original inhabitants of India:

'Quite another imputation is likewise laid against the Iran League when it tries to persuade the Parsees to lend a helping hand to Iran.' 'It is alleged in so doing the Parsees are showing ingratitude to this country of their adoption.' 'The Parsees are amongst the oldest inhabitants of this beautiful and noble land: for, really speaking, they had commenced settling in it since millenniums past, and not only after the fall of the Sassanian dominium as it is commonly

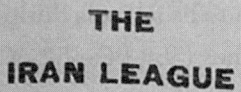

THE IRAN LEAGUE

EST. 1922.

ایران لیگ

Aims and Objects.

To renew and continue the connection between the old land of Iran and Hind ; to continue and encourage fraternal sentiment towards and interest and enthusiasm in the cause of Persia ; to confederate the Zoroastrian population in Persia with a view to increase, to ameliorate their condition and to strive for their uplift ; to make researches with reference to their religion and ancient Parsi history ; to stimulate commercial relations with Persia; to encourage Parsis to visit the old land, as businessmen or as travellers, for change of climate and health : to obtain and spread among Parsis and others, by means of literature, authentic information regarding the state of affairs in Persia ; to secure the sympathy of the Imperial Persian Government and the Persian subjects towards the cause of Parsis in relation to Persia.

President :
Sir Hormusji C. Adenvala, Kt., M.V.O., O.B.E.

Vice-Presidents :
D. J. Irani, Esq., B.A., LL.B.
F. K. Dadachanji, Esq., B.A., LL.B. } Solicitors.
The Hon. Mr. H. M. Mehta.

Patrons:

Sir Hormusji C. Adenvala, Kt., M.V.O., O.B.E.
Mrs. Dhunmai F. Arjani.
Peshotanji D. Marker, Esq.
S. R. Bomonji, Esq.

Pirojshaw R. Vakharia, Esq.
Ruttonji F. Ginvala, Esq.
The Hon. Mr. H. M. Mehta.
Khan Bahadur R. Pestonji.

Hon. Patron:
H. H. Sir S. M. S. Aga Khan, G.C.I.E., G.C.S.I., G.C.V.O., K.C.I.E., &c.

Secretary:
Kaikhosro A. Fitter, Esq.

Hon. Auditor:
Capt. Sohrab R. Bamji.

Hon. Treasurer:
Phiroze S. Guzder, Esq.

Editor of the Quarterly:
Sohrab J. Bulsara, Esq., M.A.

Office : **Kamar Bldg., Cowasji Patel Street, Fort, Bombay.**

Aims and objects of the Iran League

understood. Some large bands did indeed emigrate and settle here on that occasion also; but Parsees were known to be in India during the Achaemenian, Parthian and Sassanian times (558 BC–652 AC) as they held some portion or another of this great land as a part of their great dominion of those days. Hence it is quite long since they have become the true children of the soil; so they will love and serve it with as great sincerity and devotion as any other people settled in this country might claim to do.'

'Politically too the Parsee has greater right to her citizenship than either the Hindu or the Moslem. These claim it by right of conquest, for the Hindus conquered India from the Dravidians, and the Moslems from the Hindus. But the Parsees claim it by right of Treaty, sacrifice, and service; and so their claim to India is more sacred more certain and more deserved than any other people.'

It quoted M.K. Gandhi's message for the Parsis:

'I am glad to say that the Congress was conceived in an English brain, and nursed by two great Parsis: Pherozeshaw Mehta and Mr Dadabhoy Naoroji, the Grand Old Man of India... Now, what cannot the 2 nations of Britain and India do with their united forces and possibilities – one a brave nation noted for its fight against slavery and the other, a very ancient one, representing the two great cultures of Islam and Hinduism, and absorbing, among others, the whole of the splendid Zoroastrian stock – in numbers almost sub cognizance, but in philanthropy and enterprise almost unsurpassed.'

In this issue, Behramgore T. Anklesaria, the most accomplished Avestan scholar, wrote an article on Zoroastrian religious literature, titled Gathas and the later Avesta. He explained in Yasna, 31.8 'This stanza beautifully brings out the working of the mind of Zarathusthra, when he wanted to find out an apt attribute of the 'Omniscient Creator'. 'Mazda', whom he raised to the high pedestal of the Godhead, whilst preaching his monotheistic creed before the

Advertisment for books on Zoroastrian literature and travel to Persia in the Iran League Quarterly

orthodox multitude of 'daeva yasnas' who had become desirous of listening to his new thoughts'.

'When I held you in my mind's eye
then I realized You, O Mazda,
as the First and the Last for all Eternity,

as the Father of the Good Mind,

the true Creator of Truth,

and Lord over the actions of life.'

(Yasna 31.8 Translated by P. Nanavutty)

In the April 1933 issue, Mr N.G. Suntoke wrote an article on how conversions were taking place in America, titled *A Call to All Aryans to Unite in Zarathushtra*.

He wrote,

'Mr Sarosha A. Kaul, a civil engineer, residing in California, became interested in the religion of Zarathustra some 25 years ago and is now engaged in spreading it in the far-off land. So far he has succeeded in converting about 30 persons to Zoroastrianism and expects to increase the number at a not very distant date.'

He says Jamshedji Madan (Trustee of the Late Ervad D.B. Mehta Zoroastrian Anjuman Atash Adaran, Calcutta) distributed sudrehs and kustis and invested people into the religion:

'A robe of purple and gold was presented to me by a Parsi brother by the name of Jamshedji Madan; this brother invested me with the sudreh and kusti...'

Each issue of the journal had articles on Zoroastrian religion and Zoroastrian studies by renowned scholars. The Gathas and its interpretation were discussed in almost every issue. This must have been done to educate the community about the religion. Some of the Parsis associated with the Iran League were Sir Rustum Vakil, Dr Faredun K. Dadachanji, Khan Bahadur Hormusji Khurshedji Bhabha, Sir Phiroze Cursetji Sethna, Sir Navrozji Saklatvala, Sir Hormasji Mehta and Hormusji C. Adenwala.

The January 1940 issue records some Parsi achievements, 'Byramji Jeejeebhoy has been appointed Chairman of the Imperial Bank of India, Sir Homi P. Modi is appointed Director of the Reserve Bank of India and President of the Federated Group in

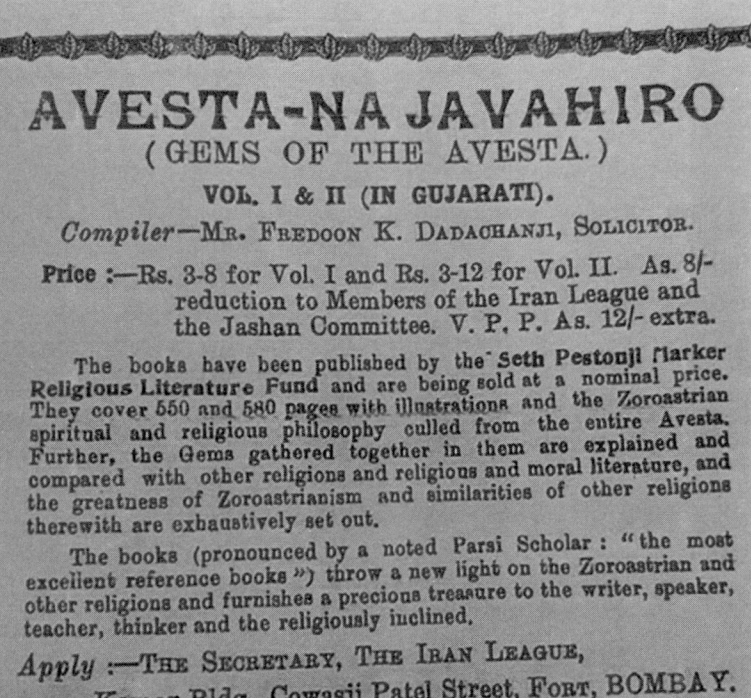

Advertisment for books on religion in the Iran League Quarterly; *there was keen interest in learning about the religion from the recently translated Gathas*

Bombay Corporation. Mr J.B. Wadia is appointed to the Board of Film Censors, Ardesher R. Dalal was elected President of the Indian Science Congress, and Chairman of The Bombay Red Cross, Mr Sorabji Rustumji was elected President of the Bombay Flying Club, Mr Rustum P. Masani has been nominated to the Permanent Famine Relief, Noshirwan P Engineer nominated to the Bar Council of Bombay, Mr Navrozji M. Dumasia nominated to the Indian Legislative Assembly. Mr Behram N. Karanjia and Prof. Sohrab R. Daver were elected to the Bombay Legislative Council. A casket was presented to Lady Ratan Tata by the Parsi inhabitants of Tardeo in

The Hon. Sir Phiroze Sethna is a Member of the Council of State and one of the leading moderate politicians of India. Having been also appointed on the Joint Select Committee, he is now in London giving his share in moulding the political future of India. And well may he do so, for, it was his ancestor Rustam Manek who had introduced the British to the great court of Aurangzeb for gaining important privileges which led to the founding of their great empire in India. He is a life member of the Iran League, and is taking a keen interest in Persia.

جناب اجل سر فیروز ستنا عضو شو رای دولتی و یکی از سیاسیین اعتدالی عمدهٔ هندوستان است و چون چندیست بعضویت کیته منتخب هم معین گردیده. اکنون در لندن متوقف و در تشکیل سیاست آینده هند سهیم و شریک میباشد چون جدش دستم مانک بود که دولت بریتانیا را از برای تحصیل امتیاز مهمی که منجر بتأسیس سلطنت بزرگ این دولت در هند گردیده بدربار عظیم اورنگ زیب معرفی نمود امید کامل انکه او هم از عهدهٔ کار خود بر آمده. استعداد ذاتی و موروثی خود را ابراز نماید

The Hon. Sir Phiroze Cursetji Sethna (Grandson of D.B. Mehta of the Calcutta D.B. Mehta Atash Adaran), Life Member of the Iranian Association.

Bombay, for the benefits she had bestowed upon them in providing them cheap tenements in memory of her husband Ratan Tata.'

Dr. Faredun K. Dadachanji, Solicitor, Vice-Chairman of the Iran League and a scholarly and public-spirited member of the Parsi community, has lately been endowed with a Doctorate in Theological Science by the Federation International des Corps Savants de Recherches of Teheran, and elected a Vice-President of the Academy of Asia.

دکتر فریدون کرشاسب دادا چانجی وکیل دادگستری نایب سرنشین ایران لیگ
عضو غیور و دانای جامعت پارسیها که اخیراً از طرف کنکاشان هیئت دانایان
بین الملل بأخذ دکتری علوم ادیان منتخر شده ست و بسمت نایب سرنشینی اکادمی
...

Dr Faredun K. Dadachanji, Persian scholar

Nauruz at Shantiniketan: Forging golden link between Persia and India

The Associated Press circulated the following news from Shantiniketan on 22 March 1933, as reported in the *Iran League Quarterly*.

'Nauruz – the Persian new year – was celebrated yesterday with great enthusiasm in Shantiniketan. The guests of honour were Prof

Aga Poure Davoud, the celebrated Persian scholar and poet whose services were lent to the Viswabharati by His Majesty the Shah of Persia, Mr Framroze Bode, the Parsi scholar who accompanied Dr Davoud from Bombay. Dr Rabindranath Tagore himself and all the others of the staff and students were present.'

Address by Tagore:

'We offer,' said Tagore, 'our gladsome greetings to the auspicious day of 'Naw Ruz' that has dawned today upon Persia's sky, and India especially rejoices in the great fact that the sun of the new year has its blessings for a new awakening in that ancient land of heroes.'

'There was a time when this festival from Persia found its way into the Imperial harem of Delhi. It only spoke of the orgies of an irresponsible power making the spring breeze drunken with the red fume of passion. But let the new year of a new life in Iran bring from now its voice to us in India of a vigorous manhood, clean and true, that of a unique reassertion of an indomitable personality and mingle with our own aspiration its hope of a luminous freedom from Asia.'

Incorporated into his book *The Religion of Man*, one of Tagore's Hibbert Lectures delivered in Oxford in 1930 mentioned Zarathustra as the Prophet. He notes, 'The most important of all outstanding facts of Iranian history is the religious reform brought about by Zarathustra. There can be hardly any question that he was the first man we know who gave a definitely moral character and direction to religion and at the same time preached the doctrine of monotheism which offered an eternal foundation of reality to goodness as an ideal perfection. All religions of the primitive type try to keep man bound with regulations of external observances. Zarathustra was the greatest of all the pioneer prophets who showed the path of freedom to man, the freedom of moral choice, the freedom from the multiplicity of shrines which draw our worship away from the single-minded chastity of devotion.'

Aga Poure Davoud

'The conscience of God transcends the limitation of race and gender and gathers together all human beings in one spiritual circle of union. Zarathustra was the first prophet who emancipated religion from the exclusive narrowness of the tribal God, the God of a chosen people, and offered it the universal Man.'

Aga Poure-Davoud said in his address to the audience:

'Today is the 21st of March – the beginning of spring. This day is called Naw -Ruz from very ancient times and up to now is celebrated with great pomp in Persia.'

'In Zoroastrian religion it is believed the Farvashis- the guardian spirits of the departed, visit the earth during this period. For this reason, it is called Farvandin or Farvandegan.'

'With the Persians this New Year begins with exact astronomical positions. This year the sun enters the first sign of the Zodiac at 11 hours, 8 minutes, and 42 seconds, in the night of Persia.'

'I wish long life and long health to Gurudeva Dr Rabindranath Tagore...on this Happy New Year.' 'The function came to a close after Mr Framroze Bode spoke and made Homazur with all and blessed a union of Iran and India through their cultural and spiritual relationships.'

Professor Aga Poure-Davoud was a highly recognized scholar of the Avesta and the *Iran League Quaterly* regularly printed his lectures on Zoroastrianism. The April 1934 issue prints his lecture on 'The Conception of Truth In the Zoroastrian Religion.' He gave a reference to the Pahlavi book of *Arda Viraf*. In this book there was a description of Heaven and Hell, as seen by the righteous Arda Viraf as he was accompanied by the angels Sarosh and Adar. In his vision of Paradise, Arda Viraf saw the delight and happiness of the truthful and righteous men, and the agony and suffering of the wicked liars in the experience of Hell. He writes, 'Zarathustra, in his Gathas Yasna 33, 3 calls paradise to be 'the house of Truth' and in Yasna 51, 14 calls hell to be 'the house of Lies'. In Yasna 51, 9 Zarathustra says that 'the untruthful will receive their severe punishment and the truthful their sweet reward'.

24
IRANI VS IRANI*

As long as I have power and am able,
I shall teach all to seek for Truth and Right.
—Yas. 28.4

In the year 1958, the meaning of the word Parsi was examined in the Bombay High Court in a case – where detailed evidence (oral and documentary) was led. In the case of Jamshed A. Irani vs Banu J. Irani, Mr Justice Mody concluded, 'I have not the slightest hesitation in concluding that the word 'Parsi' was used long prior to 1936 as meaning Zoroastrians both of India and of Iran and that it was so used both in India and Iran. As a matter of fact, it was so understood not only before 1936 but even before the Act of 1865.'[1] This case establishes that the word Parsi was used to denote not race but religion. 'Parsi' is interchangeable with the word 'Zoroastrian'.

Jamshed Irani had filed a suit for divorce against his wife Banu under the Parsi Marriage and Divorce Act of 1936. Banu contended

---

1 However earlier – in Sarwar Merwan Yezidar v. Merwan Rashid Yezidar - AIR 1951 Bombay 14 - a Division Bench of the Bombay High Court had upheld a judgment of a Single Judge that the Parsi Marriage and Divorce Act, 1936 would not apply to Irani Zorastrians – but that case was decided on legal interpretation of the Act – without oral evidence being led. Mody J. starts his judgment (in Irani vs. Irani) saying: 'I am however feeling great difficult, in following that judgment" – and goes on to state that in Sarwar Merwan Yezdiar the point whether the plaintiff or the defendant was a Parsi or not was not raised either in the pleadings or in the trial court.

---

* **The author is indebted to Mr Fali S. Nariman for his inputs in this chapter.**

that neither she or Jamshed was a Parsi Zoroastrian as they were foreigners registered under the Foreigners' Rules and the court had no jurisdiction to hear the suit...

Justice Mody heard extensive oral and documentary evidence led on the origin and connotation of the word 'Parsi'. He also clearly stated that Justice Davar's description of a Parsi in Petit vs Jeejeebhoy (1908) was an obiter dictum. He said, 'the observations of Davar J., were merely obiter dicta, but as against the same they were in the process of formulating a definition of 'Parsi' or rather in the process of formulating the full connotation of the word 'Parsi' and the same were made after considering a plethora of oral and documentary evidence. In fact Justice Mody records that contrary to the obiter dictum of Davar J., in the Petit case itself there was evidence led before Justices Davar and Beaman to the effect that Mahomedens in Persia called the Zoroastrians of Persia 'Parsis'! Before Justices Davar and Beaman the evidence of a priest (Beram Sherier) – (over-looked by Justice Davar) was that 'Parsi' was a word in common use in Persia and the following passage of the priest in his oral evidence (in the Petit Case) was reproduced by Justice Mody:

'Some Mahomedens in Persia still call us Parsis, some call us Zarthosti. The word Parsi is in common use in Persia; the word Parsi is commonly used to designate our people Zarathostis.'

The conclusion of Justice Mody that the observations in Justice Davar's judgment were obiter cannot therefore be faulted.

In Irani v. Irani the main question was what was the meaning of the word 'Parsi'. The defendants contended that 'Parsi' meant only 'Racial Parsi' and 'that Iranian Zoroastrians temporarily or permanently residing in India were not Parsis'. The plaintiffs contended that the Zoroastrians living in Iran are, and for centuries have been, known even in Iran and also in India as Parsis and they would, therefore, be Parsis within the meaning of the Parsi Marriage and Divorce Act of 1936. On the question of interpretation of the word 'Parsi' much evidence, oral and documentary, had been led. It was the plaintiff's case that from the Achaemenian dynasty the residents of Iran were known as Parsis. The Judge records:

'The religion of the country i.e., Parsa (Iran) till the Sassanian Age was Zoroastrian and up to the conquest by the Arabs. After the conquest there was extensive conversion to the Musalman religion. In the course of time Zoroastrians were called Parsis and those who were converted were called Musalman....'

'Those who migrated to India continued to call themselves Parsis because that was the name by which they had been known in their mother country Iran.'

Voluminous evidence (oral and documentary) was led including that even in the 14th century the word 'Parsi' was used in Iran in connection with the Zoroastrians of that country. In the three Colophons[2] recorded by one Mehervan Kaikhusru in his books, he had stated that he was a Parsi priest and that he came from Persia to India on the invitation from India. In each of the three Colophons, the author (Mehervan Kaikhusru) described himself as a 'priest of the Parsi caste' – and from the context it was clear that this was with reference to the Zoroastrians of Iran.

It was also in evidence that scholar and rights activist Maneckji Hataria in the 19th century had written letters to the Prime Minister of Iran, to the Governor of Yezd, and to a Minister of the King of Iran (between the years 1858 to 1862) – referring to Zoroastraians in Iran as 'Parsis'. Besides in a book on Avesta published in 1864 the author had used the word 'Parsi' only for the Persians in Iran professing the Zoroastrain faith in which he referred to the Zoroastrians of Iran as 'Parsis'.

In 1843, Rev. John Wilson the Christian missionary whose proselytising activities resulted in the conversion of three Parsi

---

2 Postscripts to the text written by the author himself.

youths, also wrote a book on the 'Parsi Religion as contained in the Zend Avesta', where he spoke of the 'Parsis of India' and the 'Parsis of Persia!'

In 1884, Dosabhai Framji Karaka in his *History of the Parsis*, the author had used the word Parsi for the Zoroastrians of Persia, and he referred to the Parsis of both India and the Persia. In a passage from page 244 of the book, the census figure of 1878 was mentioned and this passage set out the number of people professing different religions, and George Curzon (later Lord Curzon), used the word 'Parsi' as describing a religion and in the same sense as the other words used by him in that passage such as Mohammedans, Jews, Hindus etc. After he had stayed in Persia for about six months, George Curzon used the word 'Parsis' synonymously with the people of Iran who professed the Zoroastrian religion. All this has been noted and studiously recorded in the exhaustive judgment of Justice N.A. Mody.

Justice Mody also quoted from Napier Malcolm's book *Five years in a Persian Town*, A.V. William Jackson's *Persia: Past and Present* and Dr Edward William West's *Sacred Books of the East*, Sir Percy Skyes' *The History of Persia* and from Lord Curzon's *Persia and the Persian Question* and showed how the the word Parsi was used for the people of Iran who professed the Zoroastrian religion.

Evidence of a *Firman* issued by the the Shah of Iran in October 1906 was also produced in evidence in which the Shah abolished the cattle and pasture tax being levied on the Zoroastrians of Iran, who were described in the Firman as 'Parsis'!

Justice Mody then referred to dictionary meanings of the word 'Parsi' and noted:

That in Heim's Persian-into-English Dictionary published in 1934 the word 'Parsi' meant a 'fire-worshipper'.

That Murray's Dictionary (1909) Vol. VII, as well as the *Oxford English Dictionary* equated the word 'Parsi' with the religion

'Zoroastrianism', as regards which the Judge observed: 'that the first thing to be noted is that neither of the two dictionaries specifically mentions that the word is not applicable to the Zoroastraians of Iran'; and the judge then went on to add that the evidence on record before him showed that at least for the last hundred years 'the word 'Parsi' was used in Iran in respect of Zoroastrians as distinguished from other religionists like Muslims, Christians, Jews etc.' The Judge, after setting out all oral and documentary evidence, in great detail then recorded his conclusion:

'On this evidence I have not the slightest hesitation in concluding that the word "Parsi" was used long prior to 1936 as meaning Zoroastrians both of India and of Iran and that it was so used both in India and in Iran. As a matter of fact it was so understood not only before 1936 but even before the Act of 1865. I may state, though it is not relevant, that it has been so understood even after the passing of the said Act of 1936. On this evidence I unhesitatingly come to the conclusion that the word "Parsi" as used in the Act includes not only the Parsi Zoroastrians of India but also the Zoroastrians of Iran.'

The suit by the Irani Zoroastrian plaintiff against the Irani Zoroastrian defendant under the Parsi Marriage and Divorce Act, 1936 was then heard and duly decreed.

There was no appeal from this judgment and decree - even though the Parsi Anjuman of Bombay had separately applied to be heard and had appeared through counsel before Justice Mody – and this is so recorded in the judgment. No member of the Parsi Anjuman in Bombay appealed to a Division Bench of the Court challenging or questioning the judgment of the Single Judge delivered on contest and after detailed evidence and argument.

The decision in Irani vs. Irani establishes as conclusively as possible that the word 'Parsi', far from having a racial meaning, as mentioned by Justice Davar (in his 1908 Judgment in the Petit

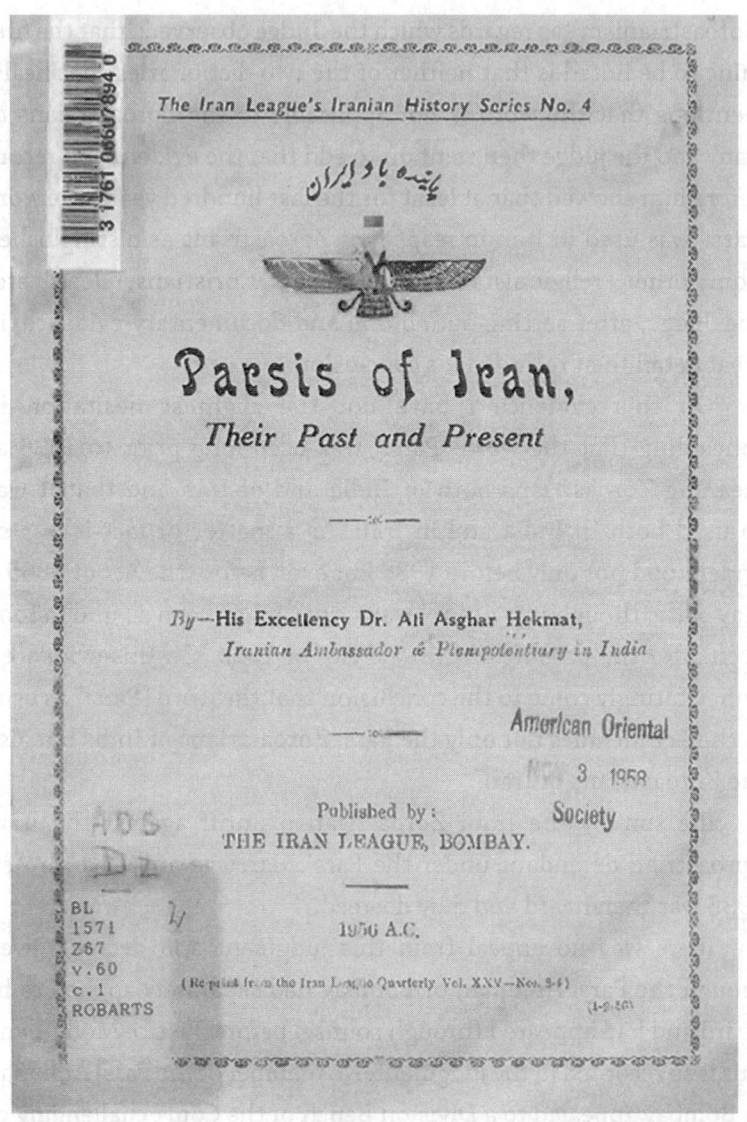

Parsis of Iran by Dr Ali Asghar Hekmat published by the Iran League, Bombay in 1956

Case), and as also observed by Lord Phillimore (in the Privy Council in Saklat v. Bella 1925) – meant, and only meant, a person professing the Zoroastrian religion – whether in Iran or in India.

25
IS ZOROASTRIANISM
A MONOTHEISTIC RELIGION?

Zarathustra boldly preached of one Supreme Being, Ahura Mazda, Lord of Life
and Wisdom, who is united with Asha, Truth and Cosmic order.
—The Gathas of Zarathushtra, Piloo Nanavutty

This was a much-debated subject in the late 1800s and early 1900s. Parsis having forgotten their ancient religion were living as a tribe amongst the Hindus and following their customs. Through the translation of the Gathas in the late 18th century, Parsis learnt that their religion was a monotheistic religion which believed in one God, Ahura Mazda.

Having lived amongst the Hindus for over 1300 years the Parsis had adopted many of their religious customs. Towards the end of the 18th century noted Indologist Sir William Jones reported similarities between Sanskrit, Greek and Latin. This prompted scholars to translate the Gathas or the holy book of the Parsis.

In 1860, Martin Hauge, who was a professor in Sanskrit at Poona Government College, first translated two volumes of the Gathas. He was assisted by Dastur Hoshang Jamaspji, High Priest of the Deccan and of the Poona Agiary. He argued that Zarathusthra taught a pure, ethical monotheism.

Lawrence Mills an Avestan scholar in his book, writes:

'It is no longer doubted that we have in the Avesta essentially the religion which prevailed in Persia when Cyrus came into contact with the Jews. The Gathas form the most difficult part of the Avesta as well as the oldest and most important. And this circumstance induced Dr Mills, during a period of ten years, to devote unusual attention to them'. From Professor Dr Eugen William of Jena, April 1888. (Our Own Religion in Ancient Persia by Lawrence Mills)

Dastur Hoshang Jamaspji, High Priest of the Deccan

The London Athenaum of 12 April 1884 described Lawrence Mills as, 'Mr Mills is considered at present the best authority on the true interpretation of the ancient Gathas.'

Lawrence Mills explains the concept of monotheism in one of his lectures, *Our Own Religion in Ancient Persia*, Page 4 'First of all He is Supreme, and therefore One. ...There can be but one 'Greatest of the Gods who made the others, with the earth and yon heaven, who made man and amenity for him. The good and morally Supreme Ahura is exalted as the only real God in our modern sense of the term, but He was One in adoration as well as in definition, supreme because His 'goodness makes Him great.'

Monotheism is what Dadabhoy Naoroji refers to when he says, 'The Parsee Religion is for all, and not for any particular nation or people.' This is what Rabindranath Tagore refers to in his essay, "The Prophet", in *The Religion of Man*. 'Zoroaster was the first man, we know who gave a definitely moral character and direction to religion and at the same time preached the doctrine of monotheism.'

Dr Irach J.S. Taraporewala translated the Gathas in his book *The Divine Songs of Zarathustra*, in which he writes, 'The place of Zarathustra amongst the prophets is unique. He was born not merely to teach and uplift the Iranian race so many thousands of years ago, but his message was meant for all humanity and for all ages. For Zarathustra was not only the prophet of Iran, but He was the world teacher, and this message is the eternal teaching of Truth, Love and Service. His message has a very special value for humanity.'

Martin Hauge

Eckehard Kulke in his book *The Parsis of India*, page 93, writes, 'the actual incentive for a religious revival came from the side of Christianity.' 'Since 1825 the Parsis in Bombay found themselves exposed to increasing criticism from the Christian missionaries.' 'They were trying to represent Parsism as a natural religion because it allegedly worshipped natural elements.' He says 'Parsism was accused of dualism...the majority of the Parsis subsequently professed a strict monotheism, which still represents the predominant religious doctrine among the Parsis today.'

Dadabhoy Naoroji had lamented about the level of education of the priests in his talk on the *Religion of the Parsis*. Kulke similarly writes 'it came to be recognized that Parsism would only have a chance of survival, if the priest's level of education was drastically raised...just so that they could recite prayers and present an intellectual exegesis of the holy scriptures.' To this purpose, the Mulla Feroze Madrasa was founded and here K.R. Cama, member of one of the wealthiest Parsi families in Bombay acquired the scientific methodology for doing research on the Avesta and Pahlavi literature. The Parsee Iranistics studies founded by K.R. Cama were pursued further by Dastur

Dr Irach JS Taraporewala

Peshotan Sanjana, Kavasji Kanga, J.J. Modi, G.K. Nariman, S.K. Hodiwala, M.N. Dhalla, S. Bharucha, T. Anklesaria and others.

*****

In the 1918 *Dastur Hoshang Memorial Volume*, Sheriarji Dadabhai Bharucha, one of the first students of K.R. Cama and member of the Expert Committee on Religion in *Petit vs Jeejeebhoy* wrote an article titled 'Is Zoroastrianism preached to all mankind or to one particular race?'

He writes.

'This is an interesting question which has lately engrossed the minds of the Parsi community. The late Ervad Tahrumas Dinshaw Anklesaria has collected in a Gujerati pamphlet, evidence, both direct and indirect, from Zoroastrian writings to prove that the Zoroastrian Religion enjoins the admission of all men into its fold.'

He quotes from various passages of the Yasna and the Rivayat and concludes:

'In the Avesta the tie of religious connection is considered therein superior to all other connections even family connections, and therefore it would be unZoroastrian and erroneous on the part of true Zoroastrians to look down, on conceited pride of blood, upon aliens, who may, out of sincere conviction and faith, wish to embrace their good religion, and seek to be admitted as members of the community.'

In short, Zoroastrianism is a monotheistic religion meant for all mankind; that Zoroastrian religion not only permits but enjoins conversion. Conversion is a tenet of the religion.

26
PARSIS TRY TO TRACE
THEIR ROOTS TO PERSIA

When the Good Mind came to me and asked:
"What wouldst thou choose?" Before Thy Fire in veneration, I replied:
"So far as it is in my power, I shall cherish the gift of Righteousness".
—Ushtavaiti Gatha Yasna 43, 9

Parsis in India learnt about their religion when their sacred book, the Gathas, had been translated from the original Avesta language to Gujarati. Having started as poor farmers, involvement in trade with the Chinese made them grow into an affluent society. They were now looking to reclaim their roots with Iran which they had recently become aware of. The Ilm-e-Khshnoom, a mystical movement founded in Persia, gained popularity. The theosophist movement also found favour with the orthodox sections. The Parsis were seriously thinking of leaving India and settling en mass at some other destination. They looked down on their past, and found the intermixing, especially with the low caste Dubras, embarrassing. They tried to create a new identity for themselves. This was an identity of having Pure Persian blood.

In 1905, the Ilm-e-Khshnoom, the Parsi mystical movement, was started by Behramshaw Shroff. They belived in reincarnation, no intermarriage for men and women, vegetarianism, spiritual vibrations and were heavily influenced by theosophy. In 1875, a young Parsi named Behramsha Shroff left Surat for Peshawar. On

ZOROASTRIANISM IN THE LIGHT OF KHSHNOOM

BOOKS FOR SALE

	Rs. a. p.
1. Zarthoshti Ilm-e-Khshnoom, Series No. I: Khshnoom the Key to unlock Zoroastrianism by the late Mr. Beramshah Navroji Shroff..	0 12 0
2. Zarthoshti Ilm-e-Khshnoom, Series No. II: Rationale of Construction of Sudreh by the late Mr. Beramshah Navroji Shroff	1 8 0
3. Khyaal on the above subject by Kaikhushru B. Jamina ..	0 2 0
4. Khshnoom Nikiz-e-Vehdin (Vols. I and II) by Dr. Framroze Sorabji Chinivala, B.A., L. M. & S., Ophthalmic Surgeon (with Charts of Iran's History and Cosmogenesis) (Authoritative Works of Reference on Khshnoom the only Master-Key to the Avesta and Pahlavi). 1st Volume deals with general outline of the Zarthoshti Religion and miraculous events of Zarathushtra's Life. 2nd Volume treats of Ahuramazda and Ameshaspends and Cosmogenesis of Spiritual Realms of Nature .. per vol.	10 0 0
4a. Four big Charts of Cosmogenesis in the Light of Khshnoom (Cloth lined) (for big halls and libraries)	1 8 0
5. Pazend Prayers, Series No. II: Pazend Setayash ba maeni by Ervad Phiroze S. Masani, M.A., LL.B., Solicitor	1 8 0
6. Pazend Prayers, Series No. III: Pazend Nirang ba maeni by Ervad Phiroze S. Masani, M.A., LL.B., Solicitor ..	1 8 0
• 7. Pazend Ashirvad (Gujerati, English and Sanskrit) by Ervad Phiroze S. Masani, M.A., LL.B., Solicitor ..	0 4 0
8. 101 Names of The Great One with correct pronunciation and introduction and meaning by Ervad Phiroze S. Masani, M.A., LL.B., Solicitor	0 1 0
9. Zarthoshti Fasli Javedan Panchang	0 4 0
10. Graphic Chart of Zarthoshti Fasli months in relation to the 12 Signs of the Zodiac with Gahambars	0 2 0
11. Five Has of Gathas (in correct pronunciation)	0 4 0
12. Khshnoom Harmala, No. I: Rationale of Construction of Kushti by Dr. Jehangir Merwanji Pavri, M.B., B.S ..	0 2 0
13. Khshnoom Harmala, No. II: Import of Gehsarna Ceremony with special reference to the 9 principles of human constitution by Dr. Framroze Sorabji Chinivala. (Very interesting booklet giving idea of the body being modelled out from soul's spiritual darkness for being transformed into its lustre)	0 6 0
14. Nam-Gravan, i.e., Name-remembering of Great Mazdayasnan Kings and Heroes of Ancient Iran by Ervad Phiroze S. Masani	0 2 0

Can be had from Parsi Vegetarian and Temperance Society,
124, Dadysett House, Cawasji Patel Street, Fort, Bombay.

Books on Khshnoom were avidly read in the early 1900s

the way he met a caravan led by members of the Saheb-e-Dilan, whom he accompanied to their home in the mountains. Here he gained an intimate knowledge of their religious practices which followed a mystic aspect of the teachings of Zarathustra. Upon his return to India, he gathered a following from among the Parsi Community who called themselves Khshnoomists after 'Khshnoom', or spiritual ecstasy, that they believed were embodied in their prayers and ceremonies.

If any movement was considered fashionable in the early 20th century, it was theosophy. The movement originated in New York in 1875, under the leadership of Madame H.P. Blavatsky and an American officer-turned journalist, Colonel Olcott. The movement shifted its headquarters to Adyar in Madras after 1878. Theosophists preached a brand of religious universalism. They also pursued the possibility of communication with the spirit world, a point reformers ridiculed relentlessly. Dastur Dhalla lamented the rise of theosophy amongst Parsis, 'the growing fondness for occult mystery, the strong passion for the marvellous and the pursuit after the visionary and impracticable, the leaning towards the ascetic virtues, do not augur well for the community.'

'Parsi orthodoxy was so closely associated with theosophy that reformists treated the two as inseparable' (Dhalla, *Zoroastrian Theology*, 366). The key figure was J.J. Vimadalal, the orthodox lawyer who led the case against Bella, and who was also a leader- and demigod-of the Bombay Theosophists. He was President of the Bombay Theosophical Society from 1909–1912.

Fighting theosophy was one of the aims of the Iranian Association which was headed by Homi Bhabha. The Journal of the Iranian Association declared that the theosophical interpretation of Zoroastrianism had distorted the religion into something unrecognizable. 'Parsi theosophists were no more Zoroastrian than we are Confucian.' The theosophists endorsed vegetarianism and

FIGURE 7.5. "When the Parsis regain Iran, their ancient Motherland, Sir Jamsetjee Jejeebhoy Baronet will be Shah-in-Shah Jamshid sitting on the Persian Throne of the Shahs of Persia."
Source: "New Year Dreams – No. 1," *HP* (6 September 1925), 6. © The British Library

Jamshedji Jeejeebhoy will be made Shah of Iran when Parsis regain their ancient motherland (Hindi Punch)

An advertisment for travel to Iran and Iraq in the Iran League Quarterly, *1933*

reincarnation, neither of which had any place in Zoroastrian belief or practice. The *Journal of the Iranian Association* (October 1912) commented snidely on Psychism which the theosophists believe in 'We have heard stories of silly Parsi women "shutting themselves up in darkened rooms and bandaging their eyes" in order, I suppose, to develop the third eye.'

There was also talk of creating a Parsi Colony outside India. They toyed with several options in 1905 ('The Economic Aspect of the Proposed Parsi Colony Out of India', *The Parsi* 1:2 February 1905 pp. 43–44). The first of these was to start a colony in East Africa. Another possibility was Sind, in India's Far West. A Parsi gentleman, B.D. Patel published a scheme in two issues of the *Rast Gofter*. His rationale was that 'as content as the Parsis were in India at the moment, they were still aliens in India. If the British left India, the Parsis could suddenly become vulnerable. The creation of their own colony would allow them not to rely on any hosts good favor for their wellbeing' (B.D. Patel, 'The Question of the Day, Do we need a Colony And Can We Found One?' *The Parsis* 1:6 June 1905).

Finally, there were fantasies of return to Persia. *The Hindi Punch* mused that leading Parsis may populate the Persian Cabinet or even occupy the throne.

The claim of being Persian became literalized, radicalized, and celebrated. Parsis wanted to create a more exclusive, radicalized identity. The notion of Persian-ness constituted the Parsi sense of self.

Externally, asserting racial purity meant restricting blood flow of non-Parsi blood at different points – adoption, concubinage, and intermarriage, concubines and their children, servants and slaves and low caste Hindus (Dubras).

There was now an internal cleansing that stigmatized Parsis that had gone native on the fringes of the Indian Empire.

27
CHILD MARRIAGE IN PARSI COMMUNITY

Some things are not fit for children – marriage is one of them.
—Unicef slogan

Child marriage was not an ancient Parsi custom. It was a Hindu custum transposed into the Parsi community. Child or infant marriage triggered lengthy debates among the members of the Parsi Law Commission in 1850. The British opposed it but the Parsis said that it was too ingrained to ban. Further, child marriage gave parental control, on who the child could marry, and it also reduced the likelihood of premarital pregnancies, which was socially stigmatized and economically problematic in colonial Parsi social life. Child marriage continued well into early 1900s. As Parsi boys and girls were already married by the age of six or seven all children born of the Parsi girl, legitimate or illegitimate, were Parsis. Men had a problem of having their illegitimate children, accepted as Parsis. As discussed earlier, morals were lax, and the sanctity of the marital tie did not exist.

In 1889, there was a widely talked about case, *Peshotan Hormusji Dastur vs Meherbai* (1889). The adult plaintiff husband argued that his 1868 marriage was invalid; he was only seven at the time of the wedding, whereas his wife was six years old. The parties had not consummated the marriage. The Bombay High Court judge, a Briton, blamed regressive Parsi practices. He failed to apply the very stringent legal test required to prove the existence of a custom. To be recognized by law, a custom had to be (i) ancient, (ii) invariable, and (iii) not repugnant to the general law (which often meant British sensibilities). Few attempts to prove a custom, according to this test succeeded in court.

The practice of child marriage continued well into the early 20th century. The Parsi priest M.N. Dhalla, recounted in his autobiography that he was 'married in 1881, at age 6 to a 5-year-old delicate beauty.'

Even in 1936, when child marriages were prohibited by law, conservative Parsis continued to push for influence over their children's marriages. They tried to prevent their children from contracting love marriages as teenagers. They wanted parental consent to prevent their teenage children from eloping. As Parsi advocate M.M. Bhesania wrote in 1928, 'requiring parental consent until the age of twenty-one would prevent the risk of impulsive or rash union in the heat of youth which can ordinarily be expected to be moved by considerations other than those of permanent and consistent conjugal harmony and domestic consistency.' He also wanted provisions invalidating any attempts by their children to convert to another religion and marry.

Child marriage being an accepted custom, Parsi boys and girls were married sometimes even at the age of three. Once the children grew up, many found their marriage incompatible. Bigamy, forced prostitution, and adultery were common. Children born outside wedlock were not an aberration and accepting them into the religion was recognized as a custom in 1905 in Petit vs Jeejeebhoy.

28
ANCIENT CUSTOM FAVOURS ACCEPTANCE

Expansion is life, contraction is death. Love is life, and hatred is death.
—Swami Vivekananda, Reply to the Calcutta Address, CW vol. 4

Questions and answers on religion were recorded in court in Saklat vs Bella. It is stated not to give up the illegitimate child of a Parsi mother with a Doorwand (alien in religion). To do so is a sin.

Transcription

Questions and answers on religion, filed before Commissioner in Saklat vs Bella.

Question XXII

There is a Baste Kustian-that is to say wearing sacred girdle round her waist-widow without a husband and she had sexual intercourse with a Doorwand (Alien in Religion). She conceived and gave birth to a child. On the death of the child, together with what(living) person's name, it's own name be recited (in prayers)

Answer XXII

If a 'Baste Kustian (wearing a sudreh and kusti) woman, by reason of having sexual intercourse with a 'Doorwand' (alien in religion) conceived and gave birth to a child, the name 'Adar Cheher' should

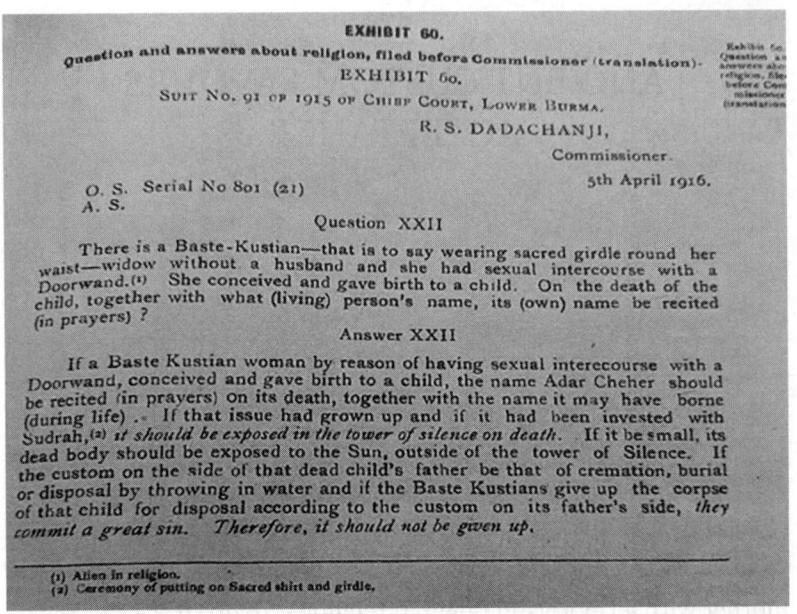

EXHIBIT 60.

Question and answers about religion, filed before Commissioner (translation).

EXHIBIT 60.

Suit No. 91 of 1915 of Chief Court, Lower Burma.

R. S. DADACHANJI,

Commissioner.

O. S. Serial No 801 (21)
A. S.

5th April 1916.

Question XXII

There is a Baste-Kustian—that is to say wearing sacred girdle round her waist—widow without a husband and she had sexual intercourse with a Doorwand.[1] She conceived and gave birth to a child. On the death of the child, together with what (living) person's name, its (own) name be recited (in prayers) ?

Answer XXII

If a Baste Kustian woman by reason of having sexual intercourse with a Doorwand, conceived and gave birth to a child, the name Adar Cheher should be recited (in prayers) on its death, together with the name it may have borne (during life) . If that issue had grown up and if it had been invested with Sudrah,[2] *it should be exposed in the tower of silence on death.* If it be small, its dead body should be exposed to the Sun, outside of the tower of Silence. If the custom on the side of that dead child's father be that of cremation, burial or disposal by throwing in water and if the Baste Kustians give up the corpse of that child for disposal according to the custom on its father's side, *they commit a great sin. Therefore, it should not be given up.*

(1) Alien in religion.
(2) Ceremony of putting on Sacred shirt and girdle,

Questions and answers about religion to expert committee on religion

be recited (in prayers) on its death, together with the name it may have borne (during life). If that issue had grown up and if it had been invested with a sudreh and kusti (on its death), it should be exposed to the Tower of Silence. If it be small its body should be exposed to the sun, outside the Tower of Silence. If the custom on the side of the dead child's father be that of cremation, burial or disposal by throwing it in water and if the Baste Kustians give up the corpse of that child for disposal according to the customs of its father's side, they commit a great sin. Therefore, it should not be given up.' (EXHIBIT 60)

*****

In 1830, a new *bandobast* (resolution) was made by the Parsi Panchayat against the practice of Parsi men and women having extra marital relationships with both Parsis and aliens, and their resulting children being accepted into Zoroastrian society.

In 1870, some Parsi women registered themselves as prostitutes and obtained a license under the Contagious Disease Act. This caused an uproar in the community and the Parsi Panchayat wanted to pass a resolution to put them and their children out of the community. Zoroastrian scholars and intelligent members of society protested against this.

K.R. Cama (the Avesta Scholar) wrote a letter to the Parsi Panchayat, in which he said, 'In the Avesta, about different kinds of punishment awarded, I have not found the punishment of turning persons out of the religion'. Many respected Zoroastrian gentlemen sent a letter of protest to the Parsi Panchayat, which was published in the Jam-e-Jamshed on 5 July 1870, protesting the attempt to outcast prostitutes and their children.

This letter establishes the practice prevalent at that time of accepting the children of Parsi prostitutes into the community.

'The Parsi prostitute crisis of 1870 highlighted anxieties over intercommunal sex'. See 'Morality among the Parsis 29 june 1870 Times of India cited in 'Patel and Paymaster', Vol. 441).

The Parsi Panchayat sought the opinion of the three priests on this matter, Jamaspji Dastur Minocher Jamaspasana, Sorabjee Rustumji Mullafram, and Peshotan Dastur Behramji Sanjana. They replied, if their navjote is done they should be admitted.

The Iranian Association in its letter of objection to the Parsi Panchayat writes, 'In page 7 of your Trust Deed of 1884, in which there is a clear recital showing that children of Parsi prostitutes (who may be presumed, in some cases, to be children of alien fathers) have been considered to be entitled to claim the benefit of Zoroastrian Trust properties to a certain extent (see Letter of Iranian Assossiation to BBP, p. 198).

The Parsi Marriage and Divorce Act of 1936 has a special provision of granting divorce to a Parsi woman, if her husband – 'forces her into prostitution.' In the Parsi Marriage Act of 1865 sex with a prostitute was not considered bigamy.

Prostitutes and their issues were very much a part of the Parsi community till 1936 when laws were made to curb such activity.

Children of Parsi women as they were born 'of a Parsi woman's womb' were always accepted as Parsis. We see this in the report of the 'Mazgaon Dock Navjotes'. The experts on religion gave a similar interpretation. Even an illegitimate child of a Parsi woman (basti kustian) should not be given up. It is a sin.

It was the men who had a problem of having their illegitimate children accepted. Justice Davar in the Petit vs Jeejeebhoy case became the champion of these illegitimate children of Parsi men and the third clause of his obiter dictum gave Parsi men a quasi-legal right to have their illegitimate children accepted.

The Special Marriage Act of 1954 allows the spouses to maintain their individual religion. It is only now that the question of acceptance of the legitimate children of intermarried men and women arose.

Though no discussion or decision was officially taken on this, men automatically took the Justice Davar obiter dictum which accepted their illegitimate children to mean their legitimate children were also accepted (Cartoon from *Hindi Punch*, p. 30).

However, that which was traditional for women from ancient times, that which was enjoined in the religious books, was suddenly unacceptable when a woman could legally have an interfaith marriage and have legitimate children in this marriage. At the same time, her illegitimate children with alien or Parsi men are accepted. There is no mention of exclusion of intermarried women's children anywhere in our religious books nor has this issue been argued in court.

Cornelia Sorabji had to go to court to be declared a 'person'

There is no custom or legal or religious reason for accepting the children of men in interfaith marriages and rejecting the children of women in interfaith marriages.

Conversion being a tenet of the religion, there is no justification in singling out the children of intermarried girls for non-acceptance into the fold. However, acceptance of the children of our intermarried men and women is not conversion, but Initiation into the faith of their choice. Conversion means they had professed another religion earlier.

The Petit vs Jeejeebhoy 1908, and Saklat vs Bella 1924, cases were closely reported in the press. However, no decision was given in the former and no injunction against Bella in the latter. Neither of these two cases and the observations made in them has been referred to in the ammended Parsi Marriage and Divorce Act of 1936. But a clause was added in the grounds for divorce 'that the defendant has ceased to be a Parsi (by conversion to another religion).'

The Petit vs Jeejeebhoy and Saklat vs Bella cases are pre independence. These judgements were made at a time when a woman was not legally considered a 'person'.

Cornelia Sorabji qualified as a lawyer in 1892 but was not allowed to practice law because 'she was not a person'. The term 'he' did not include the term 'she'. The Calcutta and Patna High Courts, while dealing with the enrollment of women held that they were not included in the term 'persons' and rejected their application. Finally in 1929, the Privy Council in a one-line ruling expressed the obvious, 'The word person may include members of both sexes and to those who ask why the word should include female the obvious answer is "why not".' Cornelia Sorabji was the first woman to be enrolled in the courts in the Allahabad High Court in India in 1929 and she was the first to be enrolled anywhere in the world under the 'person' clause, ('Pretty Ones' an article published on the 125th anniversary of the Allahabad High Court).

29
PARSI REFORMER'S LETTER PROTESTING THE OUTCASTING OF PROSTITUTES

We worship the souls of the holy men and women, born at any time, whose consciences struggle, or will struggle, or have struggled, for the good.
—Khorda Avesta, Ch XIII

Khurshedji Rustomji Cama was one of the most famous Parsi reformers of the 19th century. In 1849, he joined a trading house in Calcutta and then travelled to London where he met Dadabhoy Naoroji. Cama, like Naoroji, was a social and religious reformist, concerned with educational reform and the position of women. In 1864 he founded the, 'Zarthoshti Din No Kohl Karnari Mandli (Society for the promotion of researches in the Zoroastrian religion). In 1866, he published Zarthoshti Abhyas' (Zoroastrian Studies) in 12 volumes. James Darmesteter and A.V. Williams Jackson called him 'le Dastur laique'. In his early life, Cama had been influenced by the Christian missionary activity of John Wilson, who wrote a deatailed book on the Parsi Religion. John Wilson persuaded Cama to attend services at the St. Thomas Cathedral. Later Cama would attend small discussion groups on the Christian religion. The missionaries dubbed the teachings of Zoroaster as nature worship and accused Zoroastians of dualism. Three Parsi youths converted to Chritianity and there was a major uproar in the community. Cama later resolved to strengthen the community against such incursions through learning the religion.

Pioneer Parsee Zend and Avestic Scholars—Mr. K. R. Kama and his Pupils

Sitting, left to right :—(1) Ervad Tehmuras Dinshaw Anklesaria, 1840–1903 ; (2) Ervad Sheriarji Dadabhoy Bharucha, 1843–1915 ; (3) Mr. Khurshedji Rustomji Kama, 1831–1909 ; (4) Ervad Kavasji Edulji Kanga, 1839–1904 ; (5) Ervad Edulji Kershaspji Antia, 1842–1913.
Standing :—(1) Ervad Jamsetji Dadabhoy Nadirshaw ; 1846–1931 (2) Ervad Khurshedji Minocherji Kateli, 1826–1902.

K.R. Cama and his first students at his school for Zend and Avesta studies

He was an influential figure in the Asiatic Society and had written many religious articles in its journals. The K.R. Cama Oriental Institute was established in 1916 in his memory. Cama's son Rustomji was married to Madam Bhikaji Cama. K.R. Cama set up the first school for Zend and Avestan studies and his first students included Tehmuras Dinshaw Anklesaria, Ervad Sheriarji Dadabhoy Bharucha, Ervud Kavasji Edulji Kanga, Ervad Edulji Kershaspji Antia, Ervad Jamsetji Dadabhoy Nadirshaw, and Ervad Khurshedji Minocherji Kateli. He wrote extensively on religion, notable among them was *Pegambar Asho-Zarathust ne Janmara no Eheval* (A Life of Zoroastra based on Avestan sources). *The Collected Works of K.R. Cama* were printed by and edited by J.J. Modi in the K.R. Cama Memorial Volume, 1900.

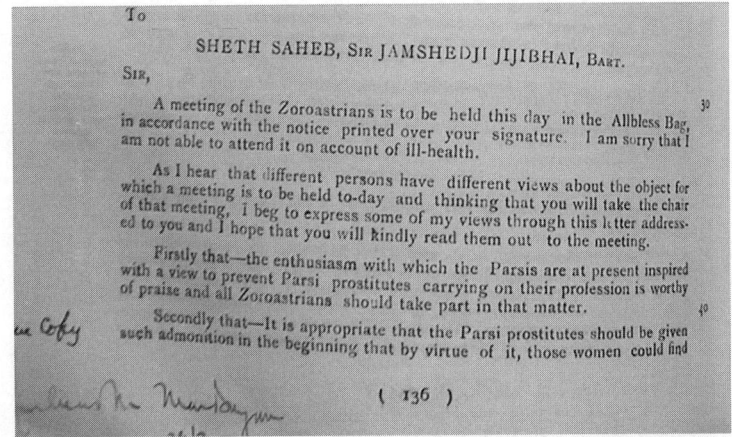

Letter of K.R. Cama to Jamshedji Jeejeebhoy objecting to outcasting of prostitutes

Transcription of Sheth Saheb, Sir Jamshedji Jijibhai, Bart

Sir,

A meeting of the Zoroastrians is to be held this day in the Allbless Bag, in accordance with the notice printed over your signature. I am sorry that I am not able to attend on account of ill health.

As I hear that different persons have different views about the object for which a meeting is to be held to-day and thinking that you will take the chair of that meeting, I beg to express some of my views through this letter addressed to you and I hope that you will kindly read them out to the meeting.

Firstly that—the enthusiasm with which the Parsis are at present inspired with a view to prevent Parsi prostitutes carrying on their profession is worry of praise and all Zoroastrians should take part in that matter.

Secondly that—It is appropriate that the Parsi prostitutes should be given such admonition in the beginning that by virtue of it, those women could find out their mistaken course and take a warning for returning to the right path, cause it is better and meritorious to reform every erring soul prior to punishing him.

out their mistaken course and take a warning for returning to the right path,
because it is better and meritorious to reform every erring soul prior to punishing him.

III. In the few authorities that are preserved in the Avesta as regards
the kind of punishment inflicted upon and the nature of expiation and religious
penitence required of the persons who would commit different kinds of offences
in olden times, I have not found the punishment of or expiation by keeping
away the adulterous man or woman from religious buildings as required by the
representationists.

IV. In the subject matter available in the Avesta about causing different
kinds of punishments awarded to and expiations made by offending persons in
proportion to their offences, I have not anywhere found the punishment of
turning persons out of the religion, fixed even for any kind of offence,
whatsover.

V. If by hasty action, these women are removed from (the fold of) the
religion, prevention will be also set up against exposing their corpses in
Dokhmas whereby they (their relations) will not but be obliged to bury or
cremate their corpses; whereas the burial or cremation of corpses is not only
forbidden in our Avesta but a duty against its prevention is enjoined and no
informed Zoroastrian should be ignorant of it.

VI. Great offenders too, were considered as having remained in the
Zoroastrian faith only, because after the death of persons committing the
" Tanafur " offence which is called a great offence, it is stated in the Avesta
that the prayers or mourning exactly similar to those observed after the death
of a righteous man, should be observed (in their case).

VII. I, therefore, humbly request that there should be great deliberation
before passing any resolution in the meeting held to-day and that care should
be taken in using words to the effect that the Parsi prostitutes getting a license
under the Contagious Diseases Act are put out of the Zoroastrian faith of or
words closely or remotely akin to that sense.

VIII. If the meeting would feel it urgent to pass the final resolutions
this day only, I hope that it will be satisfied with passing a resolution to the
effect that those women have been removed from society and intercourse of
with any other appropriate resolution of that nature.

I hope that the meeting of the Zoroastrians to be held this day will kindly
pay attention to some of my aforesaid views.

Bombay, Dated 3rd July 1870.

I am, Sir,

Your humble servant,

K. R. CAMA.

(137)

III. In the few authorities that are preserved in the Avesta
as regards kind of punishment inflicted upon and the nature of
expiation and religious penitence required of the persons who
would commit different kinds of offences in olden times, I have
not found the punishment of or expiation by keeping away the
adulterous man or woman from religious buildings as required
by the representationists.

IV. In the subject matter available in the Avesta about causing
different kinds of punishment awarded to and expiation made
by offending persons in proportion to their offences I have not

anywhere found the punishment of turning persons out of the religion, fixed even for any kind of offence, whatsoever.

V. If by hasty action, these women are removed from the fold of the religion, prevention will be also set up against exposing their corpses in Dokhmas whereby they (their relations) will not but be obliged to bury or cremate their corpses; whereas the burial or cremation of corpses is not only forbidden in our Avesta but a duty against its prevention is enjoined and no informed Zoroastrian should be ignorant of it.

VI. Great offenders too, were considered as having remained in the Zoroastrian faith only, because after the death of persons committing the "Tanafur " offence, which is called a great offence, it is stated in the Avesta, that the prayers or mourning exactly similar to those observed after the death of a righteous man, should be observed (in their case)

VII. I, therefore, humbly request that there should be great deliberation before passing any resolution in the meeting held to-day and that care should be taken in using words to the effect that the Parsi prostitutes getting a license under the Contagious Diseases Act are put out of the Zoroastrian faith or words closely or remotely akin to that .

VIII. If the meeting would feel it urgent to pass the final resolution this day only, I hope that it will be satisfied with passing a resolution to the effect that those women have been removed from society and intercourse of with any other appropriate resolution of that nature.

I hope that the meeting of the Zoroastrians to be held this day will kindly pay attention to some of my aforesaid views.

Bombay Dated 3rd July 1870.
I am, Sir, Your humble servant,
K. R. CAMA.

30
DASTUR DHALLA ON
THE SOCIAL PROBLEMS
FACED BY THE COMMUNITY IN 1942

The intoxication of religion makes every man delirious. Socio-religious customs take the place of pure, ethical and devotional faith and turn it into tradition-ridden religion as a result of which men quibble and quarrel constantly.
—The Saga of a Soul, Maneck Nusserwanji Dhalla

In his autobiography *The Saga of a Soul* written in 1942, the high priest of Karachi Dastur Dr Maneck Nusserwanji Dhalla relates his 'Atmakatha', of how a poor priest from an orthodox simple family was selected and fully sponsored by the community to go to Colombia University and study the Zoroastrian Religion under Professor A.V.W. Jackson. He enthralls us with the story of how education changed his views on many aspects of the religion. In his opinion, men and women of the community converting to their spouse's religion before marrying under the Special Marriage Act being a major reason for the decline in the population of the community.

Dhalla writes, 'A correct text of the Avesta had been prepared by Westgrade, Spiegel, and Geldner; its vocabulary had been done by Justi and Bartholomae; its translations by Spigel, Harlez, Darmesteter and Mills, its grammar had been constructed by A V W Jackson. The cuneiform writings of the Achaeminian Kings which had been like a mystery for 2,500 years, were deciphered by

MRS. COOVERBAI MANECKJI DHALLA
BORN : 7-10-1877   DIED : 24-6-1947

DASTUR DR. MANECKJI NUSSERWANJI DHALLA
BORN : 27-9-1875   DIED : 25-5-1956

Dastur Dhalla with his wife, Cooverbai

Grotenfeld and Rawlinson; travellers to the West had discovered the archaeological ruins of Iran; Critical essays were also written in the West.'

The history behind Dhalla's trip to the US is interesting. A report was being prepared on Jamshedji Tata's activities by Shapurji Dorabji Saklatwala. Dastur Dhalla was assisting him. One day, while relaxing in the evening, they decided, all of a sudden, to send Dhalla to Columbia University. Shapurji had met Professor A.V.W. Jackson at one of Jamshedji Tata's parties.

Seven weeks after writing to Jackson, a reply was received welcoming the idea with great enthusiasm. The college fees, boarding and lodging amounted to Rs 300 per month. The Tata family donated Rs 125 a month for three years towards this expense. Khurshedji Cama and Jeevanji Modi appointed a committee to help collect the rest of the funds. The Society for the Furtherance of the Faith of the Zoroastrian Religion and the Zoroastrians of Karachi also contributed to the fund. On 15 May 1905, Dhalla left the shores of Bombay to study under Professor Jackson.

In an interesting anecdote, Dastur Dhalla mentions that students spent an average of 7 to 8 pounds on food. He normally spent 3 to 3.5 pounds and tried to save as much as he could. Professor Jackson soon found out about this and informed the Dhalla that an anonymous donor had written from Bombay to pay him 15 pounds a month. 'This sounded unbelievable, and I refused to accept it,' he writes. Ultimately it came to light that Professor Jackson had made arrangements for the money to be deducted from his own account in favour of his pupil (pp. 107–8).

The Saga of a Soul contains not only the story of the Dastur's life, but also the history of the Parsis of the 20th century. Dhalla was the founder of the Zoroastrian Conference which held annual meetings on the Zoroastrian Religion. He observes quite astutely. 'After the prophets depart their disciples turn everyone into blind followers of the faith. The intoxication of religion makes every man delirious. Socio-religious customs take the place of pure, ethical and devotional faith and turn it into tradition-ridden religion as a result of which men quibble and quarrel constantly. We continue to vent our views through the Parsi press on socio-religious customs. In this era of independence of thought we must remember that in the religious life of the community it is no longer possible to drive everybody with criticism and threats along the same rut like a herd of cattle. Gone are the days when the opinion of society could dictate religious principles. Free choice has taken the place of force. Herodotus, the father of history, wrote of our 2500-year-old ancestors – the Hakaemenians – that they were valiant and courageous in envisaging changing times and circumstances and conditioning their lives according to the country and the age in which they lived.'

'Remember that the ancients had tackled the religious and ceremonial questions that arose in their own days according to light that had prevailed in the past. Those of that day had not done the thinking for all times to come, with injunctions to the future generations to act in strict accordance with them. They alone had not the monopoly to think and had not given the final mandate to acquiesce in all that they had believed'.

Dastur Dhalla lectured extensively on religion in India and abroad. In his lectures he covered the juddin (non Parsi) question, one of the social problems in the Parsi community at that time. Unfortunately, times have changed, but like their ancestors, the Parsis as a community are still debating on the same issues.

Dastur Dhalla writes almost 100 years ago, and his words are equally applicable to our community today:

Through years of burning controversy, this problem of Joodin marriages has on the whole become more confusing and difficult to solve. We have seen at the commencement that this question has not been tackled with the purpose of spreading the good faith or of increasing the dwindling population, hence the value of this has been reduced. Our religion, history and common sense tell us to spread the light of Zoroastrian faith among the unfortunate people.

Lately, such joodin marriages and Navjotes have continued. Since the turn of the century approximately fifteen such marriages have taken place.' 'Apart from that, the Navjote ceremony of the off-springs of Parsis and their non-Parsi mistresses have been performed either publicly or clandestinely.

Freedom of thought and the freedom to worship according to the dictates of conscience are men's precious rights gained during the last century. Since every individual has attained the right of such freedom in equal measure, it remains with society to ensure that the person who wishes to enjoy such privileges should exercise his right in such a manner that he does not encroach upon the rights of his neighbour.

It would be truly regrettable if a new schism is created into our small community but rather than remain within the circle in a state of constant bickering and ill-will and expand all energy on the same problem......those in opposition to the jooddin question should withdraw the resolutions passed by them up to date, because they are one-sided. Despite all their threats, mixed marriages and juddin Navjotes continue to be performed. As far as possible such resolutions will be disregarded as they have been during the last fifteen years.

No one can foretell the effect on future generations. At the moment, until the social atmosphere of the community undergoes a change, it is understandable that, due to the high deathrate, the fall in birth rate, the strength of the community shows a downward trend.

With the blossoming of man's mind through education and science he begins to examine the customs that have been handed down by his forefathers and to evaluate whether they are genuine or faked, good or bad, beneficial or harmful. During the last hundred years, thanks to higher education that has been admitted amongst the masses for the first time in history, there has been a flowering of minds of men and women of our community, and customs are being sifted in the sieve of discussion. During these hundred years there has been a change in the community's habits and mode of living. Feeble customs have been worn away by age and wiped out with knowledge.

It is possible that after decades the community may create an enlightened and educated priest-class and a popular understanding that to spread the good faith and to increase our strength is not only commensurate with the precepts of our religion but also in the interest of our social well-being.

Circumstances weaken a man's conviction and divide his opinions. I have such personal experience of Zoroastrians coming to Karachi from abroad. They would come to visit me and try to convince me about their faith in their religion by their heated discussions regarding the sinfulness in moving about bare headed, in not taking taro, or in not observing the customary taboos. Yet, perchance, should the talk turn to the juddin question, they would profess that it was obligatory to perform the Navjote of children born of mixed parentage, that it was a mandate from Ahura Mazda himself and so on. From that I would surmise that something was amiss and it would gradually be revealed that either they themselves or their close relations had been affected by the problem. When the hand of destiny strikes the greatest of the great, then within the flash of a moment their fierce opinions take a somersault.....The one-time orthodox sheds his conservative ideas and dons the garb of a reformist. Man is a strange creature and his behaviour patterns are stranger still. Life is a versatile tutor and experiences a skilled sculptor.

From my intimate personal experience of the last ten years, I have seen that those who are otherwise very conservative in their views, and who normally oppose tooth and nail the question of proselytizing, even they, when the question affects the children of mistresses kept by their relatives or friends, strangely take the lead in getting such children initiated into the faith.

'So far men have gone out of the community in search of foreign wives and have enjoyed certain privileges. These are now being demanded by Parsi women themselves. Historically man has, from ancient times, in his private and public life enjoyed certain privileges over women. Now, gradually women have begun to voice their feelings and are carrying on a battle against the privileges granted to men and demanding similar rights themselves. Yet, traditionally man believes that what he can hoodwink in his own behaviour, he has the right to suppress in the weaker sex. Mankind has now begun to realize that moral codes applicable to men and women cannot differ. Hence according to this percept, if the Parsi Anjuman made up mainly of men, wish to resolve to stop their women marrying out of the community, they will have to agree to observe the same rule themselves.

Almost a hundred years ago, the high priest of the Parsi community clearly said if men wished to intermarry, they had to allow women the same benefit. His own words express the sentiments of our intermarried girls even today.

31
THE HIGH PRIESTS OF THE COMMUNITY AS PICTURED IN LES PARSIS

So may we be like those making the world progress toward perfection; May Mazda and the Divine Spirits help us and guide our efforts through Truth; For a thinking man is where Wisdom is at home.
—Ahunuvaiti Gatha; Yasna 30, 9

Delphine Menant wrote her book *Les Parsis* on the Zoroastrian communities in India in 1897. The first three chapters were translated from the original French by Ratanbai Ardeshir Framji Vakil, B.A. The entire work was later translated by M.M. Marzban in 1917. "The first part comprises chapters devoted to the civil life of the Parsis, from birth to death, under the customs described by old travellers, and the changes of the present century." "The second part is a treatise on the religious duties of the Parsis. A succinct account is presented on the labour of scholars of the ancient Persians." She takes the reader from the Parsis of ancient Persia to the Parsis in India today.

The date of this book 1917, is important as it was the time of learning, and a time of rediscovering the forgotten connection the Parsis in India had with the Parsis in Persia. It highlights the head priests of the communities as scholars having, studied under foreign savants and authors on books of Religion.

Shams-ul-Ulama Dastur Darat Peshotan Sayanu
A scholar and linguist; Principal of the Jamsetji Jeejeebhoy" Zarthoshti Madressa" (Seminary) since 1899: Fellow of the

Shams-ul-Ulmà Dastur **DÀRÀB** *Dastur* **PESHOTAN SANJANÀ, B.A.**
Present *Dastur* (High-priest) of Wàdiaji's *Shàhanshàhi* Atesh-Beheràm,
in Bombay, since 1899.
(Born on 18th November 1857 A.D.)
A scholar and linguist : Principal of the Sir Jamsetji Jejeebhoy ' Zartboshti Medressa ' (Seminary)
since 1899 : ' Fellow ' of the University of Bombay. Author of : *The Doctrine of the Soul in*
the Avesta : *Next-of-Kin Marriages in Iràn* : *Position of Zoroastrian Women in Remote*
Antiquity. Translator, in English, of : *Zarathushtra in the Gàthàs and in the Classics*, from
Dr. W. Geiger's German work : *The Age of Avesta and Zoroaster*, from Dr. W. Geiger and
von Spiegel's works. Editor of : The Pahlavi *Nirangistàn* and *Minù-i Khrat*·(with notes and
commentaries): The *Dinkart*, (Vols. X to XVI), (with translations into English and Gujarati) :
The Pahlavi *Kàrnàmak-i Artakshir-i Pàpakàn*, (Pahlavi text· with English and Gujarati translations) : Author of a number of Papers, Lectures, and Sermons, in English and Gujarati.

Shams-ul-Ulama Dastur Darab Dastur Peshotan Sanjana, *b. 18 November 1857,*
the high priest of the Wadiaji's Shahanshahi Atesh-Beherum in Bombay, since 1899

University of Bombay. Author of: "The Doctrine of the Soul in the
Avesta": "Next of kin Marriages in Iran", "Position of Zoroastrian
Women in Remote Antiquity". Translator, in English of "Zarathustra
in the Gathas and in the Classics", from Dr.W. Greiger's German
work. 'The Age of Avesta and Zoroaster", from Dr.W.Geiger and
Von Spiegels works. Editor of: "The Pahlavi Nirangistan and Minu-
i-Khrat" (with notes and commentaries): "The Dinkart", (Vols
X-XVI) (with translations into Gujrati and English):"The Pahlavi
Karnamak-I Artakshir-i-Papakan",(Pahlavi text with English and

Gujrati translations): Author of a number of Papers, Lectures, and Sermons, in English and Gujrati. These are Dastur Darab's views on acceptance of people born in another religion and converted to Zoroastrianism as recorded in the court case Saklat vs Bella:

Exhibit 54.

Extract from pages 24-25 of Zarathushtra in the Gathas by Darab Dastur Peshotan Sanjana, filed before Commissioner. EXHIBIT 54 Suit No. 91 of 1915 OF CHIEF COURT, LOWER BURMA.

R. S. DADACHANJI, Commissioner
18th March 1916.

First, it is regarded as a sacred obligation to convert the infidels by means of words and doctrine (Yasna XXVIII, 5). The religion of Zarathushtra is a religion of culture, of spiritual and moral progress and proficiency. It penetrates through all conditions of human life, and it considers every action of life, as for instance, the clearing of the soil, the careful tending of herds, and the cultivation of the fields, from the standpoint of religious duty. Such a religion, or such a philosophy, cannot be confined to a narrow circle; the propagation of it and the conversion of all men to it, are ideas which are at the basis of its very essence. We, accordingly, find complete hymns, as Yasna XXX and XLV, which were evidently intended to be delivered before a numerous audience, and in which Zarathushtra, or one of his friends, expounds the essential points of the new doctrine for the approval of the hearers.

*****

'Ratan Tata asked for Dastur Darab's opinion before converting his wife Susaune to Zoroastrianism. This is Dastur Darab's reply:

Bombay 8 February 1903
Gracious Seth Ratanji Dadabhoy Tata

Respected Sir, we have received your letter dated February 7. I would like to thank you for your gracious invitation to participate in this Navjote ceremony that is going to take place today. For this invitation consider that you have kind feelings for me. Because of certain items, I am sorry that I will not be able to attend the gathering.

You have said in your letter that you had read the public sermon which we have published, and that you are planning to act accordingly. I am very happy to know this.

If a pious man or woman with firm belief is accepted into the Zoroastrian religion and taken into the community, then the Zoroastrian religion has no closed-door policy. This is our humble opinion that we have expressed in our sermon.

Signed
Darab Dastur Peshotanji Sanjana

Shams-ul-Ulema, Dr. Dastur
PESHOTANJI BEHERAMJI SANJANA, M.A., Ph.D.,
Late Dastur of Wadiaji's Shahanshahi Atesh-Beheram, in Bombay.
(Died on 26th December 1898.)
(From a print.)

A 'Fellow' of the University of Bombay, and a Member of the German Oriental Society. Editor of the *Dinkart* (Vols. I to IX), with Pahlavi text, transliteration in Avesta characters: and translations into English and Gujrati: of *Vijirkard-i-Denik*; *Karnamak*, of Ardeshir Babagan. in Pahlavi: and author of a voluminous Pahlavi Grammar.

His works, connected with Pahlavi literature were both numerous and important, all indicating as competent a knowledge of that complicated language as any contemporary scholar possessed.... —
Dr. E. W. West, Editor of the Sacred Books of the East Series.

The Times Press.

Shams-ul-Ulema, Dr Dastur Peshotanji Beheranji Sanjana *(father of Dastur Darab Peshotan Sanjana), d. 26 December 1898, MA, PhD, Late Dastur of Wadiaji's Shahanshahi Atesh-Beheram, in Bombay.*

A 'Fellow' of the University of Bombay, and a member of the German Oriental Society. Editor of the 'Dinkart (Vols I to IX),' with Pahlavi text, transliteration in Avesta characters: and translations into English and Gujrati: of 'Vijirkard-i-Denik;' 'Karnamak of Ardesher Babagan,' in Pahlavi: and author of a voluminous Pahlavi Grammar.

'His works, connected with Pahlavi literature were both numerous and important, all indicating as competent a knowledge of that complicated language as any contemporary scholar possessed....' Dr E.W. West, Editor of the Sacred books of the East Series.

He wrote 'Nirang-i-Zawitdinan', an explanatory treatise, with regard to the kind of ceremonies that should be performed for admission of Jud-dins (aliens) into the Mazdayasna Zoroastrian Religion. As recorded in the court case of Saklat vs Bella.

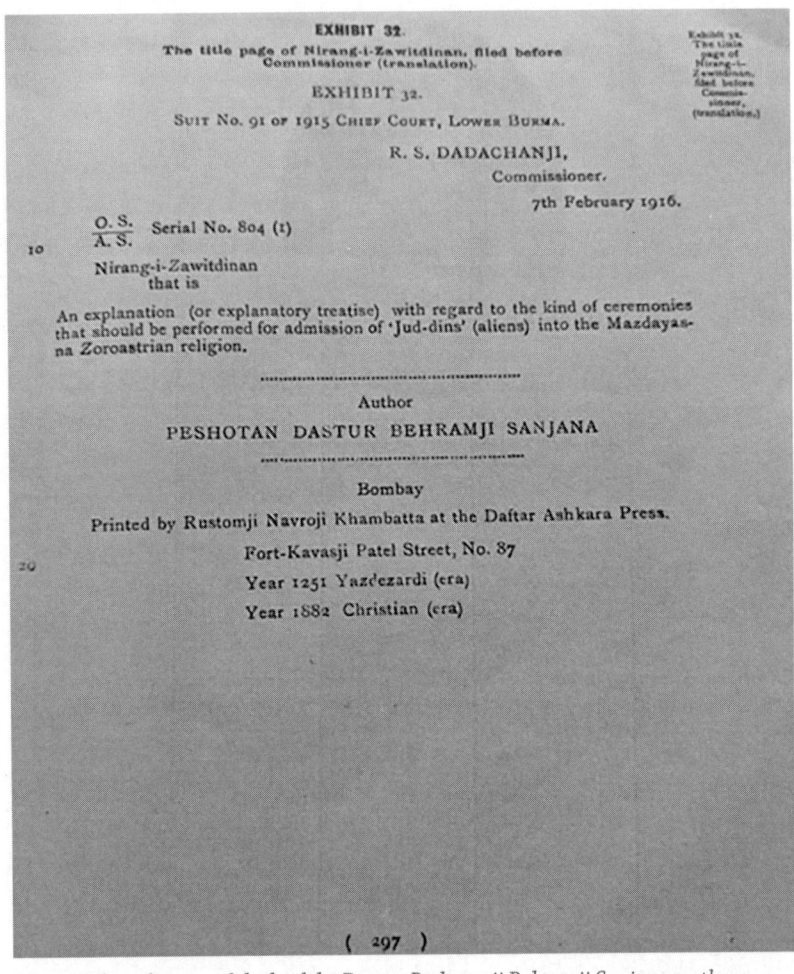

Photo of the title page of the book by Dastur Peshotanji Behramji Sanjana on the ceremonies to be performed to convert juddins

Author of 'Old Zend and Pahlavi Glossary'. Pahlavi, Gujrati and English Dictionary; the 'Pahlavi text of Ayibatkar-i-Zariran'. Translalator of 'Sardar-e-Behere Tavil', from Persian to Gujrati, and author of many Gujrati Sermons and Controversial pamphlets. Translator, into Gujrati of the Pahlavi "Vendidad", with translations.

Dastur Dr. JAMASPJI *Dastur* MINOCHEHERJI
Dastur EDALJI JAMASP-ASANA,
D.C.L. (Oxford), M.A. (Germany), Ph.D. (Germany).
Late Dastur of the Anjuman's Shahanshahi
Atesh-Beherám, in Bombay.
(Died on 26th September 1898 A.D.)
Author of: *Old Zend and Pahlavi Gossary*; *Pahlavi,
Gujrati and English Dictionary*; the Pahlavi text of
Ayôâthâ-ri Zarirân. Translator of: *Saddar-é Bêhêre
Tavil*, from Persian into Gujarati', and author of
many Gujarati Sermons and controversial pamphlets.
Translator, into Gujarati, of the Pahlavi *Vendidad*,
with transliteration.

Dastur Dr Jamaspji Dastur Minocherji Dastur Edalji Jamaspasana, D.C.L. (Oxford),
MA (Germany); Late Dastur of the Anjuman's Shahanshahi Atesh Beheram, in Bombay
(d. on 26 September 1898)

Editor of the 'Arda Viraf Namah'. In the original Pahlavi (with
introduction and Notes: Gujrati translation and Persian version of
'Zarthost Behram' in verses.

Dastur Kaekhosru (above picture) and Dastur Minocher (p.322)
performed the Navjote of Sussaune Brière and her wedding to Ratan

Dastur KAEKHUSRU *Dastur* JAMASPJI
JÁMÁSP-ÁSÁNÁ
Late Dastur of the Anjûman's Atesh-Beherâm, in Bombay.
(Died on 23rd June 1916 A.D.)
Editor of: the *Arda-Viráf Námeh* in the original Pahlavi, (with
Introduction and Notes: Gujarati translation and Persian
version of *Zarathoshi Beheram*, in verses.

Dastur Kaikhusru Dastur Jamaspji Jamaspasana, d. 23 June 1916, Late Dastur of the Anjuman's Atesh-Beheram, in Bombay; editor of the 'Arda Viraf Namah', in the original Pahlavi (with introduction and notes: Gujrati translation and Persian version of 'Zarthost Behram' in verses)

Tata by Parsi rites under the Parsi Marriage and Divorce Act. Dastur Kaikhusru was also the Head Priest of Calcuttas Banaji Agiari, the Banaji Atash Behram and the Camay Bay Agiari, Soda Water Wala's Agiari, and the Godiwala Agiari. He was in charge of the Agiaris in Aden, Colombo, Lahore and Lunoul.

The opinions of the Dasturs was sought by the sub-committee which was appointed by a committee chosen by the Zoroastrian Anjuman Council on the question of a non-Zoroastrian being accepted into the Zoroastrian Religion.

This is the reply given by Dastur Kaikhusru Jamaspji

Sir,

September 14, 1903

You have asked your opinion of whether or not to accept people of other faith into our religion, according to the teachings of our religion. You want to know whether this is acceptable or not. I am taking the permission to reply to you that according to our religion there is absolutely no restriction against accepting a non-Zoroastrian into the Zoroastrian religion. This is what the religion says. In the daily prayers of the Zoroastrian such as "Khurshid and Meher Niayesh", the person prays that May the Mazdayasna religion be spread on seven continents. (Hafta Keshvar Zamin). In the olden times the Athornan (Priest) class did not only pray this and sit around, but they went into far off countries in order to spread the Mazdayasna religion or the religion of Ashoi. (See Yajashne Ha chapter 41 paragraph 6). In several instances tyrannical people used to create problems when these Athornans went out to spread the religion. (Yajashne Ha 9 paragraph 24) We would like to point out above instances only: from the instructions or the ruling found in the Zoroastrian religion we can say that it is perfectly alright to accept non-Zoroastrians into the Zoroastrian religion.

We agree completely with the second publication of the booklet by Ervad Temurasp Dinshawji Anklasaria with the necessary proof for accepting non-Zoroastrians into the Zoroastrian religion. (Judeen No Ne Mazdayasni Din Ma Dakhel Karwa Rava Chhe Te Vishaynee Shahdato). In this, the learned Ervad points out examples from Avesta, Pahlavi, and Farsi books.

Also, our late respected Dastur Jamaspji has pointed out in the book "Pasokhay Nirangeh Javit Deenan" published in 1252 Y.D. that to accept non-Zoroastrians into the Zoroastrian religion is perfectly alright, and he has given examples. From the examples of the above booklet by Ervad

Dastur Minocheher Dastur Jamaspi Jamaspasana, b. 2 November 1870, present Dastur of the Anjuman's Atesh-Beheram, in Bombay

The Parsi Wedding Certificate Of Ratan Tata And Sussaune Braire. Officiating Priests Dastur Kaikhusru Jamaspjee And Dastur Minocheer Jamaspjee

Temurasp Anklesaria, as well as our late Dastur Jamasp, one can say that for any new student there is nothing left to search for. For this reason, we are pointing you to the examples in these booklets and are presenting them to the sub-committee.

Signed,

Kaikushru Dastur Jamaspji

Editor of an "Epitome in Gujrati prose, (in four volumes), of Firdausi's Shah Nameh" He together with Dastur Kaikhusru did the navjote of Susaune Brair and her Parsi wedding to Ratan Tata.

Shams-ul-Ulema, Dastur Hoshangji Jamaspji Jamaspasana, CIE, PhD
(d. 23 April 1908)

Shams-ul-ulama, Khan Bahadur, Sirdar, Dr Dastur Hoshangji Jamaspji Jamaspasana

Late High Priest of the Shahanshahi Parsis in the Deccan. A scholar and linguist, Professor of Persian, in the Deccan College, in Poona. Author and Editor of several works, of which the principal are: "Pahlavi Pazand Glossary: Shikana-Gumanik Vijar, (co-edited with the scholar Dr E W West.): "The Book of Adar-Viraf Nameh, with an English translation, (co-edited with Dr Martin Haug): "The Vendidad in Avesta text, with Pahlavi translation and commentary and Glossorial Index.". Editor of: "Zend and Pahlavi Izashne", and the "KHORDEH AVESTA" : "The Minokherd", etc. Author of a number of Sermons on the Zoroastrianism and many contributions on Avesta and Pahlavi literature.

Dr E.W. West and Dr Martin Hauge were two of the famous foreign scholars on Zoroastrian Religion. They established Zoroastrianism as a monotheistic Religion with the belief in one God, Ahura-Mazda.

The Dastur Hoshang Memorial Volume, papers on Iranian subjects in honour of the Late Shams-ul-ulama Sardar Dastur Hoshang Jamaspji was published in his honour by the Gatha Society of Bombay. Eminent Iranian scholars of the East and West answered the call of the society and contributed more than 75 articles for the Memorial Volume. Dastur Sheriarji Bharucha's article on the universality of the Zoroastrian Religion is published here titled 'Is Zoroastrianism Preached to All Mankind or to a Particular Race'.

Shams-ul-ulama, Sirdar Dastur Kaekobad Adarbad Dastur Noshirwan Jamaspasana

Present High Priest of the Shahanshashi Parsis in the Deccan, Calcutta and Madras and Malwa and had 23 Panthaks under

Shams ul-Ulema, Sirdar Dastur
KAÈKOBÀD ADARBÀD *Dastur* NOSHIRVÀN
JAMASP-ASÀNÀ.
(Born on 3rd November 1861 A D.)
Present High-Priest of the Shahanshshi Parsis in the
Deccan, Calcutta, and Madras.
Editor of: *Kàr–namak-i Ardesir Bàbukàn*, in the original
Pahlavi text, transliteration, (with comparative passages
from the *Shàh-Nàmeh*), with notes and translation in
Gujarati. *Zand-i Bahman Yasht* with the Pahlavi text,
transliteration and translation in Gujarati: *Dànà va
Mino-i-khirad*, with notes and translation in Gujarati.

*Shams-ul-Ulema, Sirdar Dastur Kaekobad Adarbad Dastur Noshirvan
(b. 3 November 1861)*

Dastur Kaekobad's telegram to Merwanji saying he has performed navjotes similar to Bella's, 'I am an Independent Dastur.' A report was published in the Jame-Jamshed when Dastur Kaekobad took office as High Priest (Jame-Jamshed: 21 July 1908)

him. (High Priest of the D B Mehta Zoroastrian Anjuman Atash Adaran Calcutta)

Editor of: 'Kar-na-mak-I Ardeshir Babukan', in the original Pahlavi text, transliteration, (with comparative passages from the Shah-Nameh), with notes and translation in Gujrati: 'Dana va Mino-i-Khirad', with notes and translations in Gujrati.

He represented the Community at the Parliament of World Religions where he spoke about the universality of the Zoroastrian Religion. Of a belief in one God Ahura-Mazda and that the religion was meant for all mankind

Dastur Kaekobad Aderbad Dastur Noshirwan went from Calcutta to Rangoon to perform Bellas navjote. Bella was the orphan child of a Parsi mother. He accepted Bella as a Parsi as 'she was born of a Parsi mother'. (Saklat vs Bella)

In the Parsi community presently there are three Baronets, two Knights and a Sardar and to that there is the addition of one more Sardar. The Honourable position of the Head Priest of the

Ervad SHEHERIARJI DÀDÀBHÀI BHARUCHA.

Born in March 1843. Died on 2nd September 1915 A.D.)

More than once he refused to accept the offer of a Dastur's office.

Late Instructor, of Zend, in Sir Jamsetjee Jejeebhoy Madressa (Seminary), in Bombay, from 1865 to 1870; of Zend. Pahlavi and Persian, in Sir Cowasjee Jehangir Zarthoshti Madressa, in Naosari, from 1877 to 1884. Author: of *An Outline of Zend Grammar, compared with Sanskrit*: of a Series of six brochures on *Zoroastrian Morals*, (in Gujarati): of *Nirange Rististan* (A complete account of Zoroastrian Customs and Ceremonies of the Dead): of *A Brief Sketch of the Zoroastrian Religion and Customs*, (specially written for the Religious Congress in connection with the World's Columbian Exhibition, of 1893, at Chicago): of an *Essay* on the *Disâtir*, (specially written for the Oriental Congress, in 1895, at Geneva): of Collected Sanskrit Writings of the Parsis, in seven parts (some being still unpublished): of a "Scheme for the Education of Parsi children in the tenets of the Zoroastrian Religion": of Lessons on Avesta and Pahlavi Pazand: of Pahlavi-Pazand-English and English-Pahlavi-Pazand Glossary. Translator of the Pahlavi of Adarbad Marespand's *Pand-Nâmeh*; Co-edited the Pahlavi *Dadestan-i-Dinik*, with the late Ervad T. D. Anklesharia- He has published numerous Lectures and Sermons, delivered on behalf of the 'Rah-numac Mazdayasnan Sabha', the ' Gayâo Prasârak Mandli,' and the 'Faali Sal Mandli.'

Note.—To his personal, valuable assistance *The Parsis in India* volumes are highly indebted.

The Times Press

Ervad Sheheriarji Dadabhi Bharucha

Parsis of Deccan and Malwa has been graced since many years by the descendants of Dastur Jamasp Aashana. Two Dastur Sahebs – the last of this clan – Dastur Nosherwanji Jamaspji and his brother Dastur Hoshangji held the position of the first grade of the Dasturs. Presently their successor, the new Dastur Kekobad Adarbad has also been conferred with the honour of being decorated as the Sardar of the first grade by the Honourable Government and has spread joy and cheers in the community. We have been observing that this Dasturi family of Poona has won the laurels and honours because of their wisdom, ability and determination. The native place of that family is Navsari and as a rule, the Athornan tribe of Navsari has been a success wherever they have been because of the wisdom of their heart. However, the Jamasp Aasha family of Poona have gained their fame due to their knowledge of the religion, their progressive habits in keeping with the current trends, and considering it as their ardent duty to make their fellow tribesmen achieve progress. Dasturs could be found in plenty today, but those that guide their tribe in accordance of the advanced knowledge of their religion to stride on the true path, are not known to us to be found except – those daring Dasturs from Poona.

Ervad Sheriarji Dadabhai Bharucha
(March 1843–September 1915)

More than once he refused to accept the offer of a Dastur's office.

Late, Instructor of Zend, in Sir Jamsetjee Jeejeebhoy Madressa (Seminary), in Bombay, from 1865 to 1870: of Zend, Pahlavi and Persian, in Sir Cowasjee Jehangir Zarthosti Madressa, in Naosari, from 1877 to 1884. Author of 'An Outline of Zend Grammar, Compared with Sanskrit': of a Series of 6 Brochures on Zoroastrian Morals (in Gujrati): of Nirange Rististan (A Complete Account of Zoroastrian Customs and Ceremonies of the Dead): A Brief Sketch of Zoroastrian Religion and Customs, (Specially ritten for the Religious Congress in connection with the World's Colombian Exhibition, of 1893, at Chicago): of an essay on the Distair, (especially written in the Oriental Congress in 1895 at Geneva): of Collected Sanskrit Writings of the Parsis, in seven parts (some being still unpublished): of a 'Scheme for the Education of Parsi Children in the tenets of the Zoroastrian Religion': of 'Lessons on Avesta and Pahlavi Pazand': of Pahlavi-Pazand-English and English-Pahlavi-Pazand Glossary: Translator of the Pahlavi of Aderbad Marespand's Pand-Nameh: Co-edited the Pahlavi 'Dadestan-i-Dinik', with the late Ervad T D Anklesaria. He has published numerous Lectures and Sermons on behalf of the 'Rah-numane Mazdayasnan Sabha'. The 'Gayan Prasarak Mandli' and the Fasli Sal Mandli.

Note—To his personal, valuable assistance 'The Parsis in India' are highly indebted.

Ervad Sheriarji Bharucha was one of the members of the Expert Committee on Religion appointed during the case Petit vs Jeejeebhoy to determine if conversion was a tenet of the religion. He gave evidence in favour of Ratan and Susaune. He wrote a 'Brief Sketch of the Zoroastrian Religion and Customs' which was presented at the Parliament of World Religions in 1893. Swami Vivekananda made his historical speech at this Parliament of World Religions.

His opinion on acceptance of a person born in another faith and converted to Zoroastrian Religion is expressed in the letter he wrote to the Trustees of the Anjumans Atash Behram.

Sir,

I have received your letter of this current month dated the 16th, and I am taking the liberty to answer the questions being asked in it

Any person of another faith, man or woman, who with a firm belief, free will, and a desire, wishes to enter our religion to perform his Navjote and accept him into the Zoroastrian Religion

If once an individual either born to people of another faith or born to a Zoroastrian has a Navjote performed and has made the necessary solemn declaration in the presence of the priest thereby being accepted into the Zoroastrian Religion, from that point that person should be considered for all the rights as a Zoroastrian. This is my humble opinion

Signed
Ervad Sheriarji Dadabhai Bharucha

Dr Dastur Maneckji Nusserwanji Dhalla, PhD

Present High Priest of North-Western India. (Born on 22nd September 1875 A D).

Author of: 'Zoroastrian Theology, from the Earliest times to the Present Day', (in English) : "Nyaneshis, or Zoroastrian Litanies

Dastur Dhalla says in his autobiography 'The Saga of a Soul':

It is possible that after decades the community may create an enlightened and educated priest-class and a popular understanding that to spread the good faith and to increase our strength is not only commensurate with the precepts of our religion but also in the interest of our social well-being.

Dastur Darabji Dastur Mahyarji Meherji Rana of Naosari

Dastur Darabji was described by his contemporaries as 'The Pope of the Parsis.'

The Anjuman's Atash Behram wrote a letter to experts on Religion whether it was alright to accept people of other Religions into the Zoroastrian faith. Dastur Mahyarji's reply:

January 3, 1904
Navsari

Received your letter in which you have written, 'Kindly express your opinion at your earliest with examples and arguments on the question of whether according to the teachings of our religion is it alright to accept people of other religions into the Zoroastrian religion.' I am taking the liberty to answer this question. According to the writings of our religious books, any person of another faith with a true belief, and who is anxious to enter our noble religion, has no restrictions shown him. There are certain proofs in favour of acceptance as found in:

Dr. *Dastur* MANECKJI NUSSERVANJI
DHÀLLÀ, Ph·D.
Present High-Priest of the Parsis of North-Western India.
(Born on 22nd September 1875 A·D·)
Author of : *Zoroastrian Theology*, from the Earliest
Times to the Present Day; (in English) : *Nyaeshis*, or
Zoroastrian Litanies.

Dr Dastur Maneckji Nusserwanji Dhalla, PhD

Jashne Ha (Chapter) 30 Paragraph 11 Jashne Ha (Chapter) 43 Paragraph 6

Jashne A (Chapter) 46 Paragraph 13

Jashne A (Chapter) 45 Paragraph 1

Yajashne Ha (Chapter) 8 Paragraph 7

The final paragraph of the Vendidad Progress, etc...

Signed,

Dorabjee Dastur Mahyarji

Dastur Darabji Dastur Mahyarji
Meherji Rana.
(Died in 1906 A. D.)

Dastur Darabji Dastur Mahyarji Meherji Rana of Naosari

These were the views on of religion of the high priests of the Parsi community in early 1900. These priests, we are told, were experts in religion having studied the religious texts in the original language. They have also translated and explained our holy books for us so we can understand our religion. We unlike our ancestors, can no longer claim ignorance of the teachings of Ahura-Mazda.

Sadly, today, we do not follow the teachings of our learned priests or of Ahura-Mazda the God of all.

32
WHO AM I?

Tat tvam asi (Thou art that)
—Chandogya Upanishad, Ch. VI

If you had asked me this question a couple of years ago, I would have given a clear answer. Today, I cannot do that. In the month of November 2020, my cousin found this picture while cleaning out her house (something we are all doing in this pandemic), and it set me thinking.

This is a picture of my maternal great grandfather and his two brothers. He was the first of what I thought was the Jila family to come to Calcutta from Navsari.

But the picture tells me a different story. My mother's family name was not Jila but Jila Rancuvervara. The family was not from Navsari but from a village near Surat called Rancuver. I was very attached to my grandparents and spent a lot of time with them, and to suddenly learn that my knowledge of their name and where they originally came from was wrong came as a shock.

This is the translated legend under the third picture in the photograph, (my great grandfather Hormusji).

Hormusji Edulji Jamshedji Jila Rankuvevara
Son of
Ratanbai Jamshedji Jila and Edulji Jamshedji Jila
Ratanbai is daughter of Baiai Cawasji Doodha
Edulji is son of Avabai Edulji Jila
Nephew and Palak (adopted) of

Picture of the author's great grandfather and his two brothers

Dhanbai Dorabji Sadri and Dorabji Cowasji Dhoodha
Husband of
Bachubai daughter of Dinbai Dinshawji Tariwala.
    Father of sisters Ratanbai and Dinbai and brothers Dosabhai and Minocher.
    Birth Roj 23 Mah4
    Yaz 1248
    17.1.1879
    (Hormusji Edulji Jamshedji Jila Rankuvevara, te marhoum Ratanbai Jamshedji Jila na beta, Edulji na beta, te marhoum Baiai Cawasji Doodha na beti te marhoum Avabai Edulji Jila na beta te marhoum Dhanbai Dorabji Sadri na and marhoum Dorabji Cawasji Doodha na bhanej and paalak putra te marhoum Dinbai Dinshaji Tariwalla na beti Bachoobai na khavin te baheno Ratanbai and Dinbai and brothers Dosabhai and Minocher na peeta.
    Janam: Roj 23. Mah 4
    Yaz 1248
    17.1.1879)

Strangely, the great great grandmothers' names are given but not their husbands'. Ratanbai was daughter of Baiai Cawasji Doodha and Edulji was the son of Avabai Edulji Jila.

My great grandfather was adopted as a Palak (adoption for performance of death rituals; otherwise, Parsis are not allowed to adopt) of Dhanbai Dorabji Sadri and Darabji Cawasji Doodha. I did not know this or have any idea who they are. Why is Dhanbai's maiden name given?

My great grandmother was Bachubai, daughter of Dinbai Dinshawji Tariwala. Here again only her mother's name is given not the fathers. Can anyone help me locate this part of my family?

When the mother's names are given, their maiden names have been used and often the father's name is not mentioned at all. Was lineage traced through the mothers 100 years ago?

My DNA ancestry report states my ancestry composition is 59 percent Mesopotamian, Caucasian and Iranian and that my most recent ancestor from this population was one to three generations ago. 37 per cent of my ancestry is from Northern India and Pakistan, especially from four regions Maharashtra, Gujarat, Uttar Pradesh and Madhya Pradesh. The most recent ancestor from this population is two to four generations ago.

On my fathers' side, Rusi Burjorji Gimi, I have not been able to find out anything except that he had two uncles, Pheroze and Darashaw, from the maternal side and one uncle, Nariman, from the paternal side.

So many questions about the past and no one to answer them.

After 67 years I have obtained some new knowledge of my ancestry from a chance gift of a photograph.

I wonder, with my mixed DNA and unknown parentage, would I be considered a Parsi?

APPENDIX

(A)

SAKLAT VS BELLA JUDGEMENT DATED 1918 (CHIEF COURT OF LOWER BURMA) JUSTICE C YOUNG

No. 39

In the Chief Court of Lower Burma.

ORIGINAL CIVIL JURISDICTION CIVIL REGULAR No. 91 OF 1915.

D. R. SAKLAT AND OTHERS   Vs,   BELLA AND ONE

Dated Rangoon, the 23rd of April 1918.

For plaintiffs-Mr. Connell with Mr. N. Cowasjee,

for defendants-Mr. Giles with Mr. Lentaigne

Judgement

This is a suit for a declaration that the 1st defendant is not entitled to the use and benefits of the Parsi Fire Temple in Dalhousie Street or participate in any of the religious ceremonies performed therein, and for an injunction restraining her from entering and the 2nd defendant from taking her into the said Fire Temple, and the circumstances out of which it arose are as follows: -

The trustee of the temple in question is Mr. Bomanji Cowasji a Barrister-at-law and an advocate of this Court of many years standing, and he states sometime in 1899 the mother of the first defendant came to his office and asked for his assistance. That he believed her to be a Parsi and helped her, also allowed her and her husband whose name she said was Jones to live in a room in a tenement house belonging to him in Lewis Street. That the two lived there till the husband died and that then the widow continued to live there alone till her daughter Bella the first defendant was born.

That he went to England in May 1900 at which time Bella was about three months old and that when he left, he asked his brother Sapurji that 2nd defendant to continue on his behalf the charitable work of looking after the mother and child. Mr. Sapurji, it appears, did so till the mother fell ill and died in the General Hospital sometime in 1900. He says that at one of his last interviews with the dying woman she entrusted the child to his care and begged that it might be brought up in "our" religion, which he promised to do.

He tells us that he took the child into his own house and had her taught and instructed in the Zoroastrian religion exactly as if she had been a child of his own.

He and his wife became fond of her and in course of time adopted her and when she was about 14 had the Navjote ceremony performed upon her by a priest brought from Bombay. This Navjot is admittedly one of the ceremonies required for the initiation of a person into the Zoroastrian religion. After the ceremony was performed the child in common with other members of the faith resident in Rangoon received various invitations to attend ceremonies in the temple, none of which she was allowed to accept till the 21st of March 1915 when in response to an invitation from the priest she was brought into the temple by her adoptive father the 2nd defendant. Nothing happened during the ceremony itself but shortly afterwards a storm arose culminating in the filing of this suit on the 31st of March 1915 by the Honourable Mr. Merwanji Cowasji since deceased another brother of Mr. Bomanji Cowasji and three other gentlemen.

The following issues were framed and agreed to by the parties:

1. Whether the plaint discloses any cause of action?
2. Whether this suit is maintainable?
3. Who are entitled to the benefit of the Fire Temple Trust?
4. Is the 1st defendant, the daughter of a Parsi mother?
5. Is it possible for the 1st defendant being the daughter of a non-Parsi father to be initiated (a) into the Zoroastrian religion (b) into the Parsi Community?
6. If it was possible, whether the ceremonies adopted for the purpose were defective.

The defendants applied for the first two issues to be tried as preliminary issues and after hearing arguments I decided on the 11th September1915 that the 1st defendant›s act might be viewed (1) as a trespass on to the land (2) as a trespass into the temple if this was held upon a different trust (3) as a trespass or infringement of the plaintiffs personal right to worship in the temple undisturbed by the intrusion of a person of another faith and held that the suit for the trespass on to the land or into the temple would not lie as framed as in my opinion it was a mere question of ordinary trespass which must be brought by the person in whom the land was vested, namely the trustee, but that for remaining injury namely the injury to the plaintiffs individual right to worship undisturbed by the intrusion of a person not belonging to their faith the suit would lie but that the plaintiffs would have to shew that they had such a right.

I see no reason to differ from these views.

Viewed as a mere physical trespass, the act complained of constituted an alleged wrong by a stranger to the trust against the beneficiaries and Order 31 Rule No I provides in imperative terms that in all suits concerning property vested in a trustee where the contention is between the persons beneficially interested and a third person, the trustee shall represent the parties interested; that ordinarily speaking it shall not be necessary to make the beneficiaries parties but that the Court may make them or any of them parties if it think fit.

This order is different from the English Order 16 Rule 8 which must have been before the Indian legislature and which less emphatically provides that trustees may sue and be sued on behalf of or as representing the property or estate of which they are trustees. In the first place there is the permissive may for the imperative shall, and in the second there is in the English Rule no such precision of language as is contained in the Indian Rule which expressly says that in all suits concerning property vested in a trustee where the contention is between the beneficiaries and a third person the trustee shall represent the beneficiaries.

I can only suppose that the word "shall" is used in its ordinary imperative meaning and was employed designedly.

In England in cases of trespass where though the title is in the trustee the beneficiary is in possession the fact of possession following the ordinary rule has been held sufficient ground for enabling the beneficiary to sue without joining the trustee c.p. Healey Vs. Healey 1915 1.K.B. 938. But this case of trespass and though possession apart from title would give a right of suit, the terms of the Indian order which lays down the rule that in all cases concerning property the trustee shall represent the persons in my opinion preclude me from following such authorities. In England in other cases also beneficiaries have been allowed to sue where the trustee has been asked and has refused but in these cases it is laid down that there must be the request and refusal and it is not enough merely to make the trustee a defendant (Franklin Vs. Franklin 1915 W. N. 342, Annual Practice 1918 page 235).

Here the trustee was never made a defendant, the plaintiffs filed their suit without waiting to see whether he would refuse to sue or not, and the terms of the law are as already pointed out different in that in England the word "may" is used, while in India the obligatory "shall" has been substituted.

The result is that if I am correct in my views the suit is only maintainable by the present plaintiffs, if and in so far as they can shew that their temple was polluted, and their religious susceptibilities were wounded by the intrusion into their place of worship of the defendant Bella.

It is an unsatisfactory state of affairs because unless they can prove (a) this injury to their feelings gives them a right of action (b) that these feelings were injured because she not being a Zoroastrian was present at their worship the suit will have to be dismissed altogether whether she had or whether she had not a right to worship in this particular temple under the terms of the trust deed.

The distinction seems to me to be real enough and analogous into the intrusion on to private land and into a private place of worship. If the intruder belongs to the same religion, there may be a trespass but no injury to the religious feelings, but if to a different religion or though to the same religion, yet to a different sect, then there may be both. As I have already said, I do not think the action for the alleged physical trespass is maintainable by the plaintiffs: the case of Sankaralinga Nadan Vs. Raja Rajesware 12 C. W. N. 946 was cited as an authority to the contrary, but this seems to me to be the ordinary case of addition of beneficiaries as parties which is expressly allowed by the Rule.

Furthermore, even if the plaintiffs can sue for the physical trespass, I fail to see how I can decide that it was such in the absence of the trustee.

She was actually invited into the temple by the priest through the trustee and unless it was a breach of trust on his part to issue the invitation, how can I decide that she was wrong to accept the invitation or would be wrong to accept another. It is absolutely necessary to construe the trust deed and how can I construe it in the trustee›s absence and behind his back.

The land and the temple were vested in the trustee and under the first clause of the scheme in Civil Regular No. 36 of 1889, he was given charge of temple premises and empowered to manage the same; it appears to be the practice for the priest to issue invitations to all members of the community under the supervision of the trustee and she in common with other Zoroastrians was actually invited to the ceremony by the authorities.

Both as trustee and as manager it would be for him to issue or supervise the issuing of invitations, and though he might commit a breach of trust by issuing such to persons unauthorised by the deed under which he held, yet surely it was for the plaintiffs in the first instance to prove this in a suit to which he was a party. In other words unless it was a breach of trust for him to invite her, I cannot hold that Bella did wrong in accepting an invitation, not can I hold that he has committed a breach of trust, by issuing the former invitations nor would commit further breaches by repeating them when he is not a party to the suit and has had no chance of being heard. The plaintiff asks me to declare that Bella's entry was a trespass and to restrain her from repeating it.

How can I say it was a trespass when she entered at the invitation of the manager and person in whom the property is vested and unless I can say so, how can I restrain her from repeating it. The plaintiff refrained in their plaint from mentioning the fact that she entered at the invitation of the authorities and skated round the difficulty by praying for a declaration the she was not entitled to use the temple, but now that it transpires that she did so by the invitation of the priest and trustee, it seems to me that the declaration which should have been prayed for is that she is not entitled to accept the invitation of the trustee– but why should she be not entitled to accept the invitation if he is entitled to give her one ? The Trustees seem to be an absolutely necessary party, so far as her physical entry is concerned and unless I first of all decide that it is wrong for him to extend the invitation, I cannot decide that it for her to avail herself of it. The plaintiffs could have sued for a declaration that it was a breach of trust for him to send or cause the invitation to be sent and joined her as a party with a prayer that she might be restrained from accepting the invitation if sent or from entering without one. But they deliberately refrained from doing so and now ask me in the absence of and without hearing the trustee to decide who is entitled to the benefit of the trust (Issue 3). I do not see how I can do so.

Turning then to the remaining question, which I may call the alleged moral trespass the first point to be considered is whether it affords a right of action.

The authorities seem to me to shew that it does: thus in Anandrao Bhikaji V. Shankar Daji I.L.R. 7. Bom. 123 in which 4 persons of the Chitpavan caste alleging that they and the members of their caste in common with certain other castes possessed the exclusive right of entry and worship in the sanctuary of a temple and that the defendant members of the Palske caste not being of the privileged castes infringed that right, it was held that the plaintiffs had suffered a personal injury by the pollution of their shrine for which they could sue whether they represented the rest of their caste or not.

In Jawahra Vs. Akbar Hussain 1.L.R. 7. All. 178, it was held by the full Bench that every Mahomedan who has a right to use a mosque for purposes of devotion is entitled to exercise such right without hindrance and is competent to maintain a suit against anyone who interferes with its exercise.

In Subarayada Vs. Assanali cited in Kamaraiu Vs, Asanali I. L. R. 23 Madras at p. 100 the Madras High Court held that the plaintiff as worshippers were entitled to maintain an action against any person improperly interfering with their rights to worship and in Mohiuddin vs Sayiduddin I.L.R.20 Cal. at p.816 the learned Judges approve of the reasoning in the Allahabad case. The plaintiffs claim that by the entrance of Bella not being a Zoroastrian into their temple, it was itself polluted and the service on which they were engaged would be rendered of no religious efficacy and that no future service would be efficacious till the temple was purified. I think this gave them a right of suit if such was the result of her entry and don›t understand that the defendant in any way dispute the proposition that to introduce a non-Zoroastrian into the temple particularly during worship would have this effect, what they assert, is that Bella is a Zoroastrian. The defendant's admission indeed seems to me to go further – they admit that it is not enough that a person should profess the Zoroastrian creed-he must have been duly admitted into the fold-thus Mr. B Cowasjee tells us at p, 10 of his evidence that the presence of a convert would be no shock to his religious feelings provided he had been duly initiated, and Mr.N.N. Burjorjee says the same.

I think therefore the statement of the Rangoon mobed or priest in his evidence at page 13, 22, and elsewhere that her entry or rather the entry of a non-Zoroastrian polluted the temple rendered the service inefficacious and a purification of the temple necessary was accepted by all parties, and this being so, I think that any worshipper would be entitled to sue for and restrain the repetition of such an act C. P. Sankaralinga Nadan Vs Raja Rajeswara 12 C.W.N.p946 where a similar injunction was sought and damages claimed for the pollution of a temple. Here too it was claimed that the suit did not lie, but the injunction and damages were granted, and the decision was upheld by the Privy Council.

The defendants therefore must be restrained as prayed unless Bella was a Zoroastrian and duly initiated.

This raises two main questions, the first being could Bella seeing that she was the daughter of a non-Parsi father become a Zoroastrian and be duly initiated in other words is Zoroastrianism a missionary religion and secondly was she in fact duly initiated or in other words were the ceremonies performed sufficient for the purpose?

As regards the first question on the evidence taken before me, I am in complete agreement with the conclusion arrived at on the same point by Sır Dinshaw Davar and Sir F. Beaman J. J. in the cognate case of Sir Dinshaw Petit and others Vs. Sir Jamsetji Jijibhoy 1. L. R. 33. Bom. 509 namely that the Zoroastrian religion not only permits but enjoins the conversion of a person born in another religion and of non-Zoroastrian parents». Every day the pious Zoroastrian prays that the knowledge and propagation and belief in the good religion of Mazada be over all the seven regions of the earth. (Vide evidence af 6 P. W. at p. 98.)

To this day they sing with pride of the conversion to their religion of the great Emperor Akbar.

In the 18th century we find their priests referring to Persia questions connected with converts Exhibit 51 and today we find the question referred by the Parsis of Bombay to the men most learned in their religion and the answer given in the affirmative (Exhibit 40) and two of plaintiffs own witnesses, one being the High Priest of the Shensahi Sect the largest of two Parsis chronological sects and differing from the other merely on chronological questions and himself a leading member of this committee and the other being the Deputy High Priest admitting that conversion was not only permitted but enjoined by their religion. In the face of these proofs and admissions which (Dastur Dorab Sanjana 6 P. W. pp. 16,17,98,121, Naib Dastur R. Sanjana 7 P.W.pp 59,64, 65,66). In the face of these proof and admissions it might easily be multiplied it seems idle to discuss further the doctrine that Zoroastrianism is a missionary religion which I take to be admitted. It would be equally idle to deny that for one cause or another the Parsis for many years have not as a rule attempted to convert, that there are few if any well authenticated instances in recent times of converts and that many Parsis while admitting the theory set their faces sternly against the practice of conversion.

I do not think it necessary to enquire why they thus oppose conversion. Their reasons are not in question, the point is whether 1st defendant has or has not been duly converted.

This is the main question in the case and by their pleadings the plaintiff endeavoured to throw the onus of proving that Bella was duly and validly initiated upon the defendants.

They claimed that the second defendant alleged and contented that she had been duly initiated and that it was for him to prove it.

The defendant replied that she had been taught and bred up in the faith from her earliest infancy and that when she had come to the right age, she had been questioned as to her wish to adopt the Zoroastrian religion and her belief in it and that her replies being satisfactory the initiation ceremony had been duly performed upon her by an eminent priest from Bombay, that he had invested her with the sacred *sudreh* and kusti worn by all Zoroastrians and that thereafter she like all members of the faith in Rangoon had received invitations to attend the ceremonies from the priest charged with the duty by the trustee and that she had a perfect right to accept them.

When issues were framed it was ordered that the 2nd defendant should give particulars of the ceremonies performed at her initiation and that the plaintiffs should state whether and if so in what respect they contended that these ceremonies were inefficacious.

The defendants by their letter R. F. dated 16th September 1913 stated that the ceremonies performed at the Navjot were (1) the Nahn or purification ceremony (2) the investiture with the *sudreh* and kusti accompanied by the usual prayers.

In their reply dated 13th October 1915 (Exhibit R. G.) the plaintiffs suggested (a) that Bella was not old enough to be converted (b) that a simple Navjot ceremony was not sufficient and that those required were (a) Navjot (b) Barashnum (c) A 2nd Navjot and also that she must be shewn to have complied with conditions V and VI laid down by Davar J. in the Bombay case and suggested an application to the Court to raise 2 further issues viz (1) whether the Navjot and investiture ceremonies were duly and validly performed whether such ceremonies were sufficient to convert her to Zoroastrianism.

The defendants replied by Exhibit R. H. dated 25th November 1915 and contended that Issue 6 was sufficient, as it stood when read with the particulars they had furnished of the ceremonies performed and with the particulars of the additional ceremonies stated to be requisite by the defendant, but the plaintiffs wanted further issues to be raised they must apply to the Court.

The Plaintiff replied by Exhibit R. J. dated 30th November 1915 that they had reconsidered the question and agreed that the issues were wide enough to cover all matters that might be raised.

The defendants objected to this in their letter R K. of 10th December 1915 and said that if plaintiffs wish to contend that there were defects in the performance of the Navjot and investiture ceremonies, they denied that Issue 6 covered the point.

Plaintiffs replied by R. L. claiming that it did cover the point and if defendants wished to have the matter decided it was for them to bring the matter before the Court.

In my opinion Issue 6 was intended to raise all questions both as to whether the ceremonies were properly performed in themselves and whether if properly performed they were sufficient. Particulars however had naturally to be given and were ordered and I cannot find any objection was taken that the Navjot was improperly performed in itself beyond the allegation that Bella was too young and did not comply with conditions V and VI in Davar Judge's judgment.

None of these last three points were pressed, in fact I have no recollection of their even being mentioned except by Counsel for defendant who said that he did not propose to deal with them while Counsel for the plaintiffs in his reply did not mention them at all nor indeed did either side mention the allegation that the Navjote ceremony was defective on the ground that unconsecrated nirang was used; though evidence on commission was led with regard to it. As to this last matter of the «nirang the case is stronger because no reference was made to it in any of the letters which passed between the parties. The plaintiffs must have known that the nirang was obtained from the Rangoon mobeds. There were two of these and they only called one. He denied that he had given it, but there is no evidence that his fellow priest had not done so, and Dastur Kaekobad who performed the ceremony swears that he got it from the local mobeds, but cannot say which.

In my opinion if the plaintiffs had intended to make any point of this allegation as to the nirang they were bound to mention in their objections that the ceremony was invalid because unconsecrated nirang had been used, and not having done so cannot be heard. They tried by their pleading to throw the onus throughout on the defendants, but I think that they were wrong and that while it was for the defendants to state how and why they claimed that Bella was a Zoroastrian it was for the plaintiffs who seek to restrain Bella from participating in the ceremonies of her faith, to prove how and why her claim to be a Zoroastrian failed. If I were to go into the question of the nirang, I should therefore hold that it was not shewn that unconsecrated nirang was used, but I also hold that I am not entitled to go into the matter at all.

The plaintiffs might in my opinion either have interrogated as to what was actually done at the ceremonies or called for further particulars, but they did not do so and if they had, it would still have at been for them to prove that the ceremonies were either defective or insufficient, and they cannot evade the task by pleadings as they did, that the 2nd defendant alleged that Bella had been duly initiated and by calling on him to prove it.

They were entitled to know as fully as they desired what ceremonies had been performed and how, but it was for them to do the rest and shew either that they were defective or that they were insufficient. Partly owing to their method of pleading, and partly owing to their being content with the defendants very loose and vague particulars, there has been a lamentable waste of time and money in the proceedings before the Commissioner in Bombay, where hours were spent in endeavours by the defendants counsel to prove out of the mouths of plaintiff witness that the ceremonies were in all respects sufficient onus had been placed on the defendants by the plaintiffs mode of pleading. The Commissioner regarded himself as unable to rule out any questions or any answers and the fullest license was given to the odium theologicum with the result that the questions at issue have been overlaid with masses of sometimes inadmissible and sometimes irrelevant matter. One witness alone I was told was examined and cross-examined for over 40 hours and the record of his evidence occupied over 400 pages of fullscap. The so-called evidence of these witnesses on commission was read before me and that was all, counsel on both sides agreeing that it was not worthwhile even to argue the relevancy or admissibility of much of it, and they would endeavour to base their own arguments and addresses on portions that they believed admissible and relevant, and that each in turn should be at liberty to object to such portions at that stage (vide Diary 15-2-1). Many exhibits had not been translated at the close of the case: these must be rejected and while I pass no formal order of admission or rejection, of other Exhibits, I must not be taken as admitting them. I have followed counsels' example to base my judgment on admissible evidence only. Returning to the particulars, it is clear that the objections taken by the plaintiff were

(a) that an alien could be initiated into the fold at all and (b) that a single navjote was not sufficient but that a barasnum ceremony followed by a second navjote absolutely necessary (c), that Bella was too young d), that she did not comply with conditions 5 and 6 of Davar J›s Judgment. As I have said it practically admitted that Zoroaster not merely permitted but enjoined conversion and that though the practice has fallen into disuse, in theory conversion has always been commended.

Such was the deliberate opinion of the council of experts to whom the community of Bombay referred the matter, and if it be objected that they or many of them being alive, their joint opinion was inadmissible, it is sufficient to say that the member of this committee was called by the plaintiffs and agreed that Zoroastrianism was a missionary religion (p. 10. Dastur Sanjana 6, P. W.) With regard to the question of Bella's age which as I have said was not pressed before me and which having regard to the agreement of counsel as to the conduct of the case, I feel it scarcely necessary to discuss, it seems to me sufficient to say that plaintiffs own witness Dastur Darab Sanjana (p. 21) stated that according to the Avesta children of Parsi parents should be formally initiated into the religion at the age of fifteen when he or she had arrived at the age of discretion and were able to understand religion with their own sense and judgment. This was practically the age at which Bella made her profession of faith.

The same witness at p, 42 admits that in Book I. Ch.IV, of the Aerpatastan there is a distinct reference to the conversion and initiation of minors bred up in another religion and his contention that the minors referred to were slaves and stood on a different footing is based on the very insufficient reason that the following passage relates to slaves (p. 43). Throughout practically the whole of his cross-examination he stoutly contended that the age of puberty was the age at which a convert could sufficiently understand the doctrines of the religion vide pp. 21 et seq and then in re-examination he recanted and asked to be allowed to substitute the age of majority. It looks to me as if he had learnt in the interval that his statement in cross-examination would admit Bella. Plaintiffs next witness Naib Dastur R. E. Sanjana (7.P.W.) the Deputy High Priest of the Shensahi Sect states as might be expected that in his opinion no one should be converted before he was 21 years of age, but admits he has no authority either for this proposition (p.15) or for the proposition that converts should only be admitted at a later age than other initiates and at p.40 has to admit that the sacred books contained injunctions to the effect that when an adult was converted his children also were to be admitted to the fold without any qualification as to their age being expressed.

In the face of this evidence and having regard to the facts that Bella had been bred up as a Parsi from her earliest infancy in the tenets of the Zoroastrian religion and that the priest who initiated her was satisfied as to her fitness it is impossible for me to hold that her initiation was invalid on account of her youth.

She was only technically a convert, really she was as much a Zoroastrian if she had been the actual instead of being only the adopted child of Mr. S. Cowasjee and to force me to decide that she could not be initiated before she was 21 would have required some distinct and authoritative assertion of the fact, whereas the evidence, such as it is, is all the other way,

I may also mention that neither counsel for the plaintiffs nor council for the defendants discussed the question in their addresses.

I will now turn to the question as to whether it is necessary for the Barasnum to be administered to converts.

Admittedly it was not administered and therefore if it is essential as contended by the plaintiffs, the initiation was invalid.

Now the Barasnum is an archaic and primitive ceremony of lustration, in which the whole body of the recipient is washed by the priest who perfoms the rite from head to foot during nine successive nights, and is obviously one as Beaman J. pointed out which no adult of either sex would be willing to undergo unless absolutely convinced of its necessity, and in the present day no Zoroastrian undergoes it, except certain priests who do so at their ordination and the corpse bearers (Naib Dastur R. Sanjana 7 P. W. page. 54.)

It is necessary for the priests, for unless they have done so they cannot or should not perform certain ceremonies, and it is necessary for the corpse-bearers or persons who carry the dead to the Towers of silence because their avocations bring them into immediate contact with the dead, which to the Zoroastrian is of all things the most impure. The Barasnum is prescribed in that portion of the Avesta known as the Vendidad but only for purification after contact with nassa or dead matter. (Dastur Sanjana P. 47) but nowhere either in the Avesta or in the Phelvi or Pazand literature is it anywhere either to his or his deputy's knowledge prescribed anywhere as a step for the admission of converts.(Dastur Sanjana P. 48. Naib Dastur page. 5a.)

It is indeed prescribed in certain Ravayat (answers on doubtful points of doctrine by men learned in the sacred writings) and especially in the Sad-dar Rivayat, but that in common with all Ravayats is not a book of authority (Dastar Sanjana page 49) or only a third rate authority Naib Dastur (page 53) and the Ravayats that prescribed barasnum for converts prescribe it for all Zoroastrians (Naib Dastur page 53) and when they prescribe it for converts they prescribe it not as a step towards admission, but as a ceremony to be undergone thereafter (page 53). Thus in the Ravayats it is stated that if slaves have their faith in the good religion, then it is incumbent that they should be taken into the religion by investing them with kusti and when they become clever, well conversant with the tenets of the religion and firm in their religious faith, they shall be given Barashnum.

To me this rather looks as if the Barashnum was in those days regarded not as a condition for initiation, but as an outward sign of superior knowledge and holiness, such as may be traced in the prohibition against the priests performing certain of the higher and more sacred ceremonies unless they were what is called barashnum wala mobeds.

For mere admission the Ravayat in question can hardly be said to prescribe the Barashnum, and neither does the Avesta itself, which like the Rivayats prescribes only belief (Yashna 12) (6. P.W. page. 25.) and lastly when the Vendidad prescribes the fees to be paid by the different classes of society, for its administration these persons are all already Zoroastrians. Iranians i.e. the Persians who remained in their country without succumbing to Mohammedanism neglect the rite (Jackson Persia Past and Present page 383 and 6. P. W.pg 62 etc.) and the son of the late High Priest of Yezd which is the centre of Zoroastrian Orthodoxy in Iran (6. P. W. 62) tells us that when Persians whose fathers have become Mohammedans seek to return to the ancestral faith, the Barsnum so far as he is aware is not imposed (5. D. W. page. 17.)

In 1882 when the persons known as the Mazagon converts were admitted into Zoroastrianism, the necessity for the ceremony was disputed and there was similar dispute in 1902 when a French lady was converted (6, P.W.76. But when differences of opinion prevail amongst the learned, the layman must follow the opinion of the Dastur on whom he relies (6.P. W. 64.)

In 1904 the questions (1) as to whether persons of alien faith could and should be admitted into Zoroastrianism and (2) if so under what restrictions was submitted by the Bombay Parsi Panchayat to a committee of 10 learned men. They answered unanimously that Zoroaster not only permitted but enjoined conversion but as to the restrictions that should be adopted seven voted inter alia for the barasnum, two were against it and one thought all the proposed restrictions much too severe.

Sir Dinshaw Davar at p. 88 of Exhibit 30 which is the full text of his judgment in Sir D. M. Petit and others vs. Sir J. Jeejeebhoy accepted the view that the Barashnum was necessary, but Beaman J. declined to follow him. According to him the defendants case in the suit in question was (p.23 Exhibit 31) that however perfectly converts might be admitted they were not entitled to the benefits of their (charitable) funds; and he declared that he at once and finally accepted that position as has shut the door on what might have been long enquiries into ancient ritual that appeared to him to be likely to lead to no good results.

In the present case however a decision on this point of ancient ritual is unavoidable, and let me again turn to what the High Priest and the Deputy High Priest themselves plaintiff's witness have to say upon the decision of this Council of Experts, presumable the most learned men in the community and ritual of their faith. As I have said they unanimously agreed that the prophet not only permitted but enjoined conversion and gave quotations from their sacred books in support of their conclusion, but upon the question as to the conditions ceremonies and ritual for initiation they did not cite a single authority. Exhibit 40 the report in question (says the High Priest) was fully supported whenever possible by authorities and special pains were taken to search for them but none were cited for the conditions and qualifications prescribed for converts, these were he says a piece of fresh legislation to be enforced in the future (6 P.W. p. 46). The use of the barashnum was (he says) prescribed at his suggestion (p. 16), and he had borrowed it from his father (p. 15) and the report was a species of fresh ecclesiastical legislation for new converts (p. 20). There was no suggestion of a second Navjote in the Avesta(he says) p. 22 and the initiate would be a Zoroastrian after the first Navjot (p. 33) while the Deputy High Priest owns at p. 26 of his evidence that unless the barusnum was necessary, the second Navjot also would not be necessary.

I cannot admit that either this committee of experts or the Parsi Community of Bombay have any power to introduce "by fresh ecclesiastical legislation" rules ceremonies or rites for admission which are neither prescribed by their religion or hallowed by custom.

So far as I can see in the Zoroastrian religion the power of admitting persons into the fold lies with the priests, and there is nothing authoritative to shew that the rites and ceremonies differed in the case of a convert from what is necessary in the case of a child born of Zoroastrian parents. The priest has to satisfy himself (a) that the initiate really and sincerely desires to enter the faith, (b) that he believes in its doctrines and, (c) that he is sufficiently acquainted with them for the purpose and when he has so satisfied himself the Nahn, Navjot and investiture with the Sudreh and Kusti the outward and visible signs of Zoroastrianism are all that is requisite.

The priest can demand more if he chooses, and it is here that the force of public opinion is potent, but it works upon the priest who admits, not upon the initiate who is admitted,

We see traces of this in the endeavours of Parsis to forbid the admission of illegitimate children of Parsis by women of alien faith.

In 1830 we find the Anjuman declaring that our people invest their issues by alien mistresses with Sudreh and take them into our religion and providing that as regards those already admitted it is done and finished, but that it should not be done in future, and that any Mobed or priest who did so should be punished Exhibit G, while we find a similar resolution passed in 1905 exhibit 10 also recognising the initiation of such persons as had been admitted up to that date and again threatening Mobeds who initiated such children or the future (Exhibit 10).

In other words, the community recognises the initiation by the Mobeds when it is a "fait accompli."

Here the plaintiffs have endeavoured to prove that it is not a fait accompli because the Barasnum and second Navjote were not performed.

Having regard to the evidence upon the point I am unable to hold that it is shown that either is essential. The community can of course bring pressure upon the priest not to initiate converts without these two ceremonies, but if a priest chooses to disregard such pressure, and initiate without them, the initiation is not in my opinion invalidated.

The only other grounds mentioned by the plaintiff in their letter R.J. were that the convert must be in a position to satisfy the conditions V and the VI laid down by Davar J. in the Parsi Punchayet case ILR 33 Bombay P. 515 or Exhibit 30 p. 91. Now it must again be pointed out that issue 6 related only to ceremonies, and the particulars ordered related only to ceremonies, and the party which desired to raise issues relating to other matters should have applied to the Court to raise such.

This was never done either before or after the issue of the commission, nor was the matter discussed so far as I remember in their addresses by counsel on either side.

I therefore think that either the matter was waived or that it was tacitly agreed that it could not be urged that Bella fell within their scope, and that there is no necessity for me to go into these points but in case I am mistaken, I propose to deal briefly with the matter.

The 5th and 6th conclusions at which Davar J. arrived were as follows:

(a) "That, although conversion is permissible by the religion there are certain conditions which the candidate must fulfil before becoming eligible for admission. The conditions are that it must first be satisfactorily established that he or she, in applying for admission, is animated by a good object and actuated by pure intentions, in other words, that he or she seeks admission from religious convictions and not from other considerations, and further, that the candidate is in all other respects fit to be admitted to the Zoroastrian faith.

(b). "That such an admission of a person born outside of the religion is only permissible if it is established that by such admission no harm of any kind would be done to the Zarthosti Mazdiyasnans themselves».

Now in the first place it is to be noted that Davar J. himself considered 1) this portion of his judgment to be merely an obiter dictum and (2) that he could not answer the question in the absence of the converts (Exhibit 30 p.87).

Next the Bombay case was that of Champions of converts seeking for a declaration that they were entitled to the benefits of certain funds, while the case before me is its antithesis, it is not a case of converts claiming admission, but of Zoroastrians claiming exclusion of an initiate on the ground that she has not been duly initiated and therefore has no right to enter the temple. It is thus for them to prove what they assert, namely the converts unfitness and not as in the Bombay case for the candidate to satisfy the Court of his fitness. Now Davar J. bases these conclusions V and VI (a) on the report of the Expert Committee (b) on three Ravayats. With regard to these authorities the learned Judge at p. 86 says as follow: "The plaintiffs seek the assistance of the Courts relying on the Riwayat's and a report of a committee of "Experts selected from the Zoroastrian Community. Surely if these documents are relied upon as authorities, the person on whose behalf such assistance is sought must comply with the requirement laid down in these documents. The learned Judge as a Zoroastrian does not himself attach much importance at any rate to the Ravayats. He says at p, 85 that one at least of the statements made in the question put in the first of them (Exhibit E 1 in the Bombay Court. Exhibit 51 in this Court) seems to him so startling that he hesitates to place much reliance on the accuracy of it or the other two. He refers to the allegation that Durvands or non-Zoroastrians prepared the cake or Daroons used for certain ceremonies and adds that only a Zoroastrian could understand" the gross improbability of such a thing having happened."

He however then proceeds at page 86 to set out the effect of this Ravayat Exhibit 51, and apparently understands it to lay down that the Mobeds (priest) and Behdins (layman) should not take such persons into the religion unless they are satisfied that the religion and their lives and property will suffer no sort of harm, as though the laymen had a direct voice in the matter.

A reference however to the translations shews that these precautions relate to the buying of these slaves.

The layman would buy the slaves, the layman might get them taught the religion, but it is the priest and the priest only who can admit them.

The second Ravayat set out by him at pages 87 was also an Exhibit in this case but does not contain any thing for or against the doctrine that it is the priest who admits, nor yet does the third, set out at page 88 with which I have already dealt while as for the recommendations of the Committee of Experts the High Priest admits that they are a species of fresh legislation.

Undoubtedly these suggestions as a whole were not complied with, but I cannot see that they are of any binding force. The defendants do not rely either on the report or the Ravayats; they even dispute the admissibility of the Exhibit in which the opinions of the experts are contained, while all they claim for the Ravayat is that historically they point to the practice of conversion.

So far as I can see it is for the priest who initiates the convert to satisfy himself as to his or her fitness; he is responsible to his conscience and to public opinion if he performs the ceremony from a wrong motive or without due examination, but I doubt whether any Court would go into the question of such an initiates fitness, provided that the necessary ceremonies were performed, and she was of an age and capacity to understand what she was doing. In the present such a question scarcely arises, the child had been bred up in the faith and the Rangoon priest himself admits that though he refused to initiate her, he did so not on the score of religion (p. 25) but because the feelings of the community were against it (p. 32) and because he thought that if he initiated her, he in Rangoon and his parents in India might get into trouble (p. 24) and he says he knows her well p. 3. I therefore think that this claim also fails; on all grounds therefore I must hold that the plaintiffs have failed to prove that Bella was not duly initiated and I must hold that she is, and that no Zoroastrian can complain of her presence in the temple unless such temple is meant not for Zoroastrians generally, but for a peculiar section of them to which she does not belong. In other words, I hold that the suit fails so far as what may be called the moral trespass is concerned.

As regards the physical trespass the question involves the construction of the trust under which the temple is held and I cannot construe that the trust or decide that the trustee is committing a breach of trust in causing invitations to be sent to her, in his absence and behind his back.

The questions therefore as to whether she is the daughter of a Parsi woman and whether she is one of the Parsi population, for whose benefit and the land and temple are held in trust under the Trust deeds cannot be decided in this suit and I do not propose to express an opinion one way or the other as to do so would I think serve no useful end but might even encourage litigation.

The Parsis of Rangoon so far as the evidence before me enables me to judge are in a very different position to their coreligionists of Bombay. I have heard of nothing of large charitable funds for the benefit of the Parsis of Rangoon, such as are enjoyed by the Parsis of Bombay but only of a temple and a place for the disposal of their dead. The temple has an income derived from shops which from the ground floor of the building amounting I am told to Rs.1,200 per mensem out of which its upkeep and that of the land in which the Parsis dispose of their dead is maintained. And this temple and therefore all their charitable funds of which I have knowledge the Parsis owe to the generosity of the two brothers who rescued maintained and adopted the first defendant. Whatever the law may be, it seems to me that in the present state of public feeling indiscriminate conversion is very unlikely to occur, and in Rangoon there seem to be none of those material temptations to false conversions the power of which was so dreaded by the Parsis of Bombay with their wealthy charitable institutions. All that the defendant asks is permission to pray in the temple of her faith. If the plaintiffs still desire and think they have the right to prevent her doing so, they must try their fortune in a properly constituted suit. I cannot help them in this, even if I thought them entitled. The present suit must therefore be dismissed with costs and my formal findings on the issues are as regards the-

1st the affirmative,

2nd in the affirmative,

3rd that the question cannot be answered in the present suit,

4th that it is unnecessary to decide the point in this suit,

5th (a) in the affirmative, (b) unnecessary,

6th that the ceremonies are not shewn to be defective,

C. YOUNG,

Judge, 23rd April 1918

(B)
SAKLAT VS BELLA JUDGEMENT DATED 1920 (CHIEF COURT OF LOWER BURMA) JUSTICE MCGREGOR

No 70

Judgement of Appelate Court

Civil First Appeal No 4 of 1919

For appellants-Mr. Rutledge with Mr. N. M. Cowasji, For respondents-Mr. Giles and Mr. Lentaigne,

Judgment

Dated 28th July 1920.

In our judgment of 21st June 1920 which should be read as part of this judgment and which decided the first two issues the pleadings were fully set out. We have now to decide the remaining issues. The contest centres round the third issue. "Who are entitled to the benefit of the Fire Temple Trust?" Counsel stated that if this issue was decided against the plaintiffs a decision in their favour on the remaining issues would be of every little value.

To understand the true inwardness of the questions involved and to see them in their right perspective one must have clearly before one the broad facts of the history of the case. Further to arrive at a complete decision on the main issue the facts as to the other issues must be known and a decision on them arrived at. I will therefore first deal with issues 4, 5 (a) and 6 and then consider Issue 3. Is defendant 1 the daughter of a Parsi mother.

I don't think this is a matter that is of any real importance and it may be disposed of shortly. Mr. S. Cowasji and Mr. B. Cowasji are the principal witnesses on the point. The lady visited Mr. B. Cowasji for help and she no doubt did so because he was a Parsi professing the same religion. It is clear that there was some special reason for his extending as much help to her as he did, and this was because he was satisfied that she was a Parsi. He allowed her to live in one of hie houses and helped her generously. When he went to England in May1900 he asked his brother to look after her. Both brothers had opportunities of finding out the fraud if she was merely posing as a Parsi to induce their charity and would have done so. It is also clear that she was concealing her parents' names and this they must have realized and had they had any doubt on the matter they would have acted differently. They are certain she was a Parsi and Dr. Parakh who treated her is of the same opinion. I see no reason to doubt she was a Parsi. Mr. S. Cowasji has adopted the child and has brought her up in the way a Parsi child would be brought up and in the Parsi religion and has thus practically demonstrated his opinion.

As to whether the child of a non-Parsi father can be initiated into the Zoroastrian religion this involves the question as to whether conversion is a tenet of that religion. The expression 'conversion' has been used throughout but that implies that the person concerned had before professed another religion. In the present case Bella never had any other religion. But the issue is rightly worded. There is no question that even the child of a Parsi father must be initiated and here we have to decide whether the child of a non-Parsi father can ever become a Zoroastrian by religion. That the Zoroastrian religion not merely recognizes but actually enjoins conversion cannot I think be disputed. This was stated to be so by Dastur Dorab and Dastur R. Sanjana W.P.6 and 7 in their evidence. This was held to be so in the Bombay case Sir Dinshaw Maneckji Petit v. Sir Jamsetji Jijibhai (1). The documentary evidence shows that conversion and initiation were from time to time practised.

In 1830 there was a decision of the Anjuman (Exhibit D) with reference to the practice that had grown up of Parsis initiating their children by mistresses and the practise was forbidden. In 1836 the question arose of punishing a mobed who had performed a navjot on the child of a Parsi by a mistress without the permission of the Panchayat. In 1870 the Dastur gave an opinion that such children should not be refused (Exhibits 3 and 4). Then there is the case of the children of the Mazgaon converts. These are no doubt all cases of persons who were the children of Parsi fathers. Mrs. Tata a French lady was converted in 1903 and initiated by a High Priest. This brought the matter to a head and the whole question was considered by a committee. They appointed an expert committee to consider the question in its religious aspect and their decision was that conversion was not contrary to the true religion. Both parties rely on this report in part, and it is I think clear that in view of all the available evidence it must be held that conversion of persons who are the children of non-Parsi fathers is not contrary to the religion. The report of the Expert committee, it must be remembered, was made at a time when the question was sharply dividing the community and was the subject of strongly held divergent views. Possibly neither party really thought conversion was contrary to their religion.

Founded as it was by an individual, conversion was essential to progress and conversion was no doubt practised in Persia. But when a small band of Zoroastrians fled from religious oppression and came to India and settled here the practice fell into disuse. While they lived amongst men of the same stock there would be no feeling against it; it was enjoined and was meritorious. In India the conditions were different, and they kept very much to themselves and this continued. Then when years passed the newer generations did not think of conversion. So, it is argued that though it may have been a tenet of the religion and though even it may have been enjoined on the pious Zoroastrian long disuse has created a custom that overrides the tenet. Occasions arose when the question was brought up as in the case of illegitimate children but by then the feeling of the majority of the community was against it and it was discouraged and indeed forbidden. The Parsis had acquired wealth and they had charitable institutions and the right to share in these would affect their views. All sorts of undesirable persons attracted by these benefits might seek to become Zoroastrian in order to share in them. But these are not considerations that can affect the decision of the matter. Conversion was enjoined as a pious duty and mere neglect of that duty cannot remove that tenet from the religion no custom can be established by non-performance. That would be a contradiction in terms for a custom is created by regular consistent and continuous performance. I would therefore hold that the child of a non-Parsi father can be initiated into the Zoroastrian religion.

The next question is whether the ceremonies performed at Bella's initiation were defective.

When the issues were framed the Court recorded as to this issue-" the second defendant to give particulars of the ceremonies performed at the initiation of the first defendant within one week and the plaintiffs to state within one week thereafter whether and if so in what respects they contend that these ceremonies were inefficacious".

This was done and it is admitted that in the case of the first defendant she was initiated by the performance of the customary navjot the investiture of the Sudreh and Kusti and the repetition of suitable prayers. Plaintiffs raised various objections on the ground of her age, the nirang used and so on but their principal objection was that there must have been a barushnam followed by a second navjote as essential ceremonies. This last objection is the only one now pressed. The onus is on the plaintiff to prove that barushnam is essential and there is no question that if it is not the second navjot is not necessary.

It is to be noted that the barushnam they insist on is a ceremony of lustration of the whole body by the priest on nine nights running. It is not denied or practically not denied that it is a ceremony that no convert would be willing to undergo, and it is not required for Parsi children or if it is, never performed. It was an ancient ceremony that may have been used in primitive times but is now never performed whether it be enjoined or not except in the case of priests and corpse bearers.

As to the essential character of this ceremony I will first consider what authority there is for it. There is none in the sacred writings extent. The only authority is a single Revayat. In this barushnam is enjoined for every Zoroastrian and yet it is beyond dispute that it is never observed. The revayats were opinions given based on ancient practice as opposed to inspired teachings and writings. They are admittedly of minor authority and even if this opinion was based on ancient observance the practice has evidently fallen into disuse. The witness Dastur Dorab Sanjana (page 49 etc.) says he would not ask modern Zoroastrian to observe all its recommendations and that he would not hold it incumbent on every Zoroastrian to carry out barashnum because it is not in accordance with the spirit of the religion as taught in the more authoritative books. The Vendidad lays it down only for the purification of a man who has come into contact with dead matter. This is the most unclean thing to a Zoroastrian and for that the barashnum, the highest form of purification is prescribed. The revayat prescribed it to wash away the uncleanness that had been contracted in the womb by the child feeding on menstrual matter an error which the spread of education detected and so the recommendation lost authority and was abandoned. Next, we have the Report of the Expert committee (Exhibit 40). That can quote no authority, but this Rivayat and it amounts to no more than the opinion of the majority of the members. At the time the Report was written there were two schools of thought sharply divided as to conversion and when it had to be admitted that proselytism was in accordance with the religion it may be that those who were averse to it were led to take the view that the necessary ceremonies should be made as stringent as possible. In the case of the Mazagon converts we were told that it was performed in a modified form and again that no barashnum was performed at all. I have been unable to find any proof that it was performed.

Indeed, it would appear that it was one of the subjects of dispute after they had been initiated. The father of the witness D. Dorab Sanjana was one of contentesting priests and wrote a discourse on the question of barashnum. When this witness was questioned as to authorities, he admitted there was only the one revayat and he refers to his father's discourse. He admits that the report was legislating for initiations and not enforcing ancient rules. He admits that the pious Zoroastrian is bound to follow the advice of the priest on whom he relies and it is clear that the priests were divided as to the need of barashnum for initiation.

Mrs Tata was initiated by one High Priest and defendant by another and neither enjoined barashnum. Defendant 1 was the daughter of a Parsi mother; she had never known her father or his religion; from her earliest days she had been bought up as a Parsi child in the Zoroastrian religion and it would therefore be hard to hold that barashnum, never performed in the case of an ordinary Parsi child, must be performed to render her initiation valid. Having regard to the absence of authority and to the difference in the views of the priests, it is in my opinion impossible to hold the plaintiffs have proved that her initiation was invalid by reason of the fact that no barashnum was performed.

That brings me to the main issue: -"Who are entitled to the benefit of the Fire Temple Trust?"

By a grant dated 24th November 1868 the Government of India granted to persons a parcel of land "Upon trust to build and maintain upon the said parcel of land a temple for the use of Parsi population. "

The grant further provided that if a temple was not built within one year or if the land was at any time put to any other use than that for which the trust provided the Deputy Commissioner might revoke the grant and take possession of the land and all buildings upon it.

A temple was duly built. In 1904 Mr. B. Cowasjee and Mr. S. Cowasjee, with the consent of all those interested in the temple, had it pulled down and erected, at their own expense, another Fire Temple. Mr. B. Cowasjee was at time the sole trustee and he executed a Declaration of Trust in respect of the new temple. In this he declared that he held the temple "in trust for the use of the Parsi inhabitants of Rangoon free and unrestricted but subject nevertheless to the tenets of the pure Zoroastrian religion and to the scheme prescribed by the said Court of the Recorder of Rangoon for the management of the said Trust, "

The plaintiffs contend that the words Parsi population must be read as meaning - First the descendants of the original emigrants into India from Persia who profess the Zoroastrian religion Secondly, -The descendants of Zoroastrians in Persia who were not amongst the original emigrants but who are of the same stock and have since come to India and settled there and who profess the Zoroastrian religion and thirdly - The children of Parsi fathers by alien mothers who have been admitted into the religion of their fathers and profess the Zoroastrian religion.

The defendant on the other hand contend that the grant was made for the use and benefit of persons professing the Zoroastrian religion. In short, the plaintiffs urge that the word Parsi was used to designate a race or clan or caste while defendants urge it was used to denote those professing a particular religion of whatever race they might be.

Much reference has been made in argument to the Bombay case and the conclusions arrived at therein, but I do not propose to discuss those conclusions. The learned Judges there were dealing with the meaning of the word Parsi as used in certain trust deeds creating trusts for charitable and religious uses, but they were seeking to arrive at the intention of individual donors in making charitable endowments and those donors were themselves of the Parsi race and religion. In the present case we have to find the intention of the Government. Some of the considerations which would govern the decisions would be distinctly different.

The rules of interpretation are now well known. If the words used are clear and the meaning free from doubt you cannot go beyond them. If however they are ambiguous a construction must be given as is most agreeable to the intention of the donor. The object of all interpretation is to discover the intention of the donor and to do so, the instrument is to be construed as whole. In Lloyd v. Lloyd (2) * Lord Chancellor Cottenham said: -

" If the provisions are clearly expressed, and there is nothing to enable the Court to put upon them a construction different from that which the words import, no doubt the words must prevail ; but if the provisions and expressions be contradictory and if there be grounds, appearing upon the face of the instrument, affording proof of the real intention of the parties, then that intention will prevail against the obvious and ordinary meaning of the words. If the parties have themselves furnished a key to the meaning of the words used, it is not material by what expression they convey their intention."

Moreover, in cases of the creation of trusts the Courts will all the more seek to put that construction on the deeds that will effectuate the undoubted intention of the creator or donor.

In the present case it is argued that the words "Parsi Population" are perfectly clear and unambiguous and that it is not open to the Court to go beyond them. But there is a clear ambiguity in respect of the persons to whom these words are to be applied. They may be persons of Parsi race descent, or they may be intended to indicate Zoroastrians. There is abundant indication throughout the case that the words Parsi and Zoroastrian are changeable and synonymous indeed the first plaintiff in his evidence not only says so but repeats it and deliberately insists on it in cross-examination. The grant that has to be construed was of land for a Temple and the question whether the grant was intended for persons of a particular race professing a particular religion or for all persons professing that religion irrespective of race.

I do not propose to go at any length into the meaning of the word Parsi. It was the name given to a small band of migrants fleeing from Persia to escape religious oppression. Some expression was needed to indicate these people when reference was made to them and as they came from Persia they were named Parsis. They had to preserve their religion and they and they only were the persons professing that religion and it is I think undoubted that when reference was made in early days to the religion of Zoroaster it would be described as the religion of these Parsis.

So much so that to describe one of them might be called a Parsi or equally well a Zoroastrian. This no doubt continued for long and it is quite right to say that the words in certain senses mean one and the same thing. There is therefore no reason for saying that the expression the 'Parsi population' obviously means and was intended to mean the Parsis as a race and nothing else.

To enable a Court to arrive at the true intention of the Author of the Trust it should endeavour to place itself as nearly as possible in the position of the parties at the time and to this end evidence is admissible to prove the circumstances that surrounded the Author at the time the Trust was created. Such evidence would include proof of other grants of a like nature to the same persons or to others and there is some evidence of this nature in the present case.

On the 11th January 1859 Government had made a grant of land for a cemetry for the "Parsi denomination." In 1889 suits were brought and schemes framed for the management of both these trusts. By these schemes the funds of the Temple were to be applied for the maintenance and up keep of the cemetery also.

We have then the Parsi Marriage and Divorce Act, 1865. In the bill which preceded the Act there was a definition for the word "Parsi " and it was defined as follows: - "Parsi " means or applies to a person professing the religion of Zoroaster and domiciled in British India. I do not consider that we can obtain any assistance from this, for the definition was omitted from the Act which became law, and the reason is not known. But in the Act the word 'priest' is defined as meaning "a Parsi priest and includes Dastur and Mobed." The word Parsi is used throughout the Act, sometimes as referring to a Parsi man or woman where it has a racial significance possibly and other times in a sense that clearly refers to the religion e.g., marriages are to solemnized according to the Parsi form of ceremony.

In Act X of 1865 section 331 the excepted persons are defined by their religions and in Act XXI of 1865, a similar Act for Parsis it is urged that they also are referred to by their religion.

In Act III of 1872 also the Legislature speaks of persons professing the " Parsi religion."

In the deed of Settlement of Sir Jamsetjee Jeejeebhoy Parsi Benevolent Institution (Exhibit 5) a definition of 'Parsi' is given to remove all doubt. "It hereby declared that the word Parsi means in this indenture throughout, a person or persons professing the religion of Zoroaster."

In (Exhibit 1. (A). The General Trust Deed of Panchayat Property we find the expression "the Parsi religion."

It seems to me to be clear from this that the words "Parsi" and "Zoroastrian" were interchangeable and this is not denied. Further we find that Government was, about the time the grant to be interpreted was made, frequently using the word Parsi as denoting a religion, the religion of Zoroaster.

The grant was made for the advancement of the Zoroastrian religion by providing a site for a temple in which the rites and ceremonies of that religion might be performed and it was specially provided that the land was not to be used for any other purpose under penalty of forfeiture. The scheme framed for the management of the grant of land for a burial ground was made "for burying persons who shall at his or her death be actually professing the Zoroastrian religion and no other." These two grants were subsequently renewed at the same time and it is, in my opinion, right to hold that they were both made for the benefit of the same persons.

In the scheme for the burial ground there is an explanation attached to the clause I have just quoted.

"EXPLANATION. No one shall be taken to be actually professing the Zoroastrian religion who has not been duly invested with the Sudreh and the Kusti in accordance with the rites prescribed by that religion... Here there is no suggestion that they must also be Parsis by birth and descent. It may be that at that time there was no idea of any one being Zoroastrian who was not also a Parsi by race but the grant is clearly made for the use and benefit of a religion and not for the use and benefit of a race or community and I find it impossible to hold that had that question arisen Government would have made the grant for the use and benefit of some only of those professing the religion to the exclusion of others who professed the religion. I think it is clear that the Temple grant and the burial ground were both made for the same body of persons. The word "denomination" in the burial ground grant has clear reference to a religious body, and to hold that the Temple grant was made for the benefit of the Parsi race as distinct from persons who professed the same religion but were not Parsis by descent would mean that Defendant 1 might rightly be buried in the burial ground which is maintained by the Temple funds but was not entitled to use the Temple. Such a situation could never, I think, have been contemplated by the Government.

I am therefore of opinion that the Government in the grant clearly indicated an intention to create a Trust for a particular religion, in that the land was granted for a Temple. This being so the undoubted intention must govern the interpretation to be put on the words used. Further having regard to the meaning that had been attached to the same word in the other grant and to the meaning assigned to it by the Government in its legislative enactments contemporaneous to the grant it is clear that the word in the grant may well mean Zoroastrian and that that meaning must be given to it in order to effectuate the clear intention of the Author of the Trust. I must therefore hold that persons entitled to the benefit of the Fire Temple Trust are those persons who are professing the Zoroastrian religion, whether they are Parsis by race and descent or are persons of other races duly converted and initiated into the religion.

S. M. ROBINSON,
Acting Chief Judge.

As regards the 3rd issue, the most important of those remaining, viz, "Who are entitled to the benefit of the Parsi Fire Temple Trust?" It is to be remarked that if this decided in 1st defendant's favour, that is if she is found to be one of those who have a right to use the Temple, the finding is conclusive for her, but that if it be decided that she is not one of those having that right, the finding will not be conclusive against her, for plaintiffs will have to go further, and show that her entry into the Temple, in the language of the plaint "wounds the religious feelings entertained by religiously inclined Parsis, and also causes the desecration of the said sacred Temple." This is the result of our finding in the two preliminary issues.

Before considering this 3rd issue, I desire to clear the ground by a few remarks on the case of SIR DINSHAW MANECKJI PETIT, SIR JAMSETJI JIJIBHAI the judgments in which have been freely quoted before us by both sides.

The judgements in that case are expressly confined in their application to the Parsi Community or Anjuman of Bombay and the Funds and Properties held in trust for that community. This appears from a passage in the judgment of DAVAR J and I underline the two last sentences in the following from BEAMAN J.

"The real, the plain point was simply this, that ....(the Defendants) took their stand not on religion but on caste, and when it came to a practical test, denied that anyone could become a member of the Parsi community except by birth. That in a nutshell was the whole case for the defendants, and I think that it was a good case and must prevail. In saying this I must be understood to limit myself strictly to the Trust Funds and Properties which are the subject matter of this suit. I do not want to make any general pronouncement or to go one step further than I am obliged."

As regards the Trust Funds and Properties, the question before the High Court at Bombay was narrowed down to this, viz., whether the conversion of Mrs Tata had the effect of entitling her to the use of the Godavara Agiary or Fire Temple, and more especially to the benefits of Dokhmas or "Towers of Silence" on her death. In the present case the question of the 1st defendants right to be buried in the Parsi burial ground, there being no Dokhma in Rangoon, is not in issue. Plaintiffs seek to have her excluded from the only Agiary in Rangoon on the ground that as her father was not a Parsi her presence desecrates the Agiary and wounds their religious feelings. It is not clear whether Mrs. Tata was in the habit of attending any of the Agiaries in Bombay. One gathers from the Bombay report (5) that these, other than the Godavara Agiary, were not under the control or management of the defendants.

The question, whether Mrs. Tatas' presence in an Agiary would have been regarded in Bombay as a desecration does not seem to have been specifically raised.

There are other differences also between the Bombay case and the present. There, the plaintiffs were the champions of an adult French lady, Mrs, Tata, who had been converted to the Zoroastrian religion, and their object was to have her right declared to enter into the use of certain properties. Here, 1st defendant is Parsi on the mother's side - on this question I concur with the learned Chief Judge on the grounds which he gives - has never known her father and has from earliest infancy been brought up in the religion as an adopted daughter in a Parsi family. She is not a convert to the religion, in the sense Mrs Tata was a convert. The object of the plaintiffs is to exclude her from the use of the Rangoon Agiary which she has been attending.

Again the learned Judges at Bombay were concerned with the construction of the intentions of pious Parsi founders for the benefit of the Bombay Anjuman; whereas here we have to do with a grant made to the Parsi community of Rangoon by the Government of India.

Lastly, as the learned trial Judge well points out near the end of his judgement, the Parsis of Rangoon, who probably do not number more than 150 including women and children, are in a very different position from their co-religionists in Bombay. "It seems to me" he writes, "that in the present state of public feeling Indiscriminate conversion is very unlikely to occur, and in Rangoon there seems to be none of those material temptations to false conversion, the power of which was so dreaded by the Parsis of their wealthy charitable institutions.

The remarks of the learned Judge have reference to the following passage in Davar J; judgment - " If the plaintiffs contentions prevailed, the community would very soon have no reason to boast of these characteristic of their race" (viz. the absence in the Parsi Community of street beggars and other undesirable, and the provisions made by themselves for paupers and cripples), and the Parsis would soon cease to exist as a community by reason of the rapid invasion of all pauper Sweepers and Dubras of Gujrat, who would no doubt be attracted to the Holy Mazdiasni religion by reason of the FIFTY THREE LAC RUPPEES in the possession of the defendants, and the other advantages of belonging to the Anjuman of the Holy Zoroastrians of Bombay."

Hence when Beaman J. in the passage I have already cited (7), proceeds to say.... "Perhaps, then I should say that I think .... (that) it was not the intention of the founders of these Trusts to extend their benefits to anyone who was not in the most rigid caste sense a Parsi, that is born into the community of the Indian Zoroastrians, and born of an Indian Zoroastrian father," it will be for consideration whether, in view of the express limitation of the scope of the Bombay judgments, and the differences set out above between the case and the present one, I am to feel bound to adopt that rigid definition of the term Parsi, or to attempt for Rangoon, what the Government of India has done in any of its enactments relating to Parsis, a precise definition of the limits of the Parsi community. I may say here, that in my opinion the 1st defendant is a member of the Parsi community of Rangoon; but I hasten to add that such a decision is a decision for her case only. To adopt the words of Beaman, J. I do not want to make any general pronouncement, or to go one step outside the conditions which limit the present case.

One more remark, with all due respect to Beaman J. viz. that in applying the term "caste" to the Parsi community he is not, I think it, safe to say supported by the sanction of popular usage, a tolerably sure index of the correctness or otherwise of the proposition, Parsis are not a caste, in everyday speech or writing, even - so far as my experience goes - in the loose sense in which the word is used in such phrases as " the military caste," " the noble caste and the like.

To come now to the issue - "Who are entitled to the benefits of the Fire Temple Trust?" The answer is in the grant of the Government of India referred to in the judgment of the learned Chief Judge - "The Parsi population" I agree with the learned Chief Judge, that "The Parsi population" in that grant is synonymous with "the Parsi denomination" in the grant of the end for a burial-ground. I quote here in full the relevant first article of the scheme for the burial ground settled by the Recorder of Rangoon in Civil Regular suit No. 37 of 1889:

" The burial ground shall be used for burying persons who shall at his or her (sec) death be actually professing the Zoroastrian religion and no other. EXPLANATION. No one shall be taken to be actually professing the Zoroastrian religion who has not been duly invested with the Sudreh and the Kusti, in accordance with the rites prescribed by that religion provided, nevertheless, that children born of fathers following the Zoroastrian religion, and brought up in that faith, and dying before the age of 14 years and three months, without having been invested with the Sudreh and Kusti may be taken to be actually professing the Zoroastrian religion, but children dying after having attained the age without having been invested with the Sudreh and Kusti shall not be taken to have professed the Zoroastrian religion unless his or her investiture was prevented by unforeseen and unavoidable circumstances."

It can be gathered from the records in that suit and in the connected suit no. 36 of 1889 in which a scheme for the Fire

Temple was settled, that the proviso to the explanation was meant for the children of Parsis who had married Burmese and therefore Buddhist wives.

At that time the Parsi community in Rangoon was even smaller than now, mustering about sixteen at each of their public meetings called in connection with framing of the schemes. It must have consisted mostly of men, and no Parsi women but the wives of some of them. The object of the proviso was not, therefore, to define the term Parsi so as to limit it at all times and places to the offspring of Parsi fathers, but merely to provide for certain offspring of such Parsi fathers as were in Rangoon.

I would therefore answer the 3rd issue by saying that those entitled to the benefit of the Fire Temple Trust in Rangoon are those members of the Parsi population who actually profess the Zoroastrian religion and no other and have been duly invested with the Sudreh and Kusti according to the rites prescribed by that religion. The proviso does not concern us here.

The remaining question would actually be "Does 1st defendant belong to the Parsi population of Rangoon, and fulfil the other conditions?" Plaintiff put the question in a slightly different form, viz. "Can 1st defendant belong, is it possible for her to belong, to the Parsi community and to profess the Zoroastrian religion?" and they contend that the answers must be in the negative because her father was not a Parsi. The 5th issue has been framed accordingly, Viz. "Is it possible for the 1st defendant being the daughter of a non Parsi father to be initiated (a) into the Zoroastrian religion and (b) into the Parsi community?" As one does not use initiate in connection with a community, "I take the liberty of amending (b) into 'to become a member of the Parsi community."

As regards (a), it is clear that the Zoroastrian religion, according to the intensions of its Founder, was to be a proselytizing religion; but it is equally clear that, since their arrival in India 13 centuries ago, the Zoroastrian religion has been the religion of the Parsis and the Parsis alone, and there is no authentic instance of conversion to that religion of a non-Parsi, except the case of Mrs Tata which roused a storm of controversy in the Bombay Anjuman. The learned counsel for plaintiffs appellants has said that the finding in the Bombay case are exactly what he takes his stand on; and his argument is that in these 13 centuries, during which the Parsis kept themselves apart as a peculiar people with a peculiar religion, race and descent have become so inextricably bound up with religion that the one has become a part of the other, so that no one but a Parsi can nowadays profess the Parsi religion; and 1st defendant not being the daughter of a Parsi father is not a Parsi. 1st plaintiff in his evidence says "Parsi and Zoroastrian mean the same thing are the same word". "We use one word for the other in our conversation amongst the Parsis". His first witness Burjorjee Panthaky, whose father is a priest in the old Rangoon Agiary, goes so far as to say that if a rich non- Parsi were to become converted to the Zoroastrian religion and to build his own Fire Temple for himself and for other converts, he would object to it all and have nothing to do with them. His witness Dhunjishaw B. Desai, who comes from Navsari, an important Parsi headquartering India says "I would not worship in any Zoroastrians temple built by converts themselves, as such converts have gone against the cherished sentiments of the Parsi community by converting themselves to our religion which I believe to be the true religion. We want to keep to ourselves the charitable and religious endowments and institutions raised for the Parsis".

In the last sentence we seem to hear the Bombay judgment, the preceding sentences are to be understood as seriously as they were spoke

The learned counsel for defendants - respondents relies on such statements in the evidence for plaintiffs as that 'Parsi' and 'Zoroastrian' mean one and the same thing, the statements are echoes of passages on which he relies in the Bombay Judgment. His argument is that Parsi in the Government of India grant, is used in its religious significance, to denote a religious community. The religion permits and even enjoins proselytizing the mere fact that the practice of this injunction has long fallen into desuetude can be no argument, to the mind of Government which made the grant, against the validity of a conversion now, and a convert duly initiated into the Zoroastrian or Parsi religion is entitled to the benefit of the Fire Temple Trust. Not that 1st defendant is a convert in the sense in which Mrs. Tata was.

On the Principles and spirit of the religion there is no difference between 1st defendant and any ordinary Parsi child; and the letter prescribes no peculiar initiatory ceremonies for her. The arguments in both sides have been, I think, strongly influenced by the Bombay Judgment. As these dealt with different facts and circumstances, and the point of view was determined by different considerations from those which we have here, I think it best, for the reasons which I have already given, to clear one's mind of the suggestions for the Bombay judgments and gave a decision strictly confined to the merits of the case. As I have already said, I do not intend to lay down any general proposition, nor do I understand the 5th issue, when read with my finding on the 3rd, to require answers in such a form. There are certain facts to be held in view. One is, that for however long the practice of making converts may have ceased, the religion itself enjoins it. Next, the Bombay Anjuman was divided on the question of the admission of Mrs. Tata, some being for and some against; as the evidence in this case shows that the Parsi community in Rangoon is divided on the question of 1st defendant. Again, the Government of India, in the various acts relating to Parsis, has not concerned itself to define the term. It is a reasonable influence that it does not want to commit itself to any definition. I doubt, myself, whether the term is definable. It is impossible to say, of any individual Parsi now living, that he is descended in the male line from the Parsi immigrants of 1300 years ago. A Parsi, it seems to me, is to be described, rather than defined, as a member of the well known community having, as a community, a certain origin and history, distinctive and above all a distinctive religion. That is, I think more satisfactory then definitions which when examined, reduce merely to this, that a Parsi is person whose father was a Parsi. Lastly, the defendant Bella is half Parsi by parentage. She has never known any home but a Parsi home or been taught any religion but the Parsi religion. She has been in due time invested in proper form by a Parsi High Priest of standing and repute with the Sudreh and Kusti. I may say here that on the question of the necessity of any further ceremony I am entirely in agreement with the learned Chief Judge. I am of opinion that considerations such as these would weigh with the Government of India whose intention in making the grant we have to interpret. The question in my opinion is not the general one of who a member of the Parsi community can be, but whether 1st defendant in this case is or is not, as a matter of fact, a member of the Parsi community of Rangoon. That question can, I believe, in the circumstances of this case, be answered without enquiring into the race of her unknown father. In this country a person without a community is difficult to conceive. 1st defendant does not as a matter of fact belong, and never has belonged to any other community than the one she has been brought up in and if she were cast out from it she has no other to fall back upon. My findings on the 5th issues are that 1st defendant is a member of the Parsi Commutiny of Rangoon and that she has been duly initiated into the Zoroastrian religion; and therefore, she is entitled to the benefit of the Fire Temple Trust.

A. MACGREGOR, Judge.
28th July 1920.

(C)
FINAL APPEAL MADE IN SAKLAT VS BELLA

No 73

Application for leave to appeal to His Majesty In Council

In the Chief Court of Lower Burma

Civil MISCELLANEOUS No. 68 of 1920

D. R. Saklat And 2 Others

Plaintiffs Applicants

Vs

BELLA AND ONE

DEFENDENTS APPLICANTS

The humble petition of the plaintiff- appellants abovenamed,

Respectfully Sheweth

1. Your petitioner being aggrieved at the judgment and decree of this Hon'ble Court passed in Civil 1st Appeal No. 4 of 1919 of this Court desire to appeal to His Majesty in Council on the following grounds and on other grounds as your petitioner may hereafter be advised to adopt: -

   (a) That this Hon'ble Court erred in holding that the persons entitled to the benefit of the Parsee Fire Temple Trust are those persons who are professing the Zoroastrian religion irrespective of the fact whether they are Parsees by race and descent or are persons of other races duly converted and initiated into the Zoroastrian religion.

(b) That this Hon'ble Court should have held that the only persons entitled to the benefit of the said Fire Temple Trust are members of the "Parsee population" who also profess the Zoroastrian religion. And that the respondent Bella was not a member of such population.

(c) That in determining the meaning of the expression 'Parsee population in the grant of 29th March 1868 this Hon'ble Court ought to have considered the intention of the then Parsee population who had applied for the grant and for whose benefit the grant was made, and this Hon'ble Court ought to have considered the further fact that since the foundation of the said Trust none but Parsees by race had had access to and the right of worship in the said Fire Temple.

(d) For that this Hon'ble Court ought to have held that it could not have been intended either by the Parsee population which applied for the grant, or by the Government that made the grant, that the expression "Parsi population" should comprise and include converts to the Zoroastrian religion.

(e) For that the Learned Chief Judge erred in holding that the said grant was made by the Government of India for the advancement of the Zoroastrian religion. It has never been the policy of the British Government to advance any religion either in India or in Burma.

(f) That assuming that proselytizing forms a tenet of the Zoroastrian religion this Court should have held that it cannot entitle non-Parsi converts to the Zoroastrian religion to the benefits of Parsee institutions

(g) For that this Court ought to have held that the onus was on the Respondents Bella to establish that she was properly converted to the Zoroastrian religion, and that she had failed to discharge such onus. And that even assuming that she was so converted, she was not entitled to the use and benefit of the Parsi Fire Temple for the reason that she was not a Parsi by race.

(h) for that this Court should have held that the only persons entitled to the benefit of the Parsee Fire Temple are:

First—The descendants of the original migrants into India from Persia who profess the Zoroastrian religion.

Second— The descendants of Zoroastrians in Persia who were not amongst the original emigrants, but who are of the same stock and have since that date, from time to time, come to India and have settled here either permanently or temporarily, and who profess the Zoroastrian religion.

Thirdly—The children of a Parsee father by an alien mother, if such children are admitted into the religion of their fathers and profess the Zoroastrian-religion.

(i) That this Hon'ble Court should have held that the respondent Bella admittedly not coming within the classification specified in the last preceding paragraph was not a Parsee and did not belong to the Parsee population of Rangoon and is not entitled to the benefit of the Parsee Fire Temple.

(j) For that this Court erred in holding that the respondent Bella's mother was a Parsi, it should have held that there was no legal evidence to justify the Court in finding as a fact that her mother was a Parsi.

(k) That McGregor J. erred in holding that the respondent Bella in the special circumstances of the case became a member of the Parsee Community of Rangoon. He further erred in holding that a "Parsee" could not be defined but could only be described.

2. That the decree herein and the contentions urged by the respective Parties involves directly a claim of question to or respecting property of a Value far in excess of Rs. 10,000.

3. That the questions involve in this appeal are of very great importance to the Parsi Community, and it is necessary that all such questions should be finally determined by the highest tribunal.

4. That your petitioner submits that as regards the value and nature the case fulfils the requirements of Section 110 of the Civil Procedure Code in as much as the appeal involves substantial questions of law affecting the rights of the whole Parsee Community generally, and that it is otherwise a fit and proper case for appeal to His Majesty in Council

Wherefore your petitioners pray that a certificate may be granted either as regards the amount or value and nature or to the effect that the case fulfils the requirements of Section 110 of the Code of Civil Procedure or that it is otherwise a fit one for appeal to Majesty in Council.

And shall ever pray.
COWASJEE AND DAS,
Petitioners' Advocates.
Rangoon, This 22nd of December 1920.

(D)
OPINION OF THE PRIVY COUNCIL IN OCTOBER 1925, DELIVERED BY LORD PHILLIMORE IN SAKLAT VS BELLA

Bombay High Court

Saklat vs Bella on 22 October, 1925
Equivalent citations: (1926) 28 BOMLR 161
Author: Phillimore
Bench: Phillimore, Blanesburgh, J Edge
JUDGMENT Phillimore, J.

1. The circumstances of this case are as follows:
    Some time in 1899 a Goanese Christian named Jones with his wife arrived in Rangoon. They were in humble circumstances, and the wife applied for assistance to a Parsi of good position at Rangoon, BomanjiCowasji, stating that she too was a Parsi. He befriended her till he went to England in 1900 and then asked his brother ShapurjiCowasji to look after her and the child to which she had just given birth, the respondent Bella. The father died and when her mother died shortly afterwards Shapurji, who was a defendant in this suit, but died pending the appeal, took Bella into his own house, and he and his wife treated her as their own child.

2. When Bella was nearly fourteen it was desired that the initiation ceremony into the Zoroastrian religion called Navjot should be performed for her, but the local Head Priest at Rangoon refused, chiefly because-as it appears from his evidence-he thought it

would be unpopular with the Parsi community. Advantage was then taken of the temporary presence of some other priest, who performed the ceremony; and after that invitations were sent by the Head Priest to Bella to come with Shapurji and his wife to the temple on festival days. Three such invitations were sent, the High Priest said, with the expectation that they would not be accepted; but on third occasion, being March 21, 1915, Shapurji brought her and put her within the sacred precincts facing the sacred fire, and in such a position that she went through all the ceremonies like other worshippers.

3. This proceeding gave great offence to a number of members of the Parsi community in Rangoon, and on March 31, this suit was brought by three members of the Parsi community, who stated that they brought it not only on their own behalf but on behalf of a large number of members of the Parsi community at Rangoon, against Bella and against Shapurji, stating that the temple was held on trust for the free and unrestricted use of the Parsi inhabitants in Rangoon professing the Zoroastrian faith, further stating that it was alleged that the mother of Bella was a Parsi, and that Bella had been validly converted or initiated into the Zoroastrian religion, but denying that this was so or indeed could be so, and averring that the defendants had by their acts "not only wounded the religious feelings entertained by religiously inclined Parsis, but also caused the desecration of the said sacred temple.

4. In another paragraph of the plaint, they stated that only members of the Parsi community professing the Zoroastrian religion were entitled to the use of the temple, to the access of the sacred precincts, and to attend, witness or take part in any religious ceremonies held therein, and that it was never the intention of the Parsi community that the children of non-Parsi fathers should be allowed the use of the temple. They further

said that even assuming that Bella could be duly admitted into the Zoroastrian religion, and assuming that her mother was a Parsi, even then she could not be considered a Parsi or a member of the Parsi population. They prayed for a declaration that Bella was not entitled to use the temple or to attend or to participate in any of the religious ceremonies performed therein and for injunctions to restrain her from entering the temple and Shapurji from taking her there.

5. Shapurji, in his own name and as guardian for Bella, put in their written statement. In this it was contended that the plaint disclosed no cause of action, that the defendant Bella was entitled to attend the temple and the ceremonies and caused no desecretion by her presence; and it was stated that her mother was a Parsi, that she had been brought up from early infancy as a Parsi and in the Zoroastrian faith, and that she came within the terms of the trust of the temple.

6. The following issues were then settled :
   1. Whether the plaint discloses any cause of action ?
   2. Whether this suit is maintainable.
   3. Who are entitled to the benefit of the Fire Temple Trust?
   4. Is the first defendant the daughter of a Parsi mother ?
   5. Is it possible for the first defendant, being a daughter of a non-Parsi father, to be initiated (a) into the Zoroastrian Religion (b) into the Parsi community.
   6. If it was possible, whether the ceremonies adopted for the purpose were defective (the second defendant to give particulars of the ceremonies performed at the initiation of the first defendant within one week, and the plaintiffs to state within one week thereafter whether, and if so, in what respects, they contend that these ceremonies were inefficacious): and the case was set down for a preliminary hearing on the first and second issues.

7. The Judge decided these points in favour of the plaintiffs; and thereupon some oral evidence was taken before the Judge at Rangoon, and a mass of evidence covering 664 pages of the record was taken on commission at Bombay.

8. It appears that this was not the first occasion in modern times in which the question of the admissibility of a person who was not a racial Parsi, but who had become a convert to the Zoroastrian religion, to participate in the religious services and enter the temples of the Parsis had arisen.

9. In 1903 a French woman had declared that she had become a convert to the Zoroaatrian religion and had married a Parsi gentleman of position at Bombay. Her claim to participate in religious worship had given rise to much excitement in the Parsi community, and seven Parsis, one of whom was the French woman's husband, had brought a suit in the High Court of Bombay against the trustees of the Parsi endowments, first making a general case of some misfeasances requiring the intervention of the Court, and, secondly, claiming a declaration that the trust deeds ought to be construed as admitting to their benefits any person professing the Zoroastrian religion whether a racial Parsi or not.

10. After a prolonged litigation, this suit, except in so far as it prayed for a correction of the general misfeasances, was dismissed; and the Judges, for reasons which will have to be more minutely entered into, held that the various endowments were limited to the use of people who as well as being Zoroastrian were also racial Parsis. But the controversy had not been forgotten, and its echoes are to be heard in the evidence given on commission in the present case.

11. Young J., in the preliminary judgment given in the present case, held that the plaintiffs could not sue for trepass on

land or in the temple, but that they might have a third cause of action which he described as an interference with their right to exclusive worship. He thought that they had sufficiently alleged this right and its infringement, that the right was one which had been often upheld by the Courts, and that the suit could be brought without joining the trustee or without obtaining the consent of the Advocate-General. When he came to his later decision upon the whole case, he described the injury as "an injury to the plaintiffs' individual right to worship undisturbed by the intrusion of a person not belonging to their faith," and applying his mind to the fifth and sixth issues, he held that Bella could be initiated into the Zoroastrian religion and into the Parsi community; that the ceremonies adopted for the purpose were sufficient, and that, therefore, there was no intrusion of a person not belonging to the plaintiffs' faith, and it became immaterial to decide issues three and four. Accordingly he dismissed the suit.

12. When the matter came before the Chief Court, on appeal, the Judges, though apparently they heard one continous argument, gave two judgments: the first in respect of the preliminary issues. In this they confirmed the actual decision of Young J. but enlarged the plaintiffs' cause of action, saying that they might treat it as an injury to themselves, that Bella, even though she were a Zoroastrian, yet not being a Parsi, came to the temple worship.

13. This made it necessary for the Judges in the Chief Court to determine the third issue, via,, who are entitled to the benefits of the Fire Temple Trust; and they held that it was a trust for a religion and not for a race. They then held, in agreement with Young J,, that Bella could be and was converted or initiated into the Zoroastrian religion, and

therefore they concurred with him in dismissing the suit.

14. The Judges in the Chief Court took the view that the fourth issue might also have been decided in favour of Bella, i.e., that her mother was a Parsi, but that this fact was unimportant, except as leading up to her conversion or initiation. Their lordships agree with this. In their view it is settled that as regards the racial claim, maternity is of no importance.

15. The appeal to their lordships' board has raised among other questions the actuality and validity of Bella's conversion and initiation; but on this point their lordships see no reason for differing from the judgment of the Chief Court.

16. In the great controversy in the Bombay case, Sir Dinshaw Maneckji Petit v. Sir JamshetjiJijibhai (1908) I.L.R. 33 Bom. 509 : S.C. 11 Bom. L.R. 85, the two learned Judges (one of whom was himself a Parsi), came to the following conclusions thus expressed by the Parsi Judge, Davar J. (p. 534) :-

   I.   That the Zoroastrain religion not only permits but enjoins the conversion of a person born in another religion and of non-Zoroastrian parents.

   II. That, although such conversion was permissible, the Zoroastrians, ever since their advent into India 1200 years ago, have never attempted to convert anyone into their religion.

   III. That there is not a single instance proved before the Court of a person born of both non-Zoroastrian parents ever having been admitted into the Zoroastrian religion professed by the Parsis in India.

17. It is true that as regards the quantum of the necessary ceremonial on initiation, Davar J, expressed an opinion that a piece of ritual called Burushnun was an essential part; but

in this matter he was travelling outside anything necessary for the, case before him; and their lordships do not find that Beaman J. the other Judge, concurred with him as to this, and they think that the evidence given in the present case warranted the decision to which the Chief Court came that this additional ceremonial was not necessary.

18. It follows, therefore, that the points which their lordships have now to determine are, whether the trusts of the temple are for the benefit of all persons professing the Zoroastrian religion or limited to those who, professing that religion, are also racial Parsis in the sense in which that word is understood in the Parsi community; and, secondly, whether if Bella, not being a racial Parsi, is not a person within the benefits of the temple trust, this fact gives the plaintiffs any right of direct action against her and against her guardian.

19. The contention on behalf of the plaintiffs was the same as that of the contention of the defendants in the Bombay case, namely, that all these trusts were intended for Parsis in the limited sense, i, e.:-

First. The descendants of the original emigrants into India from Persia who profesa the Zoroastrian religion.

Secondly. The descendants of the Zoroastrians in Persia who were not amongst the original emigrants, but who are of the same stock and have since that date, from time to time, come to India and have settled here, either permanently or temporarily, and who profess the Zoroastrian religion.

Thirdly, The children of a Parai father by an alien mother, if such children are admitted into the religion of their fathers and profess the Zoroastrian religion.

20. Now the origin of the temple, the right to worship at which is in dispute in the present case, is as follows:

On November 24, 1868, the Deputy Commissioner at Rangoon, on behalf of Her Majesty's Government, granted to Bejunji Cowasji and Shapurji Hirji a parcel of land in the town of Rangoon of a certain size upon trust to build and maintain upon the said parcel of land a temple for the use of Parsi population.

21. It was provided that the Deputy Commissioner might nominate new trustees, and that if a temple was not erected within a year, he might revoke the grant.

22. On August 14, 1882-probably because there had been delay in building the temple-a re-grant was made to new trustees upon trust for the same intents and purposes as the old grant, with like powers to appoint new trustees and a similar power of revocation if no temple was built within a year.

23. Previously on January 11, 1859, the then Deputy-Commissioner had granted to two Parsi gentlemen another piece of land upon trust to maintain it "as a cemetery and to the free use of persona of the Parsi denomination." There was a similar power given to the Deputy-Commissioner to appoint new trustees and a power of revocation in case the land was applied to other uses This grant was again renewed also on August 14, 1882.

24. Some disputes having arisen as to the temple, a suit was brought to have a new trustee appointed, and scheme of management framed; and on March 20, 1889, the Recorder appointed BejunjiCowasji sole trustee and ordered a scheme to be framed.

25. About the same time, a similar suit had been brought in respect of the burial ground, and by an order of the same date the Same person was appointed trustee and a similar order to frame a scheme was made. The scheme in respect of the temple gave the trustee charge of the temple and its

appurtenances with duty to manage and improve as funds permitted and power to build a range of shops on parts of the trust lands, borrowing money for the purpose. After repayment of monies borrowed the rest was to be applied for the current expenses of the Fire Temple and the Parsi Burial Ground. In this way and to this extent the two properties were brought together.

26. When the scheme for the burial ground was to be framed, there was a serious dispute with regard to children of Parsi fathers who died without having gone through the ceremonies of initiation, and eventually the scheme was framed in the following words:-

1. The Burial ground shall be used for burying persona who shall at his or her death be actually professing the Zoroastrian religion and no other.

   Explanation—No one shall be taken to be actually professing the Zoroastrian religion who has not been duly invested with the Sudreh and Kusti, in accordance with the rites prescribed by that religion, provided, nevertheless, that children born of fathers following the Zoroastrian religion, and brought up in that faith, and dying before the age of 14 years and three months, without having been invested with the Sudreh and Kusti, may be taken to be actually professing the Zoroastrian religion, but children dying after having attained that age without having been invested with the Sudreh and Kusti shall not be taken to have professed the Zoroastrian religion unless his or her investiture was prevented by unforeseen and unavoidable circumstances.

27. It is suggested for the defendants that this document shows that the stress of the matter was laid upon the religion and not upon the race.

28. One other document must be mentioned. Apparently it took a long time before the temple or at any rate the present temple was built, and on August 20, 1904, Bejunji Cowasji executed a deed of declaration of trust reciting that he and his brother had built at their charge a fire temple upon the trust lands so that the same might form part of the said trusts and be for the use of the Parsi inhabitants of Rangoon, and purporting to declare for himself and his successors in office that he held the fire temple "for the use of the Parsi inhabitants of Rangoon free and unrestricted but subject notwithstanding to the tenets of the pure Zoroastrian religion and to the scheme prescribed by the Court.

29. The defendants at their lordships' bar contended that this was an attempt to alter the trust and as such should be rejected, but in their written statement they accepted it as a valid document. So far as it goes, it rather makes in the plaintiffs' favour, but their lordships are not disposed to attach grave importance to it.

30. The Chief Court-as already stated-considered that the effect of these documents was to impose a trust for the benefit of persons professing the Zoroastrian religion and no others.

31. Their lordships agree with the latter part of this proposition. Parsis who cease to be Zoroastrians have, in their lordships' view, no claim. But upon the whole and after much consideration they think that the benefits are confined to persons who possess the double qualification of Zoroastrians and racial Parsis.

32. The judgment in the Bombay case travelled over much ground-indeed, in their lordships' opinion, much unnecessary ground-but both Judges came to the conclusion that the various trusts in that case must be construed as

being confined to persons who were of the Zoroastrian religion and racial Parsis. There were several trusts, and the expressions in the deeds were different; but the word Parsi never appeared in them, and the word Zoroastrian or some equivalent religious word was used. Sometimes the trusts were for the members of the Zoroastrian community of Bombay; other phrases were similar. Nevertheless, both Judges came to the conclusion that they must be read as has been already stated.

33. Davar J. thus expressed himself (p. 548):-

A Juddin [that is a Gentile] may become a Zoroastrian, but how he ever could possibly become a member of 'the Holy Zoroastrian Anjuman of Bombay' or be one of the members of 'the Zoroastrian Community of Bombay' or become one of the Anjuman of the Mazdiasni faith,' passes my comprehension. A Juddin converted to Zoroastrianism had never come into existence. Such a person could not possibly have been within the contemplation of the donors and founders : the possibility of such a being coming into existence would be so new and novel that if the donor ever conceived such an idea and intended to include him in his benefaction, he would certainly designate him separately and specially, and not include him is the general description of the community of his then existing co-religionists and their descendants.

34. Beaman J. said (p. 580):-

That question is not, whether the Zoroastrian religion permits conversion, but whether, when these Trusts were founded, the Founders contemplated and intended that Converts should be admitted to participate in them.

35. In their lordships' view the same line of reasoning applies to the present case, The Parsi community had grown up

to be such a distinct body, and admissions into it from outside had been so very rare, that at the time when these grants at Rangoon were made the Government must have intended that the temple should be for the benefit of professing members of the Parsi community, i.e., racial Parsis or people deemed after a long lapse of ages to' be racial Parsis.

36 But this does not exhaust the matters to be determined on the present appeal. It determines that the respondent Bella has no right of entering into the temple and may therefore be excluded or extruded from the temple by the trustees. They can treat her as a trespasser. But it does not follow that they are bound so to treat her. Still less does it follow that in an action to which the trustees are not parties, and in which therefore no indirect remedy can be obtained, a direct claim can be supported as if for a tort committed by Bella or her guardian.

37. When property is set apart for public or charitable uses, it will be a malversation to apply any of the funds for persons who are not objects of the trust. These who are objects of the trust must have all the benefits they require; and if there is a surplus, it must be left to the Courts to make a cy-pres application of it. But when the subject matter of such a trust or charity is the rendering of some convenience or service of such a nature that it will not hurt the lawful recipients if others share with them, their lordships are aware of no case in which it has been held that the trustees are bound to exclude persons who have no legal title to share. They may do so; they may treat all such persons as trespassers and say : Sic volo sic jubeo, stet pro rationevoluntas. But if they choose to admit to the benefit of some park or garden established for a particular district some persons from over the border or to admit to a

public library destined for a particular municipality persons from outside, or what is perhaps a nearer analogy, admit to the hearing of a lecture by a University professor persons not members of the University, this of itself furnishes no ground of complaint. If the numbers admitted are too large or the persons are disorderly or unpleasant in their habits or in any way substantially interfere with the convenience or benefit of those for whom the endowment was created, the trustees may be required to exclude them. But the mere claim of A that B shall not share in such a benefit because B is not within the terms of the foundation is not one that Courts would encourage.

38. Many illustrations of this doctrine could be drawn from the history of English institutions. The great schools of Westminster, Eton and Winchester arose from small nuclei, namely, a fixed number of endowed and privileged scholars taught by appointed masters. They have become what they are because unprivileged boys in greater numbers have been allowed to benefit by the services of the appointed masters, and to use the school class-room and playgrounds.

39. The statutes of the colleges in Oxford and Cambridge make provision for the education of a fixed number of students or scholars privileged and endowed. Many, if not most, of them make no provision for the admission of other members in statupupillari. But "commoners," so called, though their legal position is merely that of boarders (Rex v. Grundon, Ex parte Davison (1775) Cowp. Rep. 315, 319 have been for several centuries admitted equally with the privileged scholars to the benefits of the colleges, particularly to the use of hall, library and chapel.

40. The intrusion of an unbeliever into a place of religious worship might well be a case of substantial interference with

the devotions of worshippers. But the plaintiffs have failed to make out that Bella was not a Zoroastrian. They suggested indeed that her conversion was impossible, or at any rate that it had not been completed by due initiation; but their lordships agree with the Judge of first instance that this suggestion was not established; while, except in the evidence of one unsatisfactory witness, there was nothing to show that Bella's presence would be thought to cause desecration, if once it was accepted that she was a Zoroastrian.

41. Also, if it were a question of caste and worshippers of a higher caste would be defiled by the presence of a lower caste, as in AnandravBhikaji Phalke v. Shankar DajiCharya (1883) l.I.R. 7 Bom. 323, this would be a serious disturbance. As was said in that case (p. 329):-

This right is one which the Courts must guard, as otherwise all high caste Hindus would hold their sanctuaries, and perform their worship, only so far as those of the lower castes chose to allow them.

42. But this claim is again not established. Indeed, what may be called the quasi-caste claim is not even suggested in the pleadings. It was the wounding of religious feelings and the desecration of the temple which are put forward.

43. Their lordships have now to consider the Belief which the plaintiffs have sought in this suit. They have not sought for a general declaration as to the persons who are objects of the trust. They have not sought for a construction of the scheme, or for any order to be made upon the trustee, nor have they made the trustee a party. For this they would probably have required the consent of the Advocate General. They pray in the plaint "for a declaration that the defendant Bella is not entitled to the use and benefits of the Parsi Fire Temple in Dalhousie Street known as 'Captain's Agiary or

Dhurraymair' or to the use and benefits of the buildings standing on the said trust land or to attend at or participate in any of the religious ceremonies performed therein.

44. Then they claim an injunction to restrain the defendant Bella from entering and the other defendant, now dead, from bringing her into the temple to attend the religious ceremonies, This is a claim for an injunction to prevent the repetition of an alleged trespass. It must, therefore, first be established that there was a trespass and one for which damages, though possible only nominal, could be recovered. But for trespass upon land the only person to bring the action is the person in possession of the land, that is, the trustee. That a beneficiary or two or three beneficiaries of a trust for public purposes may bring a suit for trespass against an intruder is a novel principle of jurisprudence; and the case is not made stronger by the suggestion that several other beneficiaries agree with them.

45. It may be that in India it would be convenient in some cases to allow such a suit, and judgment in AnandravBhikajiPhadke v. Shankar DajiCharya may form a precedent. But, if so, the circumstances must be as powerful as in that case. It must be established that the juxtaposition of the two sets of persons is so repugnant to their habits of mind that the entrance of one set into the temple entails the departure of the other, so that it is as it were trespass to the person.

46. As already stated, no such case has been established, and therefore it is not necessary to discuss the principle on which the judgment in AnandravBhikajiPhadke v. Shankar DajiCharya is founded and which was indeed accepted by the Judge of first instance in the present case. The facts do not warrant the claim, if it be a sound one, and no injunction can be granted.

47. With regard to costs, the learned Judge of first instance, while giving the defendants the general costs of the action, thought that both sides were to blame for the inordinate length of the Bombay commission and made the plaintiffs pay two-thirds only of the defendants' costs of the commission.

48. If any costs of the action were to be given, some similar provision should be applied. But, upon the whole, their lordships feel that the plaintiffs have failed in the greater part of their suit, and that the giving to them of a declaration is an indulgence. They were given the costs of the preliminary issues before Young J. and the costs of so much of the appeal as related to those issues. These they keep, and the orders against them in respect of other costs in the Courts below will be discharged and there will be no costs of this appeal. Their lordships will humbly recommend His Majesty that this appeal be allowed, that the judgment of the Chief Court be varied, and that a declaration be made, namely, that Bella was not entitled, as of right, to use the temple, or to attend or to participate in any of the religious ceremonies performed therein, that except as to the costs awarded to the plaintiffs in the Court of first instance, and in the Chief Court, there be no costs in the Courts below, and there be no casts of this appeal.

(E)

TRANSLATION OF THE RIVAYATS FROM SAKLAT VS BELLA

EXHIBIT 51.

Copy of Bombay High Court translation i. e. translation of Exhibit 50 (extracts from a small Gujarati book) filed before Commissioner.

EXHIBIT 51.

Suit No. 91 of 1915 Chief Court, Lower Burma.

R. S. DADACHANJI,
Commissioner.

[Exhibit 51.
Copy of
Bombay
High Court
translation
i. e.
translation of
Exhibit 50
extracts
from a small
Gujarati
book.) filed
before Com-
missioner.

PRAYER BOOK PAGE 221.

Translation of extracts from a small Gujarati printed book at pages 52, 53
10 and 54, containing Proofs (in support) of the matter that it is lawful to
admit Juddins (a) into the Majdiasni religion, second edition, compiled by
Tehmuras Dinshaji Anklesariya.

Proof 32nd
78 Revayat.

About 132 years ago, on the occasion when the late Mulla Kaoos went to
Persia from India, taking with himself his son Peshutan who is well known by
the name of Mulla Pheroze, certain Zoroastrian gentlemen of Surat and
Broach, namely, Dasturs Darah valade (i. e. son of) Dastur Sohorab, Kavoos
Munajjam valade (i. e. son of) Dastur Faredum, Kavus valade Dastur Rustam
20 Sanjana, Noroj valade Dastur Framaraj, Rustam alias Padshah valade Dastur
Framaraj, Behedins (i.e. laymen) Sohorab alias Nekasayetkhan valade Kavus-
shah and 14 other gentlemen sent 78 questions in writing, through the late
Mulla Kavus Rustam Jalal, to the Zoroastrians of that time of the whole land
of Persia (? of the whole of Persia) and requested them to send their answers.
The Zoroastrians of Persia, on the 6th day of the 8th Kadmi month of the
Yezdezardi year 1142 (18th April 1773) having written and completed the
answers to those questions (and) the undermentioned Dusturs and Behedins
having put their signatures and seals thereon, sent them to India. The names
of the persons who have signed the same are (as follows :—) Dasture Dasturan
30 Marjban valade (i. e. the son of the) late Dastur Hosang and 17 other gentlemen. These questions (and) answers are now in existence (and they are) with
certain gentlemen. Out of those (questions), the 13th question and answer
hereof given by the aforementioned Zoroastrians of Persia are translated
rom Persian and given below:—

QUESTION—13.

Here in India Parsis buy Hindus' sons and daughters as Gulams (slaves)
and Kani jaks (female slaves) and keep them (? utilize them, to (do) their
household work, and teaching them Avasta (they) invest them, according to
the tenets of the Zoroastrian religion, with Sadra Kusti (sacred shirt and thread)
40 and having got prepared by their hands Darun (i. e. small wheaten breads) for
Ghambars and other (ceremonies or festivals), get the same consecrated, and
in the same manner all the mobeds (i.e. priests) and Behedins (i. e. laymen) of

---

(a) "Juddins" means people of other religions namely non-Zoroastrians, B. H.

Exhibit 51.
Copy of
Bombay
High Court
translation
i. e.,
translation of
Exhibit 50,
extracts from
a small
Gujarati
book.)
filed before
Commis-
sioner.

India eat and drink food and water (? touched) by their hands ; but when they (i. e. such Golams and Kani jaks) die, the said Mobeds (i. e. priests) and Behe- dins (a) (i. e. laymen) do not allow their corpses,to be placed in the Dokhmas (i.e. Towers of Silence) saying "They are children of durvands (literally infidels or unbelievers, meaning non-Zoroastrians), therefore it is not proper that their bones should lie in the same place along with the bones of the behedins. Now, when those (Golams and Kani jaks) were living, (the Mobeds and Behe- dins) got all the works relating to religion (? relating to religious ceremonies) done by their hands and when they die they prevent (their corpses) being placed in Dokhmas (Towers of Silence), such being the case, it is requested that you will be good enough to explain whether it is or it is not lawful to place their corpses in Dokhmas (i. e. Towers of Silence).

ANSWER—13.

As regards the matter of buying (a)Juddins' sons and daughters (? we say) that the Mobeds (Priests) and Behedins (laymen) should first take into consi- deration the religion and the tenets of the religion and the safety of their own persons and property in order that (by so doing they) may not suffer any sort of harm. After having been satisfied with regard to the aforesaid matter, if (they) buy (a) Juddins children and having taught them Avasta if they take them into the good Majdiasni religion, then that is a great meritorious act. But this (i. e. the following) is a matter much to be condemned and the one ill-becoming the followers of the good Majdiasni religion that the (b) Behedins of India, when the aforesaid children were alive, partook of the food (touched or prepared) by their hands and yet when they die, they should utter improper words with regard to the dead bodies of those poor paupers. Their argument to the effect that "they are Juddins' children (and, therefore it is not proper that their corpses may be put in Dokhmas (i. e. Towers of Silence) along with the corpses of Behedins", is unreasonable. To utter such words is improper, unproductive of any good and adverse to meritorious acts. And the person who puts obstacles in this matter and does not put their corpses (? and does not let their corpses be put) in Dukhmas (Towers of Silence), is an extremely great sinner in the religion, and he is Ruhsiah " (black-faced) in the presence of Meher and Sarosh. Therefore, it behoves the Mobeds (priests) and Behe- dins (laymen) of India that they should give due respect to the said children and that they should send their dead bodies to Dokhmas (Towers of Silence) according to the tenets of the Majdiasni religion ; this will be a cause of satis- faction to Ahurmazd (God) and Ameshaspands (angels). We (c) (Zoroastrians of Persia) have heard from the lips of Dastur Kavus to the effect that some of the Dasturs, Mobeds and Behedins of India have put restrictions at all places (? asking people) not to teach Avasta to such children and not to take them into the Majdiasni religion. This is a thing very much opposed to (common) sence. My dear co-religionists ! in the (d) third chapter of the Vandidad, Dadar Hormazd (God) has directed the holy Zoroaster that he should public- ly propound the Majdiasni religion to all people (c) (that is to say, he should preach religion) and that having shown (them) the good way, should himself acquire, by the benefit thereof, greatness and fame. Further, in the times of

---

(b) " Behedins " commonly means laymen. But it is presumed the word is used here to mean persons of " better religion " viz the Zoroastrians. (c) (This portion is so enclosed within brackets in the original) B. H. (d) This mark is placed at this place to indicate the [footnote on same page. That footnote is not marked for tran- slation) B. H.

Hoshedarmah, Hoshedarbami and Soshiyos all the (a) Juddins will be brought into this better Majdiasni (4) religion. So, it appears also from the said autho-*rities that it is lawful according to the Majdiasni religion to admit into the religion the children of the above description.* By doing such act, great religious merit is acquired. And those who prevent (people) from doing so are the persons, as it were encouraging Juddini And to call such persons (5) Behedins, is opposed to common) sense. Behedin is he only who propagates the good religion.

H. I. M's High Court,

Bombay.

Translator's Department

22nd November 1907.

A true translation.

(Sd.) BYRAMJEE HEERJEEBHOY,

Fourth Translator.

20th November 1907.

G. 3769.
Fols. 14.

(F)
LETTER FROM PROMINENT MEMBERS OF SOCIETY SUPPORTING RATAN TATA. 1904

EXHIBIT A 18.

Protest forwarded to the Trustees of the Parsi Punchayet Funds, filed before Commissioner.

EXHIBIT A 18.

SUIT No. 91 OF 1915 CHIEF COURT, LOWER BURMA.

R. S. DADACHANJI,

Commissioner.

20th June 1916.

Bombay, 28th October 1904.

To

SIR JAMSETJI JIJIBHOY, Bart,

HORMASJI EDULJI ALBLESS, Esq.,

JAMSEDJI CURSETJI JAMSEDJI, Esq.,

MERWANJI MANCHERJI CAMA, Esq.,

AND

BOMONJI DINSHAW PETIT, Esq.,

Trustees of the Parsi Punchayet Funds and Estates.

The proposal to place before a meeting of the Parsi Anjuman certain resolutions which are said to have been adopted by the Committee appointed to consider the several questions embodied in the requisition to the Trustees of 13th July, 1903, makes it necessary for us to address you with regard to your past and future action in the matter.

2. You are aware that, besides being subject to the general law of British India, the Parsis have special Acts of the Indian Legislature to regulate their law of marriage and succession. There is no other constituted authority to which the Parsis are subject with regard to religious, social, domestic and personal matters.

3. There have been from time to time what have been called meetings of the Parsi Anjuman, but they can claim no higher authority than general gatherings like, for example, public meetings of the citizens of Bombay convened by the Sheriff or people who have established by practice a claim to call them. The functions of such meetings are largely, in their very nature, of a formal, ceremonial and limited character.

4. Among the Parsis a practice has sprung up by which such meetings among them are convened by the Trustees of what are called the Parsi Punchayet Funds. It scarcely needs to be said that there is no such body among the Parsis as the Punchayet. The Trustees themselves are creations of divers trust-deeds executed by individual Parsis. The Parsi Anjuman has, as a body,

(8)

no voice in the election of these Trustees, vacancies among whom, as is well known, are filled up by the surviving Trustees. It is not known whether such appointments are in legal accordance with the provisions of the various trust-deeds, which have never been generally made known or published. Such as they are, these Trustees have taken upon themselves to call public meetings of the Parsis. It should be added that the present and last Sir Jamsetji Jijibhoy, Bart. were elected at such public meetings to occupy the position of what may be most nearly described as Life Chairman.

5. Holding the place of Trustees of the Parsi Punchayet Funds and Estates as above mentioned, a requisition signed by a certain portion of the Parsis was sent to you, wherein you were requested to appoint a Committee comprised of a few Parsis of education, wealth and position to enquire (1) whether it was desirable, looking at the present religious and social condition of the Parsis, to receive non-Zoroastrians into the Zoroastrian religion; and (2) if desirable, under what conditions and ceremonies they should be so received. The contention that the Parsi religion did not enjoin or permit conversion was tacitly and indirectly abandoned by the requisitionists, and they asked only for an enquiry on the basis that, according to the tenets of the Zoroastrian religion, conversion was enjoined and permitted.

6. On receipt of the said requisition the Trustees, instead of proceeding to appoint a Committee in accordance with the terms of the requisition, preferred to convene a meeting of the Anjuman by a notice dated 29th July 1903.

7. We think that the course persued by the Trustees was a course open to serious objection. Though the immediate business, to be placed before the meeting, was only the appointment of a Committee, the course acopted was capable of the construction that a general meeting of Parsis, without rules or constitution or legal validity, was a suitable machinery for discovering and determining grave religious and social questions effecting Parsis. More serious still was the further assumption involved in the action of the Trustees, that any number of Parsis could require or restrain a single individual of the Community from practising a tenet of his religion on the score of social or other considerations.

8. The meeting of Parsis, so called as aforesaid, was held on the 2nd August, 1903, and passed the following resolution :—

*   *   *   *   *

(in native characters).
The Committee thus appointed was comprised of 195 members.

9. The proceedings of this committee have been so fully reported in the Parsi papers that there is no need to refer to them in detail here. A very small number of members, scarcely a fifth of them, appear to have taken part in its deliberations. Over a hundred and fifty of them have held themselves completely aloof, and at no time have members exceeding 40 taken part in the voting.

10. We learn that a report containing the resolutions passed by the Committee will be soon submitted to you to be placed before a public meeting of the Parsis which you will be required to convene.

11. We have pointed out above that the resolution of the public meeting convened by you on the 2nd August 1903 confined itself to the appointment of

a Committee, and we venture to think that it is not incumbent on you to convene any meeting to receive the report of the Committee.

12. We desire to point out that it will not be in the best interests of the Parsi Community to convene any public meeting for the consideration and determination of the questions involved in the report of the Committee. A public gathering of a Community indefinite in its dimensions like that of the Parsis, possessing no constitution or law, will be readily admitted to be too incohesive, unorganized and miscellaneous a body to consider and pronounce upon religious and social questions. It cannot be held to possess either fitness or power, or authority for such a task, when, as in the present case, the action proposed by the Committee goes the length of requiring Parsis to abandon what they might hold and believe as tenets of their religion confessedly for social and extra religious reasons, such action cannot for a moment be admitted as within the cognizance or competence even of an Anjuman meeting properly and validly constituted.

13. For the reasons and under the circumstances above stated we think that it would be wise and in the best interests of the peace, harmony and welfare of our community that no further action in the shape of calling a public meeting of the Parsis should be taken by you. It is hardly necessary to say that those members of our Community who have definite views on the various questions that have been discussed by the Committee are perfectly welcome not only to hold them but to endeavour to propogate them in every right and legitimate manner, but we would venture to point out that the propagation of such views should be left to the operation of moral forces alone. Every one is free to try and educate public opinion of the community, and it is to that that we should all look for all such changes and reforms as may be considered desirable in the interests of the Community. We sincerely trust that the adoption of such a course would in every way promote the well being, harmony and progress of the Community which we have no doubt all Parsis, however they may differ in their views, have fully at heart.

The above Protest was signed by

Sir Dinshaw Manockjee Petit, Bart.
The Hon. Sir Pherozsha M. Mehta, K.C.I.E.
Sir J. Cowasjee Jehangir. Kt.
The Honourable Khan Bahadur Darasha R. Chichgar.
Khan Bahadur Muncherjee C. Murzban, C.I.E.
Rustomjee Byramjee Jeejeebhoy.
Dinsha Eduljee Wacha.
Meherwanjee F. Murzban.
H. J. Dadiset.
D. J. Tata.
R. J Tata
Jamsedjee Ardeshir Wadia.
Bapujee Sorabji Patel.
Cursetji Sorabji Patel.

D. N. Bahadurjee, B.A., Bar-at-law.
F. Sorabji Talyarkhan, Bar-at-Law.
F. Pestonji Talyarkhan, Bar-at-Law.
Rutom D. N. Wadia. M.A., Bar-at-Law.
M. D. Dadiset, Bar-at-Law.
H. H. Wadia, B.A., Bar-at-Law.
N. N. Saher, Bar-at-Law.
J. C. Bilimoria, Bar at-Law.
Ardeshir Framjee, B.A., LL.B., Solicitor.
Hormasjee N. Vakil, Solicitor.
F. R. Wadia, M.A., LL.B., Solicitor.
J. D. Gandy, B.A., LL.B., Solicitor.
Rustom K. R. Cama, B.A., L.L.B., Solicitor.

(9)

2

Cowasjee D. Dubash.
Dadiba Merwanjee Dalal.
Rustamjee Dossabhoy Settna.
L. N. Banajee, Bar-at-Law, Pro-
thonotary, High Court.
Jahangir Dossabhoy Framjee, Bar-
at-Law, Special Collector, City
Improvement Trust.
Rustamji Merwanjee Patel, M.A.
LL. B., Advocate, Judge of the
Court of Small Causes.
R. D. Sethna, B. A., LL. B., Bar-at-
Law, Registrar, High Court.
Pheroz H. Dastoor, M. A., Presi-
dency Magistrate.
C. M. Cursetee, B. A., (Oxon.)
Bar-at-Law, Judge, Small Causes
Court.
H. C. Coorlewala, Income Tax Collec-
tor.
Framjee Eduljee Daver.
Dinshaw Muncherjee Panthaki.
Eduljee Mervanjee Dubash.
Rustam S. Paovalla.
Cawasha S. Paovalla.
Cowasjee Jehangir.
Munchersha S. Mehta.
R. D Tata.
M. N. Wadia, B. A., Secy., Munici-
pal Corporation.
J. M. Framji Patel.
N. R. Chichgar, Editor, Akhbar-e-
Sodagar.
Dinshaw D. Davar, Bar-at-Law.
H. A. Wadia, Bar-at-Law.
P. J. Padasha, M.A., Bar-at-Law.
Dr. Ardesher D. Mody, L.M. and S.
Dr. Dara M. Dastoor, L.M. and S.
Dr. H. N. Seervai, L.M. and S.
Dr. M. D. Cama, L.M. and S.
Dr. K. M. Gimi, L. M. and S.
Dr. D. R. Burdi, L. M. and S.
N. A. F. Moose, L. C. E., F. R. CH.S.
Director, Government Observatory.
K. B. Dadi-Barjor, B.A., L.C.E.
Pestonjee Dorabjee Khandalewalla
L. C. E.
Jamsedji Dadabhoy Nadersha,L.C.E.
K. R. Wacha, L.C.E.
Manekji Sheriarjee Bharucha,L.C.E.
Maneksher K. Nadersha, L.C.E.

D. F. Mulla, M.A., LL.B., Solicitor.
D. F. Wadia, B.A., LL.B., Solicitor.
Framjee Dorabjee, B.A., LL.B.,
Solicitor.
Fardunjee M. Kanga, B.A., LLB.,
Solicitor.
Darasha Bezonji Mehta, M.A.,
Solicitor.
F. E. Dinsha, B.A., LL.B., Solicitor.
Jahangir D. Neemuchwala, B.A.,
LL. B., Solicitor.
Jahangir, B. Baman-Behram, B.A.,
LL. B., Solicitor.
Sorabjee D. Bastawala, B.A.,
LL.B. Solicitor.
Kekhashroo F. Seervai, B.A.,
Solicitor.
Jahangir K. Dadachanji, B.A.,
LL.B., Solicitor.
Ratansha E. Koyar, B.A., LL.B.,
Pleader.
Cawasjee B. Sethna, B.A., LL.B.
Pleader.
Rustam Barjorji Paymaster, B.A.,
LL. B. Pleader.
Ardeshir D. Daver, B.A., LL.B,
Pleader.
B. D. Mulla, B.A. LL.B, Pleader
Sorabjee. J. Dalal, B.A. LL.B.,
Pleader.
Hormazdiar Pheroz Dastoor, B.A,
LL. B., Pleader.
K. N. Kharas, B. A., LL. B. Pleader.
F. S. Doctor, B. A., LL. B., Pleader
Phirozsha Burjorjee Surveyor, B.A,
LL. B., Pleader.
Nadersha N. Commissariatevala
B. A., LL.B., Pleader.
Jahangir Jivanji Gazdar, B.A.,
LL.B., Pleader.
Nusserwanji Jivanji Gazdar, B.A.,
LL.B., Pleader.
Surgeon Lieut. Col. J. K. Kanga
I. M. S.
Dr. N. N. Katrak, L.M. & S.

(10)

And many others.

Exhibit D.

Copy from Record No. 6, filed before Commissioner (translation.)

In the Chief Court of Lower Burma.

SUIT No. 91 OF 1915

R. S. DADACHANJI,

Commissioner.

Serial No. 975.

P. 51 (Copy from Record No. 6).

A new Bando-bast is made.

66.

In the name of the Holy Providence Who arranges the affairs of both the worlds through the hand of nature and Who guides His favourite Mazda Yasnaſs of the pure Mazda Yasna Sect for 'Bando-bast' in respect of His Sacred Faith, through Zoroaster Aspaṇtman * Anosheh-rawan (*i. e.* of blessed soul), and by the help of the blessed souɪ of Prophet Zoroaster deputed by Him, a new 'Bando-bast' is made for enabling the excellence of righteousness to reach to the Mazda-Yasna followers of the good faith and for keeping them aloof from vice.

* of the Spi-
tama family]

On 11th August 1830 A. D. (corresponding with) Wednesday the 8th Bid of Shrawan 1886 St. and the 14th day of 11th month of 1299 (Yezd), the entire large and small Anjuman of the Zoroastrian religion met in the Aderan* of Sheth Dadibhai Nasherwanji and made the 'Bando-basts' mentioned below (viz.) that our people invest their issues by alien mistresses with Sudrah and take them into our religion—that as regards those, who were admitted into the faith up to this day, it is done and finished, but that none should be taken hereafter; and that pucca resolutions are made this day about those (above) matters and about the forbidding of adultery committed with women of our own and alien community by some foolish persons out of us who go astray. Those resolutions are stated below and all Zoroastrians should act according to them. Approved.

*a fire - temp

FIRSTLY.—As our people commenced to take the issues born of alien mistresses only recently, into our faith, and as they commenced to admit the issues born of alien women as lawful (issues) wickedness increased very much is in (the followers of) our religion these Bando-basts are (therefore) made. They are recorded in this record of our Panchayet and it is decided to print copies thereof and distribute them amongst all of the Zoroastrian Race. And it is is resolved that letters in the name of our Anjuman be written and posted to other out station leaders and a few words as would seem fit, be written to them also on this matter, so that the admission of issues of those mistresses into the faith would cease in all respects, and that they should not fail in that behalf, nor allow them to be invested with Sudrah and Kusti nor give permission for their marriage and exposures in Dokhmas. Those letters should be written in this manner with several particulars and posted to all the out stations. Approved.

Exhibit D.
Copy from
Record No.
6, filed before
Commis-
sioner
(translation.)
11-2-1916.

*(i.e. such as
could Be per-
formed by a
Mobed only)

* (laity or
clergy.)

SECONDLY:—That hereafter no one should invest the issue born of a mis-tress and brought down from out stations by any body or who may be in Bombay, with Sudrah and take him/her into the faith, that we should not accept the fact of the investiture of Sudrah got performed by any one at any place or village after going there, and moreover, if any Mobed would go to any place whatever either in Bombay or Chhasti outside Bombay or in the out stations and sur-reptitiously invest such issues with Sudrah, that Mobed should be forbidden from performing all Mobedi * Services, and no one should give (Asho dad) con-tribution to him on every good or bad occasion; and if any Behedin* or Mobed acting against the Bando-bast of our Anjuman would bring down the issue born of an alien mistress and invest him/her with Sudrah, he should be put out of our Anjuman and awarded any other punishment appropriate in the view of our Anjuman. Approved.

THIRDLY.—That if any one would hereafter bring down from any out station or Bombay, the issue born of a mistress and keep him in his house with his family, his house will be put out of (the fold of) our Anjuman; and no one should invite the master of that house, and feed him on his table and that no one should visit his place on occasions of joy or sorrow. If any one would not act according to this writing, he will be guilty before our Panchayet. Approved. The punishment thereof will be one appropriate in the view of the Anjuman in addition to what is written above.

FOURTHLY.—That in case the issues of such a mistress would come from some out station and they had been invested with Sudrah but if no one would give 'pucca' proof of their putting on the Sudrah prior to this Bando-bast of ours, their Sudrah should not be accepted, and they should not be exposed in Dokhmas also and the party bringing them (issues) should also be punished as in para. III. Approved.

* (illicit
intercourse.)

FIFTHLY.—That at present, in Bombay as well as in out stations good respectable and manly persons commit such wicked * actions; Our Panchayet Members should privately send word to them or write open letters that they should abstain from such actions. And if they would not listen to them at all they should be disgraced by the large and small Anjuman met together and in a manner deemed proper, with a view to their desisting from wickedness; and that if such persons would not desist from such wicked actions they will be awarded such punishment as will be fitting in the view of the members or the Anjuman. Approved.

SIXTHLY.—That no man having a wife of the first or second marriage should commit adultery with a woman of our own or alien community. If he will commit that act and if the leaders of the Anjuman will know of it, through a witness, they will disgrace him after awarding such, strict punishment as would be suitable. Approved.

If the adultery of any one either male or female will be definitely known to another person and if he will conceal the guilt of those two persons, he shall be guilty before the Anjuman. Approved.

SEVENTHLY.—If any woman of our Community having a husband will commit adultery with another man of our or alien community she as well as the procuress—if there be one and if she be known or caught—who had caused such actions to be committed, shall get punishment in accordance with our ancient usage, from the large and small Anjuman and they i. e. the latter) shall not allow such male in any assembly and shall keep him aloof in all matters and disallow him from entering every Dare-Meher. Besides the Anjuman shall award such other punishment as they would think fit. Approved.

EIGHTHLY :— That at present our people remain in foreign countries for many years (for sake of business) and some go there keep mistresses and spend their days in licentiousness and they do not return home or take any notice of their wives. It is therefore advisable that letters in the name of our Anjuman be written to them and their family sent to their " Mooluks " abroad if they can be sent there, and if that party be willing to return he should be sent for within a short period and made to live with his family. And in case that person would not agree to either of the two alternatives, the woman concerned shall wait for her husband for 8 to 10 years. Then after (the expiry of) that period if the said woman of her own will and pleasure ask for permission to take another husband, she will be permitted to do so. Approved. But if the said man would return (from abroad) and ask for permission to take another wife it should be refused and the Anjuman should do what would appear good to them, after considering his condition. Approved. On this arrangement being made, it will be advantageous in many other respects.

NINTHLY :—That letters in the name of our Bombay Anjuman should be addressed to the leaders of places abroad where Zoroastrians reside and where some of them may have kept Jud-din women and got issues of Zoroastrian descent born of them, stating that their whole Anjuman having met together, had made "Bandobast" in respect of issues born of Mistresses and that they (leaders) should, by their God Who is one, write and send to the Bombay Anjuman, definitely within one month, the names and surnames including age, of those Zoroastrians who have kept mistresses and got isusue born of them ; and the leaders of the (Bombay) Anjuman will arrange for the passage money of those who will bring such issues together with letters signed by leaders of out stations Anjuman—if there be any--and if they think it proper, they will give order for taking them (i. e. issues) into our zoroastrian religion. But the decision in the matter is, that permission will be given for investing Sudrah to those issues who will arrive in Bombay within 3 months of the date of receipt of the Bombay Anjuman's letters. Approved.

" True Copy "

(Sd.) JIVANJI JAMSHEDJI MODY,

(In English)

Secretary Parsi Panchayet.

11th February 1916.

11

(H)
LETTER OF PROTEST FROM IRANIAN ASSOCIATION TO PARSI PANCHAYAT

From

THE IRANIAN ASSOCIATION.

To

The Hon. Sir Jamshedji Jejeebhoy Bart.

Jamshedji Cursetji Jamshedji Esq.

Bomanji Dinshaw Petit Esq.

Sir Cowasji Jehangir Bart.

Mancherji Pestonji Kharegat Esq., i. C. S. (Retired).

Hormasji Ardeshir Wadya Esq., Bar-at-Law.

Naoroji Jehangir Gamadia Esq.

Trustees of the Charitable Funds and Immoveable properties of the Parsi Panchayat of Bombay.

GENTLEMEN,

We understand that a requisition said to be signed by a very large number of Zoroastrian ladies and gentlemen has been forwarded to you as Trustees of the Charitable Funds and Immoveable properties of the Parsi Panchayat of Bombay, and that you are therein asked to convene a general meeting of " Parsi Zoroastrians " in order to pass resolutions expressing strong disapproval of the action of Shams-ul-Ulama Sirdar Dastur Kaikobad Adarbad Dastur Noshirwan of Poona for having performed a certain Navjot ceremony at Rangoon. You are also asked to help the requisitionists and others to meet together and adopt " other proper measures for safeguarding the interests of our community." On behalf of the Iranian Association, we are directed to address this representation to you in the matter, and we trust it will be given fair consideration before you arrive at a final decision in regard to the aforesaid requisition.

1. In the first place, we believe it is essential for us to bring to your recollection a few prominent facts which are gleaned from the history of our community in this city. In remote times, when the Parsi population in Bombay was small, and when it was conveniently possible for the whole community to meet together for the discussion and determination of matters affecting the general body of the community, it appears that meetings of the general Anjuman or " Panchayat, " as it was then called, were held. Later on some of the powers of the " Panchayat " were delegated by common consent to a few individuals elected in general meetings of the whole " Anjuman, " and in course of time this smaller body to whom such powers were assigned, came itself to be designated as " The Punchayat. " With the growth of the community and the natural unsuitability of the larger or the smaller " Punchayet " to take any action in the name and on behalf of the community, the powers of the " Punchayat " altogether vanished, and the only function of the smaller " Punchayat " was to control and manage the funds and properties of the community, which were committed to its care. The smaller " Punchayat " in its turn, came in course of time to delegate its functions to a few of its members, who styled themselves Trustees of the Funds and Properties of the Parsi Punchayat, and who further arrogated to themselves the power of appointing their successors, as also

(278)

other functions which were at one time exercised by the "Punchayat," including the power of convening, when occasion arose, general meetings of the community, known as meetings of the "Anjuman."

2. The meetings that were thus called were necessarily and, at all times, of a formal, or ceremonial and limited character. In any event, at no time did the "Punchayat," large or small, profess or attempt to legislate for the community. It never ventured to set up as a propounder or interpreter of the tenets of the Zoroastrian religion, and never did it dream of questioning or repudiating them for social or other reasons, or of pronouncing verdicts on the actions of
10 individuals in religious matters, or in regard to the performance or non-performance of religious duties.

3. About a decade ago, attempts were made by a certain section of the community to induce the then Trustees of the Parsi Punchayat to convene a meeting of the Anjuman, with the object of passing certain resolutions on very delicate questions of a religious and socio-religious character. On that occasion, an influentially signed representation of a number of leading Parsees, bearing date the 28th October
1914, was forwarded and submitted to those Trustees, in which various reasons were given to demonstrate the inadvisability and impropriety of calling such a
20 meeting. After pointing out therein the facts that the Parsi community was bound to render obedience only to the general law of India and the special laws affecting it, that there was no such body as the Parsi Punchayet or any other authority possessing any powers to control the action of its members, that the meetings from time to time convened by the so-called Trustees of the Parsi Punchayat under a modern practice, adopted for the sake of convenience, were of a formal, ceremonial or limited character, whose conclusions had no binding force or validity, they requested the Trustees not to convene a general meeting of the Anjuman in the best interests of the community, for the preservation of peace and harmony among its members, on the ground that a general
30 meeting of the kind was by its character and composition unfitted to deal with delicate questions of a religious and socio religious character. We are grieved to find that this advice was disregarded by the then Trustees, mainly and ostensibly on the ground that they were bound by a promise given at a previous meeting of the Anjuman to submit before it the report of a committee which was appointed at the said previous meeting.

4. The aforesaid representation had made clear that the course sought to be adopted of placing delicate questions relating to religion and society before a mass meeting of the Anjuman, "was capable of the construction that a general meeting of Parsis, without rules or constitution or legal validity, was a suitable machinery for discussing and determining grave, religious and
40 social questions affecting Parsis. More serious still was the further assumption involved in the action of the Trustees that any number of Parsis could require or restrain a single individual of the community from practising the tenets of his religion, on the score of social or other considerations." In spite of this warning, a meeting was held on the 16th day of April 1905 when certain resolutions of a dictatorial character were adopted, and other resolutions were carried at the meeting, the purport of which was to subject to a social ban or ostracism any member of the community who offended against the prior resolutions.

(279)

5. You are aware that after these resolutions were adopted, they were submitted to learned counsel for opinion and advice as to their legal validity and efficacy. You are also aware that the joint opinion of two counsel was obtained, even before the said meeting was held, as to the validity and legal effect of such resolutions, if adopted, at a general meeting of the Anjuman by a large majority. The unanimous opinion of counsel in this matter was, to cite the words of Mr. Inverarity, " Such resolutions would have no legal effect." Mr. D. D. Davar (now the Hon. Justice Sir Dinshaw D. Davar) expressed himself thus : " I do not see how a majority of the community can enforce their views and wishes on the minority, however small that minority may be. If the minority have certain legal rights, they would be entitled to assert them and will successfully assert them in spite of any number of resolutions which the majority may pass ". The Hon. the Chief Justice Sir Basil Scott, who was then Advocate-General, was asked if the Parsi community assembled at a public meeting, either unanimously or by a large majority, could give expression to its views, so that they may hereafter at all times be binding upon and unchallengeable by the Parsi community. He said : " In my opinion they can-not effectually achieve this result." The contentions of the signatories to the representation of the 28th October 1914 were thus in substance borne out by the opinion of eminent lawyers.

6. The then Trustees accepted this opinion, and, to a certain extent, even acted upon it, despite the resolutions of the aforesaid Anjuman meeting of the 16th April 1905. Two years after the said meeting, on the 29th day of April 1907, they filed their written statement in the famous Suit No. 689 of 1906, which has become known as the Punchayat Case. They disregarded therein one of the resolutions of the aforesaid meeting, and deliberately chose to treat the same as if it was never binding on them or on the whole community, in whose interests and on whose behalf they professedly defended the action brought against them. In paragraph 14 of that written statement, dealing with the rights of children of Parsi fathers by alien mothers, which were pur-ported to be taken away and denied for all time to come by one of the resolu-tions of the Anjuman meeting of the 16th April 1905, the Trustees observed: " The right of this latter class of persons to the benefit of the trusts of which these defendants are Trustees has been questioned from time to time, and the majority of the community are against their inclusion in the Parsi Community. Having regard to the usage and practice for a good many years of admitting this class of persons into the said community and to the benefit of the said trusts, the defendants have recognised such rights, and have not disputed the same ".

7. It was expected after the wide publicity that was given to the legal opinions above cited, and after the determined manner in which the then Trustees decided to act upon those opinions, that it would not occur to thinking Zoroastrians to indulge any longer in the futile endeavour to enforce one or more of the resolutions of the 16th April 1905, more particularly because it was well known that those resolutions were entirely antagonistic to the wishes of a certain section of the community, who challenged the right of the Anjuman either to pass them, or to give them any binding aspect or legal validity, and more particularly also because an enlightened section of the community that could never be neglected, was opposed to the idea of a lay body like the Anjuman making any authoritative pronouncements on religious matters against the

declared unanimous opinion of a chosen body of experts, and also going the length
of requiring other Parsis to abandon, confessedly for social and extra-religious
reasons, what they might hold and believe to be tenets of their religion, and
what a committee of experts had declared to be special enjoinments of their
religion and their prophet.

8. As a large number of requisitionists have taken organised steps, in view
of certain events that have recently happened, to induce you to convene a meeting to enforce the resolutions of the meeting of the 16th April 1905, and " to
10 pass other proper resolutions for the protection of the community ", we are
asked by our Association to remind you of the aforesaid facts, and for the
reasons hereinafter stated, to request you, in the best interests of the peace,
harmony and welfare of our community not to take any steps or action in the
shape of calling a public meeting of the Parsis for the purpose intended by the
requisitionists.

9. In the first place, a public gathering of the community, indefinite in
its composition, and possessing no constitution or law, will be readily admitted
to be too heterogeneous and unorganised a body to consider and pronounce
upon religious and social questions. It cannot be held to possess either capa-
20 city or authority for such a task, and fortified as you are by the legal opinion of
eminent counsel, who have unanimously declared that resolutions adopted by
such a meeting, by however large a majority, can have no binding effect on
anybody, and no legal validity whatever, you can very safely and wisely decide
to say that you would not call a meeting for a purely futile end.

10. Secondly, as we have said before, the right to convene meetings of the Anjuman so-called, was arrogated to themselves by
the gentlemen who from time to time held the office of, and styled themselves
as, Trustees of the Charitable Funds and Immoveable Properties
of the Parsi Panchayat of Bombay. It is now decided by judicial authority
that the powers thus arrogated to themselves by the Trustees, and their
30 very appointment, were illegal and invalid. You are not successors of the
Trustees under the old arrangement, nor have you been appointed to hold any
of those powers which the Trustees under the old arrangement exercised,
except those specially conferred upon you for a limited purpose. Four of your
number have been nominated by the High Court and the other three elected by
the " Anjuman Committee " in pursuance of the scheme framed and sanctioned
by the Court, and your functions are now restricted to the custody and management of the funds and properties vested in you as Trustees, and you are not
authorised to convene any such meetings of the Anjuman, as it was customary
for those holding office as Trustees in the past to do. Our Association there
40 fore submits that you will see your way not to convene the meeting which you
are now asked to do, and because you as Trustees have no special power or
authority to do so, and because it is not your express duty to convene meetings
of the nature set out by the requisitionists.

11. Thirdly, your help is specially requisitioned in the present instance to
convene a general meeting for the expression of an opinion amounting to a vote
of censure on Shams-ul-Ulma Sirdar Dastur Kaikobad of Poona for a certain
religious ceremony performed by him at Rangoon. Neither the Anjuman at
Bombay, nor you have any concern with the affairs of the Rangoon Anjuman

Exhibit 11.
True copy of
letter P. A.
Wadia to Dr.
J. J. Modi
with
Enclosures,
filed before
Commis-
sioner.
19-3-1914.

or the acts of the Poona Dastur. And again, neither you nor the Anjuman have any jurisdiction or authority over them.

12. Fourthly, it must be deemed the height of presumption, if not impertinence, on the part of the requisitionists when they ask you to help them in their desire to vent their wrath upon a gentleman in the position of Sirdar Dastur Kaikobad whose religious learning and knowledge of the Zoroastrian Scriptures are well known and have received well-merited recognition at the hands of His Majesty's Government who have been pleased to bestow on him the coveted title of Shams-ul-Ulama on the occasion of the historic Darbar at Delhi; whose zeal and fervour for his religion have never been questioned during all his life; who by his sincerity and honesty of purpose and genuine concern for the welfare of his co-religionists has been an ideal Dastur and an exemplary Pastor of his flock; and who has won the esteem and veneration of all who have come into close contact with him. The report of the expert committee submitted to the Anjuman in 1905, and now in your possession, points out the unerring nature of Dastur Kaikobad's action, and the learned high priest can very well cite in support of what he has done the following well considered and weighty pronouncement of the Hon. Mr. Justice Beaman in the Punchayat case: "It is as much the duty of every pious Zoroastrian to-day to make converts as it was in the remote past". Our Association submit further that no Anjuman, however constituted, however large its numbers may be, and however "representative" its character, can ever have the right to pronounce an opinion which could be respected, on the acts of a duly constituted minister of religion like Dastur Kaikobad, and our Association, as far as they are concerned, feel that it will be setting a most lamentable precedent to give opportunities to any one section of the community to grow indignant with, and express its denunciation of, a Dastur's action, only because he did not yield to the pressure that was brought to bear on him on extra-religious grounds, to desist from performing what he, as a Dastur, considered, was a religious duty and what indisputably is in conformity with the precepts of our holy faith.

13. Fifthly, we say that it is puerile to allege and argue that whatever the tenets of the religion might be and whatever the conscientious opinion of Dastur Kaikobad may be in the matter, he had no authority or right to go against the weight of the "collective conscience" of the one-sided Anjuman which adopted various resolutions on the 16th April 1905, forbidding the performance of the Navjot ceremony in certain cases, although, as a matter of fact, the disputed Navjot forms a class by itself, and is not included in those resolutions. We beg to point out that the Trustees of the Punchayet who convened the meeting of the 16th April 1905, and who attended and participated in it, did not themselves, as we have above indicated, choose to follow the dictates of this so-called "collective conscience" of the Anjuman, even when they were not only ostensibly, but to all intents and purposes, fighting a case on behalf and in the interests of the Anjuman. And apart even from the general contention that such an ill-organised and ill-constituted body like the Anjuman has no power, authority or fitness to make weighty, valid or binding pronouncements on such questions as it did in 1905, we say that the resolutions arrived at by the Bombay Anjuman could under no circumstances be held to be morally binding or capable of exercising an influence on the conduct of a recognised Dastur like Shams-ul-Ulama Sirdar Dastur Kaikobad of Poona, or capable of being made applicable to the affairs of a far away city like Rangoon. We submit that

your assistance has been very wrongly invoked on the present occasion under these circumstances.

14. We have said in the last paragraph that the Navjot ceremony performed by Dastur Kaikobad at Rangoon, in the matter of which the requisitionists ask you to convene a meeting can in no way be said to be in contravention of any of the resolutions passed at the meeting of the Anjuman held on the 16th April 1905. We may be permitted to set out and explain this point in greater detail. You will remember that the *de facto* Trustees of the Parsi Panchayat got a notification published in the newspapers of Bombay over the signature of their Secretary Shams-ul-Ulama Ervad Jivanji Jamshedji Modi, bearing date the 9th day of February 1905, to the effect that only those persons who could prove their descent from Zoroastrian parents on both sides would be entitled to the benefit of the Trusts, vested in them. You will remember that by another notification dated the 3rd March 1905, your Secretary published an explanation in the newspapers to the effect that Zoroastrian residents of Persia, coming to India, and also the children of Parsi fathers by alien mothers would be entitled to rank as beneficiaries of these Trusts, according to ancient usage and custom. Soon after the publication of these notifications, on the 16th April 1905, the Anjuman meeting on which your requisitionists rely, was held. Your records will show that on that occasion, Dr. N. H. Sukhia of Bombay, in accordance with a notice of motion which he had sent some time prior to the meeting to your Secretary, proposed and got carried a resolution to the effect that children of Parsi fathers by alien mothers, born after the date of the meeting, should no longer be considered as members of the Parsi community, or admitted into the Zoroastrian religion. The Trustees under whose auspices the meeting which passed the resolution was convened, deliberately contravened the said resolution, as we have shown already in paragraph 6 herein. We wish to emphasise the fact that the only other substantive resolution which was adopted at the meeting was aimed against the admission of children born of alien parents on both sides, as proselytes into our community. You will thus see that nowhere, either in the two circulars of the Trustees of 1905, or in the resolution adopted by the Anjuman meeting of the 16th April 1905, was any reference made to the possible case of children of alien fathers born of Parsi mothers. This case seems for one reason or another to have been entirely lost sight of.

15. We shall state further that your Secretary was subjected to a fairly long cross-examination in the course of the Punchayat case. Your records, no doubt, contain the full shorthand notes of the proceedings of that memorable case. If you will turn over the notes of evidence recorded on the 31st March 1908, you will find various questions put to Dr. Modi by Mr. Lowndes, counsel for the plaintiffs in the case, which were all directed to point out that paragraph 14 of the written statement did not contain an exhaustive classification of the Parsi community. We are here concerned only with that portion of the cross-examination in which reference was pointedly made to page 7 of your Trust Deed of 1884, in which there is a clear recital showing that children of Parsi prostitutes (who may be presumed to be in some cases children of alien fathers by Parsi mothers) have been considered to be entitled to claim the benefit of Zoroastrian Trust properties to a certain extent. Dr. Modi was asked to say plainly if the Trust Deed was wrong. His answers as recorded were as

32

follows :—" It is more a question for lawyers than laymen. . . . I am not prepared to say it is wrong. If a case arises, I will consult my solicitors."

16.   We do not propose to comment on any of these facts or on the evidence of your Secretary, recorded in Court as above. We only wish to point out that ostensibly through oversight, the two circulars issued by the Trustees of 1906 omitted to refer to the case of the children of alien fathers born of Parsi mothers and the result of it was that the mover of the proposition was kept off the scent and prevented from moving, as we believe he would have done, an omnibus resolution prohibiting the admission of every sort of admixture of blood into the community. Your Secretary, so cautious and so keen sighted, by the admissions he made in Court and the answers he gave to the questions put to him, showed that he was all along unaware of the rights which have been enjoyed by custom by the children of alien fathers by Parsi mothers. May we ask if under these circumstances you are prepared to allow a penal resolution to be adopted against an outsider for this oversight of your Secretary and your Anjuman? You have not, your Anjuman of " Parsi Zoroastrians " has not, passed any resolution prohibiting the admission into the religion of such children. And yet your re- quisitionists without hesitation want you to assume, and have the temerity to declare that Dastur Kaikobad has "openly violated the unanimously adopted resolutions of the Anjuman," and they have not scrupled to say in language to which our Association must take strong exception, "that he has thereby done an act pernicious to the community and the religion." We have all along said and argued that the resolutions of your Anjuman never had any time, neither have they now, any binding character whatever. But even assuming that they did have such a character, and that the violation thereof would necessitate the uproar that has been now raised in our community, or justify the demand of the requisitionists, we ask you, to judge dispassionately and to say if at all the requisitionists are right in saying, as they unhesitatingly do, that Dastur Kaiko- bad has been disrespectful to those resolutions.

17.   We would add that even if, for the sake of argument, the resolutions of 16th April 1905 be taken as binding on Dastur Kaikobad, and secondly, if by parity of reasoning, the Anjuman's resolution applied equally to the case of the children of alien fathers by Parsi mothers, as to the case of the children of Parsi fathers by alien mothers, it is impossible to bring the Navjot Ceremony per- formed by Dastur Kaikobad at Rangoon within the scope of the penal resolu- tion adopted by the meeting of 1905, in as much as according to the admitted facts that have come to light, the child was born prior to the date of the said meeting, and was therefore, according to the wording of the resolution, exempted from it.

18.   We trust we have made clear our contention that the whole requisi- tion is misconceived, and based entirely on a misapprehension of facts, and is therefore valueless. We refrain from referring to the doubtful methods and misrepresentations by which the agitation against the Rangoon Navjot has been created and maintained, the artifices by which signatures to the requisi- tion have been obtained, and the personal animus against the learned Dastur which seems to pervade all the actions and representations of the promoters of the requisition. To these and such like matters brought to light by the press we trust you will give due consideration when you judge the importance, urgen- cy and genuineness of the requisition. We fully hope that you will not lend

your support to a movement made expressly for the purpose of discrediting the
character and actions of a learned High Priest in the discharge of his duties,
and demeaning him in the eyes of the general public. Such measures as are
contemplated by the requisitionists cannot reflect credit on the good sense of
our community, or promote its interests. They can only cause dissensions in
the community, such as would interfere with its future progress and happiness.
For these reasons, we earnestly appeal to you, in the name of our Association,
not to associate or identify yourselves in any way with this objectionable
movement of the requisitionists, and to desist from calling a mass meeting of
10 "Parsi Zoroastrians", as they propose.

Exhibit 11.
True copy of
letter P. A.
Wadia to Dr.
J. J. Modi
with
Exhibit 11,
filed before
Console-
sioner,
9-5-1914.

We have the honour to be,

Gentlemen,

Your most obedient servants,

H. J. BHABHA,

President.

P. A. WADIA,

BYRAMJEE HORMUSJEE,

Joint Honorary Secretaries,

Alice Buildings,

Fort.

Bombay, 7th May 1914.

20

True copy,

JIVANJI JAMSHEDJI MODI,

Secretary, Parsee Punchayet,

12th February 1916.

(I)

LETTER FROM ANJUMAN ATASH BEHRAM TO FOREIGN SAVANTS 1904

Anjuman Atash Behram
10, Sirdar's Building
Bombay
23rd June 1903

Dear Sir:

We have the honour to submit for favour of your opinion a question of Parsee religion which has been exercising the minds of the Parsee community of Bombay for some time past. The question has arisen under the following circumstances:-

A young educated lady of French birth and parentage, having expressed a strong desire to embrace the religion of Parsees or Zoroastrianism, a High Priest of the Parsees of Bombay performed her Navjote, i.e., the ceremony of investing her with the sacred shirt and thread which are recognised by Parsees as the essential symbols of the faith of Zoroaster. All the rites and formalities observed in admitting children of Parsee parents in the Zoroastrian fold were performed and observed in the case of this lady, and in addition to these she underwent a purificatory ceremony imposed by orthodox Parsee sentiments upon those who are supposed to have contracted gross impurity or contamination. The ceremony was performed by an orthodox High Priest assisted by other High and subordinate Priests, the latter subject to the spiritual jurisdiction and control of the High Priest of Navsari, which is recognised to be the stronghold of Parsee religious orthodoxy, and several leading and enlightened members of the Parsee lay community took part in the function. The young lady made a voluntary and full declaration of her new faith and her acceptance of its fundamental doctrines and teachings.

Sometime after this event a question was raised as to whether she could be admitted into the Parsee Atash Behram or Fire Temple for prayers, and the question was taken up by the Fire Temple, on whose behalf your valued opinion regarding the question is now solicited, and which is known as the "Zartoshti Anjuman Atash Behram," i.e. Fire Temple of the Zoroastrian community. At a meeting of the Governing Body of the Fire Temple held on 22nd February 1903, six of the members present voted in favour of her admission, and eight desired to have the opinion of European savants versed in Parsee scriptures before coming to a decision, and hence this reference to you. We may mention here that there is a consensus of opinion among our Avesta and Pehlvi scholars who, on being consulted, have given their opinion on the preliminary general question that Zoroastrian religion does not forbid the admission of persons of other communities or castes into the Zoroastrian religion.

We may also inform you that about a year ago, a Parsee, older than the French lady, born of Parsee parents and brought up as a Parsee, but who had since renounced Zoroastrianism and became a convert to Christianity, was some years after such conversion re-admitted into the Parsee religion by another High Priest of the Parsees of Bombay, and that shortly before the conversion of the French lady yet another Parsee High Priest, renowned for his learning and piety, publicly admitted into the Parsee religion the children of a Parsee father by a non-Parsee mother not united in wedlock, and that several years ago another High Priest performed a similar ceremony on children of Parsee fathers by non-Parsee mothers of low castes living in concubinage, many of them so admitted being considerably older than the French lady in question. In none of these cases was a question of their eligibility to admission into Parsee Fire Temple raised, and they have been freely recognised as Parsees, and admitted to all social and religious rites of members of that community. The case of the French lady being unique and quite novel, has naturally provoked keen controversy, the opposition resting their case mainly if not entirely on the social and material side of the larger question of conversion of members of other faiths to the religion of Zoroaster, a side which we may state is quite beyond and outside the scope of subject of the reference made to you, which is restricted solely to the religious object. We, therefore, request that you will be so good as to consider all the above facts, and favour us with your opinion on the question of admitting the lady into our Fire Temple. The question being one of great importance to the Parsee community, we trust your opinion will be as clear and full as possible.

Apologising for the trouble, and thanking you in anticipation,

We are, Dear sir,
yours very faithfully
SD. Sorabji Rustomji Bunshah
Sharpurji Byramji Katrak
Honorary Secretaries

REPLIES TO THE ABOVE:-

The letter of inquiry which you did me the honor of sending was received after I returned from Persia, where I had been making an interesting journey in connection with my Zoroastrian studies. In reply I beg leave to say that if all the requirements had been complied with, as your letter indicates, I should think that the lady had become accepted as a Zoroastrian, and that any question of admission to the Fire Temple had thereby been removed. Such at least would be my understanding of the spirit of Zoroastrianism so far as my knowledge goes.

Respectfully yours,
SD. A.V. Williams Jackson (New York)

If the point is raised that these religions, the Christian and the Zoroastrian, are inherently mutually too antagonistic to admit of a transfer from the one to the other; that I deny in cases where the two religions are philosophically considered, though the popular aspects of them must be worlds apart.

If it is asserted that the race of Europeans is especially alien to the Iranians, that is an error; all are Indo-germanic.

Finally, it is practically contrary to universal usage for the member of a religious community, who value their religion as helpful or necessary to salvation, to forbid any sincere person from sharing in such parts of its privileges as are thus deemed to be necessary to their eternal spiritual welfare.

I gather that you do not request my opinion as to the expediency of creating a distinction with reference to the inheritance or transfer of property in the case of converts; you simply ask for my results as above cited which I willingly afford you.

The main question which should come before us is whether the original Zoroastrian Religion discouraged the admission of proselytes. Upon this the community can then proceed to statutory action. To that point I would answer that this is to the last degree improbable as a fact, while it is positively contradictory to the letter and spirit of the original documents.

Yours obediently
SD.   Lawrence H. Mills
Professor of Zend Philosophy in Oxford
July 18th 1903

(J)
PETITION OF N N BURJORJI AND OTHERS TO BE ADDED IN AS DEFENDANTS IN SAKLAT VS BELLA AND JUDGEMENT BY JUSTICE C YOUNG, 1918

Exhibit No 52.

Petition of NN Barjorjee and others praying that they may be added as defendants
In the Chief Court of Lower Burma.
ORIGINAL CIVIL JURISDICTION.
CIVIL REGULAR No. 91 of 1915,

M. COWASJEE AND OTHERS	Plaintiff
Versus	
Bella and one	Defendant

Petition.
The Petition of N N. Burjorje, Barrister at-law and others.
SHEWETH THAT

1. This suit involves questions of great importance to the Parsi Community in Burma.
2. Advertisements of the institution of the suit appeared in the newspapers stating that the Plaintiffs claimed to sue on behalf of themselves and very many other members of the Parsi Community.

3. Your Petitioners and other members of the Community were not concerned to prevent the Plaintiffs suing in that capacity, but they learnt at a subsequent date that the Plaintiffs had in fact applied for and obtained leave to sue on behalf of all members of the said Community.

4. There are many members of the said Community who disagree with the views and contentions of the Plaintiffs and are unwilling to be represented in the suit by the Plaintiffs.

5. Your Petitioners are members of the Parsi Community in Burma and desire to be added as Defendant in order to represent the views of those members of the Community referred to in para 4 hereof.

6. There is only one Parsi Temple in the whole of Burma and all Parsis in Burma are entitled to worship and are in the habit of worshipping at the said Temple when they are in Rangoon.

7. The first and second Petitioners are residents of Rangoon and are entitled to worship and in the habit of worshipping at the said Temple.

8. The 3rd, 4th and 5th Petitioners are residents of Bassein and 6th and 7th of Mandalay respectively and are entitled to worship at the said Temple and are in the habit of so doing when they are in Rangoon.

9. Your Petitioners do not desire to raise any defence different from that raised by the original Defendants and they are prepared to accept all evidence hitherto taken on Commission without objection on the score that it was so taken before they became parties to the suit

Issue notice to the parties through their respective Advocates for 19th November 17

J. HORMASJI.

Deputy Registrar. 3rd November 1917.

GILES and ORMISTON,
Petitioner' Advocates,
Rangoon,
This 2nd day of November 1917.

Wherefore your Petitioners pray that they may be added as Defendant in order to represent their own views and those of the members of the Parsi Community in Burma who agree with them.

N. N. BURJORJEE.

A. B. MEHTA

N. S. PANRI

? ? ?

D. R. COOPER

RUSTOM H. HIRJEE

K NOWROJEE.

Petitioners

I, N. N. Burjoree, one of the Petitioners abovenamed do hereby declare that the statements contained in paras I, 2, 4. 5, 6, 7 and 9 of the above petition are true to my knowledge and that the statements contained in para 3 and 8 from information which I received and believe to be true

(Sd.) N N. BURJORJEE,
Place-Rangoon.
Dated the 3rd November 1917.

*****

No. 33
ORDER
In the Chief Court of Lower Burma.

ORIGINAL CIVIL JURISDICTION. Civil regular No of 1915.

M. COWASJEE AND OTHERS
For Plaintiffs-Connell with N. M. Cowasjee.
For Applicants-Giles with McDonnell

ORDER

This is a petition of Mr. N. N. Burjorji and four others to be joined as defendants in the above suit on the ground that the suit involves questions of great importance to the Parsi Community in Burma, and that there are many members of the said Community who disagree with the views and contentions of the Plaintiff and are unwilling to be represented by them, and they desire to be added in order to represent them.

The suit is for an injunction to restrain the 1st defendant from worshiping in the Parsee temple or from being brought in there by her guardian and defendant on the ground that she is not a Parsi.

The issues are far reaching and important. One raises the question as to who are entitled to the benefit of the Fire Temple Trust and another the still wider question as to whether it is possible for the daughter of a non-Parsi father to be initiated (a) into the Zoroastrian religion (b) into the Parsi Community. The Plaintiffs are the more orthodox or as the opponents would probably say the more narrow-minded section of the Parsees who would prohibit conversion and deny that anyone not being the child of a Parsi father can be a Parsi.

In their plaint they claimed to represent a very large number of members of the Parsee community of Rangoon who are interested in the Parsee Fire Temple

They asked for however and obtained permission under Order 1 Rules 6 to sue on behalf and for the benefit of not of many but of all persons interested in the said Fire Temple.

In the advertisement giving notice of the institution of the suit it is nevertheless stated that the suit had been instituted by the Plaintiffs on behalf of themselves and a large number of the members of the Parsee Community of Rangoon against the defendants and the petitioners state that this misled them and that they took no action as they were not concerned to prevent the plaintiffs from suing merely as representing many Parsis.

The plaint was filed on the 3Ist March 1915, leave was obtained the same day to sue in a representative capacity and the advertisement was published on the 8th May 1915.

On the 11th September 1915 this Court decided a preliminary issue as to the maintainability of the suit and in reply to one of the arguments of defendants Counsel that his clients might be ruined by innumerable suits brought by aggrieved individual pointed out that the plaintiffs were suing on behalf of themselves and all others interested and no such multiplicity of suits could be brought.

On the 30th November 1915 the Plaintiff alter reciting that the suit had been instituted on their own behalf and on behalf of the members of the Parsee Community applied for the issue of a commission to examine witnesses at Bombay.

This commission was returned executed on the 30th August 1916 and on the 2nd November 1917 the applicant presented their petition.

It is obvious that they have been excessively dilatory.

They seek to palliate this by stating that they were misled by the statements in the plaint and advertisement and by disclaiming any desire to raise any defence different from that raised by the original defendants and by consenting to accept all evidence hitherto taken on commission without objection.

They ask to be added in order to represent their own views and those of the members of the Parsee Community in Burma who agree with them. In Fraser vs Cooper Hall & Co. 21 Ch. Diva, 718: bond holder of a Railway Company sued on behalf of himself and all other bond-holders to restrain Railway Company from certain action. Another bond-holder objected to their views and was added as a defendant in his personal capacity. Subsequently a third bondholder who objected apparently to the views of every one else was also added but to create finality was added as representing all bond-holders who did not desire the injunction prayed for to be granted.

If I granted the petition which is not, as it should have been supported by an affidavit I should feel inclined to make a similar order allowing them to sue not on behalf of those members of the Parsee Community who agree with them but on behalf of all members of the Parsee Community interested in the Rangoon Fire Temple who do not desire the injunction to be granted. Their prayer to represent only those who agree with them seems to me too vague: I Might have persons seeking to come in on the ground that they did not agree either with the Plaintiffs or with Mr. Burjorjee and his fellow applicants and find all the advantages of a representative suit being gradually whittled away to the great inconvenience of the Court-c. p. Watson vs. Cave 17 Ch. Divn. 19.

I think Plaintiff made the same mistake when they stated in their plaint that they had instituted the suit on behalf of a large number of members of the Parsee Community who were interested in the Rangoon Fire Temple and I think they were correct in asking for leave to sue on behalf of all persons so interested and should have amended the title of and statements in their plaint on obtaining the leave they asked for.

To sue on behalf of those who are of their way of thinking does not seem to me to constitute a representative suit in the sense intended by Order 1 Rule 8 which provides that where there are numerous parties having the same interest in a suit, one or more may with the leave of the Court, sue on behalf of all persons so interested.

Here the persons interested are all the Parsees of Rangoon that is not necessarily all those who take the same view of their interest but all those who have as a matter of fact the same interest.

Those who disagree can if their disagreement is sufficient to make then willing to incur expense apply to be made defendants (R. 8 (2)). Watson vs Cave 17 Ch. Divn. 19. The object of the rule is to save trouble, expense and multiplicity of suits: one must know therefore who are to be bound. This is easy when the suit is on behalf of all persons having the same interest, but difficult if not impossible to ascertain it persons seek to sue or defend not on behalf of all persons interested but on behalf of all persons holding the same views. Views and interests are not the same and the law says persons may sue on behalf of all persons having an identity of interest not all persons holding a similarity of views.

Should I therefore grant this application? the Plaintiffs object to my doing so on the ground of expense, and it is clear that to grant it might increase the duration and cost of the case very considerably. The relief they claim is a purely personal one against two individuals viz, to have one declared not to be Parsi and not entitled to enter and worship in the Fire Temple of Rangoon and to have the other restrained from introducing her into the temple in question.

They have no wish to fight all the Parsis who disagree with their views they merely wish to restrain the 2nd defendant who holds these different view from translating them into action in a manner as they allege offensive to themselves and contrary to their rights of exclusive worship, and as they represent all Parsees interested in the Rangoon Fire Temple no other Parsee will be able to bring a similar action against the same individuals for the same trespass.

There will therefore be no multiplicity of suits against these defendants. Why then do Mr. Burjorji and his companions wish to be joined. They have no particular interest in the two defendants and are quite willing to leave them to fight their own battles c p.

para 3 of their petition and their long inaction, and it is obvious that they could not be joined if the matter merely concerned the present defendants and no one else. What they fear is that under explanation 6 to Section II C. P. C. the matter touches not merely the defendants on the record but all Parsees of what may be called the liberal school and that the issues as to who may sue the Parsee Pire Temple and who are and who are not Parsis will be definitely decided not merely as regards Bella and her guardian but as regards themselves.

Section II provides not only that suits but also that issues in suits may be res judicata and explanation VI provides that where persons litigate bona fide in respect of public right or of a private right claimed in common for themselves and others all persons interested in such right shall for the purposes of the section be deemed to claim under the persons so litigating.

They fear that by virtue of this explanation the scope of the suit now that the plaintiff are suing on behalf of themselves and all Parsees is automatically widened so as to include them whereas previously they recognized that it did not do so and therefore had no wish to intervene. It is for this reason they claim to be heard.

There would be risk of grave inconvenience if their views were correct.

The case would be vastly more important than it is at present. It would affect not merely the rights of the two defendants but those of all interested in the Rangoon Fire Temple who are of their way of thinking.

It is true that those who make the present application do not seek to disturb the voluminous evidence already taken, but if I granted their request and allowed them to defend the suit as dissentient, I have no guarantee that others would not come forward and say that they too had been misled by the statements in the plaint and by the advertisement issued by the Court, and while in agreement with

Mr. Burjorji and his friends in the main differed from them in being unwilling to accept the evidence taken in their absence.

It is true that the Court has discretion as to whether it shall allow fresh parties to be added, but if I allowed the present applicants to be added, it seem to me I should be raising vital question between two bodies of the community and I should be loath to allow some to join merely because their joinder would neither cause inconvenience nor delay and yet to refuse to allow others to be added who wished to cross-examine the witnesses who have been already examined.

The case would have become so important that I should feel inclined to allow every latitude.

As a matter of fact however I think that the present applicants are mistaken in their apprehensions. I think their former view that they are not concerned is the correct one, and that they will not be concerned unless I grant their request and add them as defendants.

At present it is a suit by the plaintiffs merely to restrain two persons whom they regard as wrong-doers from repeating their wrong.

They have obtained leave to sue on behalf of all interested in the temple it is true, but I do not think these others will be concluded by any decision as to who are Parsees and who may worship in the temple. Explanation VI which creates their fears is in the first place only an explanation to the section and we must go back to that and secondly its own wording must be carefully scrutinised.

All that it says is that where persons litigate bona fide in respect of a private right claimed in common for themselves and others all persons interested in such right shall for the purposes of this section be deemed to claim under the person so litigating.

It follows therefore that all Parsis interested other than the defendants are claiming not some under the Plaintiffs and some under the defendants, but exhypothesis under the Plaintiff.

Then if we turn to the section itself we see that a second suit is only barred when the same question has been decided in a former suit between the same parties or between parties under whom they or any of them claims.

Let us assume that a Parsi gentleman marries a non-Parsi lady converts her and seeks to introduce her into the Fire-Temple, are they to have no chance of being heard if the decision in this case is that no person not born of a Parsee father is entitled to worship there?

I do not think so: let us assume the present plaintiffs sue in turn to restrain them: they will be suing persons who do not claim under the defendant in the present suit who are being sued individually but under the plaintiff themselves (vide the explanation) as representing all Parsees interested. In other words all parties in the subsequent suit will be claiming under one party in the prior suit, and if so the section does not apply c. p. per the Privy Council in Ashgar Reza Khan vs. Mahomed Mehdi Hoossein Khan 1.L. R. 30 Cal: 556. 564 and Mullas Civil Procedure Code (2nd Edition p. 44).

This seems only reasonable: The Plaintiffs have brought this suit against persons whom they allege to be wrong doers. They have no wish to sue all members of the community who disagree with them on questions of doctrine in order to have it declared which view is correct, even if such a suit would be which is doubtful unless and until something more than a difference of thought arises. They apply for and obtain leave to sue as representing all Parsis interested not to any great advantage to themselves but with the result that no other Parsi will be able to sue the same defendants of the same trespass.

Certain other Parsis who did not and don't mind whether the defendants are restrained or not become apprehensive lest because the suit is brought by the Plaintiff in a representative capacity, they may be bound by the issues in this suit and therefore apply to be made defendants instead of plaintiff: the practical result of which would be to convert the suit from one for an injunction against allege wrongdoer into a suit for a declaration as to doctrine- the competence of which I doubt coupled with an injunction against the persons who are alleged to have translated their beliefs into deeds.

In my opinion their former view held when they thought the Plaintiff were suing not on behalf of all but of many Parsees interested namely that they were not concerned still remains correct. They are not interested and will not be bound. Their application is very belated and there is no reason in my opinion for granting it and strong reasons for rejecting it which 1 do with 5 Gold Mohur costs.

C. YOUNG, Judge
4th January 1918

(K)
IRANI VS IRANI JUDGEMENT OF MODY J, 1960 IN HIGH COURT OF BOMBAY

ORIGINAL CIVIL.

Before Mr. Justice Mody.

JAMSHED A. IRANI *v.* BANU J. IRANI.*

Parsi Marriage and Divorce Act (III of 1936), Sec. 2(7)—"Parsi", meaning of word—Whether Irani Zoroastrians are Parsis within meaning of Act—"Parsi" whether applies to "Racial Parsis" only.

The word "Parsi" as used in the Parsi Marriage and Divorce Act, 1936, includes not only the Parsi Zoroastrians of India but also the Zoroastrians of Iran.

ONE Jamshed A. Irani (plaintiff) filed the present suit for divorce against his wife Banu (defendant) on the ground of desertion under the Parsi Marriage and Divorce Act, 1936. He alleged that both of them were Parsi Zoroastrians at all relevant times, that they were domiciled in India, that they were lawfully married on July 20, 1951 at Bombay according to the rights and ceremonies of the Parsi Zoroastrian religion by the Registrar of Parsi Marriage under the Act and that the defendant a few months after their marriage deserted him and ceased living with him. The defendant contended that neither the plaintiff nor herself was a Parsi Zoroastrian, that both of them were domiciled in Iran and not in India, that they were foreigners and were registered as such under the Registration of Foreigners Rules, 1939, and that under the circumstances the Court had no jurisdiction to entertain and try the suit.

The suit came on for hearing before Mody J. and seven delegates and certain issues were tried as preliminary issues. One of the questions which arose during the trial of these preliminary issues was whether evidence was admissible as to the meaning of the word "Parsi" as occurring in the Act as the Act nowhere has made clear as to what was meant by a "Parsi". It was contended for the plaintiff that for the purpose of ascertaining the meaning of the word "Parsi" as occurring in the Act, oral evidence was admissible, while for the defendant it was stated that what was meant by "Parsi" had already been decided by authorities and no evidence was, therefore, admissible. Mody J. held that such evidence was admissible, and in the course of his reasons for this ruling, observed as follows:—

MODY J. I am, however, feeling a great difficulty in following that judgment [*Yezdiar* v. *Yezdiar*[1]]. Before proceeding further I may state that the question whether Iranian Zoroastrians are Parsis or not for the purposes of the said Act has become a question of great importance. I am told that it has greatly agitated the minds of Iranian Zoroastrians in India and particularly in Bombay. The importance attached is so great that the Iranian Zoroastrian Anjuman took out a Chamber Summons before me in this suit for being added as a party to this suit. In support of that summons it was pointed out to me, and with great emphasis, that the decision as to whether Iranian Zoroastrians are Parsis or not for the purposes of the said Act will have very important and grave repercussions on the members of that community. I was told that over a large number of years Iranian Zoroastrians, on the basis that they were Parsis, have contracted marriages as Parsis under and in accordance with the provisions of the said Act. The decision of the instant point would, therefore, reflect on the validity or otherwise of their marriages. Incidentally it would necessarily reflect on the legitimacy or otherwise of their children. Incidentally it would also reflect on intestate successions which have taken place in the case of deceased Iranian Zoroastrians of Bombay and India. I was also told that in India fire temples and places of religious worship as also Dakhmas or burial grounds for Zoroastrians are mostly, if not exclusively, for members of the Parsi Zoroastrian community and that Iranian Zoroastrians as Parsis are having the benefit thereof. I was also told that there are rich and varied endowments and charitable trusts for the benefit of Parsis and Iranian Zoroastrians as Parsis are receiving benefit thereunder and that the determination whether Iranian Zoroastrians are Parsis or not would affect the ability of Iranian Zoroastrians to take advantage of those places of religious worship, burial grounds, endowments and trusts. I have been given all this information not only by Mr. Khambatta who is the counsel for the Anjuman but also by Mr. Banaji who himself is one of Trustees of the Parsi Panchayat. I have mentioned all this merely for the purpose of bearing in mind that the question raised is of great importance to a community which, I am told, numbers in thousands. So far as that application for adding the Anjuman as a party was concerned, I however pointed out to Mr. Khambatta, the learned counsel for the Anjuman, but only on a *prima facie* view at that time, that in the case of an individual dispute between a particular plaintiff and a particular defendant it may not be possible for me to grant Mr. Khambatta's application to make the Anjuman a party to this suit. I however stated to Mr. Khambatta that as it appeared that the legal point involved may vitally affect a large community, I would hear submissions on law not only on behalf of the plaintiff and the defendant but also on behalf of the said Anjuman. In view of that statement made by me. Mr. Khambatta did not press his summons. Mr. Khambatta has, however, continued to appear at the hearing of this suit and I have indeed allowed Mr. Khambatta even to make submissions on the present objection raised by Mr. Chhatrapati.

Turning back to the said judgment of Chagla C. J. in *Yezdiar* v. *Yezdiar*, as I have already stated, I have studied that judgment with great care and anxiety. It has become my duty to analyse that judgment and to find out for myself how far I am bound by the same and whether I should follow the same. Needless to say, on the principle of *stare decisis*, I would be bound by that judgment. It is a judgment of a Division Bench. It is a judgment of the Appeal Court. It is a judgment delivered in an appeal from a decision of the Parsi Chief Matrimonial Court, the Court of which I am at present the sitting Judge. It is a judgment of a very eminent Judge. But having studied and analysed that judgment with great respect and with utter humility I have with great hesitation come to the conclusion which I will presently mention. The position in that case was rather peculiar. The case was tried in the trial Court only on one preliminary issue, viz. whether the Court had jurisdiction in view of the fact that the defendant in that case was not domiciled in India. The trial Court answered only that issue, the answer being in the negative. But the trial Court's judgment, as already noted earlier, makes it amply clear that the trial Court did not hold that it had no jurisdiction because the parties were not Parsis or that the said Act was not applicable to the facts of that case. Now, the judgment of the Appeal Court, however, does not appear to deal with that point at all and it does not certainly decide the appeal on that point. The appeal was decided on a different point, viz. that the parties were not Parsis and, therefore, the said Act did not apply and, therefore, the said Court constituted under the said Act had no jurisdiction. As pointed out both by Mr. Banaji and Mr. Khambatta, it is quite clear that the point whether either the plaintiff or the defendant was a Parsi or not was not raised at all in the trial Court. That was not a point taken in the pleadings. It was not a point put in issue. It was not a point argued before or decided by the trial Court. Naturally the parties did not lead evidence on that point nor did they urge their contentions in respect thereof before the trial Court. That point appears to have been taken for the first time only in the appeal. From the judgment it does not appear that the counsel for the appellant even drew the attention of the Appeal Court that the point had not been raised or argued or decided in the trial Court. It appears that the counsel for the appellant chose to argue the point raised for the first time in the appeal. Possibly, I say with due humility, the importance of the point which was being decided was not fully realised by the Appeal Court and certainly not by the counsel for the appellant in that case. In the said case of *Sir Dinshaw M. Petit v. Sir Jamsetji Jijibhai*[2], Davar J. came to the conclusion that the Iranis from Persia professing the Zoroastrian religion, who come to India, either temporarily or permanently, would be included amongst Parsis. Now, so far as that part of the judgment of Davar J. is concerned, Chagla C.J. has pointed out that it was *obiter* because the question that Davar and Beaman JJ. had to consider in that case was whether by conversion to the Zoroastrian faith a person could become a Parsi. As regards the judgment of the Privy Council in the said second case (*Saklat v. Bella*)[3] Chagla C.J. also points out that the question which they had to consider in the said case of *Yezdiar v. Yezdiar* did not arise directly for decision in the Privy Council case. That again was so because in the Privy Council case also the point was whether a Juddin, i.e. a non-Zoroastrian, upon conversion or initiation into the Zoroastrian religion, could be said to be a Parsi. In neither of the said two cases of *Sir Dinshaw M. Petit v. Sir Jamsetji Jijibhai* and *Saklat v. Bella* the point directly arose whether an Iranian Zoroastrian was a Parsi, but the point was directly considered by the Appeal Court only in the said case of *Yezdiar v. Yezdiar* and it was decided that Iranian Zoroastrians may not be Parsis. That judgment, however, expressly states that it was not necessary for the Appeal Court to decide the larger question as to whether an Iranian by being domiciled in India could become a Parsi. That point is, therefore, still open and has not been decided by that judgment. But so far as the main point is concerned, the Divisional Bench in that case has decided as aforesaid. How far am I bound to follow it? That is the question which has considerably agitated my mind. In my humble opinion such a question of great importance and involving wide repercussions was decided by the judgment of the Appeal Court without the same having been raised in the trial Court and without any evidence on that question having been recorded on either side. It appears, if I may say so, that it was a point raised only at the time of the hearing of the appeal and the counsel in that case did not even point out to the Appeal Court that the point had not been raised or considered in the trial Court and may have required evidence. In such circumstances, I feel myself not bound to follow the ratio of that judgment. As I have said earlier, it is with greatest hesitation that I come to that conclusion. But I am of the opinion that justice requires that parties must get a proper opportunity to lead evidence and to fully argue that point before it can bind not only the parties but the entire community. It may be that if in that case evidence had been led or an issue raised and decided, it would not have been open in a subsequent case for a trial Court like the present one not to follow the judgment in that case on the ground that proper evidence had not been led or that proper arguments had not been presented. In this case, however, I am not following that judgment because the point was not even raised. It was certainly not argued. There was no evidence whatever led and it was not decided by the trial Court. It was merely a point raised for the first time in appeal without the attention of the Appeal Court having been drawn to the fact that it was entirely a new point which would necessitate taking of further evidence.

In coming to the above conclusion there is another factor which has weighed with me. Undoubtedly the decision in *Yezdiar v. Yezdiar* is a decision of a Division Bench constituted of two Judges and that decision is not *obiter dicta*. But there is a contrary decision in the said case of *Sir Dinshaw M. Petit v. Sir Jamsetji Jijibhai*. Of course, that decision is *obiter dicta*. But that is a decision or rather an observation, of Sir Dinshaw Davar whom Chagla C. J. himself in his said judgment has called a very great authority on Parsi law. That decision is also a decision, not of a single Judge, but of a Bench of two Judges.

2 (1908) 11 Bom. L.R. 85.   3 (1925) 28 Bom. L.R. 161, P.C.

That is a decision which has been given, although *obiter*, in an attempt at ascertaining the complete connotation of the word "Parsi". Moreover, it appears that Davar J. made those observations after evidence was recorded in that case on that very point as to whether Iranian Zoroastrians were Parsis or not. A reference to the judgment of Davar J. appearing at pp. 113 and 115 of the said report shows that evidence in that behalf was led of one Jamsetji Dadabhai Nadershah and also of Beram Sheriar, an Irani priest. Indeed Beram Sheriar's testimony was as follows:

"Some Mahomedans in Persia call us Parsis; some call us Zarthostis. The word Parsis is in common use in Persia. It means Zarthosti. Mussalmans in Persia use the word Parsis commonly to designate our people—the Zarthostis".

There is, therefore, this conflict. Undoubtedly, the conflict is between the judgment in one case which was on a point which directly disposed of the appeal and certain observations in the judgment in another which were merely *obiter dicta*. As said earlier, although the point was directly responsible for the decision of the appeal in *Yezdiar* v. *Yezdiar*, the point was not argued and evidence was not recorded, whereas the said observations of Davar J. are merely *obiter dicta*, but as against the same they were in the process of formulating a definition of "Parsi" or rather in the process of formulating the full connotation of the word "Parsi" and the same were made after recording of evidence. I am, therefore, of the opinion that this point is open for decision by me by permitting further evidence.

H. D. Banaji, with *A. P. Talati*, for the plaintiff.
R. K. Chhatrapati, for the defendant.
P. P. Khambatta, with *P. K. Irani*, for the Iranian Zoroastrian Anjuman.

Mody J. [After setting out facts his Lordship proceeded as follows.] At the stage of address, both counsel agreed that each of the plaintiff and the defendant is a national of Iran and professes and has always professed the Zoroastrian religion and is registered as a foreigner under the Registration of Foreigners Rules, 1939....

Both the plaintiff and the defendant have given evidence. The plaintiff is 30 years old and he was born in Yezd in Iran. He was living in Iran with his father, mother, brothers and sisters. He came to India, according to him, from Iran, in 1947 for residing permanently in India. He married the defendant in Bombay on July 20, 1951. Ever since he came to India, he has not gone back to Iran at any time. The defendant is 32 years old. She was born in Yezd in Iran. She was living in Iran. She came to India in 1950, accompanied by her father. Since her marriage she has not gone back to Iran at any time.

Turning to the said first group of issues, the main question is what is the meaning of the word "Parsi". As pointed out by me earlier, neither s. 2(7) nor any other provision of the Act defines or states what is meant by that word "Parsi". The Act contains no other provisions or guidance as to what is meant by "Parsi". The defendant contended that "Parsi" meant only "Racial Parsis" and, as a matter of fact, it was because of that contention urged by Mr. Chhatrapati that issues Nos. 1 and 3 were cast in the present language. Mr. Chhatrapati's contention was expressly stated to have been based on certain earlier judgments of this Court. But, in view of the ruling which I gave when I admitted oral evidence, it is not necessary for me to refer to those judgments. The defendant's contention is that Iranian Zoroastrians whether temporarily, or even permanently, residing in India are not "Parsis" within the meaning of the Act. The plaintiff, on the other hand, contends that the Zoroastrians living in Iran are, and for centuries have been, known even in Iran and also in India as Parsis and that they would, therefore, be "Parsis" within the meaning of the Act. On the question of interpretation of the word "Parsi" evidence has been led. The material evidence on the subject is that of Rashid Irani, Mr. P.B. Vachha, Dastoor Mirza and Mr. Jamshed Tarapore and the various documents exhibited through them.

Rashid was born in Bombay and is about 55 years old. He has visited Iran four or five times, his stay in Iran being for short periods aggregating to 2 or 2½ years. He is a scholar of the Persian language, and has done research work in religion, philosophy and history of Parsis in Iran after the invasion of the Arabs. He has written some books on the subject which have been published through various associations. He has also translated the Ramayana into Persian under the orders of the Government of India. At the invitation of the Government of Iran he attended the international conference in Iran in 1954 as a delegate from India.

Mr. Vachha is an advocate of this Court of 48 years standing. Before he was enrolled as an advocate he was in the educational service of the Government of Bombay from 1906 to 1912. During that period he was for some time a lecturer in Persian in the Elphinstone College. He has published certain translations of certain Persian classics with his commentary thereon. He has also published a book in English being "A Study of the Great Iranian Historical Epic of Firdausi". He has visited Iran twice, first in 1934 in connection with the millenary celebrations of Firdausi and next in 1954 to participate in the thousand year celebrations of the great Persian physician and philosopher known to the west as Avicenna. The second visit was made by him at the invitation of the Government of Iran as a delegate from India. He has stated that he has read a large number of books on the history of Iran, both ancient and modern, published in English, Persian, Gujarati and Urdu. In 1956, on the occasion of the then impending visit of the Shah of Persia to India, he, at the request of the then Consul-General of Iran in Bombay, wrote a book entitled "Iran, Ancient and Modern".

The third witness Dastoor Mirza is an M.A. of the University of Bombay and Ph.D. of the University of London. The principal subjects for his M.A. degree were Avesta, Pehlvi and old Persian and for his Ph.D. he wrote a thesis in Pehlvi and his subject for the Ph.D. degree was Iranian languages. He has been taking active interest in Avesta, Pehlvi and Persian languages, both ancient and modern. He has taken part since 1941 in the Iranian section of the various sessions of the All India Oriental Conferences held in India. He was twice the President of the Iranian section of the All India Oriental Conferences. At those conferences he had read papers about his research in Avesta and Pehlvi.

Mr. Jamshed Tarapore is an M.A. and LL.B. of the Bombay University and for his M.A. Examination his subjects were Avesta, Pehlvi and old Iranian languages. He has translated several Pehlvi texts into English and/or Gujarathi and most of them have also been published. He also attended several sessions of the Oriental Conferences and at the Iranian section thereof he had read various papers, and had also presided over the same on two occasions. He is a member of the Managing Committee of the Iran League and is the editor of the Iran League Quarterly. He knows Sanskrit also and he has done research work in old Iranian languages and in Sanskrit.

These four witnesses were examined as expert witnesses. Each has however, mostly, by reason of his special study, produced relevant books and documents. Their own opinion evidence itself is very little.

Rashid has stated that the Achimenian dynasty reigned over Iran from 500 B.C. to about 100 B.C. and the Sassanian dynasty from about 200 A.D. to 631 A.D. He has further stated that the Arabs invaded and conquered Iran in about 631 A.D. and that the Arabs were Muslims and since 631 A.D. there has been Muslim rule in Iran.

It is the plaintiff's case that since very ancient times till the Arab conquest, almost all, if not all, the inhabitants of Iran were Zoroastrians. It is his case that since at least the commencement of the reign of the Achimenian dynasty the residents of Iran were known as "Parsa", that during the Sassanian rule "Parsa" became "Parsik" and that after the Arab conquest "Parsik" became "Parsi" and it was applied only to the Zoroastrians of Iran and not to the Arab conquerors or to the Zoroastrians converted to Islam. It is his case that the Zoroastrians of Iran have, even till today, been continued to be called and known as Parsis.

Now, the Parsi Marriage and Divorce Act was passed in 1936. It replaced the earlier Act which was passed in 1865. It is the plaintiff's case that in 1936 and even in 1865 the Zoroastrians of Iran also were commonly known and referred to as Parsis and that, therefore, when the Legislature used the word "Parsi" in the Act of 1936, and even in the prior Act of 1865, it was intended to include, and it must be construed to include, not only the Parsis of India, but also the Irani Zoroastrians, who happened to be in India, whether permanently or even temporarily.

Now, the evidence as to the use of the words "Parsa", then "Parsik" and later "Parsi" as aforesaid divides itself chronologically into two parts. The first part relates to the period commencing from the ancient times till about 100 years ago. This evidence is, I may at once say, rather vague. The second part relates to the last, about a hundred years and the evidence relating to the second period is fuller. I propose to deal with the evidence as regards these two periods separately.

I will briefly set out what cumulatively is the substance of the evidence of the said four witnesses as regards the use of the names "Parsa" "Parsik" and "Parsi" during the said first period, the documentary evidence relating to that period and certain contradictions between their testimony.

The evidence of these witnesses is that in the present day Iran there is a province called "Pars" or "Fars". I may state that in the Arabic alphabet there is no letter "P" and, therefore, the letter "F" is used instead, with the result that since the Arab conquest of Iran the letter "F" was used when written in Arabic in place of the letter "P" as used in Persian. That province was one of the important provinces of the country. That country roughly corresponds to the present day Iran. That province gave its own name to the whole country, to its people and to their language. During the reign of the Achimenian dynasty the country over which they ruled was known as "Parsa" which is the present day Persia or Iran. Herodotus and Xenophon, the two Greek historians, who lived in the 3rd and the 4th centuries B.C., referred to Iranians as Parsis. Aeschylus who also lived at about the same time was one of the great Greek tragic writers. In one of his works he has described the great battle of Salamis which was fought between the Persians and the Greeks. "Persee" is the title given by Aeschylus to his said work and the reason, according to Mr. Vachha, is that the book deals with the battle which the Greeks fought with the Persians. The words "Persia" and "Persian" in English and akin words in the European languages owe their origin to the word "Perses" as used by the ancient Greeks. The religion of the inhabitants of the country, i.e., of Parsa, from the beginning of the Achimenian dynasty, and even prior thereto, till the end of the Sassanian dynasty, following upon the conquest by the Arabs was Zoroastrian. After the Arab conquest there was extensive conversion of the inhabitants from the Zoroastrian religion to the Musalman religion. In course of time the Zoroastrians were called Parsis and those who were converted to Islam were called Musalmans. The Arab conquerors persecuted the Parsis, i.e. the original Zoroastrian inhabitants of the country. They also tried to destroy all the literature and the books of the Zoroastrian religion. Because of the persecution and the destruction a handful of Zoroastrians of Iran migrated during the seventh century A.D. from Iran into India. Those who migrated into India continued to call themselves Parsis because that was the name by which they had been known in their mother country Iran. One of the outstanding Achimenian kings was Darius who, as stated by Dastoor Mirza, reigned from 522 B.C. up to 486 B.C. Many of his inscriptions are in existence till today. They are in the cuneiform script as used by the ancient Persians. The cuneiform script was used by many ancient civilizations such as the Babylonian, Assyrian and the ancient Persian but the cuneiform script used by each of the civilizations varied. Transcriptions and translations in English of portions of some of the inscriptions of Darius have been put in as exhs. A-7, A-8, A-9, A-10 and another has been referred to in exh. A-11. Broadly stated, in these inscriptions, Darius states that "he is a Persian, son of a Persian". The actual word used by Darius is "Parsa" of which the word "Persian" is the English equivalent or translation. From these inscriptions it appears that the word "Parsa" was used during the reign of Darius for the inhabitants of Iran. Thereafter in the third and the fourth centuries the Greek historians Herodotus and Xenophon referred to the inhabitants of Iran as "Parsees". According to Rashid, during the reign of the Sassanian dynasty the word "Parsa" used in the inscriptions of Darius became "Parsik". Mr. Vachha, however, has stated that during the Sassanian times the inhabitants of Iran had come to be known as Parsis. Mr. Tarapore also stated that during the rule of the Sassanian dynasty the Zoroastrian inhabitants of Iran were called Parsis. There is, therefore, some inconsistency in the evidence of the three witnesses as to when the inhabitants of Iran came to be known as "Parsis", i.e., whether during the Sassanian times as stated by Mr. Vachha and Mr. Tarapore or after the Sassanian times as stated by Rashid, the word during the Sassanian times being "Parsik", according to Rashid. That is but natural. The words in a language do not change over-night; nor does everybody start using the new word at the same time. The change is a gradual process and this particular change has taken place more than 1,000 or 1,500 years ago, of which time there is a paucity of material. The exact time when the change took place is immaterial. It is the evidence of these witnesses that the original word was "Parsa" and that after a lapse of time it changed into "Parsi", there having been, according to Rashid, an intervening change of the word into "Parsik".

Chronologically speaking, the next piece of evidence relied upon on behalf of the plaintiff is the use of the word "Parsi" in certain Shlokas which Nairyosang, the leader of the first immigrants from Persia to Sanjan in India, addressed to the Hindu King then having suzerainty over the territory wherein Sanjan was situated. Mr. Vachha relied upon the translation of these Shlokas, or rather portions of such translation, as appearing in a book published in 1917. These portions have been put in as exh. A-5. The original book is intituled as "Les Parsis" and is written by Mlle Menant in the French language and was published in 1898. M. M. Murzban has translated that book into English and published the same with his own comments thereon. At the end of each of the Shlokas appear the words "those are we Parsi". The word as appearing in the book undoubtedly is "Parsi". That, however, is the translation firstly from French and the original writing is supposed to be in Sanskrit. Nairyosang is supposed to have addressed those Shlokas in Sanskrit. What was the actual word used in Sanskrit does not appear from the record before me. Even the date of Nairyosang is a matter of dispute. Under the circumstances, in my opinion, no importance can be attached to the word "Parsi" or "Parsis" as appearing in the English translation, exh. A-5.

Mr. Vachha has stated that even after the conquest of Iran by the Arabs the original inhabitants of Iran were continued to be called "Parsis". He further stated that originally even the Zoroastrians of Iran who converted themselves to Islam were also continued to be called Parsis in some cases. He gave two illustrations. One of them was that of Salman-e-Farsee and the other that of Majuddin-e-Hangar-e-Farsee. According to Mr. Vachha Salman-e-Farsee was a contemporary and a close friend of Prophet Mahomed, and Majuddin-e-Hangar-e-Farsee flourished in the 13th century A.D. Mr. Chhatrapati contended that from this evidence it appears that even non-Zoroastrians were referred to as "Parsis". Mr. Vachha has, however, made it clear that these were exceptions and that Salman-e-Farsee was originally a Zoroastrian but was later on converted to Islam. Now, the word "Farsee" as used in Salman-e-Farsee appears to be an appellation and it was used after Salman was converted to Islam for the purpose of distinguishing which Salman was meant. Rashid has, however, stated that there is a difference of opinion amongst scholars, as to whether Salman-e-Farsee was originally a Zoroastrian. In view of this state of evidence it cannot be concluded, as contended by Mr. Chhatrapati, that all inhabitants of Persia including non-Zoroastrians were known as "Parsis" after the Arab conquest. These are but two exceptional cases and no generalisation can be made from the same that even Muslims of Iran were known as Parsis.

After the time of Salman-e-Farsee and before that of Majuddin-e-Hangar-e-Farsee, chronologically, comes the evidence as to Firdausi. Mr. Vachha has stated that in Firdausi's writings there are a number of references to the Zoroastrians of Iran as "Parsis". Firdausi flourished between 925 A.D. and about 1020 A.D. According to Mr. Vachha, the original word used by Firdausi in his writings is "Parsi" with the plural thereof as "Parsiyan". In his cross-examination Mr. Vachha however stated that Firdausi, in his works, referred to the inhabitants of the whole country known as Iran or Persia as Iranians or Parsis. On this part of the evidence of Mr. Vachha, viz. that the inhabitants of the whole country were referred to by Firdausi as "Parsis", Mr. Chhatrapati has contended that all the inhabitants of Iran, whether Zoroastrians or Muslims, were referred to by Firdausi as Parsis and that the word "Parsis" therefore was not merely confined to Zoroastrians. From the writing of Firdausi it can be concluded that during the 10th century A.D. the word "Parsi" was in use with reference to the inhabitants of Iran. Unfortunately on the evidence as it stands there is no indication as to what period Firdausi's writings referred to. Was he using the word "Parsi" in connection with the inhabitants of Iran of his own day, i.e. of the 10th century A.D., or was he using it in connection with the inhabitants of Iran of the times preceding his and if so what? In view of this deficiency, it is not possible to properly evaluate the point urged by Mr. Chhatrapati. Mr. Banaji argued that it is well-known that Firdausi in his writing deals with Iran of the period prior to 631 A.D., i.e. prior to the Arab invasion, and that it is but natural that Firdausi should refer to the inhabitants of the whole country Iran as Parsis because prior to the Arab invasion all the inhabitants of Iran were Zoroastrians. Unfortunately for Mr. Banaji's present argument there is no such evidence on the record. The fact, however, remains that as the record stands it is difficult to ascertain as to what period was referred to by Firdausi in his writings when he used the word "Parsi" in respect of the inhabitants of the whole country Iran.

The next in chronological sequence are certain Colophons. Dastoor Mirza has explained that "Colophon" means a post-script written by the author himself to his own manuscript writing. Three Colophons have been relied upon in this case and chronologically arranged, the same are exh. A-20 (of which exh. A-21 is the English translation), exh. A-16 and exh. A-15. Each of these three Colophons itself mentions its date, the same being S.Y. 1377, 1378 and 1379 respectively, the first corresponding to 1320 A.D. and the latter two to 1322 A.D. These three Colophons are in Sanskrit although the Sanskrit language as used is poor. From these Colophons it appears that one Meharvan Kaikhushru came from Iran to India and that he has written some books and to these books he has appended these Colophons. In these Colophons, Meharvan has stated that he was a Parsi priest and that he came from Persia to India on an invitation from India. In each of these three Colophons Meharvan uses the words "priest of the Parsi caste" in describing himself. The word in Sanskrit is "Parsi" and from the context it is clear that it was used in connection with the Zoroastrians of Iran. Dastoor Mirza has stated that Meharvan was a Parsi priest in Iran and that he was invited to India by one Chahil Sangan, who was a wealthy Parsi merchant at Cambay and that Meharvan flourished in about the beginning of the 14th Century A.D.

The next in chronological sequence are the Rivayats which are, according to the evidence of Rashid, the letters written from time to time over the last three or four hundred years by various Parsis of Iran to Parsis of India. Dastoor Mirza has stated that the first Rivayat was received in 1478 A.D. and the last some time in the 18th century and that during this period there were received 22 Rivayats in all. In the book entitled "Grundrisa Der. Iranischen Philologie" which was published in 1896-1904 there are collected various articles written by various scholars. All the articles except one are in German. The one which is not in German is written in English by Dr. West, a well-known scholar, who was also a great Iranian scholar. Dr. West's article appearing in the book is on Pehlvi literature and to that article Dr. West has appended an appendix which deals with the modern Persian Zoroastrian literature of the Parsis. Dr. West has divided his article into various sections and copies of sections 123 and 124 of that article have been put in as exh. A-13. In exh. A-13 Dr. West has explained what these Rivayats are. In the article when dealing with the Rivayats Dr. West has used the phrase "Parsis in Persia" or "Iranian Parsis" or similar phrases. It is true that in exh. A-13 Dr. West has used the word "Parsis" in connection with the Zoroastrians of Iran. Unfortunately there is no evidence before me to show what is the word used in the Rivayats themselves. All that can be said from exh. A-13 is that the word "Parsi" has been used for the Zoroastrians of Iran by Dr. West, but there is nothing to show that in any of the 22 Rivayats received at different times between 15th and 18th centuries that word has been used in that connection. Exhibit A-13 is, therefore, not useful to show that the word "Parsi" was used during the period of the Rivayats.

The next in the chronological sequence come exhs. T and U which are two extracts from two articles written by Maulana Shibli Nomani in different Urdu Magazines. Maulana Shibli died in 1914. His articles were, however, subsequently collected and printed in a book form and that book is known as Maqalat-e-shabli. The said two extracts are from the 5th volume of that book. The first extract is exh. T which is an article published in the Urdu magazine "An Nudva", Volume II, No. 6 of September 1905 and exh. U is an extract from another article of Maulana Shibli also published in the same issue of An Nudva. Exhibit T mentions that at the time when Akbar (the Mogul Emperor of India) formed the religious conference and invited to it the religious heads of every religion and faith from far and wide, he carried on epistolary correspondence with Iran and at that time the Chief religious head of the Parsees was Azar Kaiwan. Mr. Chhatrapati commented that this passage does not clearly show that Azar Kaiwan was the chief religious head of the Parsis in Iran and that it is possible to read that Azar Kaiwan was at that time the religious head of the Parsis in India. In my opinion, this would not be a fair reading of exh. T because the first sentence mentions that Akbar carried on correspondence with the heads of every religion and faith from far and wide and then mentions particularly that he carried on especially correspondence with Iran. This first sentence suggests that the correspondence was carried on by Akbar with religious heads outside India because Iran is specifically mentioned. The next sentence, therefore, when it mentions Azar Kaiwan as the chief religious head of the Parsis must, in the context, be read as meaning the religious head of the Parsis in Iran. Moreover "Parsis" as occurring in exh. T must have a reference to the Zoroastrians of Iran because the passage contemplates correspondence with the heads of each religion meaning thereby a religion different from that of Akbar. Akbar was a Mogul Emperor. Mogul Emperors were Muslims, although it is a historical fact that Akbar took a broader view of religion and tried to found a different religion. But still in this context I am inclined to take the view that the reference to "Parsis" is a reference to the Zoroastrians of Iran. So far as exh. U is concerned, although Mr. Chhatrapati has offered no comment, it is quite clear that no special significance can be attached to it save that the word "Parsis" has been used in this passage in connection with religion, the words used in exh. U being "articles of faith".

I will next refer to exh. R which is the meaning of the word "Parsa" as appearing in Burhan-i-Quateh which is a Persian into Persian Dictionary. Exhibit R is the last piece of evidence relating to the first period. Rashid has stated that that dictionary was edited by Mahomed Husein-i-Tabreji, his surname being Burhan, and that the book mentions that it was edited in 1651 A.D. Now the dictionary is a Persian into Persian Dictionary and in giving the meaning of the word "Parsa" it says that the word "Parsa" is also used in the sense of "Parsee", the word "Parsee" having been used in this dictionary in the original Persian language. Exhibit R shows that the word "Parsee" was in such wide use in 1651 A.D. that it was used in this dictionary for explaining the word "Parsa". As regards exh. R, Mr. Chhatrapati commented that though it is true that the word "Parsee" has been used, there is nothing to show that it was used in connection with Irani Zoroastrians. That comment is true but I have to take it along with or in the context of the other evidence. The evidence relating to this period shows that the word "Parsi" had come into use in Iran at least since the time of Firdausi. The word "Parsi" has been used in connection with Salman-e-Farsee and Majuddin-e-Hangar-e-Farsee and also by Firdausi in his writings and in the Colophons and in Burhan-Quateh.

On this evidence, in my opinion, it is not clearly established that the word "Parsee" was used in respect of Zoroastrians or that it was used for Muslims only. I do not mean that there is any evidence that it was used for Muslims. There is no such positive evidence except in the two exceptional cases of Salman-e-Farsee and Majuddin-e-Hangar-e-Farsee. But even as regards those two exceptional cases Mr. Vachha has stated that the two persons were originally Parsis and were merely continued to be so-called. But the three Colophons, exhs. A-20, A-16 and A-15 clearly show that the word "Parsi" was used in Iran in the beginning of the 14th century in connection with the Zoroastrians of that country. The last piece of evidence as regards this period is the Burhan-i-Quateh which is of 1651 A.D. I have analysed the evidence which has been led before me as regards this period, but I am really not concerned with ascertaining whether by 1651 A.D. the word "Parsi" was applied only to Zoroastrians or not. The evidence is meagre and is not quite clear. But it is also not material for me.

Before parting with the evidence relating to this period, it may be stated that during his cross-examination Mr. Chhatrapati attempted to show that the Zoroastrians of Iran were known in Iran as "Gabr", the word being variously spelt as "Gabr", "Guebre" and "Guevre". I do not think it necessary to refer to the same for the simple reason that even if the Zoroastrians of Iran were known as "Guebre", it would not lead to the conclusion that they were not known as "Parsis". Mr. Chhatrapati has also made a similar attempt to show that the Zoroastrians of Iran were known as "Iranis". But to my mind what I have said in connection with "Guebre" applies with equal force to "Iranis".

I will now deal with the evidence relating to the second period which covers the last about a hundred years.

The condition of the Zoroastrians of Iran under the Muslim rule was far from satisfactory. Prior to 1854 a society was formed in Bombay named "The Society for the amelioration of the conditions of the poor Zoroastrians in Iran." In 1854 the Parsis of India sent an emissary, one Maneckji Hateria, to Iran and he tried to improve the condition and status of the Zoroastrians in Iran. Since long prior to 1854 there was a Zazia or Poll tax levied on the Parsis of Iran and one of the efforts made by Maneckji Hateria was to bring about its abolition. As a result of his efforts the Poll tax was ultimately abolished in about 1882 A.D. The said society has published two books, the first dealing with the period October 1, 1858 to March 20, 1861 which was published in 1863 and the second dealing with the period March 21, 1861 to March 20, 1864 which was published in 1866 A.D. Both these books are in the nature of the publication of its accounts of the said period and the report as to the work done by the society. There are certain letters appearing in these books and reliance is placed on those letters to show that in the sixth and the seventh decades of the nineteenth century the Zoroastrians of Iran were known as Parsis both in Iran and in India. The first of such letters relied upon is exh. E which is dated August 10, 1858. That is a letter addressed by Maneckji Hateria to the Prime Minister of the Government of Iran and in that letter he refers to the members of his community, i.e. the Zoroastrians of Iran, as Parsis. The next is the letter, dated August 27, 1858, exh. F, written by Maneckji Hateria to Mirza Shafi who, Rashid has stated, was the then Governor of Yezd. Then comes the letter, exh. G, which is dated August 31, 1860, and was written by Maneckji Hateria to Amin-Ul-Daulla-Farokh Khan who, according to Rashid, was one of the courtiers of the King of Iran at that time. In both exhs. F and G Maneckji Hateria has referred to the Zoroastrians in the one of Iran and in the other of Yezd and Kerman, two Provinces of Iran, as Parsis.

The next in chronological sequence are exhs. C, D and B, the dates of exhs. C and D not appearing on the record and the date of exh. B being December 29, 1862. Exhibit C is a letter written by Maneckji Hateria to Amin-Ul-Shura Pasha Khan who, according to Rashid, was a Minister to the King of Iran. Exhibit D is a letter written by Maneckji Hateria to Ala Hazrat Akdash Humayun Nasruddin Shah, the then King of Iran. In both these letters Maneckji Hateria uses the word "Parsis" for the Zoroastrians of Iran. In his work Maneckji Hateria had taken the assistance of the then French Consul in Iran who was one Count Gobineau. It appears that a letter of thanks for the assistance rendered by him was sent to Count Gobineau to which he sent a reply. That letter in reply is in the French language but Count Gobineau himself made a translation thereof in Persian and copies of both, the original letter in French and his translation thereof in Persian are to be found in the second of the said two books. Count Gobineau's said letter in French as well as in Persian and an English translation thereof are exh. B collectively. Now, in exh. B Count Gobineau uses the word "Parsis" in connection with the Zoroastrians of Iran. As regards exh. B Mr. Chhatrapati commented that the original letter to which Count Gobineau sent his reply exh. B has not been produced and that it may be that Count Gobineau happened to use the word "Parsis" of Iran, because that was the word used in the original letter of thanks sent to him. That is certainly a possibility, but in view of the word "Parsis" having been used for the Zoroastrians of Iran in the said five other letters which are of about the same date, I am inclined to take the view that it may not be that it was because of the reason suggested by Mr. Chhatrapati that Count Gobineau used the word "Parsis" in his letter for the Zoroastrians of Iran.

The next in chronological sequence is exh. S which is a portion from the introduction by Spiegel to a book on Avesta written by Arthur Henry Bleeck. This book was published in 1864. In exh. S Spiegel has used the word "Parsis" for the Zoroastrians of Iran. From exh. S there is no doubt that Spiegel used the word "Parsis" only for the Persians who were professing the Zoroastrian faith.

The next two pieces of evidence are exhs. J and K. Exhibit J is a portion from the introduction by Dr. West to Volume V of "The Sacred Books of the East". Volume V was published in 1880. In the introduction Dr. West is dealing with Zoroastrian religion and he refers to the religion and the scriptures of that religion as "Parsi Religion" and "Parsi scriptures". The way in which Dr. West uses it clearly shows that he was equating Parsis with Zoroastrians of Iran. Exhibit K appears in a foot-note in Volume XVIII of "The Sacred Books of the East" which was edited by Max Muller, which volume was published in 1882. In this foot-note Max Muller has used the word "Parsi" for a Zoroastrian of Iran. He was editing a book and was referring to religion and conversion and in that context he used the word "Parsi" for an Iranian who was professing the Zoroastrian religion.

The next in time is exh. A-14 which are various extracts from the book "History of the Parsis", Vol. I, written by Dosabhai Framji Karaka published in 1884. Karaka has used the word "Parsi" or "Parsis" or "Parsia" in these passages, exh. A-14. The context in which the word "Parsis" has been used in exh. A-14 shows beyond the shadow of a doubt that the word was used by Karaka in 1884 for the Zoroastrians of Persia. In this connection the passages from pages 61, 65, 68 and 91 are very important. The passage taken from page 61 and the one at page 65 clearly show that it was used for Zoroastrians because in the same passages a distinction has been made between Parsis and Mahomedans and Jews. What was being mentioned were the "believers" in various other religions and in that connection the word "Parsi" has been used. The passage at page 68 uses the word "Parsi" in connection with fire temples and towers of silence which can be associated only with those of the Zoroastrian faith. The passage at page 81 mentions the word "Parsis" of both India and the mother country, i.e. Iran, and the word "Parsis" has been used in the same sense both in connection with India and Iran.

The next in order come certain extracts from the book "Persia and the Persian Question" published in 1892 and written by Curzon who was later Lord Curzon and the Viceroy of India. It is the unchallenged testimony of Mr. Vachha that in 1889-90 Curzon went to Persia as a correspondent of the London Times and that he stayed in Persia for about six months and made a deep study of Persia and thereafter he wrote the said book. That book is in two volumes and certain passages from volume I have been put in as exh. A-1 and others from volume II as exh. A-2. These passages clearly show that Curzon has used the word "Parsi" in his book for the Zoroastrians of Iran. For example, the passage from page 240 (part of exh. A-2) deals with the population of the different religionists. In the same passage Curzon has used the words "Jewish", "Hindu" and "Guebre" or "Parsi". In the passage from page 244 (part of exh. A-2) the census figures of 1878 have been mentioned and this passage shows the number of people professing different religions and Curzon has used the word "Parsis" as if it was a religion and in the same sense as the other words used by him in that passage such as Mahomedans, Jews, Hindus etc. In the passage from page 493 (part of exh. A-2) Curzon gives, under the heading "Creeds", the numbers of the population professing the various creeds and in classifying the various creeds he mentions Parsis as a creed along with Shias, Sunnis, Jews etc. It is clear that Curzon, after he stayed in Persia for about six months, used the word "Parsis" synonymously with the people of Iran who professed the Zoroastrian religion.

The next are the passages which have been marked as exh. A-5 from Marzban's book "The Parsis in India". When dealing with the first period I have already referred to these passages when I was dealing with the Shlokas addressed by Nairyosang in which he has stated "Those are we Parsis". As already pointed out by me, the original Sanskrit text is not available and, therefore, the Shlokas cannot be read in connection with the first period. However what Murzban has translated is Mlle Menant's book "Les Parsis" which was published in 1898 and Murzban's translation thereof was published in 1917. As there is no positive evidence that the word "Parsi" has been used by Mlle Menant herself in her book although the title of her book itself suggests that she must have, I would place this evidence contained in exh. A-5 not in 1898 but in 1917. The passage at page 21 of the book is Murzban's own commentary and in that he has used the word "Parsis" and in the context it appears that he has used it in connection with Zoroastrians of Iran also. Exhibit A-5, therefore, shows that in 1917 Murzban used the word "Parsis" for the Zoroastrians of Iran.

The next piece of evidence is exh. A-13 which, as already seen, is Dr. West's article with an appendix attached thereto from the book "Grundrisa Der Iranischen Philologie". The book is a collation of various articles published during the period 1896 to 1904 A.D. In section 123 which is reproduced in exh. A-13 Dr. West has used the words "Parsis in Persia" as on a par with the Parsis in India, which suggests that by the words "Parsis in Persia" he was referring to the Zoroastrians in Persia.

The next in sequence are certain portions of the article written by Zokaul Mulk Foroughi published in the newspaper Tarbiyat of Iran which extracts have been put in as exhs. P and Q. Both the issues of the Tarbiyat were seen by Rashid in two libraries in Iran, which are not issuing libraries. Rashid, however, made notes of the relevant passages from the original newspapers and he has given secondary evidence of his notes. Exhibit P is the copy as made by Rashid of a portion of an article appearing in the Tarbiyat of January 27, 1905 and exh. Q is the copy of the notes as made by Rashid of the Tarbiyat of October 18, 1906. Both these exhs. P and Q show that in 1905 and 1906 the word "Parsi" has been used for the Zoroastrians of Iran. The value of exh. Q is comparatively greater because therein the word "Parsi" has been used in connection with the inhabitants of Iran in contradistinction to the Muslims of that country and, therefore, the use of the word "Parsis" for the Zoroastrians of Iran is brought out quite distinctly.

The next piece of evidence is exh. A-4 which are extracts from the book "Five Years in a Persian Town" written by Napier Malcolm and published in 1905. Mr. Vachha has stated that Napier Malcolm was an English missionary who lived in Yezd in connection with his missionary work for five years in about beginning of the 20th century and thereafter he published his said book recording his experiences. The various extracts, exh. A-4, clearly show that Malcolm has used the word "Parsis" for the Zoroastrians of Iran. That he used the word "Parsis" for the Iranis who professed the Zoroastrian religion is made abundantly clear because, for example, in the passage at page 44 he refers to the Zoroastrians as Parsis whereas he specifically mentions Jews and Mahomedans as such separately.

The next piece of evidence appertains to the book "Persia, Past and Present" by Jackson. Copies of certain passages from that book are exh. L. It is Rashid's evidence that Jackson was in Iran in 1903 A.D. and the statements made by him in the first three passages reproduced in exh. L refer to the period when Jackson was in Iran and in each of those passages he is referring to the Parsis then living in Yezd or in Iran as mentioned in those passages. The two passages from page 378 of the book clearly show that Jackson has used the word "Parsi" from the point of view of the Iranis professing the Zoroastrian religion, because in the first passage he is comparing the Irani Parsis with their co-religionists in Bombay and in the second passage he is thinking in terms of Mahomedans and Parsis from the point of view of their religion. Exhibit M are two photographs from Jackson's said book and the writings appearing under those photographs. The writings show the use of the word "Parsi" for the women appearing in those photographs. Exhibit A-6 is another extract from Jackson's said book and in this passage, when referring to certain persons of Isfahan and Yezd, Jackson says that it was he who had used the word "Guebre" for them, but that those persons themselves designated themselves as Zoroastrians or again as Parsis. This leaves no doubt that Jackson used the word "Parsis" for the people in Iran who professed the Zoroastrian religion. Moreover exh. A-6 shows that those people who professed the Zoroastrian religion called themselves Parsis.

The next in the order of date comes exh. A-18 which is a Farman issued by the Shah of Iran in September-October 1906. Rashid has stated that in about 1896 the Society which I have referred to earlier, which was established in India for the amelioration of the conditions of the poor Zoroastrians in Iran, sent another emissary named Ardeshire Reporter to Iran and he approached the then King of Iran, Muzaffaruddin Shah, for abolishing the pasture and cattle tax which was being collected from the Zoroastrians of Iran and as a result of his efforts the King issued the said Farman abolishing that tax. It is Rashid's unchallenged testimony that the tax was being collected by the Muslim rulers from the Zoroastrian inhabitants of Iran. It was that tax which was levied on the Zoroastrians, which was abolished by this Farman and in this Farman the word used is "Parsis" which clearly shows that the then ruling King when abolishing the tax used the word "Parsis" in connection with Zoroastrians who were the persons who were liable to pay the tax.

In the review of the evidence relating to this second part, I will pause here momentarily. It is to be noted that the last piece of evidence which I have referred to is of 1906. In the chronological sequence, then comes the judgment of a Special Bench of this Court which was delivered in 1908. I am referring to the judgment in *Sir Dinshaw M. Petit* v. *Sir Jamsetji Jijibhai*.[1] One of the Judges of that Special Bench was Sir Dinshaw Davar who was himself a Parsi and who has been acknowledged by Chagla C.J. as "undoubtedly of very great authority on Parsi law". In that case the question which Sir Dinshaw Davar considered was what was meant by the word "Parsis" who were the beneficiaries of certain charitable trusts and the passage from his judgment appearing at page 128 of the said report shows that according to Sir Dinshaw Davar the Parsi community included, amongst others, "the Iranis from Persia professing the Zoroastrian religion, who come to India, either temporarily or permanently". It is obvious, even on a casual reading of the judgment of Sir Dinshaw Davar, that his Lordship came to that conclusion after considering the evidence led in that case in that behalf. In any event what is to be noted is that an eminent Parsi Judge well-versed in Parsi law, gave a judgment in a case which had attracted great controversy in those days and in which the public had taken great interest that Irani Zoroastrians who were in India, permanently or even temporarily, were Parsis.

The next in the chronological sequence come exh. A-3 which are extracts from tho book "The History of Persia" by Sir Percy Sykes which was published in 1915. These extracts show that Sykes used the word "Parsis" for the Zoroastrians of Iran. There are in exh. A-3 extracts from four different pages of the said book. In respect of one of the said passages, viz. the one occurring at page 5 of the book, Mr. Chhatrapati commented that the use of the word "Parsis" in that passage was restricted to the inhabitants of the Province of Fars and that it showed that it did not apply to the whole or any other part of Iran. That comment of Mr. Chhatrapati is not justified, because the extract from page 109· specifically refers to Kerman which is not situated in the Province of Fars and in that passage which refers to the time when Sykes was living at Kerman, he has used the word "Parsis" in connection with the Zoroastrian religionists of Kerman.

Next in the order of dates comes exh. 5 which is the solitary exhibit relied upon in this connection on behalf of the defendant. It is an extract from the book "Zoroastrian Civilization" by Dastur Dhalla published in 1922. In that extract the word "Parsi" has not been used. But on the contrary it is stated that the Zoroastrians living in Persia were called Iranis. Based on this evidence Mr. Chhatrapati contended that the Zoroastrians of Iran were, at least in 1922, called Iranis and not Parsis. In this connection I must bear in mind the evidence of Rashid when he states that Dhalla merely relied upon western scholars. In any event it is not Dhalla's statement that the word "Parsi" was not used in Persia and it, therefore, cannot nullify the positive evidence of the various other exhibits referred to by me. In any event even quantitatively this is one solitary exception against the reliable evidence of so many persons such as Dr. West, Jackson, Curzon and Napier Malcolm, some of whom wrote their books and used the word "Parsis" after having spent a long time in Persia.

Then comes the oral testimony of Rashid and Mr. Vachha. Both of them had visited and stayed in Iran before 1936 when the Act was passed and even thereafter. Mr. Vachha had paid his first visit in 1934 and the second in 1954. It is the evidence of both these witnesses that during their stay in Persia they personally learnt that the Zoroastrians of Iran were called Parsis in Iran, that they were referred to as Parsis and that they themselves referred to themselves as Parsis. I have not the slightest hesitation in accepting their testimony. Mr. Vachha has even stated that on one occasion he was introduced to an official in Persia as "Parsi-e-Hind", i.e. the Parsi of India. The use of the phrase "Parsi-e-Hind" would only be for the purpose of bringing out the distinction between the Parsis of India and the Parsis of Iran but that distinc-

1 (1908) 11 Bom. L.R. 85.

tion is only as regards the country. But what is important is that the Zoroastrians both of India and of Iran were referred to as Parsis. Both of them had met Zoroastrians of Iran in different parts of Iran and Mr. Vachha has stated that he had even stayed at two places in Iran with local Zoroastrian families.

Mr. Banaji has relied upon the meaning of the word "Parsi" as appearing in Heim's Persian into English Dictionary which was published in 1934. One of the meanings given in that dictionary, which is exh. O, is that "Parsi" means a fire worshipper. I do not propose to place much reliance on exh. O because the meaning given therein is of the Persian word "Parsi", whereas I am concerned with that word as used in the English language. Of course the word "Parsi" as used in Iran would be in Persian and to that extent exh. O would be useful because it gives the meaning of the word "Parsi" as fire worshippers and, therefore, co-relates the word with a person professing the Zoroastrian religion, because so far as I know it is only the Zoroastrians who are generally referred to as fire worshippers. As against the dictionary meaning given in exh. O Mr. Chhatrapati has relied upon the meaning of the word "Parsi" as given in Murray's Dictionary, 1909 edn., Vol. VII which is as follows:

"One of the descendants of those Persians who fled to India in the 7th or the 8th century to escape Mahomedan persecution and who still retain their religion Zoroastrianism; Guebre".

A similar meaning has been given in the Oxford Shorter Dictionary. Mr. Chhatrapati relied upon the meaning of the word "Parsi" as given in these two dictionaries to show that "Parsi" means only the Zoroastrians of India and not those of Iran. It is true that according to both these dictionaries "Parsis" mean the Zoroastrians of India. The first thing to be noted is that neither of the two dictionaries specifically mentions that the word is not applicable to the Zoroastrians of Iran. I am, however, conscious that if it was applicable the dictionaries would, in normal course, have mentioned it and the absence of the mention of the Zoroastrians of Iran indicates that according to the persons who compiled those dictionaries the word "Parsi" was not applicable to the Zoroastrians of Iran. Rashid who is a scholar of the Persian language has, however, stated that the meaning of the word "Parsi" as given in those two dictionaries is not correct. His opinion has also to be taken into account. But, in any event, I have to evaluate the meaning as given in these two dictionaries in reference to the actual use of the word "Parsi" for the Zoroastrians of Iran by people like Curzon, Jackson and Napier Malcolm who had lived in Iran and who used the word "Parsi" after their personal knowledge and experience in Iran and the actual use in common parlance by the people of Iran as deposed to by Mr. Vachha and Rashid.

Mr. Banaji has also brought on the record exhs. H, I and V which were published in 1951, 1955 and 1960, respectively. He argued that the word "Parsi" has continued to be used even till to-day for the Zoroastrians of Iran. In my opinion, however, this evidence is not relevant as it pertains to a period subsequent to the Act of 1946 and I cannot construe the word "Parsi" as used in the Act by referring to what is meant by the word "Parsi" after the said Act was passed.

On this evidence relating to the second period, the position is that when the Act of 1936 was passed the word "Parsi" was in use in respect of not only the Parsis of India but also in respect of the Zoroastrians of Iran. As I have said earlier, the evidence in respect of the first period is not material for my purposes save perhaps to a very limited extent to show that the word "Parsi" was derived from the original word "Parsa" which original word with the passage of time became "Parsik" and thereafter "Parsi". The evidence as regards the second, however, shows that the word "Parsi" was used in respect of Zoroastrians as distinguished from other religionists like Muslims, Christians, Jews etc. Many of the exhibits already referred to are published books by scholars of repute. The evidence shows that since about the middle of the 19th century the Parsis of India had strived for the amelioration of the condition of their co-religionists in Iran and an Association had been formed for that purpose. That could not have been something which was not known to the public. On the contrary such an association could not have been formed unless the Parsi public in India took interest in it. The Statement of Objects and Reasons of the said Act of 1936 shows that in respect of that Act public opinion was sounded and suggestions had been made in the press, on the platform and by associations and individuals. A judgment of an eminent Parsi Judge, viz. Dinshaw Davar, had construed the word "Parsi" about 30 years prior to the passing of the Act as including Irani Zoroastrians. Moreover, Sir Dinshaw Davar had construed the word "Parsi" not as occurring in any statute but as used by a Parsi founder of charity who would have used the word in its ordinary common meaning and not in any specific meaning in which sometimes a common word is used in a particular statute. In such circumstances, it cannot be said that at the time when the said Act of 1936 was passed the Legislature was unaware that the word "Parsi" was used in India not only for that community in India but also for the Zoroastrians of Iran. A word in a statute must ordinarily be given the same meaning in which it is commonly understood. On this evidence I have not the slightest hesitation in concluding that the word "Parsi" was used long prior to 1936 as meaning Zoroastrians both of India and of Iran and that it was so used both in India and in Iran. As a matter of fact it was so understood not only before 1936 but even before the Act of 1865. I may state, though it is not relevant, that it has been so understood even after the passing of the said Act of 1936. On this evidence I unhesitatingly come to the conclusion that the word "Parsi" as used in the Act includes not only the Parsi Zoroastrians of India but also the Zoroastrians of Iran.

Suit decreed.

[The rest of the judgment is not material to this report.]

APPELLATE CIVIL.

Before Mr. Justice Gokhale.

H. M. TEJANI *v.* MRS. KULSUMBAI M. JETHA.[*]

Arbitration Act (X of 1940), Secs. 39, 19, 25, 5, 12(2)(a) & (b). 2(a) & (e), 37(5)— Court's order that arbitration agreement to cease to have effect whether appealable under s. 39—Expression "superseding an arbitration", effect of—Party promoting arbitration guilty of laches by not taking prompt steps to see that arbitrators acted and decided dispute—Consequent expiration of period of limitation for suit—Whether such party entitled to seek relief under Act to revoke arbitration—When can Court under s. 5 grant leave to revoke authority of arbitrator—Reference of dispute to named arbitrator whether should be in writing.

An order by the Court that the arbitration agreement shall cease to have effect with respect to the differences referred, is in law an order superseding the arbitra-

(L)
PETIT VS JEEJEEBHOY 1908: LINK TO THE JUDGEMENT OF THE DIVISION BENCH OF THE HIGH COURT OF BOMBAY

This judgement is available online at
Sir Dinshaw Manockji Petit And ... vs Sir Jamsetji Jeejeebhoy
And Ors. on 27 November, 1908 (indiankanoon.org)

(M)
KESHARJI DHANJIBHAI VS KAIKHUSRU KOLHABHAI JUDGEMENT, JANUARY 18, 1929: DIVISION BENCH OF THE HIGH COURT OF BOMBAY (RE-ADOPTION)

Equivalent citations: (1929) 31 BOMLR 1081, 121 Ind Cas 433

Author: K Amberson Marten

Bench: A Marten, Kt., Patkar

JUDGMENT Amberson Marten, Kt., C.J.

1. This is a most unhappy example of the possibilities of litigation in India. The suit began seventeen years ago in 1911, and we are yet at an appeal from a preliminary decree. The suit was one for the administration and division of the estate of one Dhanjibhai who died in 1901, The parties are all Parsis. The voluminous pedigree shown in paragraph 2 of the plaint exemplifies that the parties alleged to be interested are very numerous. Defendant No. 1 contends that even that list is not enough, and that there ought to be ten or eleven parties added, and he has accordingly set up a rival pedigree. Naturally with such a large number of parties the litigation is delayed, But apart from that the parties spent the first two years of litigation in raising technical points as to parties and so on, and in that way they succeeded in litigating for many years without the slightest practical result.

2. The real contest in the case is as to the position of defendant No. 1. If the plaintiff's pedigree be looked at he will be found as the son of Pestonji, a brother of the deoeasedDhanjibhiai.

Accordingly as a co-heir he would in any event claim some share. But his real claim is in effect adverse to the estate, He claimed to bs the adopted eon of Dhanjibhai and to have acquired by adverse possession or otherwise the whole of the property either before the death of Dhanjibhai or at any rate by the date of the suit in 1911. Consequently, in this administration suit, there is, so to speak, a double action going on, viz., one, as between the beneficiaries of Dhanjibhai including defendant No. 1, and another between Dhanjibhai's estate and defendant No. 1, who is claiming adversely. If only Dhanjibhai had left a will, the difficulties would have been solved, and defendant No. 1 would at once have been put to his election either to claim under the will or against it But for the moment it seems to me that he cannot be put to his election. At any rate, that point has not so far been raised in the case.

3. Now I come to a most curious circumstance, and it is this that though defendant No. 1 put forward his plea of adverse possession under two branches, namely, (1) at Dhanjibhai's death, and (2) at the date of the suit, yet the lower Court only decided against him on the first branch, and did not hear the second branch notwithstanding that defendant No. 1 put in a formal purshis asking for that issue to be determined. As regards the first branch the issue was in a wide form. Defendant No. 1 does not now contend that at Dhanjibhai's death in 1901, he defendant No. 1 had acquired a prescriptive right. That claim is now specifically abandoned at the bar.

4. But what defendant No. 1 does claim before us is that he had a right by adverse possession at the date of the suit in 1911, For that purpose he relies on Articles 142 and 144 of the Indian Limitation Act. Further, he contends that in order to take advantage of the requisite period, namely, twelve years, he will contend that his adverse possession began prior to the date

of Dhanjibhai's death although it did not crystallize into an absolute right at his death, For the respondents it is frankly and fairly conceded that the learned Judge has left this point open. That being so, we are forced to take steps to see that the point is properly adjudicated on. This involves, I think, a special inquiry.

5. This brings me to the next important part of the case, namely, the order the Judge actually made, I say this, because although the memorandum of appeal raises some thirty-one objections to the preliminary decree, counsel for the appellant has not pressed a large number of them as they are really unarguable. I accordingly appreciate counsel's statement that although the lower Court found in his favour that in the Baroda State where the parties were domiciled, the custom of adoption did prevail among the Pareis, yet it also held that this custom would not prevail in British India as regards immovable property situate there. It is elementary international law that the law which governs the land of a particular nation is the law of that nation. Consequently, land in British India is governed by the law of British India as the lex loci and not by the law of the domicile of the temporary owner. It follows, therefore, that, having egard to the law of British India and the statutory provisions which govern succession amongst Parsis, it is abundantly clear that there is no room in the law of British India for such a custom amongst the Parsis as is now put forward, Accordingly, the bulk of the points taken in appeal by the appellant must fail. Kaikhdshku But as regards the order which the learned Judge made, two C.J. mistakes have been pointed out. For some reason, which I do not altogether understand, the learned Judge, notwithstanding his experience, has apparently classed the receiver with the Commissioner, Further, he has overlooked the fact that there is no jurisdiction to delegate to any Commissioner certain matters like an inquiry as to heirs, because there is no power in that

respect in the Code. His order directed certain inquiries to be made and certain accounts taken, and it proceeded :

It is further ordered that Mr. Gulabbhai Mr. Deasi be and is hereby appointed receiver in the suit for the purpose of the above inquiries who shall take all the necessary step in the said behalf, and certify the result to this Court on or before January 15, 1926.

Now there are certain limited powers in the Civil Procedure Code under which the Judge can delegate to the Commissioner or otherwise certain investigations, but they.do not include any of enquiries Nos. (1), (2) and (3). Still less has a receiver got anything to do with inquiries of that sort. In England a Master in the Chancery Division, and in Bombay the Commissioner and Master in Equity on the original side, are judicial officers taking the place of the Judge, A receiver on the other hand is not a judicial officer. He is merely a custodian of properties by order of the Court. In that capacity it may be his duty to institute suits on behalf of the estate in the Court of the Judge. It is unthinkable that any such officer should also be the Judge in the Court in which the suits are instituted.

Nor on the other hand has there been any prior order appointing a receiver in this suit, As to whether a receiver should now be appointed, it was faintly argued that he should. But this litigation has been going on for some seventeen years. If a receiver in the ordinary sense of the word, namely, a receiver of the property, has not been found necessary for seventeen years, I do not think that the present moment is one for appointing a receiver either on the ground of equity or otherwise. If we did so, what would at once happen would be a contest as to whether certain properties claimed by the receiver were the property of defendant No. 1 by adverse possession or otherwise. Therefore, no useful object could be gained by our now proceeding to appoint a receiver of the estate.

Further the learned Judge only appointed what he called a receiver for the purpose of the inquiries. I do not read this order as having appointed anybody a receiver in the ordinary proper meaning of that word, What the learned Judge seems to have done is, by a slip of the pen, to have written the word "receiver" instead of the word Commissioner." But unfortunately even if that is the explanation, he had no power to appoint a Commissioner to make these inquiries.

9. It follows, therefore, that the order must be varied, and it must be varied in this way; Inquiry No. (1) is to stand, but it will be limited to the properties in British India. Admittedly, as regards property in the Baroda State, different considerations altogether apply. Then as regards inquiry No. (3); that will be an inquiry as to the heirs of the deceased entitled to a share in his immovable property in British India and the share payable to each. Then there must be a supplementary inquiry. I think, it should be inquiry No. (1A)An inquiry as to whether defendant No. 1 acquired a title by adverse possession at the date of this suit in 1911 to the said immovable properties or any part thereof. Next the direction about Mr. Gulabbhai Mr. Desai being appointed a receiver and so on, must be struck out entirely. The learned Judge is to hold these inquiries himself. It may be urged that alterations should be made in the law so as to give similar facilities to the mofussil Courts for delegating inquiries as exist in the Superior Courts in England and in India. But that is not a matter for us to deal with to-day.

10. Then I come to this point: Although the parties have been litigating for seventeen years there is still some uncertainty as to what the alleged immovable property in British India of the deceased consisted of. One would have thought that after this lapse of time this single point might at any rate have been cleared up. But as it has not been, there will be a direction following

inquiry No. (1A) that the plaintiff and defendant No. 1 do each furnish particulars of what he claims that the estate of the deceased Dhanjibhai consisted of at the latter's death in 1901. With regard to the particulars to be furnished by defendant No. 1, he is further to state what portions of the immovable property of Dhanjibhai he claims to have acquired by adverse possession as at the date of the suit in 1911. There is also some question as to whether the plaintiff claims any land alleged to have been purchased by defendant No. 1 out of the income or otherwise of Dhanjibhai's estate. But if any such claim is put forward, particulars are to be given to defendant No. 1

11. I would add I recognize that in some cases it would be impracticable in a suit of this nature to decide an adverse claim to the land of a third party, particularly if any eviction was sought for. But here, as I have already pointed out, defendant No. 1 has two claims, (1) as beneficiary, and (2) adversely to the estate. The litigation is already decided in part against him as regards one of these adverse claims; and it may be that the other branch of his adverse claim can also be decided in this suit. Therefore, we need not, I think, contemplate the possibility of the learned Judge having to direct a suit to be brought by some receiver to be appointed of the estate of Dhanjibhai against defendant No. 1, as a hostile party.

12. Next with regard to costs, we do not disturb the order as to costs in the lower Court, but as regards the costs of the appeal the position is this: We appreciate that much time has been saved by the course the appellant's counsel has taken, but that does not alter the fact that up to the last moment his client was putting forward a large number of points which, if successful, would have resulted in the suit being dismissed, He has failed in that. His only success is as to the modification of the terms of the actual order the learned Judge made. In those circumstances, we

think the right order will be that the appeal must be dismissed save as to the variation in the preliminary decree which I have already indicated, and that with regard to the costs of the appeal, the appellant should pay three-fourths of the costs of the respondents represented by Mr. Coyajee, The remaining one-fourth of their costs will come out of the estate of the deceased. Mr. Coyajee's clients to get one set of costs between them. As regards the other respondents represented by Mr. H.D. Thakor they support the appellant, Accordingly, they will bear their own costs of the appeal.

13. Cross-objections must be dismissed with costs.

Parkar, J.

14. I agree.

(N)
PARZOR FOUNDATION APPEAL FOR FUNDS FOR CO-RELIGIONISTS IN IRAN IN 2020

Dear All,

You must have seen Homi Gandhi's email appeal, if not it is below my letter for your reference. I am working closely with him to help all Iranians. Since this last week the situation at Yazd, Iran is critical, and many are affected by the Coronavirus.

We at Parzor have been in touch with Mr. SepantaNiknam, President Yazd Zarthusti Association and Council Member of Yazd. They are in desperate need of help and medicines. Due to Sanctions, people are dying, and we need to come together and work to help the Iranians as much as we can. Since you may be able to help, I am giving details below.

If you can contribute money by wire transfer in Indian rupees to Parzor for medicines of which we need 10,000 Tamiflu, 12,000 Kaletra and Injection of Actimera for 100 people, protective gear etc., please send your donation as per the details given below.

Iranian FM thanks Parsis for helping Iran.
The Iranian Foreign Minister mentioned that the Parsis are in fact Zoroastrians who migrated to India centuries ago.

Iranian Foreign Minister Javad Zarif thanked the Parsis of India for offering COVID-19 aid to his country in a tweet on Friday. The Parsis, as their name implies, migrated to India from Persia centuries ago. They are in actuality Zoroastrians, one of the oldest religions in the world which pre-dates Islam and Christianity.

(O)
ARTICLE IN ILLUSTRATED WEEKLY ON IRANIS

BACK TO THE LAND

Two Iranian Gentlemen Farmers

Bayram Zack

WHEN the Irani refugees came to Bombay, penniless and jobless, their first instinct was to take whatever menial jobs came their way. These were mostly as servants in Parsi households or as lowly assistants in the fire temples. Some of them however felt that this was not the life for them and they decided to go and live on farms and orchards as they had done back in Iran.

At Golwad, some three hours away by train from Bombay, there is a small concentration of Irani farmers—and their unquestioned leader and dean is 80-year-old Bayram Zack.

Bayram is a bit vague about dates but otherwise still remembers vividly the time

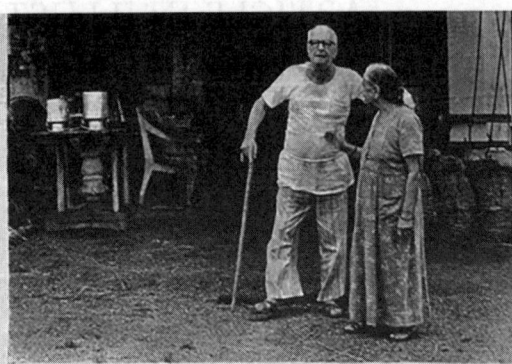

ALTHOUGH BAYRAM ZACK OWNS ALMOST 80 ACRES OF LAND, he lives in a bar which serves as his living room, bedroom and godown. He continually teases his wife al her expensive tastes.

lady, Dhunbaiji Hakim. He came to Gol to recuperate after an illness and liked place so much that he decided to stay

Though basically a farmer, he has tried his hand at many other jobs. He been in turn, a building contractor, a t tapper, a salesman and many other th "I can still do a man's job," he likes to b but actually gets tired after a little e and spends most of his time sitting in front yard supervising his workers playing with his three huge dogs and small great-grandchild.

Despite the fact that he owns almo acres of land and has given away huge s of money to charity—"I donated the e sum of Rs 2 lakhs left to me by my ado

THE ZACKS GROW RICE and vegetables as well as chickoos and mangoes. They own the largest number (over 2,000) of toddy trees in Thana district. Bayram's son, Dinshaw, does his rounds of the fields.

"I CAN STILL DO A MAN'S WORK," boasts 80-year-old Zack, the Elder. But he gets tired soon and spends most of the time sitting in his frontyard, supervising his workers.

he came here from Iran. "I was about this high," he says, pointing to his waist. His family was fairly prosperous so he came from Yezd to Bandar Abbas by palkhi. "At Bandar Abbas some Muslims tried to kidnap me, but my palkhi-bearers were loyal and saved me from them." He tells the story with much gusto and many dramatic flourishes.

Luck seems to have followed Bayram all the way to Bombay, for, whilst still a young boy, he was adopted by a rich Parsi

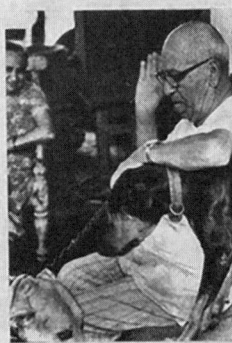

GEORGE AND MARY are Zack's favo dogs and barely ever leave his side. too live with the family in the same "b

"—Bayram. Zack lives more like a
~and than the prosperous farmer he
y is.

~e entire family—dogs and all—live in
~ge barn-like structure which serves
~ing room, bedroom, godown-cum-
~oom, all in one. "I don't believe in
~g money on show," he says, "we have
~ to eat—that is all that counts." His
daughters are now married and scat-
~ll over the country. His two sons and
~ons look after the farm.

~ayram Zack (he adopted the unusual
~ne because in Iran his family was
~ Zaqh, meaning green-eyed) has a
~tful sense of humour which bubbles
~ the most unexpected times. He once
~to trouble with a British Collector be-
~he had called two of his dogs George
~fary, and used to go around the coun-
~e loudly shouting, "Down George,
~Mary".

~ressed in typical Irani style—white
and blue striped pyjamas—he presides
~his humble home with all the aplomb
~eudal lord, now teasing his wife about
~xpensive tastes, then shouting at the
~who are forever climbing all over him,
~ling a tall story with a deadpan face.

Techniques

~he Zacks grow a variety of things—
~chickoos and mangoes to rice and
~ables. They employ 50 labourers per-
~ntly and more during the harvest sea-
~Bayram and a friend were amongst the
~farmers in the district to get a tractor
~s was 20 years ago—and he still pio-
~ new farming techniques.

~hough he has travelled almost all over
~world, Bayram Zack has never been
~ to Iran. He doesn't want to—
~ were treated like bhangis there," he
~vehemently—but it is also partly be-
~ of the Iranian rule which forbids
~ who were born in Iran but who have
~quently taken other nationalities from
~ning to Iran. The Iranian authorities,
~e, deny this but it exists in practice and
~s considerable inconvenience to many
~ Iranis who want to go back to visit
~ds and relations or to clear up busi-
~affairs.

Meherwan Irani

~ROUND 1850, an intrepid couple, Sheri-
~yar and Khorshedbanoo Irani, were
~ngst the first to trek northwards in
~ch of work. They finally settled down at
~wadi (orchard) of one Vicajee Meberji,
~modern Tarapore. Sheriyar died rela-
~y young but the formidable Khorshed-
~o brought up her six children on the
~, and they were the originators of to-
~s small but flourishing Irani colony at
~anu, a few miles from Golwad.

Khorshedbanoo's grandson Meherwan
~dadad Irani is, at 62, one of the leaders

"YES, I'M A SELF-MADE MAN," says Meherwan Irani to the author, Zarine Merchant.
With the help of his wife, he cleared the seven acres of jungle he bought in 1930. Today he
has expanded his ownership to 120 acres with a turnover of Rs 1,000 per acre.

THE PATRIARCH AND HIS DAUGHTER-IN-LAW. Meherwan Irani has a hand in most
worthwhile projects in the district. An example of his spirit of service is Dahanu's first
school. Instead of spending lavishly on his wedding, he used the money to enable his poor
neighbours to give their children an education.

a Biblical patriarch—on a prosperous estate
with his large family all around him—but
40 years ago it was a different story. "My
father was already working on a nearby
orchard but right from childhood I decided
to strike out on my own. In 1925 I bought
seven acres of land—for the then fabulous
price of Rs 2,400."

It was complete jungle land and Meherwan and his wife cleared it with their own
hands. Today at Bagh-e-Pahlevi they have
almost 120 acres of garden land and a
work-force of about 100. The returns
keep increasing each year but the crops
remain the same. "We started out with
chickoo trees and till today the chickoo is
our chief product." Meherwan also grows
beautiful roses and limes the size of grape-
fruit, breeds fish and is constantly experi-
menting with new agricultural methods.

his children and devotes most of his time
to social work. There is hardly a worthwhile project in Dahanu with which he i
not associated—be it the leper home or th
hospital, the school or the fire temple.

This tradition of service runs in th
family. His father built the first school i
Dahanu in 1928 and his daughter now run
a nursery school on the estate. Meherwa
likes to recount how the former was start
ed. "My father asked me if I would pre
fer to have a big wedding or use the amoun
spent on the festivities for a school. I tol
him not to ask silly questions and to get o
with the building."

Most of Dahanu's 45 Irani families ar
related to him in one way or another. The
are almost all orchard-owners, prosperou
and enterprising—a living tribute to th
courage and foresight of one brave woma

REFERENCES

'A Brief History of the Parsi Priesthood' in *Indo Iranian Journal*. Vol. 33, No. 3.

2005. Reprint of original judgments with explanatory articles and supplementary judgments Mumbai: Parsiana Publications.

2010 *Colonial Parsis and Law: A Culture History: Government Research Fellowship Lectures 2009-10* Mumbai: K.R. Cama Oriental Institute.

2014 *Law and Identity in Colonial South Asia: Parsi Legal Culture 1772-1947* New York: Cambridge University Press.

Antia, Kersey H. 2012. *The Argument for Acceptance in Zoroastrianism* Createspace Independent Publishing.

Bharucha, Dastur Sheriaji Dadabhai. 1918. Is Zoroastrianism Preached to All Mankind or One Particular Race?' in *Dastur Hoshang Memorial Volume*, pp. 248-57. Bombay: Fort Printing Press.

Bharucha, Ervand Sheriaji Dadabhai. 1928. *A Brief Sketch of the Zoroastrian Religion and Customs: An Essay Written for the Rahnumai Masdayasnan Sabha of Bombay.* Bombay: D.B. Toprevala Edwardes Stephen Meredyth 1923. *Kharshedji Rustamji Sons & Co. Cama, 1831-1909: A Memoir* Oxford University Press.

Bombay High Court, Kershaji Dhanjibhai vs Kaikhushru Kolhabai on 18 January 1929.

Cama, Shernaz 2016 *Threads of Continuity:Zoroastrian Life and Culture* Parzor Foundation.

Census of the Island of Bombay, Taken 2nd February, 1864 Government at the Education Society's Press, Byculla, 1864.

Conder, Josiah 1828 *The Modern Traveller: A Popular Description. Geographical, Historical and Topographical of the Various Countries of the Globe: India: Vol. IV.* London: James Duncan.

Dadabhoy Naoroji 1861 *The Parsi Religion: From the Proceedings of the Liverpool Literary and Philosophical Society.*

Darukhanawala, H.D. 1939. *Parsi Lustre on Indian Soil, Vol. 1*. Bombay: G Claridge.

Desai, Capt. Hormazdyar Jamshedji Mancheri, 2008. *History of the Parsis of Navsari* [translated from Sorabji Mancherji Desai's 1897 book Tawarikh-e-Navsari]. Mumbai: World Zarathushti Culture Foundation.

Deshta, Kiran 1995 *Uniform Civil Code: In Retrospect and Prospect* Deep and Deep Publications.

Dhall, Maneckji Nusserwanji 1975 *The Saga of a Soul: An Autobiography of Shams-ul-ulama, Dastur Dr. Maneckji Nusserwanji Dhall: High Priest of the Parsis of Pakistan.*

Dhalla, Homi and Rukhsana Nanji 2007 ' The Landing of the Zoroastrians at Sanjan: The archeological evidence' In *Parsis in India and the Diaspora* (ed Hinnels , John R. and Alan Williams). Routledge.

Equivalent citations: (1929) 31 BOMLR 1081, 121 Ind Cas 433.

Ford, Henry 1750 *A Discovery of Two Forreigne Sects in the East Indies, Viz the Sect of the Banians, the Ancient Natives of India, and the sect of the Persees, the Anceint Inhabitans of Persia: Together with the Religion and Manners of Sect* London: Lintot and Osborn.

Haug, Martin. 1907 reprint. *Essays on the Sacred Language Writings, and Religion of the Parsis* London: Kegan Paul. Kotwal, Dastur Firoze M. 1990 reprint.

Hodivala, Shapunji Kavasji 1920 *Parsis of Ancient India.*

Howard, Thomas Albert. 2018. "A Remarkable Gathering": The Conference of Living Religions within the British Empire (1924) and its Historical Significance' in *Journal of the American Academy of Religion.* 89, No.1: 126-57,46.

Irani vs Irani Suit No 45 1958 Judgement of Justic Mody.

Journal of the Iranian Association
Journal of the Iranian Association

Journals

Judges Notebook The Hon. Justice Frank Beaman: Notes in parsi Panchyat Case, Suit No. 689-06- from 7th Feb 1908 to 13th April 1908.

Judgments: Petit Vs Jeejeebhoy 1908 and Saklat vs Bella 1925.

Kabraji, Kaikhosro N. 1901. *Ehvate " Rast Goftar" yane " Rast Goftar tahta Satya Prakash"* [History of the " Rast Goftar" and " Rast Goftar and Satya Prakash"]. Bombay: Dastur Ashkara Press.

Karaka, Dosabhai Framji 1858. *The Parsees: Their History, Manners, Customs and Religion* Smith, Elder and Company.

Karanjia, Ramiyar P. 2019 *Marvels in the Life of Prophet Zarathustra* Shree Book Centre.

Kulke, Eckehard. 1974. *The Parsees in India: A Minority as Agent of Social Change.* Munchen: Welt forum Verlag.

Lala, R.M. 1993. *Beyond the Last Blue Mountain: A Life of J.R.D. Tata.* Penguin Random House, India. Mills Lawrence H. Our Own Religion in Ancient Persia. 1977. AMS Press.

Legal Petition and Documents

Madan, Dhanjishah Meherjibhai 1911. *The Complete Test of the Pahlavi Dinkard: Books Vi- IX, Part 2* Fort Printing Press.

Meherjirana, Rustomji Jamaspji Dastur 1899. *The Genealogy of the Navsari Parsi Priest* London Horsley.

Modi, Jivanji Jamshedji 2004 *A Few Events in the Early History of the Parsis and their Dates.* Reprinted by K.R. Cama Oriental Institute.

Mody, Perveez 2013 ' Love Jurisdiction' *The Cambridge Journal of Anthropology*, Vol. 31, No. 2, pp. 44-59.

Murzban, M.M. 1917 *The Parsis in India: Being an Enlarged and Copiously Annotated, up to date English Edition of Mile Delphine Menant's 'Les Parsis'* Two Volumes.

Nanavutty, Piloo 1977. *The Parsis* National Book Trust, India.

Nanavutty, Piloo. 1999 *The Gathas of Zarathustra: Hymns in Praise and Wisdom* University of Michigan.

Nariman, Fali S. 2010 *Before Memory Fades: An Autobiography* Hay House India.

Original Civil Jurisdiction Civil Regular No. 90 of 1915.

Parsiana Magazine Archives

Patel Simin 2015. *Cultural Intermediaries in a Colonial City: The Parsis of Bombay C. 1860-1921* University of Oxford.

Patel, Homi D. (tr.). 1912. *History of the Jamasp Ashana Family* [Tawarikh-e-Dastoor Jamasp Ashana, translated from Gujarati]. Mumbai: Vertman Press.

Petit vs Jeejebhoy in the High Court of Jurisdicture at Bombay, Suit No. 689 of 1906, 27 November 1908.

Petition of N.N. Barjorjee and Others (Praying that may be added as defendants) in Saklat vs Bella in the Chief Court of Lower Burma.

Rana, Framjee A. *1934 Parsi Law Embodying Marriage and Divorce and Inheritance and Succession applicable to Parsis in British India* Jame-e-Jamshed.

Rose, Jenny 201. *Zoroastrianism: A Guide for the Perplexed* New York: Continuum International.

Saklat vs Bella Privy Council Records 1925, No. 88, Vol. 24 (JSPC Suit No. 57 of 1924)

Saklat vs Bella Suit No. 91 of 1915 of the Chief Court of Lower Burma.

Sharafi, Hitra 2006 *Bella's Case: Parsi Identity and Law in Colonial Rangoon, Bombay and London, 1887-1925* ph D dissertation Princeton University.

Stewart Sarah, Alan Williams and Almut Hintzen 2016 *The Zoroastrian Flame: Exploring Religion, History and tradition*. Bloomsbury Publishing.

Stewart, Sarah (ed) 2013 *The Everlasting Flame: Zoroastrianism in History and Imagination*. Bloomsbury Acedemci.

Tagor, Rabindranath1931 *Religion of Man* (Hibbert lectures for 1930). Macmillan.

Tata Central Archives J.R.D. Tata Papers: Letters of Soon; Tata written to her mother Poona.

The Iran League Quarterly

The Parsi Marriage and Divorce Act of 1865.

Trust Deed Late Ervad D.D. Mehta Zoroastrian Anjuman Atash Adaran

Vimdalal, J.J. and Mahaluzmivala *Racial Intermarriages and Their Scientific Aspect* (1922) Bombay: The Times Press.

Williams, Alan 15September 2021. *Looking Back to see the Present: The Persian Qesseh-ye Sanjan as Living memory* Bloomsbury Collections (Web).

Wilson, John. 1843.*The Parsi Religion: As Contained in the Zand-Avasta, and Propounded and Defended by the Zoroastrians of India and Persia,Unfolded, Refuted, and Contrasted with Christianity.* Bombay: American Mission Press.

Yazdi: 17 December 2010 *Conversion Allowed in Zoroastrianism? Acceptance/ Conversion Allowed in Zoroastrianism (Learned Religious Act of Vada Dasturji Jamaspasa).*

ACKNOWLEDGEMENTS

At the very outset, I would like to acknowledge with thanks the time and effort spent by my dear friend Noshir Tankariwala, senior Trustee of the Late Ervad D.B. Mehta Zoroastrian Anjuman Atash Adaran in reading and commenting on the first manuscript of this book. In September 2020 he lost a valiant fight against the dreaded Covid-19 virus. From his hospital bed, he sent a note to my husband Noomi and me, saying that his greatest wish was to see his wife Roshni walk with 'her head held high', into the Late Ervad D.B. Mehta Zoroastrian Anjuman Atash Adaran with her two navjoted grandchildren, Anahita and Nayantara, children of her daughter Nilufer Patkar. I now have this task, to fulfil his wish, which gives me an additional impetus to what I have been striving for. Noshir wrote the foreword of my first book, *Pioneering Parsis of Calcutta* and he read and corrected, in minute detail, this book too. The questions he asked always set me thinking and led me to a better analysis. He kept repeating, a Parsi marriage is between a Parsi man and a Parsi woman, then how could there be an interfaith marriage before the Special Marriage Act of 1954.

Mitra Sharafi, the historian from University of Wisconsin Law School, shared the entire case file of the 1914–1925 judgement of Saklat vs Bella which she obtained from the Privy Council archives. Reading the cross examination of the witnesses in court makes one actually live through the entire court proceedings. It is a veritable store house of information about Parsis in the early 20th century, which has not been available to the community to date.

Mr Fali. Nariman who in a manner adopted me and this book. He made me reassemble my manuscript, which was like a jigsaw puzzle with everything mixed up and not making logical sense. He happily accepted my request for guidance, did a 'hurried look through' the manuscript and gave me a short list of changes to make. His intuitive mind quickly assessed the book and in these few words he guided me to rewrite the book in a more methodical manner. He advised gently, 'there is a mine of very useful information in all the pages of your book, but (if you don't mind my saying so) this information is spread hap-hazardly all over the book.'

It reminded me of a friend's dad, the famous architect of Calcutta, Mr Motabhai Mistry. Noomi and I were just married and wanted to design our apartment. Noomi had made these elaborate drawings and plans. Motabhai uncle came, walked around the flat, looked at the drawings, changed a few lines, put in some more, and in five minutes our flat was designed. Now we had to make it happen.

My sincerest gratitude to Mr Fali. Nariman for giving value to this book by writing the foreward. Thankyou for assisting me by writing some chapters and making the necessary corrections and additions to the manuscript. For your advice, guidance and support I am truly indebted. I hope I have managed to live up to your expectations and work as per your guidelines.

My sister-in-law Shirin Mehta, who guided me in formatting and presentation of the book, deserves mention.

Special thanks to Faroukh Jijina and Jehangir Patel of Parsiana who are always ready to answer my questions and clear my doubts.

A special thanks to Bikash De Niyogi, who gave me the confidence to write the first book and was bewildered when I presented him with a second manuscript in the first few months of lockdown. Idle time is like a workshop for an inquisitive mind.

Last but not the least, I thank my editor Indradeep Bhattacharya, who turned a series of facts and documents into what I believe is a readable book.

INDEX

Page numbers followed by 'f' and 'n' indicate illustrations and notes, respectively.